Moʻolelo

Published by University of Hawai'i Press
in Association with

Hawai'inuiākea School of Hawaiian Knowledge
University of Hawai'i at Mānoa
Dean Jonathan K. Osorio

Volume Editors: C. M. Kaliko Baker and Tammy Haili'ōpua Baker

Hawaiʻinuiākea No. 7

Moʻolelo
The Foundation of Hawaiian Knowledge

Edited by
C. M. Kaliko Baker and Tammy Hailiʻōpua Baker

Hawaiʻinuiākea School of Hawaiian Knowledge

University of Hawaiʻi Press

Honolulu

First printing, 2023

Library of Congress Cataloging-in-Publication Data

Names: Baker, C. M. Kaliko, editor. | Baker, Tammy Hailiʻōpua, editor.
Title: Moʻolelo : the foundation of Hawaiian knowledge / C. M. Kaliko Baker,
Tammy Hailiʻōpua Baker.
Other titles: Hawaiʻinuiākea monograph ; 7.
Description: Honolulu : University of Hawaiʻi Press in Association with
Hawaiʻinuiākea School of Hawaiian Knowledge, University of Hawaiʻi at
Mānoa, 2023. | Series: Hawaiʻinuiākea no. 7 | Includes bibliographical
references. | In English and Hawaiian.
Identifiers: LCCN 2022024998 | ISBN 9780824895112 (trade paperback) | ISBN
9780824895297 (pdf) | ISBN 9780824895310 (epub) | ISBN 9780824895303
(kindle edition)
Subjects: LCSH: Hawaiian literature—History and criticism. | Hawaiian
language—Semantics. | Knowledge, Theory of—Hawaii.
Classification: LCC PL6448 .M66 2023 | DDC 499/.42—dc23/eng/20221110
LC record available at https://lccn.loc.gov/2022024998

Cover image: *History of Print*. Colored pencil on paper.
Book cover illustration for Kaliko and Hailiʻōpua Baker,
by Ahukini Kupihea, 2017.

University of Hawaiʻi Press books are printed on acid-free paper
and meet the guidelines for permanence and durability
of the Council on Library Resources.

Contents

From the Dean

Welina mai kākou me ke aloha

I welcome you to *Moʻolelo: The Foundation of Hawaiian Knowledge,* a collection of essays ma ka ʻōlelo Hawaiʻi and in English about the stories composed and re-membered by Kānaka ʻŌiwi. This is the seventh volume in the Hawaiʻinuiākea Series and was the inspiration of nā Kumu Kaliko and Hailiʻōpua Baker. These Kumu, authors, and now editors have patiently collected these essays written by kumu from across Hawaiʻi pae ʻāina, and contain deeply significant reflec-tions on how we retain and remember our stories, and how they define and empower us.

The previous series volumes have focused on leadership, environment, skill, knowledge, health, and activism. This seventh volume is a worthy successor that speaks to all of those themes in the stories we tell about ourselves.

Mahalo Nui

Jonathan Kay Kamakawiwoʻole Osorio, Dean
Hawaiʻinuiākea School of Hawaiian Knowledge
University of Hawaiʻi at Mānoa

Kūkulu Kumuhana

C. M. Kaliko Baker and Tammy Hailiʻōpua Baker

Mōhala ka pua, ua wehe kaiao
—Pukui, *ʻŌlelo Noʻeau*, #2179

Mai ke ala ʻana o ka lā i kakahiaka nui poniponi, a wehe kaiao ā pualena ā ao loa, ua ao Hawaiʻi, he ʻōlinolino aloha kēia iā ʻoukou e nā makamaka heluhelu o kēia puke hou e kia nei i ka moʻolelo Hawaiʻi. Ke hoʻopuka ʻia aku nei kēia puke ma ka moʻo-pukana puke ma lalo o ka malu o Hawaiʻinuiākea: Ke Kula ʻIke Hawaiʻi, i kumu waiwai e hoʻomāʻikeʻike i ka hoʻohana ʻana i ko kākou Hawaiʻi Maoli moʻolelo, i kumu waiwai ʻimi noiʻi nowelo no ka wā i hala ʻē akula i o kiki loa mai, ā i kēia manawa iho e holo nei, ā i kēia wā aʻe e hiki mai ana, ā hala loa aku ā hiki i ke aloha ʻike kuʻuna hope loa. No ka mea, he aha ka lāhui ke ʻole kona moʻolelo? He ʻole kā hoʻi ua lāhui lā. No laila, ʻaʻole aʻe kākou e poina, he lāhui kākou Hawaiʻi Maoli i loaʻa pū nō kona moʻolelo. Hoʻomanaʻo aʻela kou mau mea kākau a luna hoʻoponopono hoʻi i ka ʻōlelo a Joseph Mokuʻōhai Poepoe i kona hoʻākāka ʻana i ka moʻolelo ma kāna pukana ʻo "Ka Moolelo Hawaii Kahiko" penei:

> E hoomaopopoia, he lahui kakou me ko kakou Moolelo Kahiko, i ano like loa aku me ka moolelo kahiko o ka lahui o Helene; a he mau mele kahiko hoi ka ko kakou mau kupuna i like aku a i oi aku nohoi ko lakou hiwahiwa ame ke kilakila i ko na mele kaulana loa o ua lahui Helene nei....
>
> "A o ka Moolelo" wahi a Cicero, "oia ka mea e hoao ai i ka manawa; oia ka malamalama o ka oiaio; ke ola o ka hoomanao; ka rula o ka hoomanao; ka elele o ka wa kahiko." (1 Feberuari)

I ka manaʻo o Poepoe, ua like a ua ʻoi aku i kahi wā ka moʻolelo a me ke mele o ka lāhui Hawaiʻi, a hōʻike hoʻi ua ʻo Poepoe nei i ke koʻikoʻi o ka moʻolelo ma ka hoʻohālikelike ʻana i ko Cicero manaʻo. Ma ka puke a ka mea Hanohano, a Kauka Pualani Kanahele, i loko o ko kākou moʻolelo kahiko i haku ʻia ai ka hana noʻeau, ka loina, ke kiʻina a kaʻina hoʻi o kēlā me kēia ʻano hana like ʻole o ka wā kahiko. No laila, ʻo ka moʻolelo ka paepae i kūkulu ai ka hale o ko kākou lāhui e noho pūkuʻikuʻi ai.

1

ʻOiai he lāhui kākou ua ʻike maka i ka mēheuheu a ke kolonaio e waiho nei i ke alo a ke ʻimi ikaika nei hoʻi ko kākou lāhui i ke kūʻokoʻa, ʻo ko kākou ʻike kuʻuna e waiho nei i loko o ko kākou moʻolelo no nā Kau a Hoʻoilo i kaʻa hope akula kā kākou e kiʻi a hoʻāla ai hoʻi i kēia au no kēia hope aku. Ma muli o kēia kūlia ʻana i ke kūʻokoʻa ka hoʻokumu ʻana i kēia puke a me kona waiho ʻana i loko o ka poho o kō lima i kēia lā.

E ka makamaka heluhelu, aia ka nui o nā mea i kākau ʻia ma kēia puke ma ka ʻōlelo Pelekania. Ua waiho ʻia ke koho i kēlā mea kākau, kēia mea kākau. Wali naʻe ka ʻōlelo Hawaiʻi iā lākou āpau, pau pū hoʻi me ka mea kahakiʻi. ʻO ka ʻōlelo Hawaiʻi ke kahua o ka poʻe nāna i hana kēia puke. ʻOiai ʻo ka ʻōlelo Hawaiʻi kekahi māhele nui o ia mea he mauli a he ea Hawaiʻi, a i ka neʻe ʻana o ke ao Hawaiʻi i mua, ke akāka mai nei nō i ka lāhui ʻo ka ʻŌlelo Hawaiʻi, ka ʻŌlelo Kanaka hoʻi, ka mea e kūʻokoʻa ai kānaka. No laila, wae a kono akula māua i nā mea kākau i wali ka ʻōlelo, no ka mea i ko māua manaʻo, ʻo ka moʻolelo i paʻa ma ka ʻōlelo Hawaiʻi ka mea e kākia mai i kekahi mau māhele ʻike e pono ai i kēia wā, i kēia au hoʻi e holo nei. I ke koho ʻana o kekahi hapa o nā mea kākau e kākau ma ka Pelekania, ʻaʻole o māua pilikia i loko nō o ke aloha i kā kākou ʻŌlelo Kanaka. Eia naʻe, ʻo ka hapa nui o ka lāhui Hawaiʻi Maoli, ʻaʻole i mākaukau ma kā kākou ʻŌlelo Hawaiʻi, ka ipu kāʻeo hoʻi o ka lāhui. No laila ka hoʻopuka ʻana i nā manaʻo nui a me nā manaʻo iki ma ka Pelekania, no ka mea ʻo kēia ʻike, he ʻike nō ia no ka lāhui. Eia hou, malia paha, i ka heluhelu ʻana o kekahi poʻe i nā manaʻo i puka ma nā mokuna o kēia wahi pūʻulu pepa nei, e ʻeu aʻe auaneʻi ka lima kīʻoʻe i ka ipu kāʻeo o nā kūpuna, ʻai, a māʻona. ʻO ia kīʻoʻe ʻana ke kiʻi a aʻo ʻana hoʻi i kā kākou ʻŌlelo Kanaka. A ʻo ia ʻai ʻana ka hoʻopaʻa ʻana i ka ʻōlelo, a ʻo ia māʻona ʻana ka wali ʻana o ka ʻōlelo. No laila, e ke hoa ʻōlelo ē, e hoʻomanawanui mai i ka ʻōlelo haole e waiho nei ma lalo mai a ma loko aʻe hoʻi o kēia puke.

No ia mea he moʻolelo: Defining Moʻolelo

Moʻolelo, loosely translated as stories and histories, are the *kūkulu* "pillars" that shoulder and chronicle Kanaka Maoli narratives and beliefs. The moʻo, or successions, of *ʻōlelo* "words" are the foundation for the many genres of moʻolelo which collectively represent the prowess of the Kanaka Maoli literary canon. Poepoe uses the terms *hoʻolou* "snares" and *hoʻopili* "connectors" to describe important interpretive elements of moʻokūʻauhau (28 Aperila). In the context of discussing the functions of moʻolelo, hoʻolou and hoʻopili are what lead to understanding *kūʻauhau* and *moʻokūʻauhau*, which in our understanding of Poepoe are individual (micro) and larger (macro) genealogies, respectively. Poepoe assures us that kūʻauhau and moʻokūʻauhau are critical in understanding our moʻolelo, and the more *kapu*, or sacred a moʻolelo is, the more likely it depends on moʻokūʻauhau. Poepoe's hoʻolou and hoʻopili are also applicable to *koʻihonua, hulihia, kanikau, mele aloha,* and other forms of poetic expression.

Haku or *paʻa moʻolelo* are individuals who were selected to learn by rote the history and lore of the land. In the series "Ka Hoomana Kahiko" in *Ka Nupepa Kuokoa,* Paul William Kaawa wrote regarding haku moʻolelo "He poe naauao keia, he poe i ao ia mai ka wa uuku mai" (These are intelligent people, people who were taught from a young age). Haku moʻolelo are also similar to what Mary Kawena Pukui ("How" 6) and George Hueu Sanford Kanahele (264–265) refer to as paʻa moʻolelo, the term we will use henceforth. In Kanaka Maoli society paʻa moʻolelo were identified at a young age by their keen ability of *ʻapo* "to retain." They were selected and trained to retain moʻolelo taught to them by master paʻa moʻolelo. These individuals then served as genealogists, historians, and poets.

Transmission of moʻolelo prior to western contact was done orally through narrative, chants, and/or incantations. Pukui states that no legend was complete without a chant ("How" 6), and a combination of narrative and chant is the traditional form of *haʻi moʻolelo* "storytelling." The narrative is Poepoe's hoʻolou and hoʻopili, linking the details of the moʻolelo together, while the mele summarizes or embellishes the moʻolelo poetically (Baker "Ke Mele"). The recitation of moʻolelo passed stories and histories of our people from one generation to the next for hundreds of years. This would rapidly change after colonization, when the colonizers replaced moʻolelo and moʻokūʻauhau, our vessels of intergenerational transmission, with stories of their own.

Weaving moʻokūʻauhau through moʻolelo is essential for understanding the connectivity of one successive genealogical or narrative line to the next. Any analysis that seeks to eliminate moʻokūʻauhau, mele, or some other form of moʻolelo will lack the necessary hoʻolou that hoʻopili the words to their intended meanings. Because our primary knowledge bases today are our Hawaiian medium resources written by nineteenth-century scholars, we are already lacking a critical element for understanding and mastering these primary sources—the pronunciation of the words, which directs and effectively defines our understanding of the paʻa moʻolelo intended. Though spelling certainly indicates pronunciation in ʻŌlelo Hawaiʻi, many words in our resources published prior to the advent of diacritical marking—that is, the kahakō and ʻokina—may remain ambiguous in terms of the intended phonetic pronunciation of a lexical item. Using *pua* and its three possible pronunciations as her example, Noenoe Silva briefly discusses this issue, arguing that nineteenth-century writers deliberately used this ambiguity for their own ends (*Power* 12). This interesting analysis points toward the creative ingenuity of our people when writing text. But because we do not have the luxury of hearing what a kupuna said before writing something such as pua, we must use contextual clues to distinguish between the possible pronunciations of *pua* as *pua, puʻa,* or *pūʻā.* Knowing the moʻolelo through the hoʻolou and the hoʻopili therefore assists modern-day scholars in addressing the issue of not knowing exactly how some word may have been uttered, and thus what the paʻa moʻolelo intended it to mean.

In an 1868 casting of aspersions on an inaccurate publication of a moʻolelo, Samuel Mānaiakalani Kamakau declares that those who publish *kaʻao* "folktale" must attend to the moʻokūʻauhau and moʻolelo of their kaʻao beforehand.[1] What this means is that authors are accountable for the facts of their kaʻao, based in moʻokūʻauhau and moʻolelo. Joseph Hoonaʻauao Kānepuʻu is renowned today for his position pieces and other contributions to the nineteenth-century literary canon of Kanaka Maoli scholarship in the Hawaiian medium newspapers (see Silva, *Power*). On October 30, 1862, he published an opinion piece in *Ka Hoku o ka Pakipika* that called on his contemporaries to publish moʻolelo in their entirety, because these publications will eventually become the repositories for future generations.[2] Moreover, by publicly criticizing other publications, Kamakau and Kānepuʻu both demand that other scholars of their own time, as well as those to come, recognize that moʻokūʻauhau and moʻolelo are important for defining who we Kānaka Maoli are as a lāhui, and are therefore key, even essential elements of being a Kanaka Maoli. In line with this ideology inherited from our ancestors, we too recognize that moʻolelo is the foundation of Hawaiian knowledge.

No kēia puke: Book Contents

The inspiration for this book stemmed from a conversation with Dean Jonathan Kay Kamakawiwoʻole Osorio shortly after our fall of 2015 Hawaiian medium theatre production of *Lāʻieikawai*. He suggested there should be a book centered on moʻolelo, and as Kumu ʻŌlelo Hawaiʻi who had spent most of our lives studying moʻolelo kahiko, this idea appealed to us greatly. This book therefore offered an opportunity to gather our *hoa paʻa moʻolelo o ke au nei* "storytellers of today" to write about the study, practice, and perpetuation of moʻolelo in their respective disciplines.

At that time, the fifth book in the Hawaiʻinuiākea series, *Kanaka ʻŌiwi Methodologies: Moʻolelo and Metaphor,* was in progress, carving out this space for Kanaka Maoli scholarship in the academy. This new book also furthers Kanaka Maoli driven scholarship rooted in traditional knowledge by expanding the current dialogue on moʻolelo as an essential element for Kanaka Maoli research and practices. The material included in this volume offers insights into *kuanaʻike Hawaiʻi* "Hawaiian epistemology" and critical analysis of moʻolelo Hawaiʻi. Bringing these authors together also consolidates modern *kālailaina moʻolelo* "narrative studies." The range of knowledge shared here crosses many disciplines, and also contributes to emerging fields of study for Kānaka Maoli and other Indigenous peoples.

A brief word about the style and spelling conventions adopted for this publication. Because this is a bilingual text and every author is a respected scholar of Hawaiian language, as co-editors, we entrusted each of them with the kuleana to decide which spelling conventions for the 'Ōlelo Hawai'i texts, such as the use of diacritical markings, were appropriate for their piece. Unless otherwise indicated, all English translations of 'ōlelo Hawai'i are by the author. In our commitment to normalizing 'Ōlelo Hawai'i usage throughout this publication, we also did not insist on English translations for words or passages. Terminology is also fluid and the choice of each author. For example, the terms Kanaka Maoli, Kanaka 'Ōiwi, and Native Hawaiian are used by contributors according to their preference.

Our hope is that *Mo'olelo: The Foundation of Hawaiian Knowledge* boosts Kanaka Maoli scholarship, enhances the traditional intellectual skills of our community, and contributes to the growing field of Indigenous Studies. We've aspired to assemble a distinguished and diverse collection of Kanaka Maoli authors and artists from across the Pae 'Āina o Hawai'i to contribute to this conversation on mo'olelo and its influence on all of our work. Each chapter displays how mo'olelo and traditional ways of knowing inform the creative and academic works of the Kānaka Maoli who have contributed to this auspicious publication. A unifying factor is that mo'olelo serve as foundational sources for every author's research and/or practice. For us to understand who we are as a people, mo'olelo is necessary, for it holds our kū'auhau, the link to our kūpuna, the history, practices, and values of our kūpuna, and the *hunahuna 'ike* "fragments of knowledge" that illuminate our path as Kānaka Maoli.

Ma loko o ka puke: Authors and Their Contributions

Each book in the Hawai'inuiākea series honors a kupuna. Since our focus is mo'olelo and 'ōlelo Hawai'i, we have selected none other than Professor Larry Kauanoe Kimura, PhD. In all honesty, where would any of us be without his efforts and leadership in the revitalization of our 'Ōlelo Kanaka? Kumu Lale is the kumu of our kumu. His personal mo'olelo, the Hawaiian language revitalization movement, and the importance of mo'olelo are some of the subjects in "He Mo'olelo Ola: Aukahi Ho'ōla 'Ōlelo Hawai'i," penned by Kamalani Johnson following an interview with Kumu Lale. He is also featured on the cover art. This publication honors Larry Kauanoe Kimura's countless efforts over a lifetime to perpetuate 'Ōlelo Hawai'i.

"Kīkohu 'ia ka Hulu 'Io me ka 'Ula'ula" is the title of the cover art by 'Ahukini Kupihea, MFA. Kupihea's art depicts the ways that mo'olelo are held, remembered, and transferred from one generation to the next. Honoring kūpuna and mo'olelo, the cover images span time and space, representing how traditional knowledge bridges to modernity. Kupihea captures the vessels of moʻolelo that have evolved over time—the printing press, microfiche, computers, and the modern era of digital media. See Kupihea's reflection for more details on his process, and the thoughts behind the artwork that holds all of the moʻolelo in this book together.

Dr. Keawe Lopes's chapter, "Retain Thy Heritage," discusses the importance of ʻauʻa, or holding on to what we have. Through his inquiry into one of our most famous traditional mele hula, ʻAuʻa ʻia, Lopes weaves his knowledge as a kumu hula and a scholar together to stress the importance of holding on to traditional knowledge. Drawing on the acts of preservation and perpetuation by Kanaka Maoli scholars Poepoe, Nakuina, Helekunihi, and Pukui, he draws parallels between Keaulumoku's ʻAuʻa ʻia, the mele that calls us to retain our heritage, and the preservation efforts of Ka Waihona a ke Aloha. Housed in Kawaihuelani Center for Hawaiian Language, Ka Waihona a ke Aloha gathers and perpetuates mele resources and Hawaiian language knowledge connected to mele practice by hosting composers and practitioners, holding yearly mele competitions, and assembling a massive repository of digitized albums.

As we heed the call to hold on, we also look to Dr. Hiapo Perreira's work to reforge kākāʻōlelo, our traditional oratory. In his chapter, " ʻEʻole Hoʻi ka Moʻolelo Kahiko, Ola Hou Ai Ke Kākāʻōlelo," he describes how moʻolelo are embedded and called upon in the art of kākāʻōlelo. For one to excel in the art of traditional oratory, Perreira explains, a thorough understanding of moʻolelo is essential.

Kumu Hula, mele medium, and epitome of traditional genius, Kekuhi Kealiʻi-kanakaʻoleohaililani provides us with a methodology for engaging moʻolelo. In describing her approach to understanding moʻolelo, kaʻao, and mele, Kealiʻika-nakaʻoleohaililani identifies three essential concerns—the Kiʻi Ākea, Kiʻi Honua, and Kiʻi ʻIaka, or meta, macro, and micro ways of engaging Hawaiian text. Her chapter, "The Charm of Kiʻi," showcases her reader friendly "Here, I show you how" style, which pulls the reader into a conversation with the author. Kealiʻika-nakaʻoleohaililani's three-tiered system of kiʻi provides the reader with tools for connecting with moʻolelo through personal, local, and global interpretations.

In "E ʻAi ā Māʻona, ʻAi ā Ea: Na ke Mele e Moʻolelo Mai i Ke Aloha ʻĀina o ka Lāhui Kanaka Maoli," Dr. Kahikina de Silva engages mele as vessels of aloha ʻāina. Through her analysis of three mele, namely "He ʻAi na ka Lani," "Nā ʻAi ʻOno," and "Aloha ka Manini," de Silva reveals hues of resistance in what might otherwise be thought of as simple food references. This chapter testifies to the importance of moʻolelo and mele for study and analysis of political movements.

In his chapter "Nā Mele Koʻokoʻo: How Mele Serve as the Koʻokoʻo of Moʻolelo," Masters of Fine Arts candidate in Hawaiian Theatre Kaipulaumakaniolono Baker discusses the importance of mele as record and rallying call for our lāhui. Paying close attention to mele lāhui that document history and movements, he discusses the process of recording through mele composition his experiences in Nā Koʻokoʻo, the University of Hawai'i at Mānoa Hawaiian leadership program. Kaipulau-makaniolono also shares his personal journey as a young composer who has been mentored by various kumu in a range of cultural contexts.

A playwright, director, and scholar, Dr. Tammy Haili'ōlelo Baker writes about hana keaka, the performance of mo'olelo on stage, as political protest in the nineteenth century. Focusing on a particular hana keaka performed in April of 1893, Baker investigates its relations to the resistance movement of Kanaka Maoli royalists following the illegal overthrow of the Hawaiian Kingdom. "Staging Mo'olelo as a Political Statement" also examines the activity surrounding the 1893 performance to provide context for the practice of hana keaka by Kānaka Maoli.

Just as mo'olelo records and preserves, so too does hana no'eau, or art. Dr. ku'ualoha ho'omanawanui brings artistic expressions by female artists to our gathering. "The Art of Mo'olelo: Mana Wahine, Aloha 'Āina, and Social Justice" centers on such wahine maoli artists as Lili'u Tomasello, Bernice Akamine, Meleanna Meyer, Haley Kailiehu, and Abigail Romanchak. Exploring their culturally and often politically conscious artwork, ho'omanawanui concentrates on the mo'olelo represented in these contemporary arts, pointing to common themes of aloha 'āina, nationalism, and political resistance. ho'omanawanui's chapter recognizes these wāhine as important figures in the current-day mo'olelo of po'e hana no'eau, whose artistic contributions express the mo'olelo and core values of Kānaka Maoli.

In his chapter, "Three Mana of a Mo'olelo about Translation," Dr. Kamaoli Kuwada advocates for the necessity of 'Ōlelo Hawai'i and of granting access to it for Kānaka Maoli non-Hawaiian speakers by providing well-translated materials for their consumption. Drawing upon the mo'olelo of Kaluaiko'olau to explain the challenges of translations, Kuwada impresses upon the reader that Kānaka Maoli should still learn 'Ōlelo Hawai'i, so that we can do our own assessments of the context, meaning, and intention of mo'olelo.

Linguistic endeavors depend on mo'olelo to answer such critical questions as *why this form now?* In "Pragmatic and Discourse Analysis of *A*-class Selection: Mo'olelo as Empirical Data," Dr. C. M. Kaliko Baker analyzes genitive subject selection through discourse and pragmatic lenses, demonstrating in the process how a firm grounding in mo'olelo Hawai'i makes possible a fuller understanding of *a*-class subject selection in nominalization and relative clause constructions.

Dr. Kalehua Krug writes about his own journey in becoming a mea kākau uhi or traditional tattoo artist. Emphasizing the importance of knowing our history, our mo'olelo, to comprehend fully the loina involved in the journey, in "Kā i ka Mōlī a Uhia!: Ke a'o 'ana i ke kākau uhi Hawai'i," he insists that for every Kanaka Maoli discipline, many valuable details are embedded in mo'olelo that we must seek out to maintain properly these practices today.

The contributions in this Hawaiʻinuiākea series volume demonstrate the breadth and value moʻolelo hold for our lāhui as the hoʻolou and hoʻopili to the mole—the roots by which we affirm and connect, awakening our mauli as Kānaka Maoli. The scholars in this volume invigorate our collective consciousness as Kānaka Maoli as they enhance and advance scholarship in moʻolelo, ʻŌlelo Hawaiʻi, performing and visual arts, traditional and modern methodologies, identity issues, and Indigneous narrative studies. Ultimately, this compilation claims Kanaka Maoli scholarship's intellectual space in academia even as it empowers modern-day Kanaka Maoli omni-sentience.

ʻO ke aloha ka i ʻoi aʻe, ʻo ka mahalo ona ukali

We extend our deepest gratitude to all of our contributing authors and artists for their trust and commitment to this groundbreaking publication that explores the intrinsic connections of Kānaka Maoli to our moʻolelo. Mahalo nui ʻia ko ʻoukou ahonui i kēia alahele o ka paʻi puke ʻana. Mahalo ā nui iā ʻolua, e Dean Jonathan Kamakawiwoʻole Osorio lāua ʻo Kauka Craig Howes no ke alakaʻi ʻana mai iā māua nei. E ʻole ʻolua, ua paʻa nei puke. Mahalo palena ʻole i ka laulima ʻana a ke kanaka nui ā i ke kanaka iki i paʻa ai ua puke nei a kākou.

Eia nō māua, nā luna hoʻoponopono, ke waiho aku nei i kēia puke me ke aloha no nā paʻa moʻolelo no ke au i hala, no ke au nei, a no ke au e hiki mai ana. Ma o ke aloha ʻāina, ka paʻa ʻike kuʻuna, a me ka mākeʻe ʻōlelo e ola mau ai ka moʻolelo o nā hulu kūpuna o ka lāhui maoli o ka ʻāina nei, ka lāhui Hawaiʻi.

ʻO māua iho nō me ke aloha,
Kaliko lāua ʻo Hailiʻōpua Baker

NOTES

1. For discussions of kaʻao, see C. M. Kaliko Baker, "Hawaiian," "Constructing," and "Ke Mele."
2. For a discussion of this passage, see Baker, "Constructing" (130–131), and Silva, *Power* 7.

WORKS CONSULTED

Baker, C. M. Kaliko. "Constructing Kanaka Maoli Identity through Narrative: A Glimpse into Native Hawaiian Narratives." In *Narratives and Identity Construction in the Pacific Islands*, edited by Farzana Gounder, pp. 119–134. Studies in Narrative Series. John Bejamins, 2015.

———. "Hawaiian Medium Theatre and the Language Revitalization Movement: A Means to Reestablishing *Mauli Hawaiʻi*." In *The Routledge Handbook of Language Revitalization*, edited by Leanne Hinton, Leena Huss, and Gerald Roche, pp. 227–235. Routledge, 2018.

———. "Ke Mele ma ke Ka'ao [Song in Folklore]." In *E Mau ai ka Puana [Continue the Refrain]*, edited by R. Keawe Lopes Jr., Ka Waihona a ke Aloha, 2014, pp. 18–26.

Kaawa, Paul William. "Ka Hoomana Kahiko—Helu 31." *Ka Nupepa Kuokoa*, Buke 4, Helu 51, 23 Dekamaba 1865, 'ao'ao 1.

Kamakau, Samuel M. "He mau mea i hoohalahala ia no na mea iloko o na kaao Hawaii." *Ka Nupepa Kuokoa*, Buke 7, Helu 7, 15 Feberuari 1868, 'ao'ao 3.

Kanahele, George Hueu Sanford. 1986. *Kū Kanaka: Stand Tall; A Search for Hawaiian Values*. U of Hawai'i P, 1986.

Kanahele, Pualani Kanaka'ole. *Ka Honua Ola: 'Eli'eli Kau Mai / Descend, Deepen the Revelation*. Kamehameha Schools Press, 2011.

Kānepu'u, J. H. "Ka poe kakau moolelo, a kaao paha." *Ka Hoku o ka Pakipika*, Buke 2, Helu 3, 30 Okatoba 1862, 'ao'ao 1.

Nogelmeier, M. Puakea. *Mai Pa'a i ku Leo: Historical Voice in Hawaiian Primary Materials, Looking Forward and Listening Back*. Bishop Museum Press and Awaiaulu Press, 2010.

Poepoe, J[oseph] M[oku'ōhai]. "Ka Moolelo Hawaii Kahiko." *Ka Na'i Aupuni*, Buke 1, Helu 57, 'ao'ao 1 a me Buke 1, Helu 131, 'ao'ao 1. 1 Feberuari a me 28 Aperila 1906.

Pukui, Mary Kawena. "How Legends Were Taught." *Hawaiian Ethnographic Notes*, vol. 1, 1602–1606. Bishop Museum Archives, pp. 1–5. http://kumukahi-online.net/haku-olelo -331/na-kumu-ike/mokuna-iv—moolelo-kaao/pukui—how-legends-were.pdf.

———. *'Ōlelo No'eau. Hawaiian Proverbs & Poetical Sayings*. Bishop Museum Press, 1983.

Silva, Noenoe K. 2004. *Aloha Betrayed: Native Hawaiian Resistance to American Colonialism*. Duke UP, 2004.

———. *The Power of the Steel-Tipped Pen: Reconstructing Native Hawaiian Intellectual History*. Duke UP, 2017.

Dr. C. M. Kaliko Baker's teaching focus is on Hawaiian grammar and worldview. His dissertation analyzed a- and o- class selection in grammatical subjects of events, that is, as subjects of nominalizations and relative clauses primarily. His analytical methodology in his research is based in discourse grammar and pragmatics. Generally speaking, by using corpora, he draws generalizations about specific structures and patterns in Hawaiian. As President of Halele'a Arts Foundation, a 501(c)3, Kaliko works at supporting, promoting, and publishing Hawaiian-medium media, for example, hankeaka 'ōlelo Hawai'i such as *Kaluaiko'olau, Māuiakamalo, Kamapua'a*, and most recently *Lā'ieikawai* and *'Au'a 'Ia: Holding On*. Within hanakeaka as a process, he serves as researcher, writer, editor, and dramaturge.

Kaliko has been a member of the Protect Kaho'olawe 'Ohana (PKO) since 1993. His major contribution to the PKO has been leading the Makahiki ceremonies since 2003 and as a kōkua with all media endeavors. Recently, he has been leading huaka'i 'ōlelo Hawai'i under the PKO to Kaho'olawe during UH's Spring Break, during which the UH Mānoa and Hilo campuses connect and work on

Kahoʻolawe using ʻōlelo Hawaiʻi as their means of communication. I mau ka ʻike a me ka ʻōlelo a nā kūpuna [So that the knowledge and language of the ancestors carry on].

Tammy Hailiʻōpua Baker is an Associate Professor in the Department of Theatre and Dance at the University of Hawaiʻi at Mānoa. As a Director/Playwright/ Theatre Educator/Scholar, her work centers on the development of an indigenous Hawaiian theatre aesthetic and form, language revitalization, and the empowerment of cultural identity and consciousness through stage performance. Baker is the artistic director of Ka Hālau Hanakeaka, a Hawaiian-medium theatre troupe based on Oʻahu. Originally from Kapaʻa, Kauaʻi, she now resides in Kahaluʻu, Koʻolaupoko, Oʻahu with her ʻohana.

He ‘umeke kā‘eo ka mo‘olelo Hawai‘i
o ka ‘ike kupuna i waiho ‘ia mai no kākou.

1

He Moʻolelo Ola
Aukahi Hoʻōla ʻŌlelo Hawaiʻi

Kamalani Johnson a me Larry Kimura

Māmā Hilo, māmā Hilo i ka ua hoʻokina
Ke nihi aʻela e hoʻopūnana i luna o ka ʻōhiʻa
Kupu hūoʻeoʻe a ka manu e kani ala i ka lehua[1]

Hoʻolauna: No Ka Moʻolelo Hawaiʻi

He ʻohina ka moʻolelo Hawaiʻi o ka ʻike kuʻuna o ka poʻe Hawaiʻi kahiko. Aia ma loko o ka moʻolelo Hawaiʻi he ʻike ʻana o ka noho ʻana o ka wā i kākau a hoʻopaʻa ʻia ai ka moʻolelo me ona mau haʻawina piha momi—e laʻa nā haʻawina waiwai, ka nohona, a me ke kuanaʻike ola nō hoʻi. I kēia au e neʻe aku nei, he mau moʻolelo Hawaiʻi ko kākou i ili ma luna o kākou ma muli hoʻi o ka hana hoʻomakaʻala a kekahi mau kūpuna ma ka hoʻomau a hoʻopuka i ua mau moʻolelo nei ma ka haʻi waha mai kekahi hanauna a i kekahi hanauna aku a ma ka nūpepa Hawaiʻi kahiko pū kekahi. No laila, no kākou i kēia wā ʻānō ka pōmaikaʻi maoli ʻo ka ili ʻana mai o ua mau moʻolelo nei, ʻoiai, aia nō ma ka moʻolelo nā haʻawina kūikawā e naʻauao aʻe ai ko kākou kuanaʻike a e ulu pū ai ko kākou manaʻo.

ʻO ia mea he moʻolelo, he kiʻina hoʻomau ʻike ia i laha ma nā lāhui o ka honua—he loina moʻolelo ko ka ʻĀsia, ka ʻEulopa, a me ka Polenesia pū kekahi. I loko nō naʻe o ka ʻokoʻa o ka moʻolelo o kēlā lāhui kēia lāhui, he kiʻina ko ka moʻolelo Hawaiʻi e Hawaiʻi ai e like me ia mea he *hualekikona*[2] me ka *meiwi*.[3] No ke kiʻina hualekikona me ka meiwi, he mea ia o ka moʻolelo Hawaiʻi nāna e kōkua mai ma ka hoʻomau a hoʻoili i ka ʻike. I laʻana, he mau huaʻōlelo ma kahi o ka huaʻōlelo laha no *offer/offering* ʻo *hoʻokupu*. Eia nō naʻe, ma kahi o *hoʻokupu*, loaʻa pū *ʻo ʻālana* lāua ʻo *kaumaha*. Ma ka unuhi Pelekānia laulā, ua like nō ka manaʻo o ua mau huaʻōlelo ʻekolu nei, eia nō naʻe, ma ka pōʻaiapili Hawaiʻi, he ʻokoʻa nō. No laila, he kiʻina hoʻomau a hoʻoili ʻike ka hualekikona ma ka moʻolelo Hawaiʻi ma ka mālama ʻike e pili pū ana me nā huaʻōlelo Hawaiʻi.

Ma kēia mokuna, ua nīnauele ʻia ke Kauka Larry Kimura no kona ʻike moʻolelo Hawaiʻi a no kona manaʻo i ke kuleana o ka moʻolelo Hawaiʻi ma ka hoʻōla ʻōlelo Hawaiʻi. Ma mua iki naʻe o koʻu hōʻike ʻana i ko ke Kauka Larry Kimura mau manaʻo e ka hoa hoʻohialaʻai, e hōʻike mua aku au no ʻekolu huaʻōlelo i puka pinepine mai ma kaʻu nīnauele i ke Kauka Larry Kimura ʻo ia hoʻi ʻo *moʻolelo, moʻokaʻao,*[4] a me *moʻokalaleo.*[5] Eia hoʻi au ke hōʻokoʻa aku nei i kēia mau huaʻōlelo ʻekolu i mōakāka koʻu mau manaʻo ma hope mai. No ua mau huaʻōlelo ʻekolu nei, he like a he ʻokoʻa ma kekahi ʻano; he pili nō i ka moʻolelo——ʻo ke ala nō naʻe i ili mai ai ua mau moʻolelo nei kona mea i ʻokoʻa ai.

No Larry Lindsey Kimura

Ua hānau ʻia ʻo Larry Lindsey Kimura i Waimea, Kohala, Hawaiʻi i ka makahiki 1946 ma kekahi wā i hoʻoikaika ai ko Hawaiʻi e hoʻoʻamelika a e ʻimi nui i ke kūlana mokuʻāina ma hope o ka hoʻopahū ʻia o Puʻuloa, ke komo ʻana i ke Kaua Kōlea, a me ka noho ma lalo o ka malu aupuni kelikoli no kanahākūmāwalu makahiki. ʻAʻohe nānā nui ʻia ka puʻumake o ka ʻōlelo a me ka mauli o ka lāhui ʻōiwi Hawaiʻi i ia wā. I kona wā kamaliʻi, ʻaʻole nō i malihini kona pepeiao i ka leo Hawaiʻi ʻoiai hoʻi ua paʻa nō ka ʻōlelo makuahine o ka ʻāina i kona kupuna wahine a me kona ʻohana Hawaiʻi o ia hanauna makua a kupuna. Ma kona hale, he ʻōlelo Hawaiʻi nō kahi a he ʻōlelo Kepanī nō kahi kai lohe ʻia. I loko nō o ke kamaʻāina o kona pepeiao i ka ʻōlelo Hawaiʻi a ʻike i ka manaʻo o kekahi mau huaʻōlelo a māpunaʻōlelo ʻana, ʻaʻole i hele a maʻa ke kamaʻilio waha ʻana i ia ʻōlelo.

No kona minamina i ka ʻōlelo Hawaiʻi, ua hū aʻela hoʻi kona hoihoi e aʻo i ka ʻōlelo Hawaiʻi i hiki ai iā ia ke kamaʻilio pū me kona kupuna wahine ma ka ʻōlelo

Eliza Lindsey, ko Kimura kupuna wahine Hawaiʻi. Author's image.

Hisamu Kimura, ko Kimura Obaasan. Author's image.

makuahine. A ʻōpio aʻela ʻo Larry, ʻae ʻia akula kona hele ʻana i Ka Hale Kula ʻo Kamehameha. I kona wā i ʻae ʻia ai e hele aku, he ʻelua hale kula i hoʻonaʻauao ʻia ai nā keiki Hawaiʻi; hoʻokahi no nā keiki kāne a hoʻokahi no nā kaikamāhine. I ka hele ʻana aku ona i Ka Hale Kula ʻo Kamehameha, ua hū kona hauʻoli i ka manaʻo ʻana he kula Hawaiʻi ana ia no laila e aʻo nō ʻo ia e pili ana i nā mea Hawaiʻi ma Kamehameha. Ma ia wā, ua ʻike nō ʻo Larry i ka makeʻe ʻole o kona mau hoa haumāna i ka ʻōlelo Hawaiʻi; manaʻo wale ʻia nō he mea hoʻonaninani ka ʻōlelo Hawaiʻi. No Larry naʻe, ua lilo ka ʻōlelo Hawaiʻi he mea e ʻike ʻia ai ka hoʻomau ola o ka lāhui Hawaiʻi.

Iā Kimura ma Ka Hale Kula ʻo Kamehameha, ʻaʻole ʻo ia i ʻike mua i ke aʻo kūhelu i ka ʻōlelo Hawaiʻi; ʻo Harriet Burrows kāna kumu ʻōlelo Hawaiʻi mua loa. Iā ia e noho haumāna ana na Burrows, ua ʻike ʻo ia no ke ʻano mālani o kona aʻo ʻana i ka ʻōlelo Hawaiʻi no ka pōkole o ka wā i ʻae ʻia ai no ia kumuhana; ʻaʻole ʻo ia i luʻu piha ma ke au nui me ke au iki o ka ʻōlelo Hawaiʻi; me he lā naʻe, he hoʻonaninani wale nō ia i manaʻo ʻia e ke Kula. Ua ʻiʻini nui nō kēia keiki koa o kona mau lā heuheu ʻole e luʻu piha i ke aʻo i ka ʻōlelo makuahine o ka ʻāina.

A hala kekahi mau makahiki, ua kō ka ʻiʻini o Kimura i kona mau makahiki hope ma Kamehameha ma ka hai ʻia o Dorothy Kahananui e ka Pelekikena o ke Kula Keiki Kāne ʻo Kamehameha, ʻo ia hoʻi ʻo Colonel Harold Kent. Na Kahananui nō i kīpaepae a hoʻoulu i ke aʻo ʻōlelo Hawaiʻi no ko Kimura ʻōlelo waha aku i ka ʻōlelo. I kahi lā āna e noho haumāna ana, lawe maila ʻo Kahananui i ka mīkini pōkaʻa līpine leo e hoʻokani ai i kekahi kamaʻilio Hawaiʻi ma waena o ka mea nīnauele ʻo Mary Kawena Pukui a me kona hoa kamaʻilio he kupuna mānaleo Hawaiʻi. Na ia haʻawina leo i hoʻohoihoi iā Larry e noi iā Pukui e hoʻopaʻa i ka leo o ko Larry kupuna wahine no ka wā e holo mai ai mai Hawaiʻi mokupuni i ko Larry puka kula kiʻekiʻe ma Oʻahu. Kamaʻilio mua ʻo Larry me Pukui i ke kelepona a laila kipa kino aku ʻo ia e launa a e hoʻopaʻa ai me Pukui i ka hui e hoʻopaʻa leo ai i ko Larry kupuna.

Dorothy Kahananui. Used with permission from Kamehameha Schools.

No Ka Moʻolelo ma ka Hoʻōla ʻŌlelo Hawaiʻi

Ua laha ka pā o ke aukahi hoʻōla ʻōlelo Hawaiʻi ma nā peʻa a pau o Hawaiʻi a ua pā pū hoʻi kekahi mau lāhui ʻōiwi ma waho o Hawaiʻi i kūlanalana hoʻi kā lākou ʻōlelo. ʻO ka ʻōmaka ʻana aʻe o ka ʻōlelo Hawaiʻi ma kekahi pae hoʻolana ola ma muli o ka hana aukahi hoʻōla ʻōlelo ma Hawaiʻi nei ka mea e hoihoi nui mai ai ka poʻe ʻōiwi o nā ʻāina mamao e ʻike maka a hoʻokolohua i kekahi hana i ʻano like ma ka hoʻōla ʻana i ka ʻōlelo ʻōiwi o ko lākou ʻāina. Eia ma lalo nei nā iwi nui ʻekolu i nīnauele ʻia ai ke Kauka Larry Kimura no kona manaʻo pili i ka moʻolelo ma ka hoʻōla ʻōlelo ʻana: 1) he mea nui anei ka moʻolelo Hawaiʻi ma ka hoʻōla ʻōlelo? No ke aha? 2) pehea i hoʻohana ʻia ai ka moʻolelo Hawaiʻi ma ka hoʻōla ʻōlelo Hawaiʻi? 3) he aha kou moemoeā nui no ka moʻolelo Hawaiʻi i kēia mua aku?

I ka mua o ka nīnau: he mea nui anei ka moʻolelo Hawaiʻi ma ka hoʻōla ʻōlelo? No ke aha? ʻaʻohe nō pane pōkole kūpono. Pane hōʻuluʻulu maila ʻo ia ma ka ʻōlelo ʻana penei:

> ʻAe. Nui ka ʻike moʻomeheu a hoʻopuka ʻia ma ka hoʻohana ʻōlelo Hawaiʻi kuʻuna waiwai ma nā moʻokalaleo Hawaiʻi e laʻa me nā mele, nā ʻōlelo ʻikeoma, nā palaualea, nā ʻōlelo noʻeau a kaulana. Hoʻohana ʻia nā meiwi kuʻinaiwi i ʻike ʻia ma nā ʻano o ke kani, manaʻo a pilina-ʻōlelo i kū i ke ʻano o ka like, pili, ʻēkoʻa, a nane paha, a me nā meiwi kīnohinohi e laʻa me nā inoa makani, ua, kai, ʻāina a kanaka a me ka helu a pīnaʻi ʻana kekahi mau ʻano meiwi kīnohinohi. ʻO kēia hoʻohana kuluma Hawaiʻi ʻana ka mea e "moʻokalaleo" ai kekahi moʻolelo Hawaiʻi kuʻuna ma waho aʻe o ke ʻano lōʻihi o ka moʻolelo a me kona palapala ʻia ʻana he koina koʻikoʻi no kona kapa ʻia he moʻokalaleo. Kū mau nā moʻokalaleo Hawaiʻi o ia au i newa aku nei no kekahi ana hoʻohālike no ko kākou au a i kumu hoʻoulu hoʻomau kākau hakuhia no kākou. No laila he haʻawina aʻo waiwai lua ʻole kā ia mau kānaka kākau o ia au i hoʻopaʻa ai a ke hoʻāla ʻia nei kākou e noʻonoʻo no kā kākou mau kākau hakuhia Hawaiʻi ʻana e kūpono ai i ko lākou mākaukau ma ko kākou ʻano he Hawaiʻi o kēia au hou. ʻO ia ka hoʻo-ikaika nui o kēia wā, ʻo ka hoʻōla i ka ʻōlelo a ʻike Hawaiʻi ma ke ʻano he mea maʻamau a kuluma i hiki ke komo i ka haku a kākau i moʻolelo he mau ʻano nowela like ʻole no kākou. Nui nā ʻaoʻao o ka ʻōlelo a me ka ʻike Hawaiʻi e hoʻopaʻa ai i ʻike ʻia ka hoʻoholomua ʻana i ka mauli Hawaiʻi i loko o nā hana haku a kākau hou ʻana.

He mea nui nō ka moʻolelo Hawaiʻi ma ka hoʻōla ʻōlelo ʻana. Ma ia mea he moʻolelo Hawaiʻi, wehewehe maila ʻo ia no ia mea he meiwi—he mea ka meiwi e Hawaiʻi ai ka moʻolelo Hawaiʻi. E like nō hoʻi me ia mea he moʻolelo ma kona ʻaoʻao he kiʻina hoʻoili a hoʻomau ʻike, ua like pū ka moʻolelo Hawaiʻi; ʻo ka meiwi naʻe kekahi mea o ka moʻolelo Hawaiʻi e Hawaiʻi ai ʻo ia a e ahuwale ai kona ʻano he "moʻokalaleo." Helupapa aʻela ʻo Kimura i nā ʻano hiʻohiʻona o ia mea he moʻolelo Hawaiʻi—he waiwai a koʻikoʻi loa nō ia i ka moʻolelo Hawaiʻi i kona manaʻo. He mea ko'iko'i nō nā meiwi i ka ho'ōla 'ōlelo 'ana, no ka mea, 'o nā meiwi kekahi mea e 'ike ahuwale 'ia ai ka Hawai'i 'ana o ka mo'olelo. No laila, no nā kānaka e a'o ana i ka 'ōlelo Hawai'i, he mea pono ka ho'omaopopo 'ana i nā meiwi i mea e ho'omau ai i kekahi mau 'ano e Hawai'i ai ka 'ōlelo.

Ho'omau maila 'o Kimura ma ka 'ōlelo penei: "Kū mau nā mo'okalaleo Hawai'i o ia au i newa aku nei no kekahi ana ho'ohālike o ko lākou au a i kumu ho'ohālike no kākou." 'O kona mana'o, 'o ka mo'olelo Hawai'i i loa'a iā kākou mai nā kūpuna mai a me nā kānaka ho'opa'a mo'olelo o ke au i newa aku nei, he hō'ike kēlā o ka nohona o ko lākou wā a no kekahi wā o nā kūpuna aku o lākou. Ma ka heluhelu 'ana aku i ia 'ano mo'olelo, he 'ike kēlā i ka 'ōlelo o ia wā a me nā hi'ohi'ona o ka noho 'ana. Ua pa'a nō ka 'ōlelo o ia wā, a ua haku mo'olelo nō ka po'e mākaukau i ka ho'opa'a kākau—he hō'ailona ho'i o ka pa'a o ka mākaukau 'oi kelakela. No laila, no kakou i kēia wā e holo aku nei, he kumu ho'ohālike kā lākou hana no kākou i kēia wā; he nui nō ka holomua ma ka ho'ōla i ka 'ōlelo Hawai'i ma o ka mo'okalaleo Hawai'i, ka 'ike ku'una, a me nā loina ku'una, he loa nō na'e ho'i ke ala e holo aku ai.

'Oiai ua 'ike 'ia ka holomua nui i loko o nā hana aukahi ho'ōla 'ōlelo a mo'omeheu Hawai'i, aia he mau ala i mua e ho'okumu a e ho'oikaika ai. 'O kekahi o ia ala ke kālailai 'ana aku i nā mo'olelo Hawai'i o ke au i newa aku nei i kumu ho'ohālike no kā kākou mau hana i kēia mau lā e ne'e aku nei. He pahuhopu nō ia e kau ana i mua a e kūlia nō kākou ma nā 'ano a pau e pa'a ai kekahi kahua ma luna o ia mau mākaukau o ia wā i hala a i kūpono ho'i no ka nohona o ko kākou wā 'oiai he wā 'oko'a loa kēia a e mau ka 'oko'a hou 'ana aku nō. 'O ka ho'okuluma aku i ka 'ōlelo ma kekahi pae o ka nohona, a 'o ka ho'okā'oi i ka mākaukau no ke komo ma nā hana hakuhia ka hō'ailona nui o kekahi holomua—he ola nō ho'i ko laila.

I ka lua o ka nīnau: pehea i ho'ohana 'ia ai ka mo'olelo Hawai'i ma ka ho'ōla 'ōlelo Hawai'i, pane maila 'o ia ma ka 'ōlelo 'ana mai penei:

Larry Lindsey Kimura. Author's image.

He kumu ho'ohālike ho'ohana 'ōlelo Hawai'i kuluma ko ia au a he waiwai ke 'ike a ho'opa'a a ho'ohana ma kekahi mau hana hakuhia hou aku e ho'opiha ai i kēia kōā nui ma waena o ke ola ikaika o ko ia au 'ōlelo a mauli Hawai'i me ka nāwaliwali o ka 'ōlelo Hawai'i a me ka mauli Hawaiʻi o kēia wā. ʻO ia kā kākou hana i kēia wā, me ka ʻike pū ʻo ka loli he lula maʻamau ia o nā lāhui kanaka a pau o ke ao. Pehea naʻe e ʻike ai i nā hiʻohiʻona hialaʻi Hawaiʻi i ka hoʻomau moʻokalaleo hou ʻana me ka ʻapo ʻoluʻolu ʻia o ia mākau makakū e kekahi lāhui Hawaiʻi i liliuloli?

No laila, he kumu hoʻohālike ko ia au mau moʻolelo i hoʻopaʻa ʻia; he mea kēlā e hoʻohana a noʻonoʻo ʻia ma ka hoʻōla i ka ʻōlelo a mauli Hawaiʻi. ʻO ia kekahi ʻaoʻao pānoʻonoʻo i komo nui i loko o nā kānaka kākau o ia wā, ʻo ia hoʻi no ka pono o ko mua aku no ka mea ua hoʻomaka lākou e ʻike i ka nalohia o ia mākaukau i ka ʻaui ʻana o ko lākou wā ola. ʻOiai ua moku ka ikaika o ka ʻōlelo Hawaiʻi mai kekahi wā a i kēia wā, a aia nō ke mālama ʻia nei nā hana e hoʻoikaika ʻia ai ka ʻōlelo Hawaiʻi o kēia wā, ke nānā ʻia nei nō ka ʻōlelo Hawaiʻi o ia au he kumu laʻana o ka noʻeau kākau e kūlia ai kākou ma kā kākou mau hana hoʻōla ʻōlelo a mauli Hawaiʻi i kēia wā. ʻAʻole nō ʻo ka maʻiʻo moʻokalaleo ʻo nā kupanaha kalakupua o nā akua a kupua o ia wā kahiko ʻoiai na ia poʻe kākau i kāmoʻo i ia mau maʻiʻo me ka ʻoi kelakela o ka ʻōlelo. He mau kumuhana a maʻiʻo ʻokoʻa a kupunaha hou paha ko kēia ola hou o ka ʻōlelo Hawaiʻi.

No laila, i ka wā e hiki mai ana, eia ka moemoeā: "E hoʻomaka e hoʻohana ʻia ka ʻōlelo Hawaiʻi ma ka hakuhia kūpono e hoʻomāhuahua ai i ka haku a kākau i kekahi mau moʻolelo pōkole a ʻano lōʻihi paha ma ka ʻōlelo Hawaiʻi. E hoʻopaʻa i nā kiʻina e hōʻoi aʻe i ko kākou mākaukau no ka ʻauamo ʻana i kēia kuleana" (Kimura, nīnauele). ʻO ke kākau ʻana ma luna mai o ka paepae ʻike kuʻuna a me ka hakuhia e kūpono ai ko kēia au nohona, ʻo ia ke kūkonukonu o ka mākaukau a ʻo ia ke keʻehina e hiki aku ai. Ua nui nō hoʻi ka paʻu ma luna o ka hoʻōla i ka ʻōlelo a e like nō hoʻi me ka hana maiau a kahi mau kānaka noiʻi nowelo ʻo ʻĪʻī, ʻo Malo, ʻo Kepelino, ʻo Kamakau, pono i ka Hawaiʻi ke hoʻomaka e hakuhia i loko o ka hoʻopaʻa moʻolelo ʻana i mea e paʻa ai ke au nui me ke au iki o kona nohona.

Panina Mokuna

He ʻohina koʻikoʻi a waiwai ka moʻolelo Hawaiʻi o ka ʻike o kekahi wā a he kiʻina hakuhia ia i loko o ka mākaukau kanaka ma ka hoʻopaʻa a me ka hoʻoili a hoʻomau ʻike mai kekahi hanauna a kekahi hanauna aku. I loko o ke kiʻina hakuhia o ka moʻolelo Hawaiʻi, hoʻopaʻa ʻia nō ke au nui me ke au iki o ko kekahi wā nohona; he hana nō hoʻi kēia i hana ʻia i loko o kona ʻano kuʻuna a he hana ia e māhuahua aʻe ai ka ʻike ʻōiwi o ka lāhui Hawaiʻi.

Ma kēia mokuna, ua hōʻike ʻia aku nō kekahi mau mea a ke Kauka Larry Kimura i hōʻike mai ai iaʻu no ka moʻolelo Hawaiʻi a me kona mau manaʻo no ke komo ʻana o ka moʻolelo Hawaiʻi ma ka hoʻōla ʻōlelo ʻana. He ʻekolu nō momi nui i puka aʻe mai kēia hana: 1) ʻo nā meiwi me ka hualekikona kekahi kiʻina hoʻomau a hoʻoili ʻike o ka moʻolelo Hawaiʻi e "Hawaiʻi" ai. Aia ma loko o kēia kiʻina no nā meiwi, ka "meiwi kuʻinaiwi" a me ka "meiwi kīnohinohi" i hōʻike ʻia aʻela ma ka ʻōlelo a Kimura. 2) He ʻumeke kāʻeo ka moʻolelo Hawaiʻi o ka ʻike kupuna i waiho ʻia mai no kākou. 3) He kumu hoʻohālike a he kumu hoʻoulu a hoʻolana nā moʻolelo Hawaiʻi i loaʻa mai iā kākou ma ke ala hoʻōla ʻōlelo, ʻoiai naʻe ʻo ka pae hoʻohana ʻōlelo ma ke kākau moʻolelo/moʻokalaleo ʻana, he pae haʻakoʻikoʻi a kiʻekiʻe ia o kekahi hoʻohana ʻōlelo ʻana. Kau nui ka manaʻo o kākou poʻe hoʻōla ʻōlelo Hawaiʻi he wā nō e kuluma aku ai ia kiʻekiʻena hoʻohana ʻōlelo i ke kūlia hoʻoikaika ma nā keʻehina liʻiliʻi a paʻa e like me ke kūkulu paepae pōhaku, ʻo nā ʻiliʻili ke hoʻokū i nā pōhaku nui a kūpaʻa pono. A lohe ʻia ke kāhea, "E ʻoni paʻa!" I ka ʻoni nō e hōʻoia ʻia ai ka paʻa.

ʻAkahi: ʻoiai he kiʻina hoʻomau a hoʻoili ʻike ko neia wā Hawaiʻi, he mea ia e "ʻōiwi" a e "Hawaiʻi" hou ai ka moʻolelo Hawaiʻi ma waho aku o ka lōʻihi a pōkole paha o ia mea he moʻolelo. He mea koʻikoʻi kēia e ʻike a e kūlia ai ka Hawaiʻi ma luna o ka hoʻokāʻoi i kēia ʻike ʻana. Aia ma loko o kēia kiʻina meiwi a hualekikona kekahi ʻaoʻao kuʻuna o ke kākau ʻana. Aia wale nō a ʻike i ka paʻa o kēia mākau a kuanaʻike hoʻi ma kekahi hoʻopānoʻonoʻo no nēia au hou, a laila e komo ma ke kākau moʻolelo/moʻokalaleo hakuhia.

ʻAlua: ʻoiai he ʻumeke kāʻeo nō hoʻi ka moʻolelo Hawaiʻi o ka ʻike kupuna i waiho ʻia mai no kākou, he pono i ka Hawaiʻi ke mālama a hoʻomau. I nā kūpuna i hoʻomau ai i kēia poʻe moʻolelo, ua hana ʻia nō me ka manaʻolana he makana ia e ola ai nō kēia kau moʻolelo i ʻole e poina ai kākou i loko o ka nui loli o ke au o ka manawa. ʻAʻole nō paha i hoʻoholo ʻia e hoʻomau ʻia ua mau moʻolelo nei i waiho ʻia ma ke kino lahilahi a waihona ʻē aʻe paha; ʻo ko nā hanauna aʻo ʻana i ka moʻolelo a hoʻomau i ua loina hakuhia moʻolelo nei kekahi pahuhopu nui—aia nō ke aʻo maoli ma loko o ka luʻu i ke kuʻuna ʻana o ka moʻolelo Hawaiʻi.

ʻAkolu: ʻoiai he kumu hoʻohālike nā moʻolelo Hawaiʻi i loaʻa mai iā kākou ma ke ala hoʻōla ʻōlelo, he kuleana ko ka Hawaiʻi ma ka hoʻoili hoʻomau ma kekahi ʻano hakuhia hou i kona waiwai i kēia wā hou. ʻOiai ua moku ka ikaika o ka ʻōlelo Hawaiʻi mai kekahi wā a i kēia wā e neʻe aku nei, aia nō ke ʻauamo ʻia nei nā keʻehina hoʻoikaika e māhuahua hou aku ai ka pae ikaika o ka ʻōlelo Hawaiʻi i pae mākaukau e ʻalo ai i ka hana nui o ke ola hou. ʻO ka nuʻu e kūlia ai, ʻo ia ka paʻa ʻike pono i nā ʻaoʻao hoʻohana ʻōlelo ma kona mau honuanua like ʻole i hiki ke komo a walea i ka hakuhia i ka moʻolelo/moʻokalaleo Hawaiʻi ma ka ʻōlelo Hawaiʻi. ʻO ke komo liʻiliʻi ma ka haku moʻolelo, ʻaʻole nō paha manaʻo nui ʻia, eia nō naʻe, he keʻehina ia e hiki aku ai i ka pahuhopu nui. No ka poʻe hoʻopaʻa moʻolelo piha akamai a kaulana a kākou i kamaʻāina ai, ua ʻike ʻia ka ʻiʻo o kā lākou hana ma ka hoʻopaʻa i nā mea nui o ko lākou wā, a no ka poʻe e hiki mai ma hope, ma ke kākau moʻolelo e ʻike ʻia ai ke au nui me ke au iki o ko kākou wā.

KUHIA O HOPE

1. "Ke Kaao Hooniua Puuwai no Ka-Miki," *Ka Hoku o Hawaii*, Buke 10, Helu 33, 2 Malaki 1916, 'ao'ao 1.

2. Hualekikona: he hua'ōlelo a māmala'ōlelo paha e pili pū ana me kekahi pō'aiapili pono'ī e ahuwale ai ka 'ike mo'omeheu; na ka pō'aiapili e hō'ike i ka hua'ōlelo a māmala'ōlelo paha e ho'ohana 'ia.

3. Meiwi: he hi'ohi'ona lawena 'ōlelo Hawai'i i ahuwale i kona 'ike alapine 'ia keu ma ka 'anunu'u ho'ohana 'ōlelo Hawai'i ha'ako'iko'i e la'a ma ka mo'olelo a mele Hawai'i paha.

4. Mo'oka'ao: he mo'olelo pōkole ia i 'ike 'ia ma o ka ha'i waha a kākau 'ia paha.

5. Mo'okalaleo: he mo'olelo 'ano nui a lō'ihi i piha pū i nā 'ike Hawai'i ku'una i palapala 'ia ma ka nūpepa paha e la'a me "Ke Kaao Hooniua Puuwai no Ka-Miki."

PAPA HELU KŪMOLE

"Ke Kaao Hooniua Puuwai no Ka-Miki." *Ka Hoku o Hawaii*, 2 Malaki 1916, Buke 10, Helu 33, 'ao'ao 1.

Kimura, Larry L. "Nā Mele Kau O Ka Māhele Mua O Ka Mo'olelo 'O Hi'iakaikapoliopele, Na Joseph Poepoe: He Kālailaina Me ke Kālele Ma Luna O Nā Ku'inaiwi Kaulua." 2002. Pepa Laeo'o. Ke Kula Nui o Hawai'i.

Kimura, Larry Lindsey. "He Kālailaina I Ka Panina 'Ōlelo A Ka Mānaleo Hawai'i: Ka Ho'ohālikelike 'Ana I Ka 'Ōlelo Mānaleo A Nā Hanauna 'Elua, 'O Ka 'Ōlelo Kūmau A Ka Makua Me Ka 'Ōlelo Kūpaka A Ke Keiki." 2012. Pepa Lae'ula. Ke Kula Nui o Hawai'i.

Kimura, Larry Lindsey, nīnauele na Kamalani Johnson. June 1, 2016.

He keiki noho papa 'o **Kamalani Johnson** o ka makani 'Āhiu o Kahana i hānau a hānai 'ia i loko o ka ho'oilina palapala mo'olelo a kona mau kūpuna. Ma muli o ua ho'oilina nei o ke ala i ma'a i ka hele 'ia e ona mau kūpuna i kā'eo ai kona 'umeke e 'auamo a e lawelawe aku ai 'o ia i kona kaiaulu. He pa'a mo'olelo 'o ia no Kahana, Ko'olauloa, O'ahu; a 'o Waiākea Uka, Hilo, Hawai'i kāna 'āina ho'okama e noho nei. 'O ka mo'olelo o ke kenekulia 19 ke kahua o kāna mau hana he kumu a'o 'ōlelo Hawai'i a mo'okalaleo Hawai'i, a he kanaka ho'omohala ha'awina a luna ho'oponopono 'ōlelo Hawai'i no Ka Haka 'Ula o Ke'elikōlani. I loko o kāna mau hana noi'i a a'o 'ōlelo, 'āwili 'o ia i ka 'ike o nā kūpuna o ka wā ma mua i maunu e ulu a'e ai ka hoihoi o ke kanaka e lu'u hou aku i ka 'ike o ke au i o kikilo aku. E like nō me kā ka pa'a mo'olelo kaulana 'o Kepelino Keauokalani i ho'opuka ai, "Ahu kupanaha iā Hawai'i 'Imi Loa!" he 'imi loa nō ka Hawai'i i kona 'ike iho nō a laupa'i; a pēlā pū ho'i ko Kamalani 'imi loa 'ana aku a laupa'i ka 'ike a pōmaika'i kēia ne'epapa 'ana aku i mua.

No ka Hō'ola 'Ōlelo a Mo'omeheu Hawai'i a 'Ōiwi o Ka Haka 'Ula O Ke'elikōlani Koleke 'Ōlelo Hawai'i o ke Kulanui o Hawai'i ma Hilo ke Kauka **Larry Kimura** a ke mau nei kāna hana ho'ola 'ōlelo Hawai'i no kanalima a 'oi makahiki. 'O ke kuamoʻo o nei aukahi ʻo ia ka hoʻomōhala ʻana i ka hoʻonaʻauao ma loko o ka ʻōlelo Hawaiʻi mai ka pae pēpē a hiki i ke kula kiʻekiʻe a hoʻomau ʻia i loko o ke kulanui. ʻO ka Luna Hoʻomalu ʻo Kimura o ke Kōmike Lekikona Hawaiʻi no ka haku huaʻōlelo Hawaiʻi hou. ʻO Kauka Kimura ka Pelekikena mua a Hoa- Hoʻokumu o ko Hawaiʻi kula kaiaʻōlelo Hawaiʻi mua loa ʻo Pūnana Leo a he Lālā Papa Alakaʻi o ka ʻAha Pūnana Leo.

He lālā hoʻōla mele Hawaiʻi ʻo Kimura o kekahi ʻāuna ʻōpio liʻiliʻi o Ke Au Mauli Hawaiʻi Hou o nā makahiki mai ka 1967 a i nā makahiki 1990. Mau kāna haku mele ʻana a kū he mau mele āna i nā kūlana makana hanohano. Ua hoʻomaka kona kāmoʻo ʻana i nā mānaleo Hawaiʻi hope loa mai ka makahiki 1966 a ʻo ka ʻoi ma o kona hoʻokumu a mālama ʻana i ka papahana lēkiō ʻo Ka Leo Hawaiʻi no ka hoʻopaʻa ʻana he 525 a ʻoi hola ʻōlelo mānaleo Hawaiʻi no nā makahiki he ʻumikumāono mai nā makahiki 1972–1988. Ke mau nei ko Kauka Kimura aʻo ʻōlelo a moʻomeheu Hawaiʻi.

. . . our kūpuna always understood the extraordinary value of moʻolelo Hawaiʻi in relation to our intellectual, emotional, and spiritual sovereignty.

2

"Kīkohu ʻia ka Hulu ʻIo me ka ʻUlaʻula"

Ahukini Kupihea

I was born in the town of Waimea on the island of Kauaʻi. I even graduated from Waimea High School. But I actually grew up in the little plantation town of Kekaha, west of Waimea. It was a thriving little community during the 1960s and ʼ70s, when the sugar plantation was still going strong. It was also a new community, with a new sugar processing mill that was large enough to accommodate all the sugar lands from Mānā to Olokele. It was an upgrade from the old mills in Waimea and Mānā that were both phased out as a result of its construction. One of the oldest towns, Mānā was furthest west on the island, originally created by one of the early South Pacific migrations that settled Kealohilani. My mother's father helped in the construction of a few buildings in Mānā, including a public swimming pool. He also played the C-Melody saxophone in one of Mānā's old Taxi-dance halls in the 1930s.

Kekaha was a great place when I was little. There was the mom-and-pop Kekaha Store, a theatre up until hurricane ʻIwa in 1982, a public swimming pool, and a huge park that was connected to Kekaha Elementary School where I attended till the sixth grade. One of my favorite things to do after school was climbing some of the big banyan and ironwood trees that bordered the park. There would always be a bunch of other boys there too, watching older siblings on the basketball court, practicing baseball, or Pop Warner football. We looked like a bunch of little brown monkeys flying from branch to branch. It might have been one of the reasons why my grandfather referred to our subdivision as "Gorilla Gahdenz." During the summer months we would all rotate, from the trees to the shore breaks of Kaupueo. Then from the beach to Kekaha Swimming Pool at Paewaʻa. I liked having the pool as our final stop because I was freezing by then and would just lie on the warm concrete that was preheated by the afternoon sun.

As far as art was concerned, it was pretty much non-existent on the west side. My influences came from the limited meager comic books I had access to, and whatever television cartoons were visible when my younger sister and I took turns rotating the antenna. There were only two art contests the entire time I was at Kekaha Elementary, and none at all when I attended Waimea High School.

I took four years of art in high school, but unfortunately so did all the kolohe kids too. The instructor never had time outside of policing the class for any kind of art instruction. So I pretty much just continued doing what I did in elementary school, which was to draw in all my other classes. My proper introduction to art came while in the Art Department at UH Mānoa. I had never seen what was truly achievable in the arts till then. However, for this I am truly grateful, because the absence of formal training during my early years has shaped me into the type of artist that I am—one who operates predominantly from the imagination. When I was young, I would just draw whatever I felt like. I had no idea of value, contour, or perspective. I had no idea how to use a pencil. But I also had no boundaries as to how I could see things. Also, I am what you would call a visual thinker. I see everything in my mind's eye before it ever makes it to paper. But when I did make it to UH, I was reacquainted with a part of myself that was always there, on the periphery, but never manifested because I predominantly worked in pencil and ink.

My rude awakening to my color blindness happened during final critique in the introduction to painting class. That was a total game changer for me, and a serious discipline changer as well. I resigned to make the best of my situation down in the sculpture department the following semester. But to my surprise and complete satisfaction, color theory was not a prerequisite for bronze casting. I also gained a wonderful mentor in the late great Fred Roster.

Now my sculpture degree has really bitten me in the ass, and taken a pretty good chunk too. As I have not "worked" as a sculptor in years, as there are a lot more monetary opportunities for illustrators and painters. I have though, come face-to-face with my old dragon during several color works I managed to complete. Which includes the cover art for this very important compendium of unique Hawaiian intellectuals. Moʻolelo is truly the foundation of us all, as I believe it to be one the most powerful displays of the imagination.

"The Plumage of the Hawk is Spotted with Red"—a play on the two who have inspired this piece. ʻIo, as in ʻIolani (Luahine). And the kī in kīkohu (kohu; appropriate) is a play on (Larry) Kimura. Both are precious (hulu) to the kuamoʻo (path) of our ʻōlelo makuahine (mother tongue), the major theme of this cover illustration. They are also adorned in red (ʻulaʻula), a color known to be sacred to our kūpuna, and indicative of the knowledge and values that we have inherited through the living breath of the ancients that still soars today.

On the front cover is the famous hula dancer ʻIolani Luahine, a powerful native icon who was well known to be a medium of the dance. Her physical skill, coupled with a mesmerizing emotional projection of the mele, allowed her to become an objective embodiment of the oral tradition that we have inherited. I envisioned her kino as a physical repository of ʻike Hawaiʻi. Flowing forth from

History of Print. Ahukini Kupihea, 2017.

this phenomenal archive are the many traditions attributed to moʻolelo Hawaiʻi in the form of her living breath. This Hā is the breadth of the spiritual and intellectual capacity of our kūpuna that has progressed since the first accumulation of the koʻe ʻenuhe who gathered the earth into mounds.

My personal choice of illustrating ʻIolani Luahine as the icon of our oral tradition stems from a few different places. The first is the Kauaʻi connection, where she climbed the ladder of the mysteries within her hula school and completed her ʻūniki, and where I myself, as well as co-author/editor Hailiʻōpua Baker, were born and raised. The second comes from my experience as a docent for the Bishop Museum Kālia (Hilton Hawaiian Village, 2000–2002). Three short videos of aunty ʻIolani were on a continuous loop during business hours that captured just enough of the dance and the dancer to flip in me an internal switch of intuitive recognition of a bona fide medium of the dance. It became apparent to me the more I watched her that she was in an altered psychological state of consciousness, induced by the living elements of the dance. She became the winds, the rain, the mountains, the maile lauliʻi on the hula kuahu. It is also interesting that the original video image of aunty ʻIolani has given us an experience similar to the cultural-technological shift impressed upon us by the printed word. The third is my family connection to ʻIolani Luahine, when my kupuna Nāhupu (k) married Kūnuiakea Makekau (w).

As the breath of our heritage encircles the body of ʻIolani Luahine, it enters the coffin of a Gutenburg style printing press. Perhaps it is ironic that the carriage of the press is called the "coffin," as it could serve as a metaphor for the passing of the oral tradition. But for the Indigenous cultural mindset, death, especially in its symbolic form, is always a given aspect of new life, and a renewal of the creative cycle interpreted through duality (black-white, male-female, masculine-feminine, life-death, so on and so forth).

When looking into Western symbolism, however, the coffin or casket is much more suggestive of protection, of preserving its sacred, or even secret contents. It is sometimes interpreted as a female symbol of the unconscious and the material, encapsulating something precious and fragile from the pressures of the external world. When conceived of as a box, the casket also symbolizes unexpected potentialities. This is definitely true in the case of the American Protestant Missionaries, who introduced the printing press to Hawaiʻi in 1822. They probably envisioned a gentle, docile nation easily enthralled into Christian servitude under the ridiculous notion of "original sin." There were a great number of buyers and takers of their ideology under the initial information monopoly of the church.

But we all know what eventually ended up happening. An 80 percent national literacy rate, and some opinionated intellectual Hawaiians opportunistic enough to initiate the dissemination of Hawaiian-owned and run newspapers. To the inevitable dismay of the growing Christian movement, they recorded ancient cultural practices, elements of our transcendent mythic philosophy, and a holistic form of spirituality. Although an astounding percentage of the native population did willingly accept Christianity throughout the pae ʻāina, our kūpuna always understood the extraordinary value of moʻolelo Hawaiʻi in relation to our intellectual, emotional, and spiritual sovereignty. This innate partiality did not allow post-contact poʻe Hawaiʻi to relinquish a millenia of cultural acquisition so easily. We stood confirmed as a nation of psychological resilience.

The voice of antiquity burst forth from the coffin—only to be engulfed in the flames. These are not the ordinary devouring flames of the physical world, but the fires of transformation. Off of the press stone emerged a genuinely new form of expression that scintillated with the light of native consciousness, recharging the voice of antiquity to reflect traditions and mysteries of the past, to highlight the sacred and profane of the present, and to illuminate our inherent native potentiality for the future.

The first of many successions borne by the printed word created a powerful paradigm shift within the Indigenous consciousness of our ancestors. Segments of the Moʻo begin to form; the compiling begins. The poets and the bards begin to step forward, chants arise in praise of the chiefs, the offspring are put in place. The resounding echoes of an ancient land spring forth from a literal darkness into the foreword of our existence. The reels are set in motion, spinning, first at the speed of sound. Collecting, assembling, the segments of the Moʻo are infinite, the wheel becomes the hub. Building, growing, evolving, the past now streams along with the present. The Moʻo, so powerful, undeniable in its becoming, is now a substantial foundation. We revisit and reflect on particular segments, working as agents of a continuous cultural evolution, giving new light and life to the voices of antiquity.

At the onset of this project, I was unsure who the male figure would be to balance aunty ʻIolani Luahine for the cover of this book. ʻIolani Luahine of course represents the female aspects of creation, fertility, birth, intuition, and motherly love from which the oral tradition has come forth. In contrast, the male represents procreation, ownership, dominance, and courage. The true power of the female for Indigenous culture is the phenomenon of bringing forth new life. The true power of the male is the potential for transcendence, the ability to move above and beyond the limits of material experience.

So I was having this discussion with Haili and Kaliko, we were eating lunch at some crappy vegetarian smoothie place at Windward Mall, trying to figure out who would be the ideal kāne for the cover. A few names were mentioned— all prominent historians, all great aliʻi, all great agents in time of change—and all of them frickin dead. So all of a sudden, we had criteria. Someone living, possibly still working, with a voice in the Hawaiian community, some expertise in or involvement with the perpetuation of 'ōlelo Hawai'i, and maybe, someone who hasn't pissed too many people off.

Then Kaliko says—

"You know, sumbody submitting one interview wit 'Lale' fo dis puke."

There was a brief moment of silence as we looked at each other... then erupted in excitement.

"Ho! Yah, Larry Kimura!, he wud be awesome fo dis book."

A veggie omelette never tasted so good! But wait. Young Kauanoe? Or old... ah mean old-ER? Hahaha! Yah, that was cool, and his reputation really preceded him in making him the perfect fit for our criteria. Mahalo e Kauanoe!

As I began to draw, images began to take shape. First was aunty 'Iolani. I moved on the page from right to left; front cover to back cover. The re-emergence of the oral tradition as the Mo'o is illustrated as the movable typeface, the visual key that takes precedence over the evolution of the printed word. Pages of print slide through the picture plane, and the voice of the ancients once again takes new form. The wax reel cylinder records the voice, printed transcriptions inevitably follow. The invention of the typewriter replaces movable type.

Although it belongs to an era in and of itself, I decided the typing element (keys) would be the best visual representation of the advances in technology that have changed along the way, as we access and interpret the original letter press printing database. Next, photography captures the print, then reels of Microfiche are cast into the roiling current of our digital era. This current pushes and pulls an ocean of information, forming the swells and the undertow of current technological applied sciences.

Kauanoe emerges as part of the swell. His phenomenal contributions to the perpetuation of our 'ōlelo makuahine have been subjected to technological change. I think of it as analogous to a onshore current, where waves bring new energy into the surf zone and onto the beach. Then the backwash and undertow take it back out again, forming a continuous cycle of regeneration. His shirt suggests the color of the projected light emitted from the microfiche lamp, symbolic of simple analog beginnings. His kīhei represents the contemporary fabric of this digital age, encoding a massive cultural field of inquiry, now accessible at our fingertips.

The pattern behind him is the resurgence of the undertow. Ostensibly moving through his po'o, it represents the cognitive and conceptual processes by which we are here, in this book, bringing ancient energies back to shore, ironically in the form of PRINT.

*The ultimate hope is that with each generation,
we will continue to adhere to Keaulumoku's foresight,
and like Helekunihi, Poepoe, Nakuina, Kukahi, Pukui,
and Ka Waihona A Ke Aloha, we ʻauʻa, we retain,
and "withhold, detain and refuse to part with" our moku.*

3
E Kama, E ʻAuʻa ʻIa
Retain Thy Heritage

R. Keawe Lopes Jr.

ʻAuʻa ʻia e Kama e kona moku
Kona moku e Kama e ʻauʻa ʻia

Oh child, look and observe thy heritage
Thy lands, oh child, retain them
—Keaulumoku[1]

Keaulumoku, born in 1716, was the son of the great chief Kauakahiakua Nui, and is noted by Samuel Manaiakalani Kamakau, a renowned nineteenth-century Hawaiian scholar and historian, as "a famous composer of different kinds of mele (Hawaiian poetic expression, songs, and chants), including compositions for war, praise, love, prophecy, and genealogy" (23 Feb.). One particular mele of importance that he composed is "He Mele Na Keaulumoku No Aikanaka." This mele is a mele wānana (prophecy) composed for Aikanaka, the maternal grandfather of King Kalakaua and Queen Liliuokalani, the last rulers of the Kingdom of Hawaiʻi.

The opening lines of this particular mele detail what seems to be Keaulumoku's view in response to the influx of foreigners, and their foreign ways, into our island home. Keaulumoku urges the kama (native) to "ʻauʻa," to retain, and moreover, "to withhold, detain and refuse to part with" their moku (heritage). It is said by many mele and hula practitioners that the illegal overthrow of the Hawaiian Kingdom in 1893 was the result of allowing too much and not withholding enough. As a result, this mele is one of our most treasured and sacred hula pahu (drum dances), and is often performed to remind and encourage our people to continue to "ʻauʻa," to retain and hold fast, even when times are unstable and turbulent.

Elisa Fiorio explains that the illegal control of our political and social structures has interrupted a highly successful history of orality, and has provoked the disappearance of our historical accounts, which are found in our oral culture: stories, poems, proverbs, riddles, enigmas, anecdotes, songs, ritual formulas, discourses, customs, and biographical accounts (68). In the midst of great change over the past 200 years, our kūpuna (ancestors) have invested tirelessly in the preservation and perpetuation of our people's cultural heritage, oftentimes in desperation to "'au'a," to preserve our historical accounts, lest they become 'ōpala (trash). Such were the words of one of my beloved kūpuna, Elia Helekunihi, a brilliant Hawaiian scholar of the nineteenth century. In the midst of such a turbulent time of turmoil surrounding the illegal overthrow of the Hawaiian Kingdom, Helekunihi produced a number of transcripts containing pertinent information concerning family mele ko'ihonua (genealogical chants), kū'auhau ali'i (royal genealogy), lapa'au Hawai'i (Hawaiian herbal medicine), and ancient Hawaiian history, or what he titled "Moolelo Hawaii."

In a personal letter to Reverend Oliver Emerson in February of 1893, Helekunihi writes "O ke kumu o ko'u kakau ana, no kuu minamina i ka Moolelo o Hawaii Nei, o nalowale ia" (The reason why I wrote (this) is because of my concern for the history of Hawai'i, lest it be lost). Helekunihi was willing to do everything possible for its preservation, even if it took years to complete and every ounce of energy from the strength of his fingers. He explains,

> Ua manao au he 10 makahiki a'u i hoonohonoho ai pau mai Aperila 1873–1883. I kuu hoao ana hiki ole oolea ke ami hoai o kuu peni i kakau ai ma waena o na manamana 3 & 4 aole ma waena o 1 & 2 ame 2 & 3.

> I think it has been 10 years for me to arrange and finish, from April 1873–1883. (At times) When I tried, it was challenging, my joints are stiff and as for my pen, I write with it between my 3rd and 4th fingers, not between 1st and 2nd or 2nd or 3rd.[2]

Helekunihi's primary goal was to "'au'a," which required that he make the necessary sacrifices to preserve this treasure of information. Helekunihi believed that "he ole hoi ka lilo i opala mahope o kuu make ana" (there would be no benefit with [this] becoming trash after my death).

Mary Kawena Pukui, one of Hawai'i's foremost scholars of the twentieth century, conveys this same thought of "minamina," or a sense of worry and concern, in her interviews with the many mānaleo (native speakers) she interviewed in the 1950s and '60s. In a session with the renowned hula master Joseph Ilalaole, a native of Puna, she explains that the reason why she was going through all the pana 'āina (places of interest) of Puna with him was so that the names would live, and that they would be documented and pronounced correctly in the future: "A o ia ka makou o ka hoopololei, i ole hoi ai e ano e ka ka aina o kaua" (That is what we are trying to correct, so that [the names of] our land would not be strange or different). Pukui continues that, "keia mau inoa a pau loa ea, minamina, minamina o nalowale" (as for all these place names, they are priceless, regretful if lost) (Interview).

Like Helekunihi and Pukui, many beloved kūpuna invested and sacrificed much to ʻauʻa, to retain our cultural heritage. With each generation that passes by, we are blessed with those who take on the responsibility of ensuring that the vast treasures of our cultural heritage live on. Over a hundred years ago, such was the case with Joseph Mokuohai Poepoe and Moses Nakuina, two remarkable Hawaiian scholars who devoted their efforts to the preservation of mele and moʻolelo using the printing press to publish newspaper columns and books. Today, Ka Waihona A Ke Aloha, an interactive resource center of Kawaihuelani Center for Hawaiian Language, dedicates its efforts to the promotion, preservation, and perpetuation of mele and mele practitioners, to ʻauʻa, to retain and preserve their moʻolelo, and to hold fast to our moku.

Hoʻopuka ma Ka Naʻi Aupuni

Prior to the overthrow of the Hawaiian Kingdom, our people's heritage was clearly visible in the most advanced technology of the time for disseminating information, the printing press. The Hawaiian language newspapers (1834 to 1948) exhibit, for the most part, at least up until the illegal overthrow in 1893, that Hawaiian was still the language of governance, power, business, trade, and education. The vast numbers of Hawaiian language newspapers tell us that our language was still very strong. The publishing of mele and moʻolelo was common in these newspapers, reaffirming that the thoughts and views of haku mele (composers) and the poʻe hoʻopaʻa moʻolelo (retainers of lore) of the time were just as important as those of journalists today.

Joseph Mokuohai Poepoe, editor of *Ka Naʻi Aupuni* (1905–1908), was one of Hawaiʻi's noted scholars of "Moʻolelo," or Hawaiian historical accounts. Poepoe explains the importance of moʻolelo by quoting Marcus Cicero, a famous Roman philosopher:

"A o ka Moolelo" . . . "oia ka mea e hoao ai i ka manawa; oia ka malamalama o ka oiaio; ke ola o ka hoomanao; ka rula o ka hoomanao; ka elele o ka wa kahiko."

Historical accounts are what enlightens the time; it is the brilliance of truth; the life of recollection; the ruler of memory; the messenger of more ancient times.

Poepoe further boasts that our mele and moʻolelo are just as valuable as those of the Hellenic people, the Greeks, who were renowned scholars of heroic legends and poetry.

In this same 1906 "Moolelo," however, Poepoe expressed the need to use the printing press as an avenue to 'au'a, and sadly, to re-kindle perhaps the interest of the "Opio Hawaii" (Hawaiian Youth) in our people's historical accounts:

> Ke hoopuka aku nei makou ma keia wahi o Ka Na'i Aupuni i ka Moolelo Kahiko o Hawaii nei, e like me ia i hoomakaukau ia a kakauia e ka lunahooponopono o keia nupepa, a ke lana nei ko makou manao e lilo ana keia mahele i mea e pulamaia e na Opio Hawaii. Ua pili keia Moolelo i ko Hawaii nei "Ancient History," elike me ia i hoikeia ma na mele ame na kuauhau a ka poe kahiko.

> We are publishing in this column of Ka Na'i Aupuni the ancient history of Hawai'i, in the manner that it was prepared and written by the editor of this newspaper, and we are hoping that this section will become something treasured by the Hawaiian youth. This particular moolelo is related to Hawai'i's "Ancient History," and is very similar to what was expressed in mele and genealogical accounts of the ancient people.

As a result, Poepoe invested in the printing of a particular series of columns entitled "Moolelo Hawaii Kahiko" (Ancient Hawaiian History) including information that was "hoakoakoaia, hoiliilia, houluuluia, a hoonohonohoia" (gathered, gleaned, compiled, and arranged) from mele and mo'olelo previously stewarded by "poe loea pili moolelo Hawaii," or experts in the field of Hawaiian history. The survival of these historical accounts rested in the assurance that the newspaper would aid in their dissemination to the community, and then, further serve as a sort of archival space where these accounts would be preserved. Poepoe's hope was to 'au'a, lest these historical accounts "become the possession of nalowale." Poepoe explains,

> O ka mea i paa a i loaa i ka mea kakau, e paa ana ia; aka, o ka mea i loaa ole a i paa ole iaia, na ka nalowale aku ia. A he nui hoi ka minamina no ka nalowale aku o kekahi mau mea ano nui iloko o ka ole mau loa.

> That which the author is familiar with, and is in his possession, will be recorded however, for that which he does not have, and does not know, it is in the possession of "nalowale." There is much to regret for the disappearing of some of the more important [information, accounts] into ultimate oblivion.

The word "nalowale" unfortunately means to be "lost, gone, forgotten, vanished, missing, hidden, extinct, disappeared" (Pukui and Elbert). This tells us that Poepoe was extremely concerned about the preservation and survival of our people's lore. This newspaper series of columns served as a repository, so that the information would not be lost to what he refers to as "ka 'ole mau loa," or "ultimate oblivion." This is an extremely regrettable reference to traditional knowledge that we would never be able to recover, the possible impetus for Poepoe's investment to 'au'a by means of the newspaper.

Inā E Pa'i Buke 'Ia

Following the illegal overthrow of our kingdom, Hawai'i was annexed as a territory to the United States of America, and English was declared the language of instruction in education. As a result, in 1902, Moses Nakuina, like Keaulumoku and Poepoe, expressed a similar urgency to 'au'a, to retain our heritage, by publishing a book, entitled *Mo'olelo Hawai'i o Pakaa A Me Ku-a-Pakaa*. Nakuina writes:

> He mau makahiki i hala ae nei, mamuli o ka imi ana i na moolelo Hawaii kahiko loa, ma ka ninau ana i ka poe kahiko, ua ikeia ko lakou waiwai ina e pa'i buke ia, a lilo i mea hoonaauao mai i ka lahui o keia au, nolaila, ua ohi, houluulu, wae a hooponoponoia ka moolelo o Pakaa a me Ku-a-Pakaa kana keiki. (Foreword)

> In some years past, through searching for very old Hawaiian stories by asking the elders, that their value would be fully realized if they were published in books and used as an educational tool for the nation in this present time, as a result, the story of Pakaa and Ku-a-Pakaa his child was gathered, collected, drafted, and edited.

Nakuina stated that the knowledge gained by the elders of his time should be published in books in hopes of educating our people. This is true with Joseph L. Kukahi, another brilliant Hawaiian scholar, who in the same year published a book entitled *Ke Kumulipo He Moolelo Hawai'i*. Kukahi explained, "hanaia i buke i mea hoomanao a i mea hoonaauao hoi" (publish it as a book to remember and to educate) (2).

There were some who thought that stories like *Pakaa a me Ku-a-Pakaa* were fictitious fairy tales that had no real value, and thus should not be considered. However, Nakuina saw a greater value in this particular mo'olelo, and lists four reasons in the foreword, of why it should be printed:

Akahi, ua kakauia ma ka olelo Hawaii oiaio o ke au kahiko.

First, (the story) was written in the true Hawaiian language of ancient times.

The very first reason why Nakuina published this moʻolelo was in direct response to the state of our language during his time, which must have been in such distress that it urged Nakuina to affirm that the moʻolelo of *Pakaa and Ku-a-Pakaa* would be written not just in the Hawaiian language, but in the true Hawaiian language of the old days. It is my conjecture that perhaps anticipating its eventual near demise, Nakuina made the decision to use the publishing of this moʻolelo as a way to preserve the Hawaiian language of old.

Alua, o na mele, na pa-ha a me na kau i nalowale kekahi a e nalowale aku ana, aole loa ia e loaa hou ina aole e paʻi buke ia.

Secondly, as for mele, pa-ha and kau that disappeared and are presently disappearing, they will never exist again if not published in books.

Nakuina explained that mele, paha (improvised chants), and kau (sacred chants) were in a dire state, and perhaps not being practiced as much. Therefore, if he did not publish them in this moʻolelo, they would eventually nalowale, or cease to exist. This informs us of how important the preservation of moʻolelo is to the survival of mele, and vice versa. The publishing of Nakuina's book would serve as a repository for this moʻolelo and ensure the survival of its mele.

Akolu, ka inoa o na makani o kela a me keia mokupuni o ko Hawaii Paeaina, a Teritore o Hawaii i keia wa.

Thirdly, the names of the winds of all the islands of Hawaiʻi, presently the Territory of Hawaiʻi.

Our kūpuna knew that the wealth of mele is embedded within their lyrics. Kamakau explained, "Ua hanaia na mele me na waiwai huna iloko o ka lehulehu loa. He nui na loina a me na kaona iloko." (Mele were fashioned with numerous valuable secrets hidden within them. There were many customs and hidden inner meanings.) (21 Dec.) Nakuina knew that preserving the mele in this moʻolelo would preserve the hundreds of wind names and places to which they belong. This particular mele, found on pages 56–58, is but one of four mele that detail the wind names of specific place names on the islands of Hawaiʻi, Maui, Molokaʻi, Oʻahu, and Kauaʻi. It provides a list of forty-six wind names and forty-six geographical place names for the island of O'ahu, most not known by the general populace. I have identified the wind names by italicizing them.

Aia la o ke ao a maua me kuu
    makuakane,
Ke kau ae la i na kuahiwi,
Ua pii ke ao a ka naulu,
Ua hina ka aukuku makani,
Ke kumu o ka ino ka ke keiki,
He ku a e-ho la i kai,
Mai kai ka ino a pa i uka,
Kiu-lua Koolau, kulepe ka
    moana,
I lawa ia a holo aku,
E pa mai ana ka makani
    Ihiihilauakea,
Oia ka makani kuloko o
    Hanauma,
He makani *kaelekai* mai mauka,
Oia makani *hu-e kapa* o Paukua,

He *Puuokona* ko na Kuliouou,
He *Ma-ua* ka makani o Niu,
He *Holou-ha* ko Kekaha,
He *Maunuunu* ko Waialae,
Huli ma-o maanei ka makani o
    Leahi,
He *Olauniu* ko Kahaloa,
He *Waiomao* ko Palolo,
He *Kuehu lepo* ko Kahua,
He *Kukalahale* ko Honolulu,
He *Ao-a-oa* ko Mamala,
He *Olauniu* ko Kapalama,
He *Haupeepee* ko Kalihi,
He *Ko-momona* ko Kahauiki,
He *Ho-e-o* ko Moanalua,
He *Moae-ku* ko Ewaloa,

He *Hinakokea* ko Mokuleia,

No Waialua ka makani ke pa mai,
He nihi mai ma ka lae o Kaena,
He Puu-kaala iho ma Kaala,
He *Kehau* ko Kapo,
He *kiu* ka makani makai mai,
He *Malualua* iho manae,
He *Peapueo* ko Kaunala,

He *Ahamanu* ko Kahuku,
He *Lanakila* ko Hauula,

He *Moae* ko Punaluu,

He *Ahiu* ko Kahana,
He *Holopali* ko Kaaawa me
    Kualoa,
He *Kiliua* ko Waikane,
He *Mololani* ko Kuaaohe,
He *Ulumano* ko Kaneohe,
No Kaholoakeahole ka makani,
Puahiohio uka o Nuuanu,

He *Malanai* ko Kailua,
Pae i Waimanalo *ka limu-li-puupuu*,
He *Alopali* ko Pahonu,
A Makapuu, huli ka makani,
Huli na Kona, huli na Koolau,
Huli mamua mai, loaa oukou,
Loaa oe e ke Alii hookuli,
Hui ae la na makani,
Pu-o ka lau o ka naenae,
Laweia'ku oe a uka o
    Awawamalu,

He *Kehau* ko Waiopua,	Loaa oe i ka lawaia upena poo iki,
He *Waikoloa* ko Lihue,	Ou auhau, komo i ka hokeo,
He *Kona* ko Puuokapolei,	O ke-panoo, o ka pa-ka no ia,
He *Maunuunu* ko Puuloa,	O ua haalualu, amu ka elepi, ka eleao,
He *Kaiaulu* ko Waianae,	Hai ke ola a ka makua,
He *Kumumaomao* ko Kamaile,	Eia mai no au, ka aumakua kanaka,
He *Kumaipo* ko Kualele,	A hoolohe mai no i ka'u ola,
He *Kopiliehu* ko Olopua,	E Keawenuiaumi–e, e pae, he ino,
Hulilua na makani o Kaena,	E holoa mai no inehinei, ka la malie.

Nakuina's intentions in preserving these wind names by publishing this mo'olelo as a book have already benefited our present efforts to recover and restore our personal relationship with our home environment. Today, this publication is an important resource, as many have drawn upon the various mele to learn the names of the winds of their neighborhood.

Nakuina finally points out that this mo'olelo reminds us that historically our kūpuna loved and cared for their ali'i, and that this was the most important reason why this mo'olelo needed to be published:

> Aha, o ka mea i oi ae mamua o na kumu mua ekolu i ha'i mua ia ae nei oia ke Aloha Alii oiaio o na kanaka Hawaii i ke au i hala a hiki loa mai no i keia au. (Foreword)

> Fourthly, what is more important than the three reasons previously mentioned, is the Hawaiian people's true devotion to the ali'i in the past and until this present day.

I believe that this was a reminder for our people to continue to care for our beloved Queen Liliuokalani, who was still living at the time this mo'olelo was published, and especially since she had been illegally dethroned and two years later imprisoned in her own palace. Queen Liliuokalani represented our nation's sovereignty, and to continue our devotion to her was to be truly loyal to the Kingdom of Hawai'i, for Liliuokalani was indeed the Kingdom of Hawai'i. Although, it has been over a century since Queen Liliuokalani's rule, Nakuina's mo'olelo is still an encouragement for us today to continue to remember, celebrate, and care for our ali'i, our 'āina, our kūpuna, and our kumu, and to be constantly mindful of their well-being.

What is obvious is that over a hundred years ago, Nakuina knew that our cultural knowledge and language were in a dire state, and proposed that in order to best preserve and maintain them, it was imperative to seek out, gather, and ironically print in books the knowledge of our kūpuna, which had been handed down orally from generations past. The printing press was a powerful way to ensure the preservation and maintenance of our people's mele and moʻolelo. Nakuina's introduction to *Pakaa a me Ku-a-Pakaa* is a clear reflection of his thoughts in response to colonization, which caused this very unstable time in Hawaiʻi's history.

Poepoe and Nakuina both plead for our people to retain our cultural knowledge, which not only reiterates Keaulumoku's mele urging our people to ʻauʻa, but also confirms that Keaulumoku's prophecy did in fact come to pass, and that Nakuina and Poepoe were forced into interceding on behalf of the survival of our cultural heritage. Although both Nakuina and Poepoe advocated for more modern and non-traditional ways of retaining our lore, they were both making serious recommendations regarding preservation, so that our mele and moʻolelo would not become the possession of "nalowale," or lost to "ka ole mau loa."

Ka Waihona A Ke Aloha

For the past three decades, there has been a surge amongst Hawaiian language educators and cultural practitioners to invest in the further preservation of Hawaiian language newspapers, manuscripts, personal diaries, video documentations, oral histories, mele, and hula that are in archival resource centers and in private collections. Like Helekunihi, Poepoe, Nakuina, Kukahi, and Pukui, Ka Waihona A Ke Aloha also believes that it is imperative for our generation to engage the puana of Keaulumoku and ʻauʻa, retain and preserve, these invaluable heirlooms of our kūpuna, and to invest in the best technology today to put them in formats that would first preserve them, and then create ways for the information preserved to be accessible.

Ka Waihona A Ke Aloha is an interactive archival resource center for the promotion, preservation, and perpetuation of mele and mele practitioners. The mākia (motto) for Ka Waihona A Ke Aloha is "Hoʻoheno ka puana i lohe ʻia," "Cherished is the refrain that has been heard," or "Cherished is the refrain so let it be heard." Both translations provide the understanding that Ka Waihona A Ke Aloha was established to preserve and care for the many wonderful pearls of mele "that have been heard," and to further perpetuate them "so that they be heard." To increase accessibility to this knowledge, the preservation, perpetuation, and the dissemination of our peoples' puana is therefore the primary focus.

Since 2002, Ka Waihona A Ke Aloha has created, established, facilitated, advised, promoted, and cared for projects where mele are placed at the focal point of preservation, perpetuation, discussion, presentation, and performance. Ka Waihona A Ke Aloha recognizes the importance of mele practitioners, and values the moʻolelo embedded within their repertoire.

Ka Waihona A Ke Aloha has established five major research projects: Nā Mele o Hawaiʻi Nei, Ke Welo Mau Nei, Ka Papa Mele Kauwela, Hoʻokani Mānoa, and Lā Mele. Below are descriptions of these projects.

Nā Mele O Hawaiʻi Nei focuses on the digitization of mele from vintage vinyl recordings that feature revered mele practitioners, who, for the most part were native speakers or trained by those who were learned in the art of mele performance. These include 45, 78 & 33 1/3 rpm recordings from the Bishop Museum Audio Disc Collection, the Kimo Alama Keaulana Collection, the R. Keawe Lopes Jr. Collection, the House of Music Collection, and the University of Hawaiʻi at Mānoa Sinclair Library Vinyl Collection. To date, Ka Waihona A Ke Aloha cares for 14,784 digital mele recordings.

Ke Welo Mau Nei is a guest lecture series featuring revered mele practitioners, and, sponsored in collaboration with Kawaihuelani Center for Hawaiian Language's mele courses. To date, Ka Waihona A Ke Aloha has organized twenty-three series and welcomed one hundred fifteen guest lectures. The digital collection of these guest lecture series events accounts for one hundred seventeen hours of video footage that include a variety of personal moʻolelo told by the mele practitioners themselves.

Ka Papa Mele Kauwela is a mele course series offered during the Summer for students of both the academy and community at large. To date, Ka Waihona A Ke Aloha has offered Ka Papa Mele Wahi Pana for six consecutive summers, 2003—2008 and, Ka Papa Mele Inoa in the summer of 2011. These summer mele courses were all taught by revered mele scholar Kimo Alama Keaulana. Presently, Ka Waihona A Ke Aloha stewards over two hundred six hours of video documentation of Keaulana teaching and sharing moʻolelo for five hundred and ninety-eight mele from his personal collection.

Hoʻokani Mānoa is a guest mele performance series which features the musical talents of mele practitioners. In 2002, Ka Waihona A Ke Aloha created two very unique programs: Hoʻokani Mānoa Reminisces and Hoʻokani Mānoa Continues, featuring both seasoned and aspiring mele practitioners. To date, Ka Waihona A Ke Aloha stewards over one hundred one hours of video documentation featuring one hundred ten guest mele performances.

Lā Mele is a program which brings those of the community and the academy together to celebrate mele and mele practitioners. Lā Mele features intellectual and engaging sessions on the topic of mele including Mele Panel Discussions, Mele Performances, Mele Sing-a-long Sessions, and a Mele Choral Competition featuring Hawaiian Immersion and Charter Schools. To date, Ka Waihona A Ke Aloha has documented eight annual Lā Mele programs, thirty-five Guest Lecture Performers, thirty-four school choir participants and thirty-two hours of video documentation.

Ka Waihona A Ke Aloha is truly invested in the documenting, digitizing, and indexing of cultural knowledge gleaned from the repertoire of mele and the personal moʻolelo shared by mele practitioners featured in these five projects. The indexed information or the papa kuhikuhi include inoa ua (rain names), inoa makani (wind names), inoa wahi (place names), inoa kanaka (people names), inoa hui hīmeni (musical groups), nā mea kanu (plants), nā holoholona (animals), nā mea pili lani (terminology pertaining to the sky), nā mea pili honua (terminology pertaining to the earth), nā mea pili kai (terminology pertaining to the sea), and other natural phenomena and unusual sayings. The indexed information is inputted into a searchable database, first for preservation sake, and second, to enhance accessibility, so that we are able to gain knowledge, increase understanding, and perpetuate the information. To be clear, however, Ka Waihona A Ke Aloha is not a substitute for the traditional way of learning mele and moʻolelo. "He alo a he alo" (face to face) is teaching and learning at its finest, and it requires that a relationship bound by respect and commitment is first established between teacher and student, and that the relationship is cared for and maintained.

To honor the relationship I have with my Kumu, Kimo Alama Keaulana, I have chosen to exhibit the papa kuhikuhi created for his visit as a featured guest for Ke Welo Mau Nei. "Uncle Kimo," as he is more affectionately called, is a respected authority on ancient and modern hula and music, and his impressive professional career, cultural knowledge background, and academic credentials allow him to straddle both the Western academic and the Hawaiian cultural practitioner worlds. Uncle Kimo is an exceptional teacher, un-matched in many ways, and his experiences with the masters of old shine through his teaching. He is indeed a walking and breathing archive of mele and moʻolelo.

Uncle Kimo has been more than generous with his knowledge and his time. To date, Uncle Kimo is the only scholar who has been featured in all of Ka Waihona A Ke Aloha's five projects:

Nā Mele o Hawaiʻi Nei:	In July of 2009, Uncle Kimo gave permission to Ka Waihona A Ke Aloha to digitize his collection of five hundred seventy-four 45 rpm vinyl recordings.
Ke Welo Mau Nei:	Uncle Kimo was featured as a guest lecturer for Ke Welo Mau Nei three times (4/8/08, 3/7/12, and 4/3/14). I also invited him on five occasions to my mele classes outside of Ke Welo Mau Nei (3/17/09, 3/31/09, 4/1/10, 9/24/10, and 10/1/10).
Ka Papa Mele Kauwela:	Uncle Kimo taught all six summers of papa mele wahi pana (2003–2008) and one summer of papa mele inoa (2011).
Hoʻokani Mānoa:	Uncle Kimo was featured at Hoʻokani Mānoa with his award winning musical group Lei Hulu three times (9/17/04, 10/21/05, and 4/28/07).
Lā Mele:	Uncle Kimo was invited to present on a panel of revered mele practitioners, including Noelani Mahoe and Nina Kealiiwahamana, at the inaugural Lā Mele in 2012.

ʻAnakala Kimo Keaulana. Used with permission from Ka Waihona A Ke Aloha.

Here is an example of the papa kuhikuhi for Uncle Kimo's visit as the featured guest lecturer for Ke Welo Mau Nei on April 1, 2008. The information Uncle Kimo shared at that visit included sixteen inoa kanaka, five inoa hui hīmeni, nineteen inoa wahi, one inoa ua, and fourteen mele. Uncle Kimo also shared other pertinent information about the City and County Department of Parks and Recreation and its sponsorship of the Hawaiian Song Writing and Composing Contest.

Ka Waihona A Ke Aloha
Ka Papahana Hoʻoheno Mele
Kawaihuelani, Ka Hālau ʻŌlelo Hawaiʻi
Dr. R. Keawe Lopes Jr.

Waihona	Ke Welo Mau Nei
Lā	2008-04-01
Wahi	Spalding 257
Wehewehena	Ke Welo Mau Nei (KWMN) Video Collection. Ke Welo Mau Nei spring 2008; HAW 384: Ka Papa Mele "Ka Haku Mele" Kumu Keawe Lopes. 1 Quicktime
	(Original source includes: 2 MDVD [Located in CABINET C; 4th Shelf]; Digital copy located: KA WAIHONA A KE ALOHA MAIN EXT HD 8TB - Ke Welo Mau Nei Wikiō KWMN 2008 SPRING - KWMN SP08 KEAULANA, KIMO ALAMA 04-01-08).
Inoa Hoʻopaʻa/ Haku Mele	Kimo Alama Keaulana (Haku Mele)
Helu	KWMN SP08 KEAULANA, KIMO ALAMA 04-01-08
Manaʻo ʻē aʻe	Note:

Inoa Kanaka: Charles E. King, Adeline Lee, Katherine Maunakea, Pukui (Mary Kawena), Bill Aliʻiloa Lincoln, C.S. WO, Cindy (Alama), Edith McKenzie, Abigail Kawananakoa, Kinoiki Kekaulike, Dutchie Saffery, Lanihuli (Lee), Frank Sinatra, Little Joe Paauau, Alice Namakelua, Johnny K. Almeida; *Inoa Hui Himeni:* Halona, McGuire Sisters, Ink Spots, Ka Leo O Kalani Trio, Kaʻau Crater Boys; *Inoa Wahi:* Mānoa, Maui, Pali Luahine, Nānākuli, Akaaka, Waiakeaakua, Halelani Drive, Mānoa Playground, California, Borthwick Mortuary, Halekoa Hotel, Maunakapu, Puʻu Heleakalā, Palikea, Kahala Hilton, Pohakus, Shindig Bar, Midway Bar, Hawaiʻi, Washington State; *Inoa Ua:* Ua Tuahine; *Pili lani:*

Ānuenue, Lani Kelakela; *Pili kuahiwi:* Wai ʻĀnapanapa, Valley, Nahele, Kahawai, ʻAuwai; *Pua:* Pua Melia; Kumulāʻau: Kiawe; *Mele:* Nani Mānoa, Pua Melia, Kinoiki Kekaulike, Ka Poli o Nānākuli, The Nearness of You, Satin Sheets, You Don't Know Me, Kaulana Nā Pua, Ka ʻŌiwi Nani, Uluhua Wale Au, I'm Just A Sunbeam for Jesus, At The Cross, Makalapua, Molokaʻi Nui A Hina. *ʻŌlelo Noʻeau:* "I ka ʻōlelo ke ola i ka ʻōlelo ka make." *Puanaʻi:* "I think one of the hallmarks of at least 20th Century kind of songs...you got to keep the language simple, so that it can appeal to a wider audience...Like Mrs. Pukui's songs...Bill Aliʻiloa Lincoln, all these other wonderful composers, you look at their language and it's simple. Look Mrs. Pukui, she made the dictionary and her words are simple. She had 30,000 words at her command, sometimes, nowadays, composers try get too fancy and try impress us. That only impresses us to know that you have good dictionary skills."; "...the royal symbol is the rainbow."; "...as I understand Hawaiian music composition, you keep it simple... you just watch for those kinds of words that might have other kinds of meanings and if you do have to use a word like that...you make sure you balance it off with another word to neutralize the word." *Nā Mea ʻĒ Aʻe:* City & County Department of Parks and Recreation, Hawaiian Song Writing & Composing Contest, Nā Hōkū Hanohano Awards, Haku Mele Category, Hawaiian Language Category, South Pacific Arts Festival, Mele Lāhui, Waltz, Church Songs.

The information provided above is but one of one hundred fifteen papa kuhikuhi that are housed at Ka Waihona A Ke Aloha for the Ke Welo Mau Nei series. As previously mentioned, Ka Waihona A Ke Aloha has five major research projects, and stewards over 14,784 digital recordings, 410 hours of video documentation, and a collection of 598 mele wahi pana and mele inoa. Since 2002, over 2,000 university students and faculty, schools, community members, cultural practitioners, kumu hula, and recording artists have accessed Ka Waihona A Ke Aloha's information to aid in Hawaiian language curriculum development, research projects, and components for hula competitions in the form of fact sheets and liner notes for compact disc recordings.

Ka Waihona A Ke Aloha represents a renewed access to the ingenuity of our kūpuna. Ka Waihona A Ke Aloha's commitment to this endeavor challenges our present to invest sincerely in the preservation of mele and mele practitioners, and to engage earnestly our people with their moʻolelo. Ka Waihona A Ke

Aloha further encourages us, the kama, to "kama," to make secure, to learn well, and actively produce, for the real preservation and survival of mele and moʻolelo is in the actual doing, the actual performance. The ultimate hope is that with each generation, we will continue to adhere to Keaulumoku's foresight, and like Helekunihi, Poepoe, Nakuina, Kukahi, Pukui, and Ka Waihona A Ke Aloha, we ʻauʻa, we retain, and "withhold, detain and refuse to part with" our moku.

ʻAuʻa ʻia e Kama e kona moku
Kona moku e Kama e ʻauʻa ʻia

NOTES

1. Keaulana, Lei Hulu, trans. Mary Kawena Pukui.
2. Unless noted otherwise, all translations are the author's.

WORKS CONSULTED

Almeida, John K. Papakolea [Recorded by Julia Nui's Kamaainas with John K. Almeida and His Hawaiians], [Hawaiian Vinyl Recording]. 49th State Record Company 4549.

Fiorio, Elisa. "Orality and Cultural Identity: The Oral Tradition in Tupuri (Chad)." *Museum International*, vol. 58, nos. 1–2, 2006, pp. 68–75.

Fornander, Abraham, and Thomas G. Thrum. *Fornander Collection of Hawaiian Antiquities and Folk-lore*. 1916–1920. Kraus Reprint, 1974.

"He Moolelo Hawaii." *Ka Nupepa Kuokoa*, vol. 33, no. 19, 12 May 1894, p. 1.

Helekunihi, Elia. Letter to Rev. Oliver Emerson. Haiku, Hawaiʻi. February 1893. Family Collection.

Humu Moolelo: Journal of the Hula Arts, vol. 1, 2006, p. v.

"Ka Papa Kuhikuhi Makahiki O Na Mea Kaulana o Hawaii Nei!" *Ka Nupepa Kuokoa*, vol. 4, no. 28, 13 July 1865, p. 4.

Kamakau, Samuel Manaiakalani. "Ka Moolelo o Na Kamehameha." *Ka Nupepa Kuokoa*, vol. 6, no. 8, 23 February 1867, p. 1.

———. "Ka Moolelo o Na Kamehameha." *Ka Nupepa Kuokoa*, vol. 6, no. 51, 21 December 1867, p. 1.

Kanahele, George S., ed. *Hawaiian Music and Musicians: An Illustrated History*. U of Hawaiʻi P, 1979.

Keaulana, Kimo Alama. Ka Papa Mele Kauwela: *Nā Mele No Nā Honolulu and Nā Mele No Nā Waiʻanae*. R. K. Lopes Jr., instructor. Ka Waihona A Ke Aloha. Honolulu. Unpublished manuscript.

———. Lei Hulu Hula School. With R. K. Lopes Jr. Honolulu, 1997–2002.

———. *Na Mele No Nā Waiʻanae*. Honolulu, 2003. Unpublished manuscript.

———. Personal Conversations with R. K. Lopes Jr. 1997–2010.

———. *Puke mele: A Book of Hawaiian Songs.* Ishi Enterprize, Inc., 2001.

Keaulumoku. "He Mele Na Keaulumoku No Aikanaka" *Ka Makaainana,* 8 June 1896, p. 6

Kukahi, Joseph L. *Ke Kumulipo.* Honolulu: T.H. Grieve Publishing Company, 1902.

Lopes, R. Keawe, Jr. *Ka Waihona A Ke Aloha: Ka Papahana Hoʻoheno Mele; An interactive resource center for the promotion, preservation and perpetuation of mele and mele practitioners.* 2010. University of Hawaiʻi at Mānoa, PhD dissertation.

"Mookuauhau Alii." *Ka Makaainana,* vol. 5, no. 3, 8 June 1896, p. 6.

Nakuina, Moses. *Moolelo Hawaii o Pakaa a me Ku-a-Pakaa, na kahu iwikuamoo o Keawenuiaumi, ke alii o Hawaii, a o na moopuna hoi a Laamaomao!* Kalamaku Press, 1991.

Poepoe, Joseph Mokuohai. "Ka Moolelo Hawaii Kahiko." *Ka Naʻi Aupuni,* vol. 1, no. 57, 1 February 1906, p. 1.

Pukui, Mary Kawena. "How Legends Were Taught." *Hawaiian Ethnographic Notes,* vol. 1, 1602–1606. Bishop Museum Archives, pp. 1–5. http://kumukahi-online.net/haku-olelo -331/na-kumu-ike/mokuna-iv---moolelo-kaao/pukui---how-legends-were.pdf.

———. Interview with Joseph Ilalaole. Honolulu: Bishop Museum, 1960.

Pukui, Mary Kawena, and Samuel H. Elbert. *Hawaiian Dictionary: Hawaiian–English, English–Hawaiian,* rev. and enlarged ed. U of Hawaiʻi P, 1986.

R. Keawe Lopes Jr. he kupa nei kumu ʻōlelo no Nānākuli akā, ke noho nei nō naʻe ʻo ia ma Pūʻahuʻula, Koʻolaupoko, Oʻahu me kona ʻohana. ʻO Tracie Kaʻōnohilani Farias kāna wahine o ka male ʻana a he ʻekolu a *lāua kaikamāhine:* ʻo Piʻikea, Kaʻōnohi, me Hāweo. He polopeka ʻo Kumu Keawe a ʻo ia ala nō hoʻi ke poʻo o Kawaihuelani, Ka Hālau ʻŌlelo Hawaiʻi o ke kula nui nei ʻo Mānoa. Ma laila nō ʻo ia e aʻo nei i nā papa mele, i mea hoʻi e hoʻoikaika ʻia ai ka ʻaʻapo ʻana o nā haumāna i ka ʻŌlelo Hawaiʻi. ʻO ka luna hoʻolaukaʻi nō hoʻi ʻo ia no Ka Waihona A Ke Aloha, Ka Papahana Hoʻoheno Mele o Kawaihuelani. ʻO Keawe lāua ʻo kāna wahine nā kumu hula o Ka Lā ʻŌnohi Mai o Haʻehaʻe.

R. Keawe Lopes Jr. is a native of Nānākuli, Oʻahu. He currently resides in Pūʻahuʻula, Koʻolaupoko, Oʻahu with his wife, Tracie Kaʻōnohilani Farias and three daughters, Piʻikea, Kaʻōnohi, and Hāweo. Keawe Lopes is an associate professor, and at present director of Kawaihuelani Center for Hawaiian Language, University of Hawaiʻi at Mānoa. He currently teaches Hawaiian language courses that include the study and performance of mele as an enhancement of Hawaiian language acquisition. He is the director of Ka Waihona A Ke Aloha, an interactive resource center for the promotion, preservation, and perpetuation of mele and mele practitioners. He and his wife are the kumu hula of Ka Lā ʻŌnohi Mai o Haʻehaʻe.

e kiaʻi mau i ka ʻoi mau o ka ʻike ʻōlelo Hawaiʻi
me ka ʻike moʻolelo kahiko ma nā kumuhana
me nā pōʻaiapili like ʻole.

4

'E'ole Ho'i Ka Mo'olelo Kahiko, Ola Hou Ai Ke Kākā'ōlelo!

Hiapokeikikāne Kichie Perreira

Eia ma lalo nei he pō'aiapili i 'ike 'ia ai he hi'ohi'ona 'ōlelo ha'ako'iko'i[1] o ka ho'okipa 'ana mai ka mo'olelo hiwahiwa mai o Kawelo (Ho'oulumāhiehieika'on imālieapualīlialanaikawai 124–126).[2] I ka ho'ea 'ana aku o ua 'o Kawelo nei me kona alo o ka holo pū 'ana i Wai'anae, iho akula ke kahuna o ke Ali'i Ka'ihika-puakākuhihewa e hō'oia ai i ko Kawelo kūlana ali'i ma ka ihu o ka pua'a penei:

> Hele maila ua kahuna nei, a he mau anana ka mamao mai kahi a Kawelo e kū ana, kū ihola ia, a 'o kona manawa ia i oli a'e ai i ke mele pule o Kawelomahamahai'a, a ho'ohiki a'ela i nā inoa 'o Kamalama, Kaweloleimakua, Kawelohea, Kawelolauhuki a me nā inoa o ko lākou mau mākua, 'o ia 'o Mālaiakalani a me Ma'ihuna Ali'i. 'O ia pule o ua kahuna nei a pau, 'o kona ho'oku'u ihola nō ia i kahi pua'a hiwa i lalo a 'ōlelo ihola 'o ia, "E [ka] pua'a hiwa, e [ka] pua'a 'olomea, e ka pua'a 'eku i ka honua, e ka pua'a nānā i ka lani, 'eku 'ia, nānā 'ia ka lani, 'o Wai'ale'ale ke kuahiwi."
>
> Holo akula ua pua'a nei, 'oiai ho'i nā maka o nā mea a pau e nānā ana iā ia, a hō'ea i kahi a ke kanaka Kaua'i e kū ana me ka lawakua o kona mau 'ōiwi a pau. I ka hō'ea 'ana o ua wahi pua'a nei ma nā wāwae o Kawelo, ua moe ihola 'o ia i lalo me ka 'oni'oni hou 'ole a'e, a 'o ka wā ia i 'ike a'e ai nā kānaka a pau o ka Makani Kaiaulu o Wai'anae, he ali'i nui nei kā'e'a'e'a a ka ikaika nui wale i hō'ea mai i ko lākou wahi.
>
> 'O ka manawa ia i hele mai ai 'o ke kahuna a hiki ma kahi a Kawelo e kū ana, hā'ule ihola kona mau kuli i lalo me ke kūlou 'ana o kona po'o i lalo. A li'uli'u iki ke kukuli 'ana o ua kahuna nei, hopu ihola ia i kahi 'ouo pua'a hiwa, pa'a ma ka lima, a laila, kū a'ela i luna. "E Kaweloleimakua, mo'opuna a Kawelomahamahai'a o ka maha i'a, o nā hapuna maka o Kawelo i ke kai, eia ka pua'a, he 'ālana, he mōhai, he noi aku iā 'oe, e ka moopu [*sic*: mo'opuna] lei hulu, lei hiwahiwa a Mālaiakalani, e kipa i ka hale. He 'ai, he i'a, he kapa a he nohona ko ke ali'i. Ua ho'ouna 'ia mai nei au e Ka'ihikapuakākuhihewa, ka lani o O'ahu nei, e ki'i mai iā 'oukou, e nā Ali'i pali kū mokomoko o Kaua'i,

e kipa i ka hale o ke aliʻi e ʻike, he mau mākua, a he ʻohana no ʻoukou, eia lā i Oʻahu nei. Pehea ka leo o ke kauā?" i nīnau aku ai ua kahuna nei iā Kawelo.

Pane maila ʻo Kawelo, "Ua ʻae akula au i kāu kiʻi, e ke kanaka, i ka ihu o ka puaʻa, ka mea iā ia ka ipu ʻōlelo a ke aliʻi."

ʻO ka wā ia o ua kahuna nei i huli aʻe ai i mua o nā kānaka a kamaʻilio maila i mua o lākou, "E nā uʻi o ka Makani ʻŌlauniu o Pōkaʻī! E nā mailelauliʻi o Koʻiahi! E nā ʻōhiki moe one o nā ʻŌhikikolo! E nā hala puna [sic: puīā] i ke onaona o nā Keaʻau! E ke one ʻōpiopio o Mākua! E nā kalo ʻūlina ʻaʻala o Lehano! E nā niu haohao o Waiʻanae! E ʻike ʻoukou i nā aliʻi kū mokomoko o Kauaʻi. ʻO kekahi mau moʻopuna kēia a Kawelomahamahaiʻa o Wailuahoʻāno. Eia lā, ua pae mai i Waiʻanae nei. No laila, e lawe ka puaʻa, e lawe ka ʻīlio hānai ʻai, e lawe ka moa, e lawe ka iʻa, e lawe nā kāmau ʻai, e lawe nā kapa paʻiʻula, e lawe nā mea a pau e pono ai nā malihini aliʻi o Kauaʻi. Eia mākou ke piʻi nei no uka o Lualualei.

Mai ka makahiki (MH) 1997 koʻu komo ʻana i ka walea haʻiʻōlelo, a mai ka MH 2003 koʻu hoʻokolo ʻana ma nā palapala kahiko i mea e hoʻomohala ʻia ai he haʻawina e haʻiʻōlelo ai nā haumāna o ke kula kiʻekiʻe ʻo Nāwahīokalaniʻōpuʻu me ko ke Kulanui o Ka Haka ʻUla O Keʻelikōlani ma ke aukahi hoʻōla ʻōlelo Hawaiʻi o Hilo Hanakahi. Kiakahi mau nō kaʻu pahuhopu mai ia mua mai a hiki i kēia wā, ʻo ka hoʻōla i welo kupuna he kākāʻōlelo: "Orator, person skilled in use of language; counselor, adviser; storyteller; oratory; to orate. *Lit.*, to fence [with] words" (Pukui and Elbert 119).[3]

Ma nā makahiki hoʻi o koʻu kilo ʻana i ka nūpepa me nā moʻolelo kahiko, a no koʻu noiʻi hele pū ʻana i ka MH 2008 ma nā hale waihona palapala kahiko o Oʻahu a puni ma ka mea e mākaukau ai wau no ke kākau ʻana i kaʻu pepa laeʻula no ke kākāʻōlelo hoʻōla, ua ʻike kino ihola wau i ka nele nui loa, ʻane loaʻa ʻole loa he ilina ʻike o kekahi ʻano piha pono no ke kākāʻōlelo, oki loa ko ke kākāʻōlelo hiʻohiʻona haʻiʻōlelo haʻakoʻikoʻi.[4] No ia noiʻi ʻana ma nā hale waihona palapala kahiko i ʻike ʻia ihola, ʻaʻole nō palapala piha, a hapa palapala paha o kekahi ʻano i kākau ʻia no ke kākāʻōlelo ponoʻī iho nō; ʻaʻohe nō ʻatikala (ʻatikala nūpepa kahiko a mea like paha) a moʻolelo pilikino i ʻike ʻia no ia kākāʻōlelo ʻana; a ʻo kahi ʻike i loaʻa, aia ma ka puka wale aku o ka huaʻōlelo ʻo "kakaolelo" ma ʻō a ma ʻō o ka nūpepa Hawaiʻi kahiko o ke au aliʻi kuʻuna me ka wā huliau Kalikiano pū. Aia naʻe hoʻi ma ka hoʻokuʻikuʻi ʻana i kēlā hunahuna kēia hunahuna ka hoʻomohala ʻana aʻe he manaʻo. ʻOiai pū ʻaʻole i lilo ka lola mānaleo he kūmole o kēia noiʻi ʻana, ua kilo ʻia nō e aʻu ka papa ʻinideka o Ka Leo Hawaiʻi (Hale Kuamoʻo 1996–1997), a pēia hoʻi nā papa ʻinideka lola mānaleo o ka Hale Hōʻikeʻike o Pīhopa. Ma ia mau waihona nui a ʻelua, ʻaʻohe nō kuhi ʻana, ʻaʻohe nō kumuhana i kālele ma luna o ke kākāʻōlelo ma ka hāiki, a ma ka haʻiʻōlelo haʻakoʻikoʻi ma ka laulā.[5]

He mauhili nō paha nā pahuhopu nui ʻelua o kēia pepa nei. ʻAkahi hoʻi i ka pae o ka haʻawina laulā o kēia pepa, ʻo ia ka nānā ʻana i kaʻu mau "haʻawina ʻuhane" i kilo ai a i wae ai mai loko mai o koʻu noiʻi ʻana i ka haʻiʻōlelo haʻakoʻikoʻi a ka Sāmoa, he *lāuga*, a pēia hoʻi ka haʻiʻōlelo haʻakoʻikoʻi a ka Māori o Aotearoa, he *whaikōrero*. ʻOiai he ʻokoʻa loa ia mau kaila a ʻōnaehana haʻiʻōlelo ʻelua kekahi mai kekahi aku, ea aʻela he mau haʻawina pili ʻuhane e lōkahi ai ia mea he haʻiʻōlelo haʻakoʻikoʻi. ʻAʻole loa ʻo kaʻu he hoʻopilipili ma ka hāiki i nā loina o ia mau haʻiʻōlelo ʻana, he mea nō naʻe kaʻu e hoʻomanaʻo ai i nā aoʻao mea nui o ka ʻuhane ʻana o ia mau kaila haʻiʻōlelo, e hoʻomanaʻo pū ʻia ai pēlā i loko o ke kākāʻōlelo hoʻōla a ka Hawaiʻi.

ʻAlua hoʻi i ka pae o ka haʻawina hāiki kuʻikoʻi iho o kēia pepa, ʻo ia ka hoʻomanaʻo ʻana, pehea lā ka nui me ka laulā o nā haʻawina ʻuhane e hoʻomanaʻo ʻia i loko o ke kākāʻōlelo hoʻōla o Hawaiʻi nei, ʻo ka iwi nui o ia hoʻōla ʻana, no loko pono mai ia o nā moʻolelo Hawaiʻi kahiko. Inā hoʻi ua ʻalaneo ka ipu o ka ʻike, ʻo ia hoʻi, inā paha ʻaʻole i kūlia pauaho ʻole nā kūpuna ma ke kākau ʻana a lehulehu kohu palena ʻole nā moʻolelo kahiko o nā ʻano like ʻole a pau e nanea nei a e ola nei nā kiʻina hoʻōla ʻike Hawaiʻi o kēia wā; a inā paha ʻaʻole i hoʻomanawanui nā mea hoʻopaʻa leo i ka ʻimi hele i nā kūpuna ʻike o ka wā, a hoʻopaʻa ʻia ai ko lākou mau leo i hoʻoilina no kākou o kēia au me ko kēia mua aku; a inā paha ʻaʻole i kiʻi aku nā kumu waele o nā anahulu makahiki 60 a 70 paha e aʻoaʻo mai ma ka hoʻohana ʻana i nā moʻolelo kahiko me nā lola mānaleo ma ka mea e mau ai ka Hawaiʻi ʻana o kā kākou ʻōlelo Hawaiʻi a hiki i kēia lā, ʻaʻohe nō a he ala e manaʻo iki ʻia mai ai ē, he ala e hoʻōla ai i ka haʻiʻōlelo haʻakoʻikoʻi Hawaiʻi, he kākāʻōlelo. No loko mai o nā moʻolelo Hawaiʻi kahiko (palapala me ka lola mānaleo pū kekahi) ke ola e hoʻolaupaʻi hou aʻe ai. ʻAʻole wale nō ʻo ka ʻike, ʻo ke ʻano pū nō naʻe kekahi i hoʻopaʻa ʻia ai a i hoʻopuka ʻia ai ia ʻike, ua paʻi a paʻi ke koʻikoʻi o ia mau hiʻohiʻona ʻelua ma ka hoʻōla ʻana i ke kākāʻōlelo. ʻAʻohe ola o ke kākāʻōlelo hoʻōla inā ʻaʻohe moʻolelo Hawaiʻi kahiko. I loko nō paha o ke kālele o kēia pepa ma luna o nā haʻawina ʻuhane o ia mau ʻano haʻiʻōlelo haʻakoʻikoʻi no ka ʻohana Polenesia mai, ʻaʻole loa hoʻi e poina ʻia ke koʻikoʻi haʻalele loa o ka moʻolelo Hawaiʻi i loko o ke kiʻi ʻana e hoʻōla i ke kākāʻōlelo, i kekahi ʻike hoʻi e Hawaiʻi ai ka Hawaiʻi i loko o kēia au hou e naue nei.

He Haʻawina ʻUhane no ka Lāuga me ka Whaikōrero mai

ʻOiai ʻaʻole nō i mōakāka pono ka ʻaoʻao haʻiʻōlelo haʻakoʻikoʻi o ke kākāʻōlelo a hiki aku i ka huliau ʻana o ka lāhui i loko o ka hoʻomana Kalikiano, ke kālaiaupuni ʻaha ʻōlelo kau kānāwai, me ka ʻoihana loio pū kekahi (Perreira, *He Haʻiʻōlelo* 190–219), eia ke hoʻomoeā aʻe nei pēlā no ke ʻano nō paha o ka ʻōlelo e lawelawe ʻia ai ai ka noho 'ana o ka 'aha kūkā malū, ka 'aha 'ōlelo ali'i ho'i, a me ka ho'okō 'ana aku i ka 'ōlelo o ia 'ano 'aha i waena o ka nui maka'āinana (152–158). Eia ho'i ma lalo nei ka'u e ho'omoeā aku nei he kākā'ōlelo mai loko mai o ka nānā 'ana i nā "ha'awina 'uhane" a me nā hi'ohi'ona e pili pū ana i ka ha'i'ōlelo ha'ako'iko'i a ka Sāmoa he *lāuga*, me kā ka Māori o Aotearoa he *whaikōrero*.

I ko'u wā e mea aku ana e kākau i ka'u pepa puka lae'ula, ho'okama'ilio maila ke Kauka Charles "Kale" Langlas (Po'o Kōmike) no ke ki'i 'ana aku e nānā i ka ha'i'ōlelo ha'ako'iko'i a ko kekahi hoa lāhui Polenesia hou aku i mea e ana pū ai. Ma ia wā, 'a'ole nō i kau iki aku ko'u ohohia no ko'u po'o pa'akikī 'ana ho'i e 'i'ini ana e kaulona pono ma luna o ka hana a ka Hawai'i, me ka ho'onui 'ole i ka luhi ma luna o ka nānā 'ana i kā ha'i. Malia o kapa 'ia ka'u hana he mea e ho'opili aku ana i "kā ha'i mea'ai" (Pukui and Elbert 330) ma ka mana'o ho'i, o 'ōhumu 'ia wau i ko'u ho'opili 'ana aku i ke kākā'olelo ho'ōla i loko o ka welo 'ike o ha'i. Ua hewa loa ia no'ono'o 'ana o'u, a ua 'ike 'i'o ihola wau ma hope mai, 'a'ole wale nō ia kilo 'ana i ko Polenesia he mea waiwai e pa'a ai he kuana'ike ākea no ka ha'i'ōlelo ha'ako'iko'i Polenesia, he ala pū nō na'e ia e hiki ai ia'u ke kia'i i ka Hawai'i 'ana o ke kākā'olelo, 'a'ole ho'i e maha'oi a lilo i loko o ka welo o ha'i. Inā nō na'e e maha'oi aku, he ki'ina ia i loko o ka pō'ai Polenesia pili ma luna o ka na'auao kuana'ike Hawai'i, 'a'ole ma muli o ka lalelale wale 'ana nō i ka nani hinuhinu o kekahi hi'ohi'ona *lāuga* a *whaikōrero* paha e pā wale ai ka na'au ke nānā a ke lohe aku. Pēia ho'i i ki'i 'ia ai e nānā aku i ka *lāuga* me ka *whaikōrero*, a inā pēlā, e pa'a mai nō he 'elele 'ike o ka ha'i'ōlelo ha'ako'iko'i o Polenesia komohana (*lāuga*) me Polenesia hikina (*whaikōrero*).[6] 'Oiai he 'oko'a loa nō nā loina ho'okō i ka *lāuga* me ka *whaikōrero* kekahi mai kekahi aku, ua ahuwale 'i'o nō ke 'ano Polenesia pili o ia mau 'oihana a 'elua ma ke kilo 'ana i nā "ha'awina 'uhane," 'o ia ho'i, nā ha'awina pili kuana'ike nui o ka ha'i'ōlelo ha'ako'iko'i o ia mau mo'omeheu 'oko'a 'elua.

Hele nō a 'alawa wale ka maka i ka 'ili kai hohonu o nā loina *lāuga* me ka *whaikōrero*, a pēia ho'i nā hi'ohi'ona pohihihi a lāli'i 'oko'a o nā 'ano like 'ole e pili pū ana, 'a'ole nō pa'akikī iki ka ho'ohihi 'ana aku i ia mau ho'oilina 'o'ole'a e mau nei ia 'ano ha'i'ōlelo 'ana a hiki i kēia wā. He ma'alahi wale nō ka lele kāpulu 'ana e ho'omāoe aku i ko ha'i nani, a pono hāpuku wale aku nō me ka 'ōkomo pū iho i loko o ka 'oihana kākā'olelo, a kapa 'ia aku ho'i, he ho'oilina Hawai'i mai o kikilo mai.[7] 'A'ole loa pēlā ka 'oia'i'o o ko'u 'imi 'ana e ho'ōla i nā hi'ohi'ona ha'i'ōlelo i loko o ke kākā'olelo. He kōkua nui ke kilo hāiki 'ana i ka 'oihana ha'i'ōlelo ha'ako'iko'i o nā lāhui pili Polenesia i mea e pa'a ai he na'auao laulā o ia 'oihana nui; i mea pū nō ho'i ia e ho'oholo a e kia'i pono 'ia ai ka 'ao'ao Hawai'i mau o kā ka Hawai'i iho nō. 'A'ole kēia kilo 'ana he mea e kīko'o kāpulu ana i loko o ko ia mau lāhui Polenesia e piha ai ka ipu o ka 'ike a La'amaomao. 'Oiai 'a'ohe nō ku'u pololei 'ana mai he ilina kākā'olelo pono'ī iho nō mai nā kūpuna mai e kino pono ai he ki'ina ho'omau i loko o kēia au, e like me ka mea e 'ike nei i ka *lāuga* me ka *whaikōrero*, e ku'u iho ka nae o ka na'au haunaele i ia nele ma ka ho'omana'o 'ana i ka noʻeau ʻōlelo manomano i paʻi lehulehu ʻia i loko o ka waihona moʻolelo Hawaiʻi kahiko ana ʻole. ʻO ke kuanaʻike kanaka i kākau ʻia aku ai a paʻa ia waihona moʻolelo kahiko, ʻo ia kuanaʻike like ke hiki ke hoʻōla i nā hiʻohiʻona haʻiʻōlelo haʻakoʻikoʻi o ka ʻoihana kākāʻōlelo, e like me ka mea e ʻimi ikaika ʻia nei i loko o kēia kākau ʻana. ʻEʻole hoʻi ka moʻolelo kahiko, ola ai kānaka!

ʻO kekahi ʻaoʻao hoʻōla koʻikoʻi loa e hoʻomanaʻo ʻia, ʻo ia ke akamai kanaka[8] i loko o ka hana. ʻO ia hoʻi, e like me ka mea e ʻike ʻia ma lalo nei no ka hiki wale ʻana ke lumaʻi iho i loko o ke "koina" e ʻike ke kākāʻōlelo i nā ʻike kuʻuna a pau me ona ʻōlelo kuʻuna piha e pili pū ana, a e maʻalea hoʻi ma nā lawena a pau e hua ai ia kākāʻōlelo ʻana aku i loko o ka ʻuhane, ʻaʻole naʻe pēlā ke kanaka ʻana, oiai hoʻi, he kanaka! Ke nānā aku i ka *lāuga* me ka *whaikōrero*, he mau ʻoihana kuʻuna loa ia i ulu ai ke akamai kanaka o ka mea haʻiʻōlelo ma ka pili mau ʻana i ia ʻike ma nā ʻano pōʻaiapili like ʻole e haʻiʻōlelo ai; a ulu aʻe ia ʻike kino, a ulu aʻe ia ʻike kino, hele nō hoʻi a mākaukau loa a loea wale aku ma ia hana ʻana. Pēlā pū me ke kākāʻōlelo ʻana: E hoʻomanawanui ʻia ka ʻike kino ʻana ma ka nui e hiki, ma ka nui pōʻaiapili e hiki, e pili mau ai ka ulu i ka ʻiʻo. ʻO ia hoʻi kekahi kumu nui i kilo ʻia ai nā ʻoihana *lāuga* me ka *whaikōrero*, i mea hoʻi e kamaʻāina iho ai i nā hiʻohiʻona nui e pili ai kēlā kuanaʻike haʻiʻōlelo kēia kuanaʻike haʻiʻōlelo ma nā haʻawina o ka ʻuhane, a e nānā ʻia paha he haʻawina ʻuhane like e pono ai ke kākāʻōlelo ʻana. Pēlā pū hoʻi e lōkahi ai ke kākāʻōlelo i loko o ia ʻoihana haʻiʻōlelo haʻakoʻikoʻi Polenesia, ma ka ʻuhane nō hoʻi, ʻaʻole ma ka lawena kino hāiki—ma ke kuanaʻike nui hoʻi o ka welo haʻiʻōlelo haʻakoʻikoʻi Polenesia laulā e pili pū ai. ʻO ia ʻano kōkua kai ʻimi ʻia, i mea hōʻoia naʻu he kuanaʻike hoʻomohala i ke kākāʻōlelo i loko o kēia au hou. Eia ma lalo nei he ʻehā haʻawina ʻuhane wae aʻu i manaʻo ai he mau mea koʻikoʻi ke hoʻomanaʻo ʻia i loko o ke kākāʻōlelo hoʻōla hou. Pau, ua hoʻokūkū wau i ia mau haʻawina wae ma luna o kaʻu i ʻike ai he mea pili i loko o nā māhele nui ʻehā o ke Kumu Honua Mauli Ola.

(1) Ma ka *lāuga* me ka *whaikōrero*, paʻa ihola he ʻolokeʻa haʻiʻōlelo nōhie e hahai ai ma ka ʻoaka ʻana aku i nā noʻeau like ʻole a pau o ka ʻōlelo mīkololohua me ka hoʻānoano. ʻAʻole hoʻi ma ka mea e like ai nō a like kēlā me kēia hahaʻi ʻana a kēlā me kēia mea haʻiʻōlelo, ma ka mea nō naʻe e hoʻokō ana ma ka manaʻo lōkahi i nā loina kuʻuna e kūlana pono ai ka mana kupuna o ka *lāuga* me ka *whaikōrero*. I loko hoʻi o ka paʻa mau o ka ʻolokeʻa kuʻuna, minamina pū ʻia ka nani hakuhia[9] e komo ai nā manaʻo hou i loko o ka hana kahiko. He aha hoʻi ka manaʻo kahiko loa i pau wale kona waiwai i loko o kēia au hou nei? A he aha hoʻi ka mea hou loa o kēia au nei i pili ʻole iki kona kahua noʻonoʻo i ka mauli kupuna? I loko o ka makamae nui loa ʻia o ka ʻōlelo haʻakoʻikoʻi, ka ʻōlelo mele hoʻi me ka ʻōlelo kuʻuna e hoʻoholo ai ka mea haʻiʻōlelo he kiʻiʻoniʻoni ma ke au noʻonoʻo o ke anaina hoʻolohe, ʻo ka pilina o ia mau ʻike/ʻōlelo kuʻuna a pau i loko o ka nohona o kēia wā ka "pāʻani hoʻokaulike" e kūlia ʻia. I nā wā a pau e haʻiʻōlelo ai no ka "nani" o ke au kahiko, he kui lima ia e ʻimi ana e hōʻoia mau i ka waiwai e pā ai ko kākou

Hawaiʻi ʻana o kēia au i ke ʻano mauli kupuna o ka wā ma mua. E hāpai mau ʻia nā ʻaoʻao like ʻole o ka haʻiʻōlelo (ka manaʻo, ka ʻōlelo, me ka lawena kino) i loko o ke kūlana kiʻekiʻe a maʻemaʻe, i ʻole hoʻi e hāʻule ia haʻiʻōlelo ʻana i kekahi hopena kuʻuna o ka *lāuga* me ka *whaikōrero*, ʻo ia hoʻi ke ʻoki ʻia i mua o ka lehulehu ākea ma muli o ka pāhemahema.

(2) ʻO ia ʻano ʻoki ʻana, kiʻi ʻia e ʻoki pēlā no ke koʻikoʻi aʻe o ka mālama ʻana i ka mana o ka nui, a he mea ʻole hoʻi ka ʻeha o ka naʻau o ka mea haʻiʻōlelo hoʻokahi e ʻoki ʻia pēlā. ʻAʻohe pāʻani ʻana ma ka haʻiʻōlelo haʻakoʻikoʻi, ʻoiai, nānā ʻia ia kaila haʻiʻōlelo me ke kapu nui—he ala hoʻi ia e moamahi ʻia ai nā moʻokūʻauhau kupuna o nā ʻano like ʻole. Hoʻokali lōʻihi ʻia hoʻi ka hōlona, ʻaʻole e kū koke aʻe i luna e haʻiʻōlelo wale ai. ʻAʻohe pū minamina ʻana i ka hemahema o ka mea ʻike hapa a ʻike ʻole—inā e komo ana i loko o ka *lāuga* a *whaikōrero* paha, he pono e ʻike, he pono e maiau ka lawelawe ʻana, a ʻo ka hua maʻemaʻe, he mea pai ia i ka moʻokūʻauhau nui, ʻaʻole i ke kanaka hoʻokahi. ʻIke ʻia kēia ʻano ʻoki ʻana i loko o ka *seu* ʻana i ka *lāuga* (Perreira, *He Haʻiʻōlelo* 19–20, 43–45, 59–60), me ke kū ʻana aʻe paha o ka nui Māori o kekahi ʻaoʻao a haʻalele wale aku i ka *marae* ma ke ʻano kūʻē ʻokoʻa i ka *whaikōrero* i hele hoʻi a pelapala (131). E like hoʻi me ka holomua ʻana o ke au o ka manawa, a hoʻi nui ka Hawaiʻi i loko o ke kākāʻōlelo ʻana, pēia hoʻi paha ka hoʻomanaʻo ʻana i ia ʻano lawena e ahuwale aku ai ke kūʻē ʻana i ke kūlana hemahema kūpono ʻole loa o kekahi haʻiʻōlelo ʻana. ʻO Kekūhaupiʻo nō paha ke kumu hoʻohālike ma kona hoʻopaʻi ʻana i ka hewa o ke kaʻina hoʻohāinu ʻawa ma waena o Kīwalaʻō me Kamehameha mā (Kamakau 71:18).

(3) Ma ka *lāuga* me ka *whaikōrero*, kiaʻi pono ʻia ke aʻo ʻana a paʻa maikaʻi nā hiʻohiʻona haʻiʻōlelo me nā lawena kuʻuna kūpono e hoʻokino ai (ka lawena hoʻi o ke kino, ka pohā pono o ka leo, ka hoʻāli pono i ka mea paʻa lima). Pēia hoʻi ia kiaʻi ʻana, i mōkū paʻa maikaʻi nā māhele ʻike kuʻuna manomano e mau ai ka ʻiʻo o ka haʻiʻōlelo haʻakoʻikoʻi. I ka hele ʻana a walea ma nā ʻike me nā ʻōlelo kuʻuna, pēia hoʻi e hiki ai ke hakuhia ka mea haʻiʻōlelo a e hoʻohua i ka ʻike kahiko ma kekahi ʻano noʻeau hou o kēia wā.

(4) Ma ka *lāuga* a me ka *whaikōrero*, ʻike ʻia nō he pōʻaiapili haʻiʻōlelo kūmau, ʻaʻole wale iho nō ma ka ʻākoakoa ʻana o kānaka i loko o nā ʻaha kiʻekiʻe o ka *malae* a *marae* paha, ma ka mea pū nō naʻe e ʻike ai ke kanaka i ka mea nui o ka hoʻopuka manaʻo ʻana ma ke kaila haʻakoʻikoʻi e paʻamau ai ke kiʻina moʻomeheu i mua. Ma nā ʻoihana haʻiʻōlelo ʻelua, haʻaheo pono ʻia ka ʻuhane e ea aʻe ana i loko o ka lawelawe pono ʻana i kēia ʻano haʻiʻōlelo haʻakoʻikoʻi. ʻO ka sila nui hoʻi ia e ʻōhū aʻe ai ka umauma welo lāhui a kehakeha ke aloha mauli kupuna.

ʻO ia mau ʻaoʻao nui a pau i kūkā ʻia ma luna, he mea pono hoʻi ke hoʻomanaʻo ʻia ia mau hiʻohiʻona i loko o ke kākāʻōlelo hoʻōla hou, i mea hoʻi e ili ai ma luna o nā hanauna hou ke ʻano Hawaiʻi koʻiʻi o ka haʻiʻōlelo ʻana. He mea nō naʻe e hoʻomanaʻo ʻia iho, ma kēia kinohi hou o ke kākāʻōlelo ʻana aku, ʻaʻole ana e lele paukikī wale aku a hōʻea palupalu ko kākou haʻiʻōlelo ʻana ma nā keʻehina like o nā loina nohihi a lāliʻi hoʻi o ka *lāuga* me ka *whaikōrero*. Ua kino iho ua *lāuga* me ka *whaikōrero* ala ma muli o ke ʻano kūakahiko mai ka piko mai hoʻi, ʻaʻohe nō moku pū ʻana a hiki loa i kēia lā. Pēia hoʻi, aia ana ke ola ehuehu o ka ʻoihana kākāʻōlelo i ka hōʻoia ʻana i ke ola o ke kuanaʻike hanauna ma ka pūlama mauli Hawaiʻi i loko o ka ʻōlelo Hawaiʻi piha. Inā pēlā, na ka hanauna hou, a ia hanauna aku, a ia hanauna hou aku e ʻimi, e hoʻonui, e hoʻomāhuahua, a e hoʻolaupaʻi i kēia kiʻina hoʻōla hou ma nā hiʻohiʻona me nā loina Hawaiʻi kūʻiʻo e kūpono ana i ka nohona kanaka holomua o kēia mua aku. A hala aku ka haneli makahiki, a ui aku ana ka Hale Nauā i ka hōʻoia hanauna, e ʻī ʻia aʻe ke kuluma paʻa iho o ka ʻoihana kākāʻōlelo hoʻōla hou i loko o ka naʻau kila o nā keiki uaua o ka lāhui.[10] ʻOiai pēlā, koʻikoʻi loa ka hoʻomanawanui ʻana ma ke kāpilipili ʻana, a kāpilipili hou aku, a kāpilipili hou aku e ika hou aʻe ai ka haʻiʻōlelo maoli ʻana, ʻaʻole wale nō i kēia kākau ʻana, a mahalo ʻia kona nani, a pau! He mea koʻikoʻi loa ka hoʻohiki lōkahi ʻana o ka lāhui ma luna o ke ola laupaʻi o ka mauli Hawaiʻi i loko o ka ʻōlelo Hawaiʻi piha; a inā pēlā, e lilo ʻo ke kākāʻōlelo ʻana kekahi mānowai nui e ʻike ʻia ai ka lāhui Hawaiʻi ma kona Hawaiʻi ʻana. He mea koʻikoʻi ka hoʻomau ʻana ma ia hoʻohiki, i loko nō paha o ka naʻau ʻehaʻeha o ka hapa emi e hōʻole ana, ʻaʻole nō hiki ke hana ʻia, ʻaʻole nō hiki ke kākāʻōlelo. E kūpaʻa nā ʻōpio o kēia wā ma ka hoʻomāhuahua ʻana e ʻai hou ai nā moʻopuna i ka ʻāina o ia kuluma ʻana.

He Kālailaina ma Luna o ke Kumu Honua Mauli Ola no ke Kākāʻōlelo

Ma ka hoʻomanaʻo ʻana i nā ʻaoʻao nui ʻehā o ke kālaimanaʻo hoʻonaʻauao Kumu Honua Mauli Ola (ʻAha), i kuhi lahilahi ʻia aʻela ka lawena (kino) ma luna, ʻo ia kālaimanaʻo hoʻi ka mea e hoʻomanaʻo ʻia ai ka ʻike kuʻuna me ona ʻōlelo Hawaiʻi, ka lawena me ka pili pū i loko o ka ʻuhane Hawaiʻi. Pēia nō hoʻi wau e kiʻi aku nei i nā haʻawina ʻuhane o ka *lāuga* me ka *whaikōrero* a hoʻomoeā aku i loko o ka hiʻohiʻona haʻiʻōlelo haʻakoʻikoʻi o ke kākāʻōlelo ʻana. E nānā pūʻulu ʻia ma lalo nei ka ʻike kuʻuna i loko o ka ʻōlelo Hawaiʻi piha, ʻoiai, ʻo ka ʻike kuʻuna mai loko wale mai nō o ka ʻōlelo Hawaiʻi piha ka mea mau e pono loa ai ke kākāʻōlelo ʻana. ʻAʻohe pili o ka moʻolelo Hawaiʻi kahiko o ka ʻōlelo Pelekānia i loko o ke kākāʻōlelo ʻana, ʻoiai, he nele akāka ke kino e lau ai ke ahi o ka lua. He pono e hoʻomanaʻo ʻia ka moʻolelo kahiko i loko o kona mau hiʻohiʻona ʻōlelo Hawaiʻi piha.

ʻŌLELO ME KA ʻIKE KUʻUNA. ʻOiai pēlā, ʻo ka mea koʻikoʻi mua, a e pili pū ana i ka ʻōlelo Sāmoa e *lāuga* ai me ka ʻōlelo Māori e *whaikōrero* ai, kākoʻo pau pū ʻia ke kākāʻōlelo Hawaiʻi, he ʻōlelo Hawaiʻi piha wale nō, ʻaʻole ma kekahi ʻōlelo ʻē e kākāʻōlelo ai. ʻO ka ʻōlelo Hawaiʻi ka hōkeo nona mai ke kākāʻōlelo ʻana, a ma laila wale nō e mau ai hoʻi ke kahukahu ʻana i kona mana. ʻAlua, ʻaʻohe nō hoʻopaʻapaʻa iki no ka waihona ʻike manomano o ke kākāʻōlelo mai o kikilo mai, he ʻike puaʻi o kēlā me kēia mānowai nui like ʻole o ka moʻolelo kahiko. Ma waho aku nō naʻe o ia paʻa ʻike pēlā, he mea koʻikoʻi hou aku nō paha no ko kēia au ka 'imi pū 'ana aku i nā loina e pili pū ana me ka 'ike kupuna. Pehea ho'i e kino ai ka 'ike ku'una he Hawai'i ma ke kākā'ōlelo 'ana? Aia nō ho'i paha he mahu'i 'ana i loko o kā Kamakau (238:8) kākau 'ana no ka haku mele.

'O ia "haku mele," 'a'ole nō paha i no'ono'o 'ia kēlā me kēia ka'aka o 'ō a 'ō e pā wale ana ka na'au, a "haku" 'ia aku ai he mele. Ua no'ono'o 'ia nō na'e ho'i he kanaka kūlia nui ma ka ho'opa'a 'ike a loea ma nā loina o ka 'oihana haku mele, ka mea nāna e ho'oholo ana a e ho'opa'a ana i nā au nui me nā au iki o kēlā me kēia wā o Hawai'i nei i loko o ke mele e ko'ihonua iho ai ka lāhui. Pehea lā ho'i kākou o kēia au e hō'ea aku ai i ia pae manomano o ka 'ike haku mele? Ma nā ki'ina ho'omaka ma'amau nō ho'i o nā loina o ia 'oihana! 'O ia ho'i, ua hiki ke pa'a pela he 10,000 mele Hawai'i o nā kaila like 'ole, he aha lā nō na'e ia pa'a 'ana ke 'ike 'ole aku no nā loina mele Hawai'i e haku hou ai. Pehea e mōakāka iho ai nā hua'ōlelo koho (he kapu kekahi mau hua'ōlelo, he pono kekahi); ke kāpilipili laina mele Hawai'i me ke kumu o ia 'ano kāpilipili 'ana ma ke 'ano o ka "raima" Hawai'i (i 'oko'a loa mai kā ka Haole); ka 'oloke'a laulā o kēlā kaila mele kēia kaila mele 'oko'a (he ho'oipoipo, he ho'ohanohano, he kanikau, he ho'ālohaloha paha); oki loa, he na'auao no ke kaona me ke kuana'ike Hawai'i no loko mai o ke mele ku'una e 'oi a'e ai ka mōakāka o ke 'ano no'ono'o au kupuna, e hiki ai i ka haku mele o kēia au ke ho'ohua hou aku ma ia 'ano no'eau Hawai'i pili.[11] Inā na'e he pa'a hua'ōlelo mele wale nō, pau ka 'ike kupuna no ka haku mele 'ana, moku ka welo. Hele nō a pa'a nā loina haku mele, 'o ka lolo pū 'ana nō ho'i ia ma kēlā me kēia 'ike e pili pū ana ma ia ao. 'O ia ho'i, no ke kanaka o kēia wā e ake ana e kū ma nā ke'ehina o ke kākā'ōlelo 'ana, he ko'iko'i ha'alele loa ka 'imi 'ana e pa'a a mōakāka iho nā loina o ka 'ike ku'una, a i loko o ia 'ike loina ku'una e hua pū ai a launa i loko o ke kākā'ōlelo 'ana.[12]

Hele a 'ike ma ka haku mele, a ho'okolo aku pēia ma kekahi māhele 'ike aku, a komo aku ana ma kekahi māhele 'ike hou aku, e ahuwale a'e nō ho'i auane'i he kuana'ike Hawai'i kā'oko'a e ho'opūnana pono 'ia iho ai ke kākā'ōlelo 'ana aku, me ka malihini 'ole ho'i ma nā hi'ohi'ona e lawena hou iho ai i waena o kānaka. 'O ka pahuhopu hiki koke o kēia pepa ka ho'okahua hou 'ana i ke kuana'ike ha'i'ōlelo ha'ako'iko'i i loko o ke kākā'ōlelo 'ana ma ke ala 'imi na'auao mo'olelo kahiko. 'O ka hopena nui nō na'e e kau pono ana i ka maka, he ki'ina ho'āla pa'a i ke kākā'ōlelo e 'ike hou 'ia ai ia lawelawe 'ana he Hawai'i e ka Hawai'i iho nō, 'akahi. 'Alua, e 'ike hou 'ia ka Hawai'i he mea ha'i'ōlelo o ia kaila hanohano nui, e like ho'i me ka 'ike 'ana i ka *lāuga* me ke *whaikōrero* o nā pō'aiapili ha'i'ōlelo ha'ako'iko'i o ia mau lāhui. I loko ho'i o kēia mau pahuhopu no ke kākā'ōlelo 'ana e ho'omana'o 'ia ai ka ho'ona'auao laupa'i e 'ike ai i ka 'ike kupuna, 'a'ole 'o ka ha'i'ōlelo wale 'ana nō. E 'ike 'ia ke kākā'ōlelo he kino e ho'oulu 'ia ai a māhuahua ka na'auao Hawai'i kā'oko'a i loko o ka 'ōlelo Hawai'i piha.

LAWENA. Ma ka 'imi 'ana i ka 'ao'ao lawena Hawai'i o ke kākā'ōlelo 'ana, 'a'ole nō e ahuwale koke mai, 'oiai, he mea pa'a wale mai nō ka lawena Hawai'i mai ka hānau me ka hānai ʻana aʻe nō a nui ke kanaka i loko o ka pōʻai ʻohana a pilina Hawaiʻi. Hala aʻe nā kūpuna, nā kūpuna Hawaiʻi hoʻi o ka noho ʻana, hala pū nō lākou me kā lākou lawena Hawaiʻi hoʻi o ka noho ʻana; me ka hana nui nō i kēia au e hoʻokino hou iho ai i ia lawena inā ʻaʻohe ʻike maka a kamaʻāina mua. ʻAʻole nō naʻe ia he mea i hiki ʻole loa ke hoʻīnana hou ʻia, me ka hana nui loa nō naʻe a pili koke me nā kūpuna a mākua ʻike e waiho mai nei, māhuʻi aku nō paha ma ia mau hiʻohiʻona Hawaiʻi. Koʻikoʻi ka lawena ʻana o ke kākāʻōlelo he Hawaiʻi, ʻoiai, ma ka māhuahua ʻana aʻe o ka haʻawina naʻau a hū wale aʻe he ʻōlelo mai loko mai o ka ʻuhane o ke kumuhana e kākāʻōlelo aku ana, he mea nui ka ʻike ʻia o ia hū ʻana he Hawaiʻi, e like hoʻi me ka mea e ahuwale ana ma ka lawena kino kanaka Sāmoa e mōakāka ai ka *lāuga* he Sāmoa, a pēia hoʻi me kā ka Māori he Māori, e ʻike ʻia ai ka ʻokoʻa nui o ia mau lawena haʻiʻōlelo haʻakoʻikoʻi kekahi mai kekahi aku. Ma ka nui loa i hiki, e pono nō hoʻi e hōʻoia i ka Hawaiʻi ʻana o ke kūlana kino—ke kūnou ʻana iho o ke poʻo, ka leha ʻana aʻe o ka maka, ke kuhi ʻana aku o ka lima, ke kaʻi ʻana aku paha, kaʻi ʻana mai paha o ka hele ʻana—ʻo ia mau ʻaoʻao nō hoʻi a pau kekahi e pono e makaʻala loa ʻia a e hoʻoulu akahele ʻia i mea e pono ai ke kākāʻōlelo ʻana. ʻO ka hula kahiko nō paha kekahi e kilo ʻia e hoʻonaʻauao iho ai; ʻo ka moʻolelo kahiko pū kekahi mea e hoʻopiha pono ai i ka ʻike no ka lawena kino ma nā pōʻaiapili like ʻole o ka nohona moʻomeheu Hawaiʻi o ka wā ma mua. Mai loko mai o ka heluhelu hāiki loa ʻana e hiki ai ke unuhi mai i nā manaʻo hoʻokele e akāka hou aʻe ai ka lawena Hawaiʻi. E pili pū ana i ka hoʻoulu i ka lawena Hawaiʻi, he mea nui pū ke kiaʻi loa ʻana, ʻaʻole e komo kolohe ke ʻano lawena Kahiki no waho mai o ke kaila kuhi lima o ke ʻano pāleoleo paha, ke ʻano peʻa lima nō paha o ka Haole i ke kua, me ia mea like aku, ia mea like aku. Ke kō nā ʻaoʻao hoʻoulu ʻike i helu ʻia ma luna, pau pū nō me ka ʻike i ka lawena kūpono e hoʻohua ai, ʻo ke ala nō hoʻi ia e komo ai i ka ʻuhane o ke kākāʻōlelo ʻana e ea aʻe ai a lewa.[13]

ʻUHANE. ʻAʻohe oʻu manaʻo nui e kākau ai ma kēia māhele no ka ʻuhane o ke kākāʻōlelo ʻana, ʻoiai, ma ka hana ka ʻike e ʻuhane ai. ʻO kahi manaʻo nui wale nō e hoʻomanaʻo ʻia, inā paha e manaʻo ʻia ʻo ka paʻa ʻike i nā au nui me nā au iki o ka moʻolelo kahiko i loko o ka ʻōlelo Hawaiʻi piha ka pae mua o ka lanakila; a ʻo ka walea ʻana o ke kino ma ka lawena Hawaiʻi ka lua o ka pae lanakila; hele nō hoʻi a "lalilali ʻole ka ʻili o ke akamai"[14] ma ia mau ʻaoʻao, ʻo ka hemo nō ia o ke ala e ʻike ai i ka ʻuhane o ke kākāʻōlelo ʻana. Ma ka noke mau ʻana a pau ka wā ʻakahi akahi, a hala ka wā hōlona o ka hoʻāʻo ʻana e hoʻomanaʻo i kēlā ʻike kēia ʻike a uʻuʻu wale iho ana i loko ka haʻiʻōlelo ʻana; ma ka hāʻawipio ʻole ʻana a paʻamau i ka haʻiʻōlelo ʻana, a ia haʻiʻōlelo aku, ia haʻiʻōlelo aku; a ma ka hele ʻana a nanea i ka haʻiʻōlelo ʻana, e haʻalele ai i ka ʻaoʻao kanaka ʻo ka hoʻopaʻanaʻau, a komo i loko o kekahi ʻaoʻao o ke kino pāpālua e haʻiʻōlelo ai mai loko nōkī mai o ka naʻau ma ke kuanaʻike nui, ʻo ke ala akāka nō ia e lēhei aʻe ai i loko o ka ʻuhane o ke kākāʻōlelo ʻana.

He Mana'o Pani

I ka wā mua o ko'u kākau 'ana i nā mana'o o loko o kēia pepa nei, e kau nui ana ma ko'u no'ono'o nā kūpuna kāka'ikahi o ka 'ōlelo Hawai'i piha e koe mai ana. E kau mai ana i ku'u maka nā mākua poeko loa a holomua ikaika ma nā 'ike 'ōlelo Hawai'i, e la'a ho'i me nā mākua mānaleo ikaika, nā polopeka 'ike Hawai'i o nā kulanui, me nā kumu kaiapuni 'ōlelo Hawai'i 'o'ole'a ho'i, pau pū nō me nā haumāna o'o lololo ho'i ma ka 'imi 'ike Hawai'i. E ake ana wau e komo koke ia mau hulu kānaka aloha i loko o ka ho'īnana pū 'ana i ke kākā'ōlelo. I loko ho'i o ka naue 'ūlōlohi 'ole 'ana o ke au o ka manawa i mua, pēia ho'i ka papaha o ka nalo honua 'ana o ke kūlana lahilahi māhunehune o ke kākā'ōlelo o kēia wā e waiho nei i loko o nā kumu me nā haumāna kāka'ikahi e pili pū ana ma ia mau pō'ai a'o. Ke komo pū kānaka a puni kēia pae moku i loko o kēia ho'īnana 'ana, pēia ka ulu 'ana a'e o ka papaha e ikaika ai he kumu ho'ohālike lawa e mau ai kēia ki'ina i loko o ka hanauna hou. 'A'ole ho'i e 'ole ka 'oko'a o ka ha'i'ōlelo 'ana o kekahi kaila i kekahi kaila hou aku nō ho'i. Inā nō na'e e lōkahi ma ka na'au: 1) e kia'i mau i ka 'oi mau o ka 'ike 'ōlelo Hawai'i me ka 'ike mo'olelo kahiko ma nā kumuhana me nā pō'aiapili like 'ole; 2) e 'o'ole'a ma ka ha'i'ōlelo piha 'ana e komo aku ai i loko o ke kākā'ōlelo 'ana (ka 'uhane); a 3) e 'o'ole'a ma ka ho'oili 'ana i ka 'ike i ma'ema'e ka mau 'ana aku, 'o ia ho'i ke ke'ehina hana e ahuwale ai kaua mea 'o ke ola. Ke ho'oili a a'o aku i ka 'ike, e ho'oili ku'upau, "kūkae a na'au."[15] Inā he ha'awina 'ōlelo a mo'omeheu o ke a'o 'ana, inā ho'i paha he ha'awina lawena ho'ohālikelike o ka ha'i'ōlelo 'ana aku, he ko'iko'i loa ka hō'ea 'ana o kēia kākā'ōlelo ho'ōla hou i loko o ka 'uhane hahana o ka hanauna hou. 'O laila ho'i kahi e pau ai ka ha'i'ōlelo o kona 'ano ha'awina, a ao maoli a'e ai ka 'ikena i ka nani o Nōla'ela'e.[16]

KUHIA O HOPE

1. **Ha'ako'iko'i** rhetorically complex (vocabulary, grammar, *élan*, often highly poetic and metaphoric in content).

2. Ua nānā pū 'ia he la'ana wae hou aku o ia ho'okā'au 'ana ma loko o kā Nakuina (40–45) o ke 'ano 'ōlelo "ho'okipa," he ho'ohenehene nō na'e i nā ali'i o nā moku o Hawai'i Mokupuni ma lalo o Keawenuia'umi e hiki pākahikahi aku ana i o Kūapāka'a mā i Moloka'i.

3. Ua mohala kēia kākau 'ana mai loko mai o ka'u pepa puka lae'ula, *He Ha'i'olelo. . . .* No ka 'ike piha hou aku, e nānā aku nō i laila.

4. I ia MH 2008, ma lalo o ka ha'awina kālā noi'i na ka Hawai'i Council For The Humanities, ua kālele ihola ko'u noi'i 'ana i nā palapala kahiko ma ka Hawai'i State Archives, ka Hawaiian Historical Society me ka Hawaiian Mission Children's Society Library, a pēia ho'i ma ka Bishop Museum Archives and Library. Ua nīnauele pū 'ia 'o Janet Zisk (kūka'i 'ōlelo kelepona, Mei 2008), ka mea mālama palapala kahiko o Nā Kula 'o Kamehameha, Kapālama, no ia kumuhana 'o ke kākā'ōlelo me ka ha'i'ōlelo Hawai'i ha'ako'iko'i, a hō'ole mai ana nō ua Zisk nei, 'a'ohe nō 'ike palapala a 'okina leo paha e waiho aku ana iā ia no ia kumuhana. I mea pāku'i, ua kilo pū 'ia ka 'ohina kōlamulamu mo'omeheu a

Thrum (1875–1933) a me ka ʻohina kōlamulamu nūpepa moʻomeheu Hawaiʻi a Taylor (18 Pepeluali 1949–25 Kekemapa 1961).

5. Ma ka nīnauele pū ʻana i ka mea nāna i hoʻokumu a i alakaʻi iā Ka Leo Hawaiʻi ma nā MH 1972–1988, iā Larry Kimura (27 Iulai 2010), hōʻoia pū maila ʻo ia no ia kūlana nele hoʻokahi nō. ʻOiai ua hoʻomau ʻo Ka Leo Hawaiʻi ma nā MH 1989–2001 ma lalo o Puakea Nogelmeier me kona mau hoa nīnauele pū, hōʻoia pū maila ʻo ua Nogelmeier nei no ia kūlana nele hoʻokahi (kūkaʻi ʻōlelo ma Iune 2010; hōʻoia hou ʻia ma ke kūkaʻi leka uila 6 Iulai 2011). Mahalo nui iā Leah Calderia o ka Hale Hōʻikeʻike o Pīhopa no ke kōkua ʻana ma laila.

6. I ʻike laulā hou aku, e nānā i kā Kuipers me kā Watson-Gegeo.

7. Ua kuhi aku kā Chun (33), penei no kēia ʻano hoʻomāoe ʻana: "Today Hawaiian oratory is slowly being heard again, although it is restricted to community gatherings and meetings. It is greatly influenced by speakers who have some relationship to the Māori of Aotearoa, those who have either traveled there or have hosted or been in the presence of Māori who have come here. This imitation may not be a bad thing, for at least the Hawaiian speakers follow a Polynesian format, though it is a Māori one. Recently during personal introductions at a retreat for a Hawaiian organization, a woman introduced herself as ʻMy mountain is such-and-such, my land is such-and-such, my river or water is such-and-such, and my sea is such-and-such.ʻ That is a form taken straight from the oratory and song of the *marae* (meeting house) of the Māori. . . ." ʻOiai hoʻi he ʻōlelo ahuwale kēia i ka Māori o Aotearoa, a e pili ana hoʻi i kaʻu ma luna no ke kilo ʻana i nā haʻawina ʻuhane, hoʻomau ʻo Chun (17; McKinzie 52–53) ma ka hoʻike ʻana no kekahi ʻōlelo Hawaiʻi hoʻoholo moʻokūʻauhau o ka makuahine o Samuel Mānaiakalani Kamakau penei:

Ma ka aoao o ka makuawahine o Manaiakalani S. M. Kamakau, Kihapupu, ke keiki a Kaoaoakahaiao, kaikamahine a Kaonohiokala me Leihulunuiaka-manu, ke kaikamahine a Kukalnihooneenuu [sic] me Kahoowahakananuha. He Ewauli a Laakona, he Ewa a Laakea a Hoalani, ku ae Ewa noho iho Ewa.

O ka aina o Manuaula i Kamananui kewe, mai na pali Lihue a Kukaniloko, a Wahiawa i Pooamoho ka honua, o koʻu poe kupuna no koʻu makuakane. O kewe a me ka honua o koʻu makuahine mai Waikele a Kalauao; o ka Ewa a Laakona. He kanaha mookuauhau a keu, e pili ana i koʻu mau makua, wahi a Kalanikila. He loaa ia oe la ea, loaa i ka ama, ke ike ia la ka makaukau a me ka pololei ("On. J. Koii").

8. **Akamai kanaka** common sense.

9. **Hakuhia** creativity.

10. ʻOiai e hoʻokāʻau ana wau ma luna o ka manaʻo o ka Hale Nauā, e nānā aku i kā Malo (191–192), pau pū nō me kā Emerson haʻakuhi ʻana (199–200) no ia mea he Hale Nauā.

11. I manaʻo hoʻākāka no ia "pili" ʻana o ka noʻeau ʻōlelo Hawaiʻi, e nānā i kā Perreira (*He Haʻi ʻōlelo* 253).

12. Ua like pū koʻu manaʻo ke noʻonoʻo aʻe i ka ʻōlelo noʻeau (a he aha hou aʻe lā ka ʻike kuʻuna e kilo ʻia), ʻo ia hoʻi, ua hiki nō hoʻi ke paʻanaʻau iho nā ʻano ʻōlelo noʻeau a pau e waiho ana ma ka ʻohina ʻōlelo noʻeau (Pukui, ʻŌlelo), inā naʻe e makaʻala i ke ʻano i kāpilipili ʻia ai, ka pōʻaiapili nona mai ka ʻōlelo noʻeau, a inā laki, ka moʻolelo piha i kino ai ka ʻōlelo noʻeau, ʻo ia ʻike haku ʻōlelo noʻeau ka mea e pūnohunohu aʻe ai ke kuanaʻike e pono ai ke kākāʻōlelo ʻana. Inā pēlā, ʻaʻole pono e hoʻopaʻanaʻau hele i nā ʻōlelo noʻeau paʻa mua a pau,

'oiai, hele nō ho'i a pa'a iho ia kuana'ike, pa'a pū ka hiki ke kāpilipili he 'ōlelo o ke kaila no'eau o ke kuana'ike Hawai'i e ho'okā'au hou aku ai. 'O ia ihola ka pono nui o ke kuana'ike e mākau ai ke kākā'ōlelo 'ana aku.

13. E nānā hou aku i kā Perreira (*He Ha'i'ōlelo* 47–49) no kēia 'ano kālailai pili i ke Kumu Honua Mauli Ola.

14. He lālani mele kēia o "He Mele He'e Nalu" (Pukui me Korn 36–41) e 'ike 'ia ai ka mea akamai loa ma ka he'e nalu 'ana, 'a'ole nō pulu kona 'ili i ke kai. Ho'ohana wau i kēia 'ōlelo ho'ohālike ma ka ho'omoeā 'ana a'e i ka mea akamai loa o ke kākā'ōlelo 'ana.

15. He 'ōlelo kēia e pili ana i ka lawe hānai 'ana i ke keiki. Ke lawe hānai 'ia he keiki, "The child was given outright; the natural parents renounced all claims to the child. This became a binding agreement when the parents said in the hearing of others, '*Nāu ke keiki kūkae a na 'au*,' I give this child, intestines, contents and all" (Pukui, *Nānā* 49; e nānā hou aku i kā Handy me Pukui 72). Ma kēia pepa nei, ke ho'ohana nei wau i kēia 'ōlelo ma ke 'ano, ke a'o aku, e a'o piha aku, 'a'ole e 'au'a. E a'o aku i nā haumāna a kākou ma ka nui loa e hiki, i māhuahua ka 'ike o ka haumāna e kākā'ōlelo ai.

16. He pā'ani kēia ma ka mana'o o "nōla'ela'e" (Pukui me Elbert 270) he " 'āina" 'ike ia e hō'ea ai ka mea pa'u ma ka 'imi na'auao.

PAPA HELU KŪMOLE

'Aha Pūnana Leo and Ka Haka 'Ula O Ke'elikōlani, ke Kulanui o Hawai'i ma Hilo. *Kumu honua mauli ola: He kālaimana'o ho'ona'auao 'Ōiwi Hawai'i*. 2009. http://www.olelo.hawaii .edu/documents/pdf/KHMO.pdf.

Chun, Malcolm Nāea. *Kākā'ōlelo: Traditions of Oratory and Speech Making*. Ka Wana Series, Book 8. University of Hawai'i Curriculum Research and Development Group, 2007.

Handy, E. S. Craighill, and Mary Kawena Pukui. *The Polynesian Family System in Ka-'u, Hawai'i*. 1958. Charles E. Tuttle, 1972.

Ho'oulumāhiehieika'onimālieapualīlialanaikawai [Ho'oulumāhiehie]. 1909–1910. *Ka moolelo hiwahiwa o Kawelo, ka hiapa'i'ole a ka ikaika, ka mea nāna i ho'oha'aha'a ke 'o'ole'a o Kauahoa, "ka u'i o Hanalei." 'O ka mea nāna ka lā'au kaulana 'o Ku'ika'a, a nāna ka wahine ho'olei 'īkoi 'o Kānewahineikiaoha*. Edited by Hiapokeikikāne Kichie Perreira. Bishop Museum Press, 2009.

Kamakau, Samuel Mānaiakalani. *Ke Kumu Aupuni: Ka mo'olelo Hawai'i no Kamehameha, Ka Na'i Aupuni a me kāna aupuni i ho'okumu ai*, edited by M. Puakea Nogelmeier. Honolulu: Ke Kumu Lama, 'Ahahui 'Ōlelo Hawai'i, 1996.

Kuipers, J. "Oratory." *Journal of Linguistic Anthropology*, vol. 9, nos. 1–2, 2000, pp. 173–176. Stable URL: 10.1525/jlin.1999.9.1-2.173.

Malo, David. *Hawaiian Antiquities (Moolelo Hawaii)*. 1898. Translated by Nathaniel B. Emerson, and edited by Eloise Christian, 2nd ed. Bernice Pauahi Bishop Museum Special Publication 2, 1951.

McKinzie, Edith Kawelohea. *Hawaiian Genealogies Extracted from Hawaiian Language Papers*, vol. 2. The Pacific Institute, Brigham Young University–Hawai'i, 1986.

Nakuina, Moses K. *Moolelo Hawaii o Pakaa a me Ku-a-pakaa, Na Kahu Iwikuamoo o Keawenui-aumi, ke Alii o Hawaii, a o na Moopuna hoi a Laamaomao! Ke Kamaeu nana i Hoolakalaka na*

Makani a pau o na Mokupuni o Hawaii nei, a uhao iloko o kana Ipu Kaulana i Kapaia o ka Ipumakani a Laamaomao. Honolulu, 1902.

"O. J. Koii, kau i Kapua." *Ke Au Okoa*, vol. 2, no. 14, 23 July 1866, p. 3.

Perreira, Hiapokeikikāne Kichie. *He Haʻiʻōlelo Kuʻuna: Nā Hiʻohiʻona me nā Kiʻina Hoʻāla Hou i ke Kākāʻōlelo*. 2011. University of Hawaiʻi at Hilo, PhD dissertation.

———. "He Kiʻina Hoʻokuanaʻike Mauli Hawaiʻi ma ke Kālailai Moʻokalaleo." *Hūlili: Multidisciplinary Research on Hawaiian Well-Being*, vol. 9, 2013, pp. 53–107.

Pukui, Mary Kawena. *ʻŌlelo Noʻeau: Hawaiian Proverbs & Poetical Sayings*. Bishop Museum Press, 1983.

Pukui, Mary Kawena, and Samuel H. Elbert. *Hawaiian Dictionary: Hawaiian–English and English–Hawaiian*, rev and enlarged ed. U of Hawaiʻi P, 1987.

Pukui, Mary Kawena, E. W. Haertig, and Catherine A. Lee. *Nānā I Ke Kumu (Look to the Source)*, vol. 1. Hui Hānai, 1972.

Pukui, Mary Kawena, and Alfons Korn, trans. and ed. *The Echo of Our Song: Chants & Poems of the Hawaiians*. U of Hawaiʻi P, 1973.

Taylor, Clarice B. "Tales About Hawaii." *The Honolulu Star Bulletin*, 18 February 1949–25 December 1961.

Thrum, Thomas G. *A Compendium of All Articles of Historical and Cultural Interest from Thrum's Almanac and Annual, 1875–1933*, compiled and edited by Richard Bordner. SRSC Press, 2006.

Watson-Gegeo, K. A. "The Study of Language Use in Oceania." *Annual Review of Anthropology*, vol. 15, 1986, pp. 149–162. Stable URL: http://www.jstor.org/stable/2155758.

He Polopeka Kōkua ke Kauka **Hiapokeikikāne Kichie Perreira** ma Ka Haka ʻUla O Keʻelikōlani o ke Kulanui o Hawaiʻi ma Hilo, kahi e kau nui nei kona hie i ke aʻo i ka moʻolelo Hawaiʻi kahiko ma ka mea e paʻa mau ai ka Hawaiʻi ʻana o ka ʻike me ka ʻōlelo Hawaiʻi. Noho ʻo ia ma Kaʻūmana, Hilo me kāna wahine aloha ʻo Hanakahi, a me kā lāua mau kaikamāhine pulakaumaka ʻo Keanokualani me Keakamaluhiwa.

*If we allow them, the kiʻi in our moʻolelo, in our kaʻao,
and in our mele can help us meet our greatest challenges
with better questions, because within these texts,
namely these kūpuna, are the experiences and wisdom of
a billion stars, a billion births, and a billion deaths.*

5
The Charm of Kiʻi

Kekuhi Kanae Kanahele KealiʻikanakaʻoleoHaililani

Preparing for the Journey
Kū mākou e hele me koʻu mau pākiʻi aloha
ready yourselves for departure my dearest kin
Ka ʻāina a mākou i ʻike ʻole ai ma lalo aku nei
headed towards the southernmost regions of my soul
Aʻe mākou me kuʻu pōkiʻi, kau i ka waʻa
I am not afraid to board the canoe because you are with me
Noʻiau ka hoe a Kamohoaliʻi
Our brother's blade knows many oceans
. . . Ke kū nei mākou e ʻimi kahi e noho ai a loaʻa ma Peleʻula
to turn back is not a choice . . . lavish intimacy invites me to her home
ʻO Kapōʻulakīnaʻu ka wahine a loaʻa i ka lae kapu o Makapuʻu
my dreams are famished, starved at the siting of land, of infinite possibilities
I laila pau ke kuleana, e ʻimi iā Kānehoalani
I extend my heart towards Kānehoalani. Have I arrived?
A loaʻa i ka lae o Makahanaloa
I have journeyed too far from myself
He loa ka uka o Puna, ʻelua kāua i ke kapa hoʻokahi
my body aches to dance, my soul desolate, my mind racing
Akahi au a ʻike, hāʻupu mai walohia wale ā
this is the first time I am left to ponder, alone
E Kānehoalani ē, Kānehoalani ē, aloha kāua
Aloha Grandfather Sun, my timeless consciousness
Kau ka hōkū hoʻokahi hele i ke alaloa
Ascension on the path towards the zenith, purposeful, knowing
Aloha kama kuku kapa a ka wahine
while I struggle to felt the fibers of my own meaning
He wahine lohiʻau, nāna i ka makani
Oh, goddess divine, possess me!
He makani lohiʻau, hāʻupu mai ʻo loko
a wind that folds time, my innards are alive, journey is begun!

Who and what is this chant all about? For the moment, let's not look at the mele's relationship to the narrative, or the value of the Hawai'i cultural objects embedded in the text…although you want to. For now, just take another look at the mele and answer the question, who and what is this chant all about?

What Is the Charm of Ki'i?

Aloha friends of poetry, oratory, and narrative. I thought it might be fun and useful to dedicate this chapter to "The Charm of Ki'i." Hawai'i stories and poetry illuminate Hawai'i lifeways. They have been our constant companions over the last sixty years during the restoration of ourselves and reintroduction of who we are and our contributions in the world. We depend on mo'olelo, ka'ao, and mele for their layers of value, especially when it comes to Hawai'i cultural objects such as 'ōlelo no'eau and ritual, and traditions such as farming, kilo i'a, loko, hula, kālai ki'i, and many others. Just as the 'āina and kai are our landscapes for physical and spiritual subsistence, mo'olelo, ka'ao, and mele have been our landscapes for intellectual and psychological subsistence.

In "The Charm of Ki'i," I would like to introduce the possibility of our relationship with each and every mele and/or story beyond our interdependence on them for Hawai'i cultural objects. I would posit that each mo'olelo, mele, and ka'ao has more layers of messaging than what we are ma'a to observing and absorbing, and that if we begin a more-than-third-party relationship with each mo'olelo, ka'ao, and mele, we will have gained an immense interpersonal relationship with these literary "people." Each mele and story has a name and a birth date and a purpose for being created; they are therefore our relatives in nature, and therefore humanity, and therefore ourselves.

What is the use of that? Well, that confidence, that attitude, moves us toward a path of limitless creation, mau a mau. We add our individual contributions to the Hawai'i Life corpus of knowing. And that keeps growing, so that we are touching every part of the Hawai'i Universe, the Earth and Cosmos and our own spirit. This chapter is about how to access the MORE of what mo'olelo, mele, and ka'ao have to share with us beyond our material relationships with them. Excavating ki'i for meaning is not a new concept; nor is the idea of creating personal, communal, and global relationships to ki'i an original theory. My personal offering of the AHI approach helps all levels of learners get closer to the timelessness of ki'i in a timely, somewhat efficient, meaningful way.

A ki'i is an image. A charm is that which absorbs and reflects magic. So, the Charm of Ki'i is the magic that ki'i absorbs and then reflects out in story, chant, hula, and memory. When we look through the kaleidoscope of a mo'olelo, a ka'ao, or a mele, the Charm of Ki'i is what looks back at you. What you are seeing in the kaleidoscope is a multi-dimensional, multi-layered image that shifts with each rotation. Moʻolelo, kaʻao, and mele live in this multi-dimensional world of multi-layered shapes and images, shape-shifting to form a different reflection of kiʻi with each turn.

Isn't that delightful? What if the charm of kiʻi that present themselves in abundance in each moʻolelo, kaʻao, and mele are meant to shift our dimensional perception of how we view the world and ourselves? Would that be helpful, perhaps even a gift?

We will talk about these kiʻi people in more detail later on.

> *Note: When I say, forest people, or ocean people, or kiʻi people, I mean all of the elements that make up a particular community. It is like saying poʻe iʻa, poʻe pua, poʻe kalo, but only "thing" in English. People for me don't only have two feet and two legs, lungs, and a heart. My community is HUGE, so people, in my language, means essentially everyone from bird people to slug people (ewwww!) to soil and microbe people.*

Alright, back to our narrative.

For now, my pōkiʻi aloha, before we entrust our journey to the skillfulness of Kamohoaliʻi's paddle, we are going to turn our attention to three conscious shifts that I entreat you to consider before reading any further. Play with me here. OK? Ready?

Conscious Shift #1: Be willing to shift freely and non-judgmentally between the material and immaterial—because the immaterial, in the reality of the entire Hawaiʻi Universe, makes up 99 percent of our lived world. With this shift, we can begin to cultivate our relationship with kiʻi... and Hawaiʻi literary works are REPLETE with them! If we resist this shift, and cling to the linearity of text as we perceive it on the page, the whole energetics of Hawaiʻi narrative, musicality, and poetry doesn't necessarily disappear, but it does go dormant. But I am guessing the whole point of a book on Moʻolelo is not to send our relationships to texts into dormancy.

Next shift. Mākaukau?

Conscious Shift #2: Let's just get rid of—I mean, simply throw out—the notion that what's in our moʻolelo, kaʻao, and mele is what the Hawaiians USED to do. In 2022, we can afford to have a little more imagination. Stories, storytelling, story-listening, story-singing, story-dancing, story-chanting, and story creation develop a cognitive altering experience because of the orality of it, and because we are in fact in the exact space where these stories are created. This allows us to navigate back and forth and in and out of several different realities at the same time. The information, the lessons, and the images in ancient texts, spoken or read, were created from a life experience that happens to be happening... right this moment!

And Shift #3. Be READY for this one!

Conscious Shift #3: Here's the gut shift, the SUPER Kanaloa-ness, the Uli-ness of the whole sacred text talk. When we talk, chant, sing, dance, orate the experiences in moʻolelo, kaʻao, and mele, we're not talking "about" them, we LIVE them again, and again, now. *Not metaphorically.* You don't just moʻolelo about ʻUmi, you live with him. You don't kaʻao the Kana story, you are the eternal cord! You don't dance about divinity. You BECOME it!

Deep breath...and here we go.

The Morphic Kiʻi

So now we're ready to dive. Moʻolelo, kaʻao, and mele are far from being locked in time. Because a moʻolelo speaks to a particular time does not mean it is fixed there; it has merely begun there. The kiʻi in moʻolelo link time. Kaʻao are wonderfully spacious; hence, the kiʻi in them bridge spaces, both material and immaterial. And mele, if you can imagine, are expansive outward and inward, so the kiʻi in them and the leo, hula, or ritual used to expand that kiʻi harmonize frequencies in space and time.

WOW!! What does it all mean?

What it means depends on what level you relate to the moʻolelo, kaʻao, and mele. You can be sure that your level of accessing their charm is proportionate to your relationship with them. If you relate to moʻolelo, kaʻao, and mele from the level of entertainment, then to be sure, what you walk away with is a feeling of being entertained. Not bad, not good, not lasting—just pleasantly entertained. At the very least, this level of relationship to text will lure you into the magic of the story. But entertainment is momentary if this relationship is not cultivated.

If you relate to moʻolelo, kaʻao, and mele from the level of curiosity, then what you leave with are more questions. This is good, and a little bit more lasting, because now you've energized new synapses in your mind and in the Hawaiʻi universe's brain, so to speak. You are drawn to find answers.

If you relate to moʻolelo, kaʻao, and mele from the level of inheritance, then what you will find are the treasures that our kūpuna have left us, that inform us, and that make our lives more waiwai. Those discoveries multiply with each moʻolelo, kaʻao, and mele that you commit your energy to learning, reiterating, and teaching. As an inheritance, then, moʻolelo, kaʻao, and mele become ways by which you could potentially connect to other people in other places.

But what if entertainment, curiosity, and inheritance lead you to yet a deeper relationship to moʻolelo, kaʻao, and mele through the kiʻi? Some folks already experience this level of relationship. But for folks who are not maʻa, or accustomed to this notion, think about this.

Kiʻi are images that are captured in the time in which a text is created—not captured as in imprisoned, but captured as in video or film. But unlike a video tape, a ki'i is not a static visual. A ki'i is sensual and sentient in that it develops as you develop. Isn't that cool? The meaning of ki'i morphs like all other dynamic entities in nature—like us in fact. Ki'i are most effective when we are aware that they are there, in multiple layers.

Who are these ki'i? They are the hero, the goddess, the wise woman, the warrior, the mo'o, the dark cave, the snake, the purity, the dark, and the light. We experience them as the cosmic cord, the intelligence of animals, the trees who rise to battle, the bad guy, the child, the raging river, the birth of the savior or a chief, a sunrise, a sunset, and the creation of islands.

Ki'i are born out of a geography, and interestingly linger in that geography's memory. And not just born out of a single geography, but born out of its relationship to the geographies of the world. What makes ki'i numinous is that they are thought, connected to Hawai'i texts, emotionalized, and taken them wherever we are. Like I said, ki'i can be expansive. Or, ki'i can induce introspection. The latter is where the undiluted potency of the charm is generated.

So let's go back to the very first question above and the mele at the beginning of our chapter. Who and what is this mele all about?

Go ahead. I'll wait.

Indeed, the text is about Pele's migration—on one level. From a broader lens, the text is about the journey and transition. But now, look beneath the layers of entertainment, curiosity, and inheritance, and ask these questions through the lens of **Conscious Shift #3**:

> *Who is the navigator?*
> *Who is the land never before experienced?*
> *Who is the wa'a?*
> *Who is Pele'ula?*
> *Who is Kapō'ulakīna'u?*
> *Who is experiencing Makapu'u?*
> *Who is experiencing Kānehoalani?*
> *Who is the makani lohi'au?*

The text, "Kū Mākou," is, essentially, about YOU! And it is, essentially, about ME! At a very visceral level, the message is essentially about all of our reflections in the story, WHO are the same reflections in the universe.

Too much? Hold on to your makaaniani! Because the MORE you delve into the charm of ki'i, the more chaotic and confusing it may become…which in the larger scheme of things, creates the perfect circumstance to experience regrowth and profundity. But I assure you, more about the charm of ki'i is actually very simple. **Remember Conscious Shift #2.**

The Kiʻi Process

During this time with me, I'd like to look at three steps in a process that I have simplified for my use when I am teaching or simply creating a relationship with text. It seems to work for most, so we'll try it out here too. If it works for you, maikaʻi. If it makes absolutely no sense, then…oh well! Toss it out. But in any case, I invite you to nanea with us as we explore the world of kiʻi.

First, I will describe three scales from which we will be deciphering kiʻi: a meta-scale, a macro-scale, and a micro-scale, or the Kiʻi Ākea, Kiʻi Honua, and the Kiʻi ʻIaka. Then, in the following section, we'll look at some texts—moʻolelo, kaʻao, or mele—and identify, just play, with the kiʻi that stand out for you. This is a continuous process.

Kiʻi Ākea, Kiʻi Honua, Kiʻi ʻIaka: Meta, Macro, Micro
The general attitude to approach this process with is "What do the kiʻi in this story have to teach me?" It is wonderfully titillating to know that no matter what story I read or hear, that story is my own personal lesson to learn how people think, what people's land is like and how they relate to it, why people's belief systems are the way they are, and who's important in the worldview of the folks from whom the story comes. Those are the things we learn from stories and song when we dig a little deeper. If we know this about Hawaiʻi texts, our relationship with them expands.

That Hawaiʻi stories are very similar to Okinawan stories or Germanic stories in terms of their kiʻi is mind-blowing. Be aware that if we reduce our relationship to Hawaiʻi texts to just the Hawaiʻi universe, we could relegate the fate of our Hawaiʻi contribution in the world to the same fate as Hina-i-ka-wai in the text about Puʻu Hālaʻi and Puʻu Honu in Hilo. Playing with kiʻi is all about flexing. Let's start.

The AHI (Ākea, Honua, ʻIaka) scale method I am sharing here is not the only method there is to identify kiʻi and identify WITH kiʻi, but it is a method that makes our stories accessible to people no matter their level of familiarity with the Hawaiʻi landscape, history, language, and culture.

What does this AHI look like?

Let's imagine an egg shape made of dashes or dots—whichever you like, anything but a solid line—for our purposes. And let's think about the orientation of the eggs as our relationship to the images or kiʻi. And let's also think about the open spaces between the dots as the ways in which our relationship to kiʻi morphs. And finally, let's think about the space beyond the egg shapes—THAT is the possibility for creating the next moʻolelo, kaʻao, or mele.

The first large east-west-oriented egg is the Kiʻi Ākea, the meta images. The

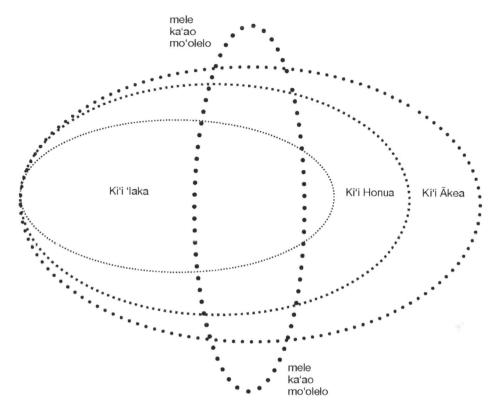

mele
kaʻao
moʻolelo

Kiʻi ʻIaka

Kiʻi Honua   Kiʻi Ākea

mele
kaʻao
moʻolelo

Kiʻi diagram. Author's image, 2017.

Kiʻi Ākea are the kiʻi that on a world scale just about any culture will recognize. Some examples of Kiʻi Ākea are sacrifice, rebirth, transition, transformation, death, birth, mother earth or mother nature, sky father, journey, gender roles, wisdom…and the list goes on. These are represented by certain characters or situations in a moʻolelo, kaʻao, or mele. We'll visit that a little later.

Within the next dotted circle of the Kiʻi Ākea live the Kiʻi Honua. The Kiʻi Honua are macro-images of region and community. Time is not a determining factor here. Just space. Kiʻi Honua are the images/themes recognizable to a particular geography, community, or ethnic group. For instance, in Hawaiʻi, the kiʻi of Wākea is pretty recognizable as a sky/space/time/father/restriction/societal image. The image of a raven may be recognizable in a number of Native American tribes. Corn may well be recognizable in Native American and Maya clans, and therefore by certain regions. The list goes on and on. As for Kiʻi Honua in communities, the scythe and mallet is a popular image recognized by the construction industry, while the medical/healing profession recognizes the image of the Asclepius, or serpent on a rod. But don't confuse the communal kiʻi as only a symbol. The ki'i could very well be a symbol, but really, it's what's behind the symbol that is the ki'i.

And lastly, the Ki'i 'Iaka. 'Iaka, Kūka'iaka, Lele'iaka, and kakahiaka are all images for Hi'iaka, which is both a name and a ki'i. In our terms, the Ki'i 'Iaka is the reflection, the shadow. That is YOU, your own image. The 'Iaka are all the facets of you, but the ones that show up in the story are usually the ones that want your attention the most. A Ki'i 'Iaka is a very special and magical personal image or theme. I say special and magical because no matter how cerebral we want to get about identifying and defining images/ki'i in the text, and no matter how good we become at memorizing the meta and macro ki'i in world texts, the thing that matters most about why a particular story is standing out for you at any particular time is because the Ki'i 'Iaka needs to speak to you. And needs to speak to you NOW!

The Ki'i 'Iaka could be the same as the Ki'i Ākea and Ki'i Honua, but you relate to them differently. On the other hand, the Ki'i 'Iaka can just be that one image or one theme that resonates with you because of your current life happenings. Let me also mention that the images or ki'i that we're speaking about here come from the same place as your dream images, your Ki'i Moe. Yes, indeed. But that's for another time.

And finally, around these three-nested east-west-oriented egg shapes who are the ki'i, there is another north-south-oriented dotted egg shape that looks like it's rotating around the ki'i. That's the mo'olelo, the ka'ao, and the mele. The dotted lines imply that energy and information pass throughout the whole system, and different ki'i are recognized depending on how the story or mele is positioned.

Let's practice. In the short text below, who are your Ki'i Ākea, Ki'i Honua, and Ki'i 'Iaka?

> *Pele comes from Kahiki, a space beyond the Hawai'i horizon. In her homeland, Lonomakua teaches Pele the science of fire—not domestic fire, the elemental fires of the earth and the sky. As Pele's gift develops, she knows intuitively that she would have to leave the comfort of her home to fulfill her purpose of creating landscapes around the world. Hence, when the time comes, Pele announces to her family that she is to leave Kahiki and take those family members with her whose functions would contribute to her task of building land. With heavy hearts, the rest of Pele's family gathers at the shore, where the great canoe Honuaiākea waits. As Pele and the chosen family members embark on the canoe, Pele's mother, Haumea, hands Pele an egg-child, a seedling, a healer in embryo; one who would become a most beloved sister and progenitor of hula. She is Hi'iakaikapolioPele, the egg who is kept safely in Pele's bosom.*

My Kiʻi Ākea: transition, "Pele knows intuitively that she would have to leave. . . home"
My Kiʻi Honua: Hiʻiakaikapoli, a Hawaiʻi way to recognize younger-older sibling rela-
tions; that there must be a continuum of sorts, and that we're responsible for that
My Kiʻi ʻIaka: The transition image really stands out for me now, since I am transition-
ing professionally—and therefore personally. So I guess, my Hiʻiakaikapoli, my
egg, is a promise of restoration for me once I settle

Who are:
Your Kiʻi Ākea:

Your Kiʻi Honua:

Your Kiʻi ʻIaka:

Who Are the Kiʻi Ākea?

In the study of mythography, kiʻi or archetypes are global images found in all stories around the world—from the Himalayas to the Amazon rain forest, from Ubud to Milfordhaven, from the Salish to the Tuwharetoa. We cannot deny, no matter how piko-centric (geo/ethno-centric) we are designed to be, that kiʻi are everywhere in all stories. And two out of three times, kiʻi convey the same or very similar meanings! Isn't that bizarre? How is it that kiʻi in my story of Kana in Hilo, Hawaiʻi, could possibly have the same kiʻi and meaning as a story from Jeju, Korea?

My first reaction is "Boy, my people got around." But the connection is bigger than just people transmigrating from place to place. The kiʻi actually exist in the fabric of places. It's the memory of the ʻāina, and everyone has access to that fabric. Meta-images belong to the collective unconscious. **Remember Shift #1?**

The point of this is to introduce you to your kiʻi, not to do a whole treatise on mythography and the meta-physical dimension. If you want more learning in this area, Joseph Campbell is a good place to start. Now, back to Kiʻi Ākea.

We will be looking for Kiʻi Ākea or global archetypes found in text, but in a little more interactive form down below. Rather than provide a list, here are some Kiʻi Ākea that both you and I can work on. The question is: "When you see the words below, what are some of the meanings, images, and ideas that you associate with the kiʻi?" We'll start with five kiʻi. I'll begin, and then you can add to the list. Think meta-image.

Moon—harvest, tidal changes, feminine illumination
WRITE THREE MORE HERE

    1.

    2.

    3.

Sun—consciousness, the illumination born out of deep darkness
WRITE THREE MORE HERE

    1.

    2.

    3.

Father—structure, society, ascension, teacher
WRITE THREE MORE HERE

    1.

    2.

    3.

Grandfather/mother—wisdom, transference, continuity
WRITE THREE MORE HERE

    1.

    2.

3.

Sunrise—newness, rebirth, seasons
WRITE THREE MORE HERE
   1.

   2.

   3.

Good fun, yeah? Let's have another go at AHI, but this time with a different type of text—mele. Rely on (if you need to) a good Hawaiian dictionary to help with unearthing your ki'i. Remember, what you experience at the topical layer is one experience, but our exercise here is to *excavate* for ki'i. This time, instead of playing with three different ki'i, like we did for the Pele story above, we are just going to pull out ONE ki'i, then relate to that one ki'i on three different scales. Think meta, macro, micro... global, geo-communal, and personal.
Hold on to the pola of your malo!! This is going to be fun!

   A Waiākea i Hilo Hanakahi
   Ala i ka wā pō iki, ala i ka wā pō iki
   I ka lei lehua o Hilo ē
   Paukū 'ia ka hala me ka lehua
   Maika'i Hilo, Hilo Hanakahi

My Ki'i Ākea: *awakening from the dream world; night turning to day (ala i ka wā pō iki); the globe experiences this same phenomenon at each rotation of the earth*
My Ki'i Honua: *in hula, coming out of the trance state after dancing a forty-five-minute set of hula pele is the same as night turning into day. New information comes through in this state.*
My Ki'i 'Iaka: *don't wake up too suddenly to my list of things to do; my body and mind is transitioning; ala i ka wā pō iki is to bring myself into a relaxed rhythm*

Who are:
Your Ki'i Ākea:

Your Kiʻi Honua:

Your Kiʻi ʻIaka:

Who Are the Kiʻi Honua?

Kiʻi Honua are macro-images, that is, themes or images shared by a community, a geographical or national group. The Kiʻi Honua is a kiʻi that is closer to home for me—well, for most of us. These include the images of our cosmologies, our moʻokūʻauhau, our 400,000 deities, the history of our migrations, the sum and total of our prayers, hula, carving, crafts, fishing, mahiʻai, music, intellect, technologies, the ideas of our very existence and our more than physical relationship to these islands, and on and on. The Kiʻi Honua are those images in moʻolelo, kaʻao, and mele that reflect how and why Henua Enana people, Japan people, Hopi people, Niʻihau island people, or Hawaiʻi island people relate to the world the way we do. It is our shared relationship to our geographical and communal worldview.

The Kiʻi Honua expand to the most universal attitudes that belong to a nation, and can contract down to village lifeways. Kiʻi Honua are useful for industry folks who belong to the same occupational or religious communities. This Kiʻi Honua is a tricky one, because it's so close to us, but just remember, the kiʻi or the image/theme suggests our relationship to the story at different scales. Some examples of Kiʻi Honua images could be ocean, naʻau, seasonality, kalo, waʻa, turtle, loyalty, teamwork, retirement, promotion, and on and on.

Kiʻi Honua are less obvious specifically in moʻolelo, due to the historical and linear nature of the narrative. But no matter how historically accurate we claim them to be, Hawaiʻi moʻolelo are essentially kaʻao in the making. (That's for another chapter.) I mean that Hawaiʻi narrative cannot help but include any number of out-of-the-mainstream activities, events, and characters because the moʻolelo is laced with Hawaiʻi worldview—and that isn't always historically bound to the element of time.

Below is a truncated excerpt from the moʻolelo of ʻUmi that I am retelling here as I found it related by various authors. Let's AHI again, shall we?

> *Līloa has a son Hakau by his mother's younger sister, Pinea. Later he begets*
> *ʻUmi upon a pretty chiefess of low rank whom he surprises at her bathing*
> *pool and with her consent makes his wife. He leaves with her the usual rec-*
> *ognition tokens and ʻUmi makes his way to his father's court and becomes a*
> *favorite. Līloa at his death leaves the land to Hakau but the god to ʻUmi, and*
> *warns this favorite younger son to remain in hiding when his father is no*

longer living to protect him. ʻUmi withdraws from Waipiʻo with his three comrades ʻOmaʻokamau, Piʻimuiwaʻa, and Koi, whom he has adopted from boyhood, and hides in the country between Hāmākua and Hilo, where he takes two wives and engages in fishing and husbandry. The kahuna Kaʻoleiokū observes a rainbow hovering over the boy's head as he repairs to the place where his god is hidden in order to lay before it the first offering of fish. To make certain of his rank, the kahuna lets loose a pig, and when the pig approaches the youth, the priest guesses his identity and takes up his cause against Hakau. (Beckwith, 389–390)

My Kiʻi Ākea: *succession of the second son. This image stands out for me as my mentors get older; a common theme in traditional and world monarchies*

My Kiʻi Honua: *first offering to the god. A common practice in most of Hawaiʻi. My current relationship to this kiʻi is a gentle reminder for me to stay close to the elements not just spiritually, but physically*

My Kiʻi ʻIaka: *my personal message from this part of ʻUmi's story is again the idea of succession, and identifying potential leadership in my immediate community*

Who are:
Your Kiʻi Ākea:

Your Kiʻi Honua:

Your Kiʻi ʻIaka:

So here we are, nearing the end of our conversation. The final kiʻi are the most evasive, and the ones we tend not to look for, because we are trained to have a third-party relationship to our world. OR, sometimes we just don't want to see ourselves differently, because we've got life all figured out. In any case, we are trained to believe that the person or images in moʻolelo, kaʻao, and mele cannot possibly be for us, or they cannot possibly be reflections of ourselves, because the story is about "them," NOT ME. Well, if that's the case, the Kiʻi ʻIaka really mess us up!

It doesn't matter if we engage the Kiʻi ʻIaka or not. They are still present. These are the micro-images or the personal themes based on our own experiences, intuitive processes, and personal interpretation of the information. They are our MOST POWERFUL allies for learning the world before the world "learns" us. Kiʻi ʻIaka really put us into perspective. These images try their best to tell us what's going on in our wailua because, as I said before, they are reflections of us in a textual and oratory form. THIS is the "more" part of stories and poetry that I was talking about in the beginning of our time together. The more part is beyond entertainment, beyond curiosity, beyond inheritance. The Ki'i 'Iaka, if nothing else, reveal exactly what we need to know when we need to know it, and will only speak to us if we begin to ask the questions such as the following:

> *What does this mo'olelo have to teach me?*
> *What message does this ka'ao have for me?*
> *Why is this mele showing up now?*

Now if we don't listen to them in this form, guess what? They'll certainly find us in our dreamscape!

Let's do one last exercise together. My biggest challenge here is deciding whether we end with a mo'olelo, and of the tens of thousands we have, which one?! Or do we end with a ka'ao, of which I have personal favorites. Or do we end with a mele? Hmmmm...

Okay, then. A mele it is! But this time, I'm not going to play with you—and it takes me some amount of energy not to play with you. I WANT to!

I'll be an observer as you suss out your ki'i from this short mele. Grab your 'aunaki and 'aulima, friends! We are going to build our AHI.

> *Ho'opuka e ka lā i kai o Unulau*
> *E lulumi ana i nā 'ale o Kaunā*
> *Haki kākala mai ana e ka makani*
> *Pua (puka) ka hala, ka lehua o Pana'ewa*
> *Hele i kai, kūnini i ka papa lohi o 'Āpua*

Who are:
Your Ki'i Ākea: sunrise. Surf is breaking, caused by the wind
Your Ki'i Honua: new beginnings. Sunrise marks a new day, a new era. These new things are coming quick, for example, lulumi. Yet freshness is brought nonetheless.
Your Ki'i 'Iaka: I should look forward to my new opportunities that lie ahead, knowing wholeheartedly that the transition isn't without obstacles

Well, I hope you've enjoyed our travels, and liked the AHI process. Use it if it is useful to you. Kamohoali'i's hoe has surely skillfully navigated us in and out of the swells and the surf of the ki'i dimensions perfectly! Mahalo, big brother!

So, what the heck does all this mean? And what does it have to do with me, my career, my family? It's all about navigation, dear friends. The Charm of Ki'i is all about how we navigate what society is telling us is a complex life. The Charm of Ki'i helps us to see that our nemesis in life is our struggle NOT to see that nemesis in ourselves.

I swear, THE greatest question of the last four or five decades for us Hawaiians has been "How to live in two worlds—in the Western world and Hawaiian cultural world?" Cow dung! Wrong question. Our greatest challenge is to ask ourselves the right questions, the questions that will allow our wailua to interact purposefully with the fabric of our Hawai'i here, the Hawai'is far away, and the Hawai'i inside of us. If we allow them, the ki'i in our mo'olelo, in our ka'ao, and in our mele can help us meet our greatest challenges with better questions, because within these texts, namely these kūpuna, are the experiences and wisdom of a billion stars, a billion births, and a billion deaths.

What's the next step? Ask the questions. Each time you listen to a mele, reread a favorite ka'ao, or do research in mo'olelo, ask them. Ask the ki'i in the texts, "What can I learn from you today?" Whether the answers come from the most desirable ki'i or the most undesirable ki'i, they will tell you exactly what you need to know.

THAT IS THE CHARM OF KI'I!

WORKS CONSULTED

Beckwith, Martha W. *Hawaiian Mythology*. 1940. U of Hawai'i P, 1970.

Campbell, Joseph. *Myths to Live By*. Penguin, 1993.

———. *Mythos: The Complete Series. Mythos I—The Shaping of Our Mythic Tradition; Mythos II—The Shaping of the Eastern Tradition; Mythos Three—The Shaping of the Western Tradition*. Athena, 2012.

———. *Pathways to Bliss: Mythology and Personal Transformation*, edited by David Kudler. New World Library, 2004.

Chopra, Deepak, M.D., and Rudolph Tanzi, PhD. *Super Brain: Unleashing the Explosive Power of Your Mind to Maximize Health, Happiness, and Spritual Well-Being*. Harmony Books, 2013.

Emerson, Nathaniel B. *Unwritten Literature of Hawai'i: The Sacred Songs of the Hula*. Bureau of American Ethnology Bulletin, Smithsonian Institution: Washington Government Printing Office, 1909.

Kanahele, Pualani Kanaka'ole. *Ka Honua Ola, 'Eli'eli Kau Mai (The Living Earth: Descend, Deepen the Revelation)*. Kamehameha Publishing, 2011.

Pele chants. Hālau O Kekuhi. Nā Kumu Hula Pualani Kanahele and Nālani Kanaka'ole. See also Emerson.

Von Franz, Marie-Louise. *Creation Myths*, rev. ed. Shambala, 2001.

Kekuhi Kanae Kanahele KealiʻikanakaʻoleoHaililani is an educator who has trained in the tradition of Hula ʻAihaʻa and Hula Pele, chant, and ritual, for thirty-nine years under Hālau O Kekuhi. Named for her grandmother, Edith Kekuhi Kanakaʻole, she was ritually elevated to the status of Kumu Hula (hula master) of Hālau o Kekuhi by her mother, Kumu Hula Pualani Kanahele, and her aunt, Kumu Hula Nalani Kanakaʻole.

Kekuhi has co-produced some of Hālau O Kekuhi's most significant contributions to oral and ritual arts stage performances, namely Holo Mai Pele, Kamehameha Paiʻea, Kilohi Nā Akua Wahine, Hānau Ka Moku, Wahinepōʻaimoku, Ka Hana Kapa, and CD resources Uwolani, Puka Kamaʻehu, and Hiʻiakaikapoliopele.

In an effort to broaden her service to people beyond the hālau, Kekuhi has developed Ulu Ka ʻŌhiʻa-Hula Consciousness Seminar & Hālau ʻŌhiʻa-Hawaiʻi Stewardship Training to teach basic Hawaiʻi practices that can connect anyone, anywhere, to their inner and outer landscapes. Kekuhi and her husband Tangaro offer an annual Kū E Ke Olioli: Chanting for Wellbeing Series. She is currently developing an online chant course, OLI HONUA, to support learners worldwide.

No laila, ʻo ka ʻai hoʻonuʻu ʻana o ka poʻe Kānaka Maoli,
ʻaʻole paha ia he ʻai ā manō, me ka nānā ʻole ʻana aku
i ka pono o ka ʻāina a me ke kai nāna e hānai mai.

6
E ʻAi ā Māʻona, ʻAi ā Ea
Na Ke Mele e Moʻolelo Mai

Kahikina de Silva

Ke moʻolelo ʻia ke aloha ʻāina o ka Lāhui Kanaka Maoli a me ke kūʻē politika o ua Lāhui nei, i loaʻa ai ka pono o kona ʻāina aloha, kau nui nō ka manaʻo o kākou i ʻelua wā i hala aku nei, ʻo ia hoʻi ka wā i hoʻokahuli ʻia ai ke Aupuni Mōʻī, a me ke au i hoʻāla hou ʻia ai ko kākou lāhui ʻana mai—ke au hoʻi i kapa ʻia ʻo ka *Hawaiian Renaissance.* ʻO kēia nō paha nā wā i nui loa ai nā moʻolelo aloha ʻāina i laha iā kākou, a i kuʻi ai kona lono i nā kihi ʻehā o ka honua nei. Eia hou, kākoʻo ʻia paha kēia ʻikena e nā ʻano o nā mele i puka pinepine ma ua mau wā nei nō—he Mele Lāhui a he Mele Kūʻē, ma laila nō hoʻi i moʻolelo ʻia ai nā hana aloha ʻāina o ia au. Eia naʻe, ma muli o ke kaukaʻi nui ʻana i keia ʻikena, mahuʻi pinepine ʻia kahi kōā i ka moʻolelo aloha ʻāina o ko kākou Lāhui, ma waena o ka puka ʻana mai o nā Mele Lāhui o nā makahiki 1893–1898 a me ke ea hou ʻana mai o ka leo mele kūʻē i nā makahiki 1960–1980. A, ʻo kēia kōā hoʻi, he wā ia e mahuʻi ʻia ai ke emi, a i ʻole ka nalo ʻana aku o ke aloha ʻāina politika i ka lāhui Kanaka maoli.

ʻIke ʻia kēia ʻano kuanaʻike ma kā Elizabeth Tatar hoʻonohonoho ʻana i ka "History of Hawaiian Music" ma loko o ka puke *Hawaiian Music and Musicians.* Hoʻokaʻawale akula ʻo ia nei i ʻewalu māhele o kēia moʻolelo, "according to the major non-Hawaiian (Polynesian) musical trends of the time" (xliii). Ahuwale koke maila ke kuanaʻike i loaʻa ai kēia mau māhele, a hiki ke wānana ʻia nā pilikia e hua mai ana, e laʻa ka manaʻo ē ma ka wā wale nō e hui ai nā mele a, ke pau kona wā, pau nō ia ʻano mele; a me ke kaukaʻi nui ʻana aku i ke alakaʻi ʻana mai o waho, me he mea lā mai laila wale mai nō ka loina a me ka leo mele e puaʻi ai kahi māhele hou o ke mele ʻana aku o ke Kanaka Maoli. Ma kā Tatar nei moʻolelo ʻana mai, hulikua ʻia nō hoʻi ka wā mua i laha loa ai nā Mele Lāhui ma ka ʻāina nei, a wehewehe wale ʻia nō ia wā (Māhele II, 1872–ca. 1900) no ke alakaʻi ʻana mai o Henri Berger i ka Bāna Lāhui Hawaiʻi, ka haku ʻia ʻana o nā hīmeni Hawaiʻi e nā aliʻi, a me ke ea ʻana mai o ka hula kuʻi. Aia a ʻike ʻia ma Hawaiʻi nei ka "social unrest that had convulsed the American mainland from the mid-1950s" (xliv), ʻo ia hoʻi ma ka hopena o nā makahiki 1960, a laila i hoʻomaopopo ʻia ai nā mele kūʻē a me nā mele pai lāhui o ke Kanaka Maoli.

Ua ʻane like nō hoʻi kā Berger moʻolelo ʻana mai no nā mele hoʻāla Ea a ko kākou lāhui aloha ʻāina, ma ua puke like nei nō. I loko nō o kona kuhi lihi ʻana aku i nā mele i haku ʻia no ke kūʻē ʻana i ka hoʻokahuli aupuni a me ka hoʻohui ʻāina (e like hoʻi me "Kaulana nā Pua"), kūpaʻa nō hoʻi ʻo ia nei i ka hoʻohāiki ʻana i ka wā i puka ai ka hapanui o nā "Sovereignty Songs," ma hope hoʻi o ka haunaele sivila o ʻAmelika ma nā makahiki 1950–1970. Eia hou, mea mai ʻo ia ala: "With the exception of 'Kaulana Na Pua' [sic], 'Hawaiʻi Ponoʻi' [sic] and 'Hawaiʻi Aloha,' the well-known sovereignty songs of the 20th century and beyond are products of the modern era and grow out of the American tradition of 'protest songs'" (776).

Eia kaʻu nīnau e hāpai aku ai i mua ou, e ka mea heluhelu, inā pēlā—inā i ʻano pio aku ke Mele Lāhui a me kona moʻolelo aloha ʻāina ma hope o ke kāʻili ʻia ʻana o Hawaiʻi i Teritore no ʻAmelika; inā hoʻi mai ua ʻāina anu lā mai ka hapanui o kā kākou mau mele kūʻē a hoʻāla Ea—ua aha ʻia lā ke aloha ʻāina i ʻōmau ʻia a paʻa i ka houpo o nā mamo a Ka Naʻi Aupuni? Ua aha ʻia lā ka ʻōlelo a James Keauiluna Kaulia, i hele a laha loa i kēia au o ka piʻi hou ʻana o ka Lāhui, ʻo ia hoʻi:

> …e like me ka lokahi o ka lahui i keia la ma ke kupaa i ke aloha i ka aina, pela ka hiki ole i keia Aupuni Repubalika e hana aku i na mea e ae mai ai o Amerika e hoohui, o ke kaula kaohi no ka hooholoia o keia kumuhinu a ke Aupuni, aia no ia ia kakou ka lahui.…
>
> Nolaila, mai makaʻu, e kupaa ma ke Aloha i ka aina, a e lokahi ma ka manao e kue loa aku i ka hoohui ia o Hawaii me Amerika a hiki i ke aloha aina hope loa. (4–5)

Ua pio maoli anei nō ke aloha ʻāina a me ka makeʻe lāhui, a ua hoʻi paha i Kahiki me Kanekuaʻana? ʻAʻole paha. Akā, e like me ka luʻu ʻana a ea ka honu ke holo ʻo ia ma ke kai, he luʻu a he ea paha ko ke aloha ʻāina. I ko Noelani Goodyear-Kaʻōpua ʻikena, pili nō hoʻi ke *ea* ʻana mai o ka lāhui i ka lōkahi ʻana mai o nā manaʻo politika a me nā loina kuluma o ka poʻe Kānaka Maoli. Kākau ʻia maila e ia:

> As "life," ea encompasses the cultural, the political, the economic. In observing the rhythms of Hawaiian movement over time, one sees peaks—or catalytic events—when the arbitrary boundaries between activities represented as merely cultural (such as hula or voyaging) and those cast as political (such as land rights protests or sovereignty rallies) are blurred. When people explicitly assert the ways cultural practice is political, and political movement is cultural, Hawaiian social movements leap forward. (12)

ʻIke ʻia, ʻaʻole nō ke Ea he mea kūmaumau o ka ʻeleu a me ka holomua—he wā hana ʻiʻo a he wā hoʻomaha nō hoʻi. E like nō me ka honu, ka mea nona ia inoa hoʻokahi ʻo ke Ea, he luʻu nō hoʻi kona i lalo o ke kai, a ʻike ʻole ʻia e ka nui lehulehu o uka kāna noke mau ʻana i ke ola. I ka wā hoʻi e pono ai ka laha ʻana mai o kēia honu, ea mai nō, a nanahu aku paha. E like me kā Goodyear-Kaʻōpua e kuhi mai ana, ke hana ʻiʻo kākou no ke kālai hou ʻana i nā palena i hoʻokaʻawale ʻia ai ia mea he *culture* a me ka politika hoʻi, loaʻa auaneʻi ka pono. Pēlā i ola hou ai ʻo Kahoʻolawe, a i kūpale ʻia ai nā kuleana ʻohi lāʻau a ʻohi iʻa paha o ka ʻōiwi; pēlā nō hoʻi e hoʻohemo ʻia ai ka ʻeleao puni kiʻei o Maunakea.

ʻO kaʻu nīnau naʻe, no ka wā ia e luʻu ai ka honu i lalo o ke kai—no ka wā i mahuʻi ʻia ai ka mālie o ke kai, a me ka wā e kaʻa ana ma waena o nā " ʻou" i poʻi hānupanupa ai nā manaʻo aloha ʻāina o ka lāhui ʻōiwi.

E laʻa hoʻi ka wā ma hope pono mai o ka hoʻohui hewa ʻia ʻana o kēia ʻāina me ko ʻAmelika, i kapa ʻia aku ʻo ke au Teritore ia o Hawaiʻi nei. ʻOiai ʻaʻole paha i manaʻo ʻia he wā kēlā i ulu nui ai ke aloha ʻāina a me ka makeʻe lāhui i nā keiki papa o Hawaiʻi nei—ʻaʻole i loaʻa ke kaua kūloko, ka palapala kūʻē, a me nā hanana ʻē aʻe i ʻike ʻia ma ke au hulihia o nā makahiki 1890—akā ʻaʻole paha i pio ke aloha o ka lāhui Kanaka Maoli i kona ʻāina a me kona lāhui ponoʻī. Ua mau nō, a ua mau nō kona moʻolelo ʻia mai ma nā mele nahenahe (Basham 99)[1] i haku ʻia ma ia wā, a hiki mai nō hoʻi i ka wā nei.

I kēia mokuna o ka puke nei, e hāpai ʻia ana a e kālailai ʻia ana ʻekolu mele nahenahe o ke au Teritore, me ko lākou kamau ʻana i ke aloha ʻāina a me ka makeʻe lāhui Kanaka. ʻOiai he mau mele nahenahe kēia, i haku ʻole ʻia nō paha me ka manaʻo o ka haku mele e hoʻolaha a hōʻoia aku i ke kū ʻana o nei mau mele ma ke ao politika, ʻaʻole kona moʻolelo he mea ahuwale o ke kūʻē i ka hoʻokolonaio, e like me nā Mele Lāhui i puka ma ka wā i hoʻokahuli ʻia ai ke Aupuni Mōʻī, a me nā mele kūʻē hoʻi e puka mau ana i kēia lā.

Akā, eia au ke mahuʻi nei, ua like—a ʻoi aʻe paha—ka mana o kēia ʻano leo aloha ʻāina o ka lāhui Kanaka Maoli, ʻo ia hoʻi ka leo e "kaohi ana i ka noho Kuokoa Lanakila ana o [kona] one hanau ponoi" ma o ka hoʻomau ʻana i nā loina a me ke kuanaʻike o ka lāhui Kanaka Maoli ("Ke Aloha…"). ʻO ka leo hoʻi ia e hoʻolaulaha i ko kākou kūlana kūʻokoʻa, me ka noʻonoʻo ʻole paha; ʻoiai ua paʻa hemo ʻole kēia ʻano aloha ʻāina i ka naʻau o ke Kanaka, hiki ʻole ke ʻalo ʻia kona puka ʻana mai a me kona halihali ʻia ʻana e ka leo o ua Kanaka nei. ʻAʻole e kani mōakāka ana kēia leo aloha ʻāina ke lohe ʻia, akā he ʻūlāleo paha kona hoalike, e paʻē mai ana i ka pepeiao, a lilo auaneʻi i kani mumuhu e hoʻohuoi ai ka mea nona ka pepeiao kani i kahi manaʻo nui e hoʻouna ʻia nei i ona lā. E like hoʻi me ka leo hula i loaʻa ai ʻo Pele, ka mea i lilo i pulakaumaka (pulakaupepeiao paha) nona a i hoʻouna ʻia e Kanikawī me Kanikawā, nā akua o Lohiʻauipo i Hāʻena, pēlā e hoʻolāʻau ai kēia ʻūlāleo pai Kūʻokoʻa iā kākou e hahai i kona kani a loaʻa ke kumu, he aloha ʻāina. ʻO ka leʻaleʻa ka mea e ʻumeʻume ʻia ai kākou e kēia poʻe mele, akā he mana nō hoʻi kona i hiki ke hoʻokamaʻāina hou i ke Kanaka i ke ala i alahula ʻia e ka meheu o nā kūpuna, ke hoʻopaʻa hou iā ia i ka ʻike e kū ai kona Lāhui, a ke alakaʻi hou iā ia i ka waele ʻana i ala hou e ola ai ka pulapula e hele ma hope ona. Ma o kēia mau mele e ʻike lihi ʻia ai kēia ʻano mana—ke ea hoʻi—e ola nei i ka iwikuamoʻo aloha ʻāina o ke mele Hawaiʻi.

I ke mele hoʻonuʻu[2] e ea ai

Eia hou kahi manaʻo nui o ka mokuna nei: ʻo ke aloha ʻāina, a me nā manaʻo politika i ulu aʻe ma muli ona, ʻaʻole ia he mea i haki, i nalo, i poina, a i pau aʻela paha i ke au hoʻokolonaio a me kona kai eʻe i luku ʻia ai nā ʻaha kū moku o kēia pae ʻāina. Akā, e like me ka iwikuamoʻo o ke kino Kanaka, ka mea nāna e hoʻopili i kona iwi poʻo me kona hope; e like me ka iwikuamoʻo o ka waʻa, e kīkoʻo ana mai ka ihu o mua a i ka manu o hope; e like nō hoʻi me ka iwikuamoʻo o ka mokupuni, ka mea iā ia e hui ai kahi kai me kahi kai o ia moku, nā kaha o ka ʻākau me ka hema, a pili mai ʻo uka me kai—pēlā ka mau ʻana mai o kēia iwikuamoʻo aloha ʻāina, mai ke kumu mai o kēia lāhui Kanaka Maoli a i kēia wā nei nō, mai ka ʻelemakule a i ke keiki, mai ka lae ʻo Kumukahi a i ka mole ʻo Lehua.

Ma o kēia iwikuamoʻo i paʻa ai ke kino o ke Kanaka a me ke kino o ka lāhui Kanaka Maoli. No laila, ma ona lā nō hoʻi i paʻa ai nā loina i kō i kēia lāhui, a puka mai i ke ao mālamalama. Pēlā i loaʻa ai ka mahiʻai, ka hoʻokele waʻa, ke kūkulu hale, ke mele, a me nā loina ʻē aʻe a pau i hele a walea i ka poʻe Kānaka. A, ke puka ia, ea mai nō hoʻi kēia iwikuamoʻo aloha ʻāina, ke ʻike a ʻike ʻole ʻia paha e ka lehulehu.

Inā pēlā, hiki nō paha ke koho wale ʻia kekahi mau mele nahenahe, me ka nānā ʻole ʻana aku i ke ʻano, ke kumu, a me ke kino o ua mau mele nei, a ʻike ʻia nō kona iwikuamoʻo aloha ʻāina, me kona paipai ʻana hoʻi i ke au politika a kākou e hoʻokele nei. A he pāʻani leʻaleʻa paha kēlā no nā hoa aloha ʻāina i puni i nā mele Hawaiʻi. ʻAʻole naʻe ia ʻo ka pahuhopu o kēia mokuna.

No laila, ʻo ke mele aʻu e kapa nei he "mele hoʻonuʻu," ʻo ia ka lāhui mele nāna e halihali mai i ke aloha ʻāina a pili pū me kāua a ʻelua, ma o kēia mau ʻaoʻao lahilahi nei. He mau mele kēia i haku ʻia no ka hoʻoulu ʻana, ka ʻohiʻohi ʻana, ka hoʻomākaukau ʻana, a me ka haupa ʻana i nā ʻono o ka ʻāina kulāiwi o kākou. ʻO ka hapanui o kēia mau mele, he leʻaleʻa nō ke lohe a ke mele aku, a ʻo ia nō kekahi o nā kumu aʻu e hāpai nei i ua mau mele nei ma ʻaneʻi. He ʻano lou ia leʻaleʻa, i ulu ai ko kākou hoi i ke mele, a lilo akula iā ia. Ke mele hou kākou i kēia mau mele kū i ka hialaʻi, komo hou ke aloha ʻāina i loko o kākou, a ʻumeʻume ʻia nō hoʻi nā hoa aloha ʻāina no ke kū like ʻana, a ulu hou aʻela nō. Eia kekahi, ʻoiai ʻo ka ʻāina a me ka hua ʻana mai o ka ʻāina ke kumu o kēia mau mele, ahuwale maila kekahi ʻano o ka pilina o ke Kanaka Maoli me kona ʻāina ʻōiwi, i ola ai a māhuahua lāua a ʻelua. A ma laila nō e ea mai ai nā manaʻo politika i mau ai ke kū ʻana o ka lāhui Kanaka Maoli i ka moku.

ʻEkolu mele hoʻonuʻu a kāua e moni ai, e kuʻu makamaka heluhelu. ʻO ka mua, ka pūpū hoʻi e ʻono ai ka puʻu i ka ʻai hou, ʻo ia ʻo "He ʻAi na ka Lani," i haku ʻia e

Lili'u no kona kaikunāne Mō'ī, no Kalākaua. Pāhola 'ia nei mele ma 'ane'i i hō'oia no ka pili pono 'ana o ka pā'ina me ka ho'okele aupuni, a i 'ike le'a ai kākou ē, ma ke mele nō e loa'a pono ai ia pilina. Ma hope mai ona, e ho'onu'u kāua i "Nā 'Ai 'Ono," a e ho'ōho like 'ia ka puana ē, "Aloha ka Manini."

> **"He 'Ai na ka Lani"—He 'Ai Aupuni**
> Mai noho a pane a'e,
> Ua kapu 'ē ka 'aha i ke ali'i.
> 'Ai ē, 'ai lā.
>
> (Lili'uokalani 119)

Ma mua o ka hīmeni 'ana mai o ka Sons of Hawai'i i nei mele, ka ho'opa'a 'ia 'ana ma kā lākou pā CD i ka makahiki 1973, ka ho'opa'a hou 'ia 'ana ma kā Dennis Kamakahi pā CD i ka makahiki 1999, a me ke pa'i 'ia 'ana o kona mau hua 'ōlelo i ka puke a ka Hui Hānai, 'a'ole kēia he mele i laha ma waho o kekahi hui li'ili'i o ka po'e puni mele Hawai'i. 'Oi loa aku ke kaulana o nā hīmeni hiehie a me nā mele haipule a kona haku mele, 'o ia ho'i 'o Lili'uokalani, e la'a 'o "Aloha 'Oe," "Ku'u Pua i Paoakalani," a me "Ke Aloha o ka Haku." Pēlā pū ke 'ano o ke kaulana o nei haku mele, o Lili'uokalani ho'i: he wahine akamai i ka wili pū 'ana i nā loina haku mele o ka Hawai'i a me ka haole, a he wahine kū ho'okahi i ka nani o ka leo a me ka maiau o nā hua'ōlelo āna i haku ai (Kanahele, updated Berger 504–507). 'A'ole nō i mana'o nui 'ia he haku mele aloha 'āina ua wahine nei, nāna i ho'olaha i nā mana'o politika o kona wā ma o kāna mau mele.

'O kēia mele 'aha'aina ho'i, 'ano like paha kona kūlana, 'oiai hiki ke kuhi wale 'ia he mele "nani" ia a he mele "le'ale'a" paha, no ka pā'ina pinepine 'ana o kekahi ali'i i hele ā kaulana loa i ka ho'ole'ale'a 'ana a me ka ho'onu'a 'ana i ka 'ai 'ono o ka 'āina. A, 'oiai 'o Kalākaua ke ali'i nona nei mele, ma kekahi 'ano he 'oia'i'o nō (Imada, 443–454). Eia na'e, e like me kā Kīhei de Silva e kuhi mai ana, "[This is] more than a song about satisfying the appetite," a 'o ke pani e wehe 'ia ai kēlā mana'o, 'o ia ho'i ka hua 'ōlelo ho'okahi 'o " 'ai," a me kona mau mana'o 'elua—no ka ho'opiha 'ana i ka lua o ka inaina, a no ka noho ali'i 'ana no kekahi moku a ahupua'a paha. Aia a maopopo kēia mana'o pālua o ka hua'ōlelo ho'okahi, a laila, e ahuwale maila ke 'ano o kēia mele, he mele make'e lāhui a he mele kīpū lani nō.

Ho'ākāka maila 'o Noenoe Silva i kona 'ike 'ana i nā mana'o politika o "He 'Ai" ma ke 'ano he mele "that talks back to [Kalākaua's] detractors and defends [his] right to the throne." No kāna kālailai mele, he mea nui kahi i loa'a ai nā mea 'ai i lawe 'ia i ka 'aha'aina a hānai 'ia i ka Mō'ī. Wahi āna, 'o ka hapanui o ke mele, "[it] refers to food being brought to the king from the uplands, the kula (plains), the freshwater streams, and the sea, indicating in the usual language of Hawaiian poetry that he rules over the entire country" (185). 'O ia ho'i, ke 'ai ka Mō'ī i nā 'ono o ka 'āina, 'ai nō ho'i 'o ia i nā moku nona ia 'ono.

No kā de Silva wehewehe ʻana mai i ke ʻano politika o nei mele, ʻo ke ʻano o ka mea ʻai ka mea nui, a me ka mana e hoʻolalelale ʻia a hoʻoulu ʻia ma o ua ʻai ʻana nei. Pili kēia i ka ʻai ʻahaʻaina ʻana me nā akua a me ka hoʻolaʻa ʻana i ke akua a i ʻole ka hoʻoulu ʻana i ka mana i loaʻa i kahi mea ʻai ma muli o kona pili akua (kī) a i ʻole kona inoa (limu kala) (Pukui, *Nānā* 2–3). Pili nō hoʻi kēia kālailaina i ka ʻai ʻana i loaʻa i ke kanaka ka mana o kāna mea e ʻai ai, e like me ka mea i ʻike ʻia i ka ʻailolo a ka poʻe hula. Inā pēlā, ʻaʻole wale nō ka ʻai he mea e ola ai ke kino, akā he mea e kū ai ke aliʻi i ka moku: na ka ʻoene e hāʻawi i ka mana i koe i nā aliʻi i hala; na ka poi lehua ka hoʻoulu lāhui; na ka ʻōpae māhikihiki ka mahiki ʻana i ke ʻino; i ke aʻukū ka mana e naʻi ai i ke aupuni. No laila nō i ʻōlelo ai ʻo de Silva penei:

> "He ʻAi na ka Lani," then, is an extraordinary composition, one that operates, simultaneously, on levels of innocent festivity and ritual solemnity. On the first level it celebrates the pleasures of satisfying the chiefly appetite and palate: "Hush, the chief is enjoying his favorite foods; eat, enjoy; eat, enjoy!" And on the second level, it invests that chief with the symbolic meanings of the food he consumes: "The kapu is invoked; eat this for mana, eat this for fertility, eat this to cast out evil, eat this to conquer and rule; eat and rule, eat and rule."

Pākolu ka haʻawina e loaʻa ma kēia mau kālailaina ʻelua. No ka ʻai ʻana, he mana a he koʻikoʻi ko ka mea i ʻai ʻia, kahi i loaʻa ai ka ʻai, a me ka mea nāna i hoʻomākaukau. No laila, ma kā Silva wehewehe ʻana, ʻike ʻia ko Kalākaua noho ʻAimoku ʻana no ka pae ʻāina holoʻokoʻa; ma kā de Silva hoʻi, hoʻopili hou ʻia ka ʻai ʻana i ka hoʻomana—i ke akua, ke aliʻi, ka ʻāina, a me ka lāhui. ʻO ka mea kupanaha hoʻi, ʻo ia nō ka hiki ke hala kēia mau manaʻo ʻoiaʻiʻo, ma muli wale nō o ka hoʻohāiki ʻana i ka manaʻo o ka "ʻai" ʻana. E like me kā Silva i hōʻike maila, "The single-meaning translation of ʻai as dine effectively depoliticizes the song" (185). A pēlā nō hoʻi. I ka wehewehe ʻia ʻana o ke mele i ka puke *The Queen's Songbook*, ʻaʻole nō he wahi ʻōlelo iki no ka ʻai Aupuni ʻana o Kalākaua. Kuhi wale ʻia nō ka hoʻopau ʻia ʻana o nā loina a me nā kapu kahiko o ka ʻai ʻana, a me ka mau ʻana nō o ka hāmau ʻana aku o ke anaina, ke ʻai ke aliʻi (Liliʻuokalani 120).

Ma muli o ka hoʻēmi ʻia ʻana o ka mana politika o nei mele, hoʻēmi ʻia nō hoʻi ka mana politika o kona haku—o Liliʻuokalani—a me kona kūlana he Mōʻī. Hoʻēmi ʻia nō hoʻi ka mana o ka ʻahaʻaina, ka ʻai ʻana, ka hānai ʻana, a me ka hoʻoulu/hoʻomākaukau ʻana i ka mea ʻai. A, hoʻēmi ʻia auaneʻi ka mana politika me ka makeʻe aloha ʻāina o nā mele like ʻole, i noho wale nō ua mana nei ma nā mele lāhui i haku ʻia no ke kūkala moākāka ʻana i ke Ea ʻana o ka lāhui Kanaka Maoli.

Eia naʻe, ua pili nō a paʻa ua mau manaʻo politika nei i kēia mele hoʻokahi a me nā mele ʻē aʻe nāna e hoʻonani a paipai i ka ʻai ʻana o kākou i nā ʻono like ʻole o ko kākou ʻāina kulāiwi. ʻO ke mele ʻahaʻaina o kēia au, ʻaʻole paha i like kona kapu me ko "He ʻAi na ka Lani"; ʻaʻole nō i like kona kauoha ʻana e ʻai (a māʻona) a e ʻai (Ahupuaʻa). A he kūpono nō, ʻoiai he mau mele ia no kākou poʻe makaʻāinana. Akā nō naʻe, ma muli o ka hoʻomaopopo ʻana i ke kino kālaiʻāina o kēia mele a Liliʻu, ʻaʻole anei i hōʻeuʻeu ʻia ko kākou nānā pono ʻana i nā manaʻo politika o nā mele ʻahaʻaina hou, ka mana hoʻi o ka ʻai i hoʻonuʻu ʻia a me ka ʻāina nona ia mau ʻono? A, ʻaʻole anei i hoʻoulu ʻia ko kākou ʻono i ka mana a me ka haʻaheo i loaʻa i ka ʻai a me ka iʻa o ka ʻāina, i nā "ipo" nāna i hoʻomākaukau, a i ka momona o ko kākou ʻāina, nāna e hānai mai ana i ke ola?

ʻO ke aʻo ʻana, ke mele ʻana, a me ka haku ʻana i kēia mau mele, he māhele ia no ko kākou kaheāwai ma ke ʻano he lāhui ʻōiwi a he Kanaka Maoli nō hoʻi. Pēlā e pili hou ai kākou i ka ʻōlelo, ka loina, a me ka ʻāina o kākou; a ʻoiai ma o ka ʻai ʻana a me ka hoʻomākaukau ʻana i ka ʻai e pili hou ai, he mea maʻa mau nō ia, e like me ka mea i paipai ʻia e Jeff Corntassel mā, ma ka inoa ʻo ka *everyday resurgence*.[3] ʻAlua, e ʻole ko kākou hoʻomau ʻana i ke mele ʻana, ka hoʻoulu ʻana, a me ka ʻai ʻana i nā ʻono like ʻole o ko kākou ʻāina, mau ai lākou, a hoʻonalowale ʻole ʻia e ke kai ʻeʻe a ka hoʻokolonaio. Inā e pau ko kākou mele ʻana no ka ʻai a me ka iʻa a ka Hawaiʻi, ʻo ka pau nō ia o lākou, a pani koke ʻia kona hakahaka i ka *poke bowl* a me ka *plate lunch* e laha mai nei ma nā kaha alahula a kākou. A inā e pau ka ʻai a ka Hawaiʻi, ʻo ka pau nō ia o ka lāhui Kanaka Maoli. Mio aʻela nā mea e kū ai kākou he lāhui ʻokoʻa, a lilo aʻela ka Lāhui i mau kānaka hele hoʻokahi nō, e ʻauana ana me he mau lapu lā o Milu.

He pale nō kēia mau mele hoʻoleʻaleʻa i ua ʻino hoʻonalonalo nei. A he ʻai paʻa ia e ikaika ai nā iwi o kākou, i mau ai hoʻi ke kīkoʻo ʻana o ka iwikuamoʻo o ke aloha ʻāina a pili mai i ka hanauna nei.

> *"Nā ʻAi ʻOno"—ʻOno ka ʻai i ka hoʻomākaukau ʻia e ke Kanaka*
> I ʻono nō ka poi lehua
> I ka wali pono ʻōwili ʻia,
> Kō ʻia ʻana, ka hoʻowali ʻana

ʻO kēia mele a Clarence Kinney i haku ai, hoʻokō ʻo ia i kekahi hiʻohiʻona i ʻike pinepine ʻia ma kēia mau mele hoʻonuʻu, ʻo ia hoʻi ka lilo ʻana i ka helu papa, a me ka pīnaʻi ʻana mai o ka ʻōlelo like ma nā paukū pākahi o ke mele. Penei ʻo "He ʻOno," na Bina Mossman: "Hoʻi iho ʻoe i kahi ʻanae lā / Me ka manini pūlehu ʻia lā / ʻO ke kole ē ka iʻa maka onaona lā" (48–49). Penei ʻo "Pipi Kaula": "Pipi kaula / Limu kohu / Nīoi wela / Lomilomi aku / ʻInamona / ʻUlaʻula salt." Penei nō hoʻi ʻo "ʻAmaʻama," na Sam Alama: "He aloha ē ka iʻa lā / ʻAi a ka ʻamaʻama / ʻAi a ka iʻa lā / ʻAi a ka lāwalu / ʻAi a ka hoʻomoemoe." A ʻaʻole nō e nele kā Kinney haku like ʻana i kāna mele nei.

ʻO ka mea naʻe i kū ʻokoʻa ai ʻo "Nā ʻAi ʻOno," ʻo ia hoʻi ke ʻano o nā mea i helu papa 'ia. I ka hapanui o nā mele ho'onu'u, helu papa 'ia nā 'ono i moni 'ia: 'o ka i'a 'oe, 'o ka 'ai 'oe, 'o ka 'īna'i paha, a ia mea aku nō. Eia na'e 'o Kinney ke helu papa nei i nā *hana* like 'ole a ke Kanaka i kona ho'omākaukau 'ana a me kona ho'onu'u 'ana i nā 'ono o ka 'āina. 'O ka poi lehua ka 'ai ho'okahi āna i hea akula; he nui na'e nā 'ōlelo i loa'a no ka ho'omākaukau 'ana i ka 'ai (wali, 'ōwili, kō) a me ka i'a (lāwalu, hulihuli, wahī, pūlehu, mo'a, 'ōlali, moemoe), a he nui ho'i no ka 'ai 'oli'oli 'ana o ke kanaka (momoni, naunau, pāhe'ehe'e, ale, mikomiko, haupa, hā'ale, tomi, pepenu, mūkā). He 'ono ho'i tau!

'Elua paha hopena o kēia 'ano helu papa 'ana. 'Akahi, mōakāka maila ke kauka'i nui 'ia 'ana o ke Kanaka—a me ka mikioi o kona lima—*i 'ono* ka 'ai. E like me kā "He 'Ai na ka Lani" i hō'ike maila, he mea nui kahi i loa'a ai ka 'ai, a me ka mea nāna i ho'olako i ia 'ai, i mana ai ka 'aha'aina a me ke ali'i nāna e 'ai. Eia hou ma nei mele a Kinney, ke kuhi 'ia nei ke Kanaka no kona ho'okō pono 'ana i ka loina ho'omākaukau 'ai a kona lāhui; e 'ole ka "wali pono," ka "mo'a pono," ka "wahī pono," a pēlā aku, 'ono ai ka 'ai a me ka i'a o kēia papa'aina.

'O kekahi mea nāna e kuhi ana penei, 'o ia ka pilina 'ōlelo i ho'opuka 'ia ai ka puana mua o ke mele. He mea ma'amau ke kuhi 'ana i ka 'ākena 'a'ano ma o ka "i," penei: "Ua 'ono ka mea 'ai i ka maika'i o ke kuke 'ana." Eia na'e, ke ho'opuka mua 'ia kēlā "i" ho'okahi ma ke 'ano he māka painu no ua 'a'ano nei, kālele 'ia ka 'ākena, i maopopo mua i ka mea ho'olohe ē, na kekahi i ho'oulu i ka 'ono o ka mea 'ai. No laila, ke puana 'ia ma ke mele, "*I* 'ono nā mea 'ai . . . ," ua mahu'i ē ka mea ho'olohe i ka loa'a 'ana mai o ke *kumu* i 'ono ai ia mea 'ai. A 'o ka pane ho'i, 'o ka hana maika'i a ka mea nāna i kuke. Kāko'o nō ho'i kā Margaret Titcomb i kēia mana'o i ke kuhi 'ana mai, penei: "Fish were never brought to the serving place without some preparation. Fresh fish were always salted, if only a little, the salt allowed to permeate the flesh to some extent" (21). I 'ono nō i ka hana a ke kanaka.

Ma o kēia wehewehe 'ana i ka pono o ka lima kanaka, i 'ono ai ka mea'ai, pēlā nō ho'i e maopopo ai ke kuleana a ke Kanaka e 'auamo pono ai a ho'okō, i loa'a pono ai ka hua o ka 'āina, a i ola ka 'āina, ke Kanaka, a me kona lāhui. Ma kēia mele, ho'ohui pū 'ia kēia mau mea 'ehā—ka 'ai, ka 'āina, ke Kanaka, a me ka lāhui Kanaka Maoli—no ka mea, he 'ohana kākou, a aia nō ke ola o kekahi i ka pono o kekahi. 'A'ole nō hiki ke ho'oka'awale 'ia, o pau auane'i ka pono, hā'ule auane'i i ka pohō. Ke 'ike 'ia nei na'e ka puni ka'awale a ke au ho'okolonaio a kā'ili 'āina; ke 'ike 'ia nei nō ho'i ke kipa 'ana o ia au i ke ali'i nui o O'ahu.

I ka lā 20 o Iune, makahiki 2012, ho'okumu a'ela ka Army Corps of Engineers o 'Amelika Hui Pū 'Ia i ko lākou papahana ho'ōla manu 'ōiwi ma loko pono o Kawainui, ma Kailua, Ko'olaupoko, O'ahu. 'O kona hana nui ka 'eli 'ana a me ka mālama 'ana i 'umikūmākahi ki'owai ma loko o Kawainui, he kanahā 'eka ka nui, i wahi e hui ai a ola ua mau manu nei. Kapa 'ia kēia papahana 'o ke *Kawainui Marsh Environmental Restoration Project*, a 'ehā ona pahuhopu nui, 'o ia ho'i: 1) ka ho'oulu 'ana i nā 'āuna manu 'ōiwi ('o ke kōloa, ke ae'o, ka 'alae 'ula, a me ka 'alae ke'oke'o), 2) ka ho'onui 'ana i ka "scenic open space" ma Kailua, 3) ka ho'ēmi 'ana i ke kahe wale 'ana o ka wai mai ka 'āina mai a i ke kai kohola, a me ka 4) ka ho'ohemo 'ana i ka nāhelehele i uluāhewa i loko o Kawainui ("DLNR"). Kāko'o pū 'ia kēia papahana e ke Ke'ena Forestry and Wildlife o ke aupuni noho hewa o Hawai'i, a hō'oia maila kona po'o, 'o Paul Conry, i ka waiwai nui o ua papahana nei, 'o ia ho'i: "to ensure we have these populations of endangered native birds in the future."

I loko nō o ka waiwai a me ka maika'i o ka ho'oulu 'ana i nā lāhui manu 'ōiwi o ka 'āina nei, mau nō ke kānalua o kekahi po'e o ka lāhui Kanaka Maoli o Hawai'i nei, no ka lilo 'ana o kēia papahana i mea e ho'oka'awale 'ia ai kākou a me ka ipukai kaulana 'o Kawainui, 'o ia ho'i kekahi o nā loko i'a a me ka 'āina mahi kalo nui loa o O'ahu nei i ka wā kahiko, kahi ho'i i pili pono ai ke Kanaka a me ka 'āina kulāiwi ona, i kō nā kuleana o ke kua'āina me ke kaikaina. 'O kēia mahu'i ho'oka'awale a'u, hō'oia 'ia nō e ka 'ōlelo o ka palapala ho'olālā o ua papahana ho'ōla manu nei: ho'okahi wale nō kuhi 'ana i ka mo'olelo a me ka loina a ka Hawai'i, no ka lilo 'ana paha o kēia papahana i "integral component in ongoing governmental and community public education and interactive efforts by drawing public attention and providing opportunities to display and discover the marsh's natural resource significance and *past* historical and cultural practices" ("Kawainui Environmental" 4).[4] 'Ike le'a 'ia ē, 'a'ohe mana'o o kēia papahana a me kona mau lima ho'okō i ka ho'omau 'ana i ia mau loina, a i 'ole ka ho'iho'i 'ana aku i ke Kanaka e noho, e mālama, e ho'oulu, a e ho'āla i kona 'āina pono'ī.

Ma uka iki o kēia mau ki'owai a ka pū'ali 'Amelika e mālama nei, ke ho'omākaukau nei ke Ke'ena DLNR a me ke Ke'ena DOFAW i papahana 'anelike, i lilo ke kanaono 'eka o Kawainui i 'āina ki'owai no ka māhuahua 'ana o ia mau lāhui manu like: ke kōloa, ke ae'o, ka 'alae 'ula, a me ka 'alae ke'oke'o. Ma ka palapala ho'olālā o nei papahana, 'a'ole nō he 'ōlelo iki no ka mo'olelo a me ka loina o ke Kanaka Maoli, i pili i ua loko i'a nei mai o kikilo mai. Loa'a nō na'e kekahi mau māhele o ka papahana nāna e ho'onui a hō'olu'olu i ke kipa 'ana o ka lehulehu i ia wahi no ka "passive recreational enjoyment of the environment" (*Kawainui Marsh*). Akāka hou maila ka ho'okumu 'ana o nā aupuni noho hewa o Hawai'i nei i kūlana hou e kū ai ke kanaka, 'o ia ho'i he mea nānā wale 'o ia, e kūki'i ana ma ka 'ao'ao o ia mea he *nature*, i mea e nanea wale ai i ka nani o laila, a i 'ike maka no ka ulu 'ana a me ke ola 'ana o ka 'āina. 'Ike 'ia kēia kuana'ike like i ke kapa 'ia 'ana 'o Ulupō he "Cultural Park and Ethnobotanical Garden." 'O ka hana a ke kanaka ma kahi i kapa 'ia he "Park" a he "Garden" paha, 'o ia nō ka "passive recreation": 'a'ohe ona huli 'ana i ka lima i lalo, 'a'ole nō he 'ike e loa'a i kāna hana 'ana. Me he mea lā, ua ho'oka'awale 'ia ke kanaka mai ka 'āina mai, a ma kēia mau wahi e lilo ai 'o ia i malihini kipa i ua 'āina nei, no ka mahalo 'ana i ka nani āna e 'ike ai a me ka ho'onanea 'ana i kona mana'o a me kona na'au. 'A'ole kēia 'o ka pilina e pono ai ka ʻāina momona o Hawaiʻi; ʻaʻole ia ʻo ka pilina e pono ai ka lāhui Kanaka Maoli o Hawaiʻi nei.

Ua hoʻomaka ʻia aʻela ka papahana a ka pūʻali koa ʻAmelika i ka makahiki 2012; a ʻo kā ka DLNR, ma ka 2011 ia. I ka makahiki 2015, ua hoʻokumu ʻia kekahi papahana ʻokoʻa loa ma kahi o ka heiau ʻo Ulupō, i komo iki ʻole ʻia e ia mea he "passive recreation." I ia makahiki nō i hoʻomaka ai ke alulike ʻana o Hikaʻalani, ka ʻAhahui Sivila o Kailua, ʻAhahui Mālama i ka Lōkahi, a me ka DLNR, i hoʻoulu pono ʻia ka ʻāina a puni ʻo Ulupō (kahi e kapa ʻia nei ʻo Ulupō Nui), a i hoʻoulu pono ʻia nō hoʻi ka pilina o ia ʻāina me nā kupa a me nā kānaka e noho ana mai ka lae o Mokukapu ā i ka lae o Wailea. ʻOiai he mea nui ka hoʻōla hou ʻana i ka ʻāina a me ka hoʻohemo ʻana i ka nāhelehele i uluāoʻa, ʻokoʻa iki ka pahuhopu nui o nā papahana ʻē aʻe, ʻokoʻa ko Hikaʻalani, ʻo ia hoʻi:

> ...to grow the interdependent relationship between land, people, and community at Ulupō Nui through the retelling and reliving of our cultural stories, replanting and eating of our ancestral foods, and reviving of our land- and water-based practices through huli ka lima i lalo, turning our hands down towards the earth in the restoration of some of the most significant wahi pana in Kailua: Ulupō heiau and Kawainui fishpond. (*Hikaʻalani*)

I ka makahiki 2019, ua ulu aʻe mai loko mai o Hikaʻalani he ʻahahui hou nona ke kuleana ʻo ka mālama me ka hoʻoulu ʻana iā Ulupō a me Kawainui. ʻO Kauluakalana ka inoa o kēia hui hou; ua like a like nō naʻe kāna mau pahuhopu: "to restore and grow healthy relationships between people and place through the aloha ʻāina practices of retelling our Kailua-specific stories, replanting and eating our ancestral foods, and caring for the sacred sites, lands, and waters of our beloved ahupuaʻa of Kailua" (Kauluakalana).

ʻO kēia papahana nei, he hoʻokē a he kūʻē maoli nō i ka hoʻokaʻawale ʻia ʻana o ka ʻāina, ka poʻe kānaka, ka moʻolelo, a me ka loina Hawaiʻi, kekahi mai kekahi aku. A he kūpaʻa nō i ka hōʻike ʻana a me ka hoʻokō ʻana i ko kākou ʻike ʻoiaʻiʻo ē, he pono ka hui like ʻana o ke alo a me ka mauli o kēia mau mea ʻehā, i ola ai lākou a pau. Inā hala kekahi i ka maka, inā kāpae ʻia kekahi ma ka ʻaoʻao, ʻo ka nāwaliwali maila nō ia o nā mea ʻē aʻe, a pau auaneʻi.

I loko o nā makahiki ʻelima i hala akula mai ka wā i hoʻomaka ʻia ai ko Hikaʻalani hana ma Ulupō Nui, a me ka makahiki hoʻokahi i piha i ko Kauluakalana kahu ʻana, ua "kipa" ʻia ua ʻāina nei e kekahi mau kaukani kānaka—nā kāne, wāhine, keiki, a ʻelemākule hoʻi—ʻaʻole naʻe ma ke ʻano e kipa ʻia ai ka Pāka, a e mākaʻikaʻi ʻia ai paha ka Ethnobotanical Garden. Ma o ke alakaʻi ʻana o Kaleomanuiwa Wong (ke kahu o Ulupō Nui a me ka luna hoʻokele o Kauluakalana), ua huli ka lima i lalo, ua hehi ka wāwae i ka lepo, ua huki ka lima i ka nāhelehele, a ua moni ka puʻu i ka ʻai kamahaʻo o Kailua. Ma mua o ka 2015, ʻelua wale nō loʻi e waiho ana ma Ulupō Nui, akā ʻike ʻia nā aka o nā loʻi kahiko he nui, e moe ana ma lalo o ka lepo a me ka nāhelehele. I kēia manawa, he kanahākūmākahi ka nui o nā loʻi kalo, kahi e laupaʻi ai ʻo Hāloa, a ke ulu nei nō nā ʻano mea kanu Hawaiʻi like ʻole e pono ai ke ola ʻana o ka lāhui: ʻo ka ʻulu ʻoe, ʻo ka ʻuala ʻoe, ka wauke, ka pūhala, a he nui hewahewa hou aku nō. A ke hoʻi hou nei nō nā kupa o ka ʻāina i ka piko o Kailua.

ʻO ka hua naʻe i mahuʻi ʻole ʻia, ʻo ia hoʻi ka hoʻi hou ʻana mai o nā manu ʻōiwi e noho ma nā lihiwai o Ulupō Nui, kahi e puka ai nā ʻauwai o ua mau loʻi nei, puka pū me nā mea like ʻole e ʻono ai nā manu a me nā iʻa o Kawainui. A no laila, e like me kā Wong i hōʻike maila, ʻike ʻia nō nā manu ʻehā a ka pūʻali koa a me ka DLNR e ʻumeʻume ana, e noho i kahi wahi e komo ʻole ʻia e kānaka—i kēlā me kēia lā, ʻike ʻia ke aeʻo, ke kōloa, a me nā ʻano ʻalae ʻelua; pili mai nō kekahi mau ʻohana manu i kahi e kanu ʻia nei ke kalo a e ʻeli ʻia nei nā ʻauwai hou. A i kekahi manawa, ʻoi aku nō nā manu e noho ana ma ka lihi o Ulupō Nui ma mua o nā manu e kipa ana i kahi ʻāina hoʻoulu manu o uka (Wong, Kaleomanuiwa). Me he mea lā, ma muli nō kēia o ka hoʻi hou ʻana o ke Kanaka i Ulupō, a me ka ulu ʻana o Hāloa a māhuahua. Aia a hoʻi ka ʻāina a me ke Kanaka i ka pilina kuʻuna e kaukaʻi ai kekahi i kekahi, a e hoʻoulu ai nō kekahi i kekahi, a laila e loaʻa ai ka pono.

A ʻo kēia nō ka puana a kā Kinney mele no "Nā ʻAi ʻOno"—aia a pili pū ke Kanaka, ka ʻāina, ka hua o ka ʻāina, a me ka loina Hawaiʻi, a laila e ʻono ai ka ʻai me ka iʻa. ʻO kā ia ala mele ʻana penei, ʻaʻole paha ia he ʻōlelo leʻaleʻa wale nō o ka hoʻopuka ʻana aku, ʻaʻole nō he ʻōlelo hoʻopulelehua, i mele wale ʻia nō no ka ʻoliʻoli a me ka nanea o ke anaina hoʻolono mele. Akā, he ʻōlelo hoʻokūpaʻa ia e hōʻike ai ke Kanaka i kona kūlana pili pono i kona ʻāina a me ka momona o ua ʻāina nei. Ke mele ʻia penei: "I ʻono nā mea ʻai i ka maikaʻi / O ke kuke ʻana," kūkala ʻia nō hoʻi ke kuleana o ke Kanaka nona nā loina hoʻomākaukau ʻai o nā kūpuna, a me ka hiki ʻole ke hulikua ʻia, o nalo auaneʻi ia ʻono. A i ka wā nō hoʻi e hoʻēmi a hoʻohaʻahaʻa ʻia ana ke kūlana o ke Kanaka Maoli, he ʻōlelo pai Ea nō hoʻi kēia, i kona kūpaʻa ʻana i ka hiki ʻole hoʻi ke hulikua ʻia ka Lāhui Kanaka Maoli, o nalo auaneʻi ka waiwai a me ke ola o ka pae ʻāina hoʻoheno nei.

ʻO ka lua o ka hua Ea e loaʻa ma nei mele, ʻo ia hoʻi ka nui huaʻōlelo i puka no nā ʻano hana i pili i ka hoʻomākaukau ʻana a me ka ʻai hoʻonuʻu ʻana i nā ʻono o ka ʻāina. E like me ka mea i hōʻike mua ʻia ma ka mokuna nei, hoʻopuka ʻia i kēia mele he ʻumi hua ʻōlelo i pili i ka hoʻomākaukau mea ʻai, a he ʻumi nō hua ʻōlelo no ka haupa ʻana o ke Kanaka i ia mau ʻono. ʻO kekahi o kēia mau hua ʻōlelo, ua ʻano laulā, a laha iā kākou, e laʻa ke kuke, ka moʻa, ka wahī, a me ka ʻono. A ʻo ka hapanui hoʻi, he pilikahi nō i kekahi ʻano o ka mea ʻai (hoʻowali), kekahi ʻano o ke kuke ʻana (lāwalu), a i ʻole kekahi ʻano o ka ʻai ʻana (pepenu). I ia hele ʻana ā pilikahi nā hua ʻōlelo, ʻike ʻia auaneʻi ka hana i kū nō i ka loina kūmau o ka poʻe 'ōiwi o nei 'āina no ka hoʻomākaukau a me ka haupa 'ana i ka 'ai. No laila, no ka hoʻowali 'ana i ka poi, hoʻopuka 'ia kekahi mau hua 'ōlelo i 'ane like, 'o ka wali pono, ka 'ōwili, a me ka hoʻowali. A laila, puana 'ia hoʻi kekahi hua 'ōlelo i maʻa 'ole paha i kekahi hapa nui o kākou, 'o ia hoʻi ke "kō" 'ana i ka poi. Wahi a Pukui, 'o kēia ke kōmi 'ana i nā puʻupuʻu o ka poi ma ka 'ele o ka 'umeke, i mea e pau ai nā puʻu, a wali loa ka poi (Pukui and Elbert).

Ma ke aʻo 'ana mai o ke mele i kēia hua 'ōlelo, ma loko hoʻi o kēia pōʻaiapili ona, 'ike (hou) kākou i kēia hana kuluma a ka poʻe Kānaka Maoli, aʻo (hou) kākou i nā loina e mālama pono ai iā Hāloa, a 'aʻapo (hou) kākou i ka hua 'ōlelo kūpono nāna e wehewehe. Inā 'aʻole kēia he hana i maʻa i ka mea hoʻolohe, maliʻa paha, e hoʻomaka ana nō 'o ia i ke kō 'ana i ka poi, a hoʻōla hou 'ia kēia loina i kona 'ohana. A i 'ole, ua maʻa paha ka hana, akā hana 'ia me ka maopopo 'ole ē he hana kuluma ia mai kinohi mai; eia nō ka hōʻoia, a me ka hua 'ōlelo e hoʻomaopopo 'ia ai. No laila, ma ke mele e hoʻohui 'ia ai kēia mau ao 'elua o ka nohona Hawaiʻi Kūʻokoʻa, 'o ia hoʻi ke ao i pili i ka noʻonoʻo a me ka 'ōlelo, a me ke ao i pili i ke kino a me nā hana like 'ole ona.

Kākau maila 'o Melissa Nelson i kona 'ike 'ana i ke 'āʻumeʻume o kēia mau ao 'elua, penei:

> It is a common conundrum, feeling the difference between the world of thought and the world of my other senses. Do I read through the wetlands ecology essay or that classic piece on Zen Buddhism, or do I work with my hands in the garden repotting lupine and sage and revel in the smell of sweet-smelling medicine plants and fresh dirt? Do I sit and pull black-and-white words from full-spectrum thoughts or walk in a damp redwood forest to feel like a small mammal? There is a profound relationship between these different activities. (231)

E like me kā Nelson i wehewehe maila, he mau ao 'okoʻa loa kēia, akā 'aʻole nō i kaʻawale loa; he pilina hemo 'ole nō. Ma kekahi 'ano, pili kēia noʻonoʻo 'ana o Nelson i ko ka Hawaiʻi wehewehe 'ana i ia mea he *knowledge, experience,* a me ka *sense* ma ka hua 'ōlelo hoʻokahi: " 'ike." Hōʻoia maila ka 'ōlelo a ka Hawaiʻi i ka like a like o kēia mau hana: he 'ike ko ka maka, ka pepeiao, ka ihu, ka puʻu, a me ka 'ili kekahi, a ma o ka 'ike 'ana o ke kino ma o kona mau māhele like 'ole, pēlā e loaʻa ai ke aʻo a me ka naʻauao.

Hōʻike nō hoʻi 'o Kapāʻanaokalāokeola Oliveira i kēia pilina hemo 'ole o ka noʻonoʻo me ka lonoa o ke kino ma o kāna i kapa maila he "sense abilities" o ka poʻe Kānaka Maoli. Kuhi mai 'o ia nei i ke kūlana *sensual* o ka 'ikena Kanaka, 'oiai loaʻa ka 'ike iā kākou ma o nā 'ike like 'ole o ke kino a me ka naʻau. A, 'o kāna haʻawina no kākou, 'o ia hoʻi, 'aʻole nō he mea kupu wale ka 'ike i loaʻa ma ka hana: "engaging in an activity in and of itself does not ensure knowledge acquisition," a pēlā pū me ka lilo 'ana o ke Kanaka i loea o ua loina nei (12). 'O ka mea e pono ai, 'o ia ho'i ka 'ike pū 'ana i ka hana a ke kino a me ke a'o 'ana nō ho'i i ka 'ōlelo a me ka na'auao i pili ai nā ao 'elua a pa'a i ka 'ike o ke Kanaka.

No laila, 'a'ole lawa ke kō 'ana i ka poi me ka ho'omaopopo 'ole 'ana i ia hana ma o kona hua 'ōlelo pono'ī 'o ke kō; 'a'ole nō i lawa ka ho'omaopopo 'ana i ka hua 'ōlelo me ka 'ole o ka ho'okō 'ana i ia hana kuluma a ka Hawai'i. Ke hala kekahi māhele iā kākou—ka no'ono'o a i 'ole ka hana a ke kino—hā'ule pohō ka loina, a hala loa iā kākou ka noho Kū'oko'a 'ana he Kanaka Maoli. 'O ka hana a kēia mau mele, e like me kā Kinney "'Ai 'Ono," ho'olako mai nō ia i nā hua 'ōlelo a me nā 'ōlelo no'eau a ho'okā'au paha, i hiki ai iā kākou po'e Kānaka ke 'ike a ho'okō i nā hana ma'amau o kēlā me kēia lā, ma o ka 'ike a me ka 'ōlelo i wali i ko kākou lāhui. Ma o ka ho'opili hou 'ana a pa'a ka loina, ka 'ōlelo, a me ka no'ono'o Hawai'i, ma laila wale nō kākou e pakele ai i ka noho kala'ihi 'ia maila e ke au ho'okolonaio a me ke kai ho'īliwailike o 'Amelika. A, ke mele mau 'ia kēia mau 'ōlelo, 'ike 'ia nō ke Kū'oko'a o ka lāhui Hawai'i, ma o kona ho'omaopopo 'ana a me kona ho'omau 'ana i nā loina ona, i pili i ka 'ai, ka mālama 'āina, a me nā mea like 'ole o kona nohona.

> ### "Aloha ka Manini"—Ua lawa i ka i'a o ka laupapa
> Aloha ka manini me ka pōpolo
> He i'a noho ia i ka laupapa
>
> (Kauwē 15)

'Oiai he mele 'ano laha 'ole ke mele i ho'omaka ai kēia mokuna, 'o ia ho'i 'o "He 'Ai na ka Lani," he mele laha loa nō kēia, i pā ai paha ka hapanui o ko kākou mau pepeiao. Mai ka wā i haku 'ia ai 'o "Aloha ka Manini" e Lot Kauwē, ma kahi o ka makahiki 1920,[5] a i kēia makahiki nei, ua 'oki 'ia kēia mele a pa'i 'ia ma luna o ka iwakāluakūmālua a 'oi pā leo (Ortone 10).[6] Hīmeni mau 'ia ma nā pā'ina Hawai'i, ma nā papa 'ōlelo Hawai'i, ma nā 'aha mele nui a me nā mea li'ili'i ho'i, a ma kahi ho'olaha wikiō 'o YouTube. Ma waena o kēia mau pāleo he nui i puka, 'o ka mea hoihoi loa paha i loa'a iā ia kēia mele, 'o ia ho'i kā Blayne Asing pā CD i kapa 'ia 'o *Young Old Soul*. He 'umi mele o ua pāleo nei, a 'o ka hapanui nō, he mau mele 'ōlelo haole, i haku 'ia e Asing a me nā haku mele kaulana 'ē a'e. Ua hele ā kaulana 'o Asing i ua po'e mele nei, a no kāna ho'opuka 'ana i kēia CD, loa'a akula iā ia ka makana Hōkū Hanohano i ka makahiki 2016, ka mea i kuhi aku 'o ia ka pu'ukani hou i 'oi loa i ia makahiki.

Aia na'e ma kēia pāleo 'ekolu mele Hawai'i, i ho'īli 'ia i ka hanauna nei e nā kūpuna 'ōpio, 'o ia ho'i 'o "Ka Na'i Aupuni," "Moloka'i Nui a Hina," a me "Aloha ka Manini." Ma o ka ho'ohui 'ia 'ana o kēia mau mele 'ekolu ma ke pāleo, 'oko'a iki maila ko kākou ho'omaopopo 'ana i nei pu'ukani a me kāna 'oihana. Me kona ho'omaopopo 'ole 'ana paha, ua koho ua pu'ukani nei i 'ekolu mele nāna e hō'ike mai ana i ʻekolu ʻano o ke aloha ʻāina. Mōakāka loa kēia ʻano o nā mele mua ʻelua, ʻoiai he mele lāhui ʻo "Ka Naʻi Aupuni," a he mele wahi pana ʻo "Molokaʻi Nui a Hina." Laha loa lāua a ʻelua, a me ko lāua mau manaʻo aloha ʻāina. No laila, ke noʻonoʻo ʻia ke ʻano o kēia puʻukani, pili mai nō ua aloha ʻāina nei iā ia, i loko nō o kona mele pinepine ʻana i nā mele ʻōlelo haole o ke au hou. Maopopo loa ka paʻa ʻana o kona mole i nā mele a me ke aloha ʻāina o ka lāhui ʻōiwi. A, ke nānā ʻia kēia mele hoʻokahi ʻo "Aloha ka Manini," hoʻolalelale ʻia kona mau manaʻo politika a aloha ʻāina hoʻi, i ʻano ʻekepue akula i ke ʻano leʻaleʻa a "ʻono" o ua mele ʻai iʻa nei.

Ma kēia pā CD a ke kāʻeʻaʻeʻa ʻōpio, ʻike ʻia nō hoʻi, ʻaʻole wale nō i ka poʻe oʻo a me ka puʻukani o nā mele *traditional* o Hawaiʻi nei i paʻa ai a laha ai hoʻi kēia mele; ʻaʻole wale nō na Genoa Keawe, Gabby Pahinui, a me Myra English. Akā, ma muli o kona puka ʻana mai ma nei pāleo ʻo *Young, Old Soul*, hiki ke ʻike ʻia ka laha loa o kēia mele—ma waho aku o nā pōʻai pūlama mele kahiko—a me ka halihali ʻia ʻana o kona leo i nā hanauna ʻōpiopio o ka lāhui Kanaka Maoli a me nā kupa o Hawaiʻi nei. No laila, ke hāpai ʻia kēia mele ma ke ʻano he iwikuamoʻo e pili mau ai ka lāhui Hawaiʻi i ke aloha ʻāina, maopopo iā kākou ke ākea o kona manamana ʻana aku, a pili nō ka hapa nui loa o kākou. Eia kekahi, hōʻoia ʻia paha ke kumumanaʻo o nēia mokuna, ʻo ia hoʻi, ua ola nō ke aloha ʻāina i nā mele like ʻole a ka poʻe Kānaka Maoli i haku a hīmeni ai, ma kēlā me kēia au, a no kēlā me kēia māhele o ka nohona. ʻOiai he mea kēia aloha i paʻa i ka naʻau o ke Kanaka Maoli, ʻaʻole hiki ke hemo, mai loko mai ona, a mai loko mai nō hoʻi o kāna mau hana waiwai e lawelawe aku ai. A no laila, alakaʻi nō ke aloha ʻāina i ko kākou noho aupuni ʻana, a me ka haupa ʻana i nā ʻono o ka ʻāina.

E like me ka hapanui o nā mele hoʻonuʻu i loaʻa iaʻu, lilo ka nui o "Aloha ka Manini" i ka helu ʻana i nā ʻono e moni ai ka puʻu. A, e like nō hoʻi me ua hapanui nei, ua kālele kēia mele ma ka ʻaoʻao o ka iʻa ma kahi o ka ʻai.[7] Puka mai nā inoa o ʻeono iʻa i loko o kēia mele pōkole wale nō: ka manini, ka pōpolo, ke kala, ka nenue, ka nahawele, a me ke āhole. He ʻai nō, akā hoʻokahi wale nō puka ʻana mai, a he poi ʻuala ia.

Maliʻa paha, ʻelua wahi haʻawina liʻiliʻi e loaʻa iā kākou ma o nei ʻano mele ʻana mai. ʻO kekahi, ʻo ia nō ka hoʻonohonoho pono ʻana i ka papaʻaina Hawaiʻi, i loaʻa ka ʻai a me ka iʻa. Mai loko mai o ka lāhui mele hoʻonuʻu, loaʻa he hoʻokahi wale nō mele e helu mai ana i ka ʻai wale nō, me ka ʻole o kahi iʻa. Loaʻa he ʻeono mele e helu mai ana i ka iʻa, me ka ʻole o ka ʻai. A, loaʻa nō he ʻumi mele nāna e helu mai i ka ʻai a me ka iʻa. No laila, ma kēia mau mele e ʻike leʻa ai kākou i ke ʻano o ka papaʻaina Hawaiʻi, ua piha i ka loaʻa ʻana o ka ʻai a me ka iʻa, me he mea lā ʻo ka hoa kēia o ko ʻAmelika huina mea ʻai ʻehā: ka ʻiʻo, ka lau, ka waiū, a me ka ʻanoʻano.

Kākoʻo ʻia kēia hui koʻolua ʻana o ka ʻai a me ka iʻa e ka wehewehe ʻana i nā manaʻo o ua mau hua ʻōlelo nei, a he koʻolua maoli nō ke ʻano. Penei kā Pukui i wehewehe maila:

'ai: Food or food plant, especially vegetable food as distinguished from
i'u, meat or fleshy food; often 'ai refers specifically to *poi*

i'a: Meat or any flesh food. Any food eaten as a relish with the staple
(*poi*, taro, sweet potato, breadfruit), including meat, vegetable, or even
salt. Also *'īna'i*. *Ka i'a lauoho loloa o ke kuahiwi*, the long-haired relish of
the mountain [greens]. (Pukui and Elbert)

Ua ahuwale maila ka pilina o ka 'ai a me ka i'a ma kēia wehewehe 'ana: 'a'ole
paha i hiki ke wehewehe i ka mana'o o kekahi hua'ōlelo me ke kuhi 'ole 'ana aku
i kona ko'olua. A 'ike 'ia nō ho'i ka pono o kekahi i kekahi, ke 'ai 'ia e Kānaka. A
no laila, ke mele mai 'o Lot Kauwē, penei: "Poi 'uala kāohi pu'u," 'a'ole wale nō ia
poi he mea e emi ai ka lihaliha o ke āhule, akā he ko'olua ia no ka i'a i hele a nui
ma nei mele, i loa'a iā ia kona ko'olua pono'ī, a i pa'ewa 'ole ai ka papa'aina i
ho'omākaukau 'ia. Pēlā pū nō paha ke kuleana o kā Lili'u 'oene a me ke kalo mana,
kā Kinney poi lehua, kā Alama miki poi, a me kā Ichimura poi 'awa'awa. Ke hui
pū ka 'ai me ka i'a, 'o ia nō ka 'ai ma'amau a ka Hawai'i, ka mea nāna e pale aku i
kā Enrique Salmón i kapa ai he "Big Gulp culture," nāna e hānai mai i ka nui
lehulehu i ka 'ai i palai 'ia, ho'omomona 'ia, a ha'aliu 'ia. Wahi a ia nei, ma Mekiko
'ākau-komohana, 'o ka pa'akikī o ka loa'a 'ana o kēia 'ano mea 'ai ke kumu e ola
ai ka po'e 'ōiwi o laila i ka 'ai maoli o ko lākou 'āina (25). Eia 'o Kauwē ke paipai
nei i ia ola like, ma o ka ho'ohanohano 'ana a me ka ho'olaha 'ana i ka 'ono loa o
kā kākou papa'aina 'ōiwi.
    'O ka lua paha o ka ha'awina li'ili'i i loa'a i kēia nānā 'ana i ke kino o kā Kauwē
mele, 'o ia ho'i ka 'ike 'ana i ke kūlana o ia mea he 'ai a he i'a paha, ma ka papa'aina
Hawai'i a i ka mana'o o ka lāhui Kanaka Maoli. Mea maila 'o Pukui no ke ko'iko'i
o ka 'ai, penei:

'Ai may designate food or eating in general, but specifically it refers
to the paste termed *poi* made from the corm of the taro (Hawaiian *kalo*).
The Hawaiian diet was built around *poi*. (Pukui and Handy 2)

Hō'oia 'ia nō kēia 'ikena i ka wehewehe 'ana i ka 'ai a me ka i'a, i puana 'ia ma
luna a'e nei. 'O ka mea 'āpiki na'e, 'a'ole paha i kāko'o nui 'ia e kēia po'e mele
ho'onu'u. Mai loko mai o nā mele he 'umikūmāwalu i loa'a, he ho'okahi wale nō
mele nāna i helu mai i ka 'ai me ka 'ole o ka i'a. A, 'oiai helu mai ka hapanui o nā
mele i ka 'ai a me ka i'a (he 'umi nō mele), kuhi ka hapanui o lākou (he 'eiwa) i
ho'okahi 'ai, i ko'olua no nā i'a he nui hewahewa e ho'onu'u 'ia.[8] No laila, 'a'ole
paha hiki ke kuhihewa. 'Oiai 'o ka 'ai, ka poi, a me ke kalo nō ho'i ka 'ai nui a ka
po'e Kānaka Maoli, a ma laila nō ka mana e ola pono ai ke kino, ka lāhui, a me
ka 'āina, 'a'ole ma laila ka nui o ka 'ono e miko ai ua ola nei. Aia ia i nā i'a like 'ole

o Nā Kai ʻEwalu: ka iʻa holo o ke kai, ka iʻa pili pōhaku, ka iʻa holoholo ʻāina, ka iʻa lau lupalupa, a me ka iʻa mili i ka lima. A, ʻo ia kai mele ʻia i loko o kēia poʻe mele, e like me "Aloha ka Manini."

Inā pēlā, ʻeā, maopopo paha iā kākou ē, i loko nō o ka mana a me ke ola e loaʻa iā kākou iā Hāloa, ʻaʻole i lawa no ka hoʻoulu ʻana i ko kākou Lāhui—ua lawa ia no ke ola a me ka mau ʻana o ka lāhui, ʻaʻole nō naʻe no kona ulu ʻana aʻe a māhuahua. Ma kēia mau mele, ʻaʻole nō e mele ʻia ana ka māihi ola o kākou me ka lana ʻana paha i ka ʻauwae. No Kauwē mā, ʻaʻole i lawa. Mele ʻia ka ʻono, ka miko, ka lihaliha, ka leʻaleʻa, ka lupalupa, a me ka uluwehi—mele ʻia ka uluāoʻa ʻana o ka lāhui nei a me ko kākou ʻuhane i piha i ke aloha. E like me nā lālani mele i haku ʻia e Helen Desha Beamer, "Ua ʻai, ua inu a kena / ʻAʻohe mea e koe aku."

Ua ʻano pili kēia kuanaʻike no ke ola i kā Gerald Vizenor i kapa ai he *survivance*, a i wehewehe ʻia maila e King, Gubele, a me Anderson ma ke ʻano he hoʻohui pū ʻana i nā manaʻo o ka *survival* a me ka *resistance*. Ma o kēia ʻano haʻi moʻolelo a moʻomoʻolelo ʻana mai, pakele akula ka poʻe ʻōiwi i ka hoʻopau loa ʻia e ka hoʻokolonaio, a kūʻē/kūpale aku nō hoʻi i nā ʻōnaehana aupuni o kēia mau lā e hoʻomau ana i ka hana hoʻokolonaio i kala loa akula (7). Hoʻākāka hou maila ʻo Vizenor i kona mau manaʻo penei:

> The character of survivance creates a sense of native presence over absence, nihility, and victimry.
>
> Native survivance is an active sense of presence over absence, deracination, and oblivion; survivance is the continuance of stories, not a mere reaction, however pertinent. Survivance is greater than the right of a survivable name.
>
> Survivance stories are renunciations of dominance, detractions, obtrusions, the unbearable sentiments of tragedy, and the legacy of victimry. (1)

Ma kēia mele ʻo "Aloha ka Manini," a ma nā mele ʻē aʻe i mele ʻia ai ka ʻai a māʻona a me ka inu a kena, ʻaʻole nō e nele ka hoʻomaopopo ʻana i ka Hawaiʻi, ma muli paha o ka noho piha ʻia o nei mau mele e ka iʻa i maʻa iā ia. Kuʻupau nō kēia mau mele i ka ʻono i loaʻa i ke kai momona, a he ʻano kūkala hilahila ʻole ia i ua momona nei, i ka waiwai a me ka ʻono lua ʻole o ka ʻāina kulāiwi o kākou a me kona Lāhui ponoʻī. ʻIke ʻia ka nui iʻa e noho ana ma ka laupapa; honi ʻia ke ʻala o ka iʻa ke hoʻomākaukau ʻia no ka ʻai ʻana, a moni ʻia nō hoʻi kona ʻono, me ke kāohi pū ʻana mai o ka poi ʻuala. He aloha wale nō, a he aloha ʻauʻa ʻole ʻia. Ma ia ʻano, he mau moʻolelo nō hoʻi kēia mau mele no ka *survivance*, no ko lākou hōʻole ʻana i nā moʻomoʻolelo hoʻokolonaio i haʻi mai no ka naʻaupō, ka nāwaliwali, ka hepa, a me ka lokoʻino o ko kākou Lāhui aloha.

Eia kekahi, pili aku nō hoʻi kēia mau mele, a me ko lākou kuanaʻike e kālele ana i ka ʻono o ka ʻāina, me ka manaʻo i hāpai ʻia e Ernest Stromberg. ʻOiai ʻaʻole paha i mahalo nui ʻia kāna kālailaina e Vizenor (kuhi maila ʻo Vizenor he ʻōlelo "derivative" wale nō kā Stromberg no ia mea he *survivance,* i nānā ʻole i kona mau pōʻaiapili) (20), he mea hoʻoulu manaʻo kā Stromberg wehewehe ʻana penei: "While 'survival' conjures images of a stark minimalist clinging at the edge of existence, survivance goes beyond mere survival to acknowledge the dynamic and creative nature of Indigenous rhetoric" (19–20).[9]

Pēlā nō hoʻi ke ʻano o kēia mau mele hoʻonuʻu. Helu ʻia ka ʻono o ka ʻāina—ʻo ia hoʻi nā iʻa o ke kai—a he nui nō. A, eia hoʻi, moʻala ʻia a haupa ʻia nō ke ʻai ʻia, ma luna aʻe nō o ka mahalo wale ʻana nō i ka mea i loaʻa. Me he mea lā, ʻo kēia hoʻonuʻu piha ʻana i nā ʻono o ka ʻāina, ʻo ia hoʻi ke ʻano e pono ai ke Ea ʻana o kākou a kū hou i ko kākou moku ponoʻī. ʻAʻole lawa ke ea hapa ʻana, ka ulu pipī ʻana, a me kā hoʻomau wale ʻana nō i nā pono i koe iā kākou i kēia wā nele nei. Aia nō a kāʻeo ka ʻumeke, a piha ka ipu kai, a mikomiko aʻela i ka paʻakai, a laila, e loaʻa mai ai ka pono.

ʻO ka haʻawina hoʻi i koe, he manaʻo nui ia, a ua pili nō i nā manaʻo ʻelua i hāpai ʻia e Silva a me de Silva i ka maka mua o nei mokuna, ʻo ia hoʻi ke koʻikoʻi o kahi i loaʻa ai ka ʻai (a iʻa paha), a me ke ʻano o ka ʻai (a iʻa paha) i hoʻonuʻu ʻia. Wahi a Silva, ma muli o ka loaʻa ʻana o ka ʻai a me ka iʻa mai nā wahi like ʻole o ka pae ʻāina, mele ʻia a hoʻomana ʻia ko Kalākaua noho Aliʻi ʻAimoku ʻana no ka Pae ʻĀina holoʻokoʻa, mai Kumukahi a i Lehua. A ʻo kā de Silva hoʻi, ma muli o ke koho pono ʻana i nā ʻano mea ʻai o kā Kalākaua ʻahaʻaina, ua hoʻomana ʻia kona noho Aliʻi ʻana, a kūpale ʻia ka ʻōhumu ʻana mai waho mai.

Ma nei mele nō hoʻi ʻo "Aloha ka Manini," ʻike ʻia ko Kauwē minamina i kahi i loaʻa ai nā iʻa ʻono āna. Ma ka lalani ʻelua o ua mele nei, hōʻoia ʻia nā iʻa mua i helu ʻia ma o kahi a lāua e noho ai, ma ka "laupapa," a ʻike ʻia auaneʻi, mai laila mai nō nā iʻa a pau loa i hoʻohanohano ʻia e kēia mele: ʻo ka manini, ka pōpolo, ke kala, ka nenue, ka nahawele, a me ke āhole (Titcomb). ʻAʻole kēia he mau iʻa o ke kai hohonu, a eia nō hoʻi, ʻaʻole ia he mau iʻa i kakaʻikahi o ka loaʻa ʻana mai. Lēʻia naʻe ke kai papaʻu i kēia mau iʻa, e like me ka mea i hoʻākāka ʻia i ka puke kilo iʻa a Margaret Titcomb:

[No ka manini:] Mrs. Pukui relates: "It was one of the commonest fishes of my birthplace, Kaʻu, in Hawaii." (106)

[No ke kala:] This fish is so abundant that it is eaten considerably for that reason. Mullet and *moi* and other fish are more popular, but *kala* is easier to find and catch. (85)

[No ka nenue:] Paʻahana Wiggin Says: "A choice fish in Kaʻu.... We call it *iʻa papa* ... because it remained inside the reef close to shore." (114)

[No ke āhole:] A common shore fish, found in both salt and fresh water, the young abundant along sandy beaches, chiefly in shallow water. (59)[10]

Ua akāka maila ke 'ano o kā Kauwē mele a me ka 'ono āna e ho'ohanohano nei, he mea i pili i ke one hānau, i laha loa a nui ho'i, a i ma'alahi ka loa'a 'ana mai. He mau i'a nō ho'i kēia i hiki ke 'ai 'ia i kēlā me kēia lā, a hopohopo 'ole paha ka lawai'a i ka pa'akikī o ka loa'a 'ana mai a me ka lō'ihi o ka māhuahua hou 'ana mai o ua mau i'a nei o ke kai. 'O ka mea e 'oi a'e ai kēia mahalo 'ana i ka i'a noho laupapa, ke nānā 'ia nā mele ho'onu'u he 'umikūmāwalu i loa'a mai, ua like nō a like ke 'ano. Ma ua mau mele nei, helu 'ia he kanakolu kūmālima 'ano i'a, a mai loko mai o ia hui, noho ke kanakolu kūmālua ma kai papa'u. 'O ke a'u, ke akule, a me ke aku wale nō kai noho i kai hohonu, a ma 'elima wale nō mele i hea 'ia ai ko lākou mau inoa. No laila, he mea ma'amau loa kēia ho'ohanohano 'ana i ka 'ono o ka i'a o ka laupapa, a me he lā ua 'oi a'e ka mahalo a me ka 'oli'oli o nā haku mele i ia 'ano i'a.

Na kēia 'ikena paha e ho'ākāka maila i ka haupa a me ka ho'onu'u 'ana o ke Kanaka Maoli. 'Oiai mana'o 'ia paha i kēia mau lā, 'a'ole wale nō i pili ka *feast* i ka nui o ka 'ai i loa'a, akā i ke 'ano kūikawā a kāka'ikahi nō paha o ke 'ano o ua 'ai lā, 'a'ole nō pēlā ka mea i mele 'ia maila. Ma kā Kauwē mele, 'ike 'ia 'elua mea nui i mahalo 'ia: ka loa'a koke o nā i'a a me ka like 'ole ho'i o nā mea i loa'a. Ma laila nō ka 'ono, a ma laila nō ka waiwai. Ua lawa ka haku mele i ka 'ono o kēia mau i'a ma'amau, 'a'ole no kona hā'awi pio 'ana a hoka nō ho'i me ka mana'o 'ana, 'o ia wale nō ka mea i loa'a. Akā, ua lawa 'o ia no ka mea 'ike 'o ia i ka 'ono maoli nō o ia mau i'a, i ka nui launa'ole o nā 'ano i hiki ke ho'omākaukau a 'ai 'ia,[11] a i ka waiwai o ka 'ono ma'amau o ka 'āina. Kāko'o 'ia nō ho'i kēia mana'o i ka 'ai a Kauwē i ho'owali ai i ko'olua no ka nui i'a o kāna papa'aina, 'o ia ho'i ka poi 'uala. 'A'ole kēia 'o ka poi lehua i hānai 'ia ai 'o Kalākaua, 'a'ole nō 'o ka manaulu e ulu ai ka mana o ka lāhui. He 'uala wale nō, i loa'a i nā 'āina like 'ole, a i nā wā like 'ole, i loko nō o ka loa'a me ka 'ole o ka poi kalo.[12] A, he 'ono.

Puana 'ia maila kahi mana'o like i kā Bina Mossman mele i kapa 'ia nō 'o "He 'Ono." E like me kā Kauwē helu i'a, mele mai nō ho'i 'o Mossman no nā i'a o ka laupapa: 'o ka nenue 'oe, 'o ka 'ō'io 'oe, 'o ka 'anae 'oe, 'o ka manini 'oe, a ia mea aku nō. Akā, ha'i pololei mai nō 'o ia ala i kona make'e 'ana i ka i'a o kai papa'u, me ka pono 'ole o ka 'imi nui 'ana i i'a o kai hohonu, ma ka 'ōlelo 'ana penei: "Mai pi'ikoi 'oe i ke akule lā," a me "Ho'i iho 'oe i kahi 'anae lā." Ua 'ike 'ia, 'a'ole kēia he mele i pili wale nō i ka i'a o kai, akā pili kona kaona i ka 'ume'ume 'ana i huapala—a pēlā nō ho'i ka ho'omaopopo ākea 'ana i kā Kauwē mele no nā i'a noho laupapa. Akā na'e, 'ike 'ia nō ho'i ka pili 'ana o nā mana'o aloha 'āina i ua mau mele nei. Ma kekahi 'ao'ao, he mau mana'o politika ia. Inā pēlā, 'ano like kā Mossman kauoha 'ana mai i ka "ho'i" 'ana i nā i'a o kai papa'u me ke mele 'ana aku o Kekoaohiwaikalani i kāna lālani mele kaulana, "Ua lawa mākou i ka pōhaku / I ka 'ai kamaha'o o ka 'āina." Ua pili nō ka 'ai ho'onu'u 'ana me ka 'ai ahupua'a, a no laila, ke koho kākou i ka i'a o ko kākou kai pono'ī, a me ka pōhaku o ko kākou 'āina pono'ī, koho ho'i kākou i ke kūpa'a 'ana ma hope o ua 'āina nei.

A, ma kekahi 'ao'ao ho'i, he mau mana'o mālama 'āina a mālama kai ko loko nei. Mea 'ia mai no ke kala, ua 'ai nui 'ia ma muli nō o ka nui i loa'a ma kai, a hiki iā kākou ke mahu'i i kona hoa kū'ē: ke li'ili'i maila ka loa'a, emi maila ka nui o ka 'ai 'ana, i ulu hou a'e ai ka nui o ua mau i'a nei. No laila, 'o ka 'ai ho'onu'u 'ana o ka po'e Kānaka Maoli, 'a'ole paha ia he 'ai ā manō, me ka nānā 'ole 'ana aku i ka pono o ka 'āina a me ke kai nāna e hānai mai. A, ke ho'ohanohano kākou i nā i'a ma'amau o kai papa'u ma o ke mele a me ka 'ai 'ana aku, paipai kākou i kekahi 'ano kiko'ī o ka haupa 'ana, i hiki paha ke kapa 'ia he *everyday feast* a i 'ole he *everyday indulgence*. E like me kā Corntassel i kākau ai no ka *everyday resurgence,* he 'ano kēia o ka 'ai Hawai'i i kauka'i a ho'oulu i nā pilina o ka 'āina a me ka lāhui, a he mea nō ho'i ia i hiki ke hana 'ia i kēlā me kēia lā, 'oiai 'a'ole ia he 'aha'aina e pono ai ka hana nui a me ka 'ai ho'oulu mana. A e like nō ho'i me ka *resurgence,* koi maila kēia 'ano 'ai i ko kākou mālama pono 'ana i ka 'āina nāna e ho'olako mai ana i ua mau i'a nei.

'O ia lālani mele kaulana a Kekoaohiwaikalani, 'o ia ho'i, "Ua lawa makou i ka pōhaku," ua laha nō i kēia au, i puana na ke aloha 'āina no ka hō'ike 'ana i kona kūpa'a 'ana no ka pono o Hawai'i nei, me kona kū'ē a hō'ole 'ana nō ho'i i ka limanui kā'ili 'āina a ho'okākāuha kanaka o 'Amelika. 'Ike 'ia ma kā Kauwē kaena 'ana i ka lawa ona i ka poi 'uala a me ka i'a o ka laupapa, he mana'o nō kēia i hele a pa'a i ka na'au o ke Kanaka, a ke ō mai nei nō i nā mele, nā mo'olelo, a me nā loina 'e a'e a kēia lāhui Kanaka. I laila nō e loa'a ai kēia 'ano o ka mo'olelo 'ana i ke aloha 'āina a me ka paio politika o ka lāhui Kanaka Maoli.

I Ea i ka 'Aha'aina

'O ka mea nani loa o kēia 'ano 'aha'aina a Kinney lāua 'o Kauwē i mele maila, 'o ka 'ai ma'amau nō ia, a ua hiki ke lilo ia, 'o ia ka papa'aina ma'amau e ola ai, a e ea ai, ka lehulehu kanaka e noho ana ma kēia mau kaha o ka moana nui ākea. I ka wā i piha ai ka *loko i'a* 'o Kawainui i ka 'anae, ke awa, a me ka 'ama'ama—i ka wā nō ho'i i uliuli ai kona mau kaha i ka uluāo'a 'ana o ka lau kapalili o Hāloa a me nā lau nahele 'ē a'e o uka—he kini a he lehu ka po'e o Kailua, i hānai 'ia nō mai loko mai o ia ipukai momona. No laila, maopopo iā kākou, ua hiki nō i ua 'āina nei ke hānai i ka nui lehulehu o ko kākou wā. Aia na'e i ka pono o ia 'āina, a me ka pono o kona pilina me kākou po'e Kānaka. A 'o kēia pilina, 'a'ole nō ia he kipa aku a ho'okipa mai, no ia mea he nanea i ka nani o ka 'āina. 'A'ole pēlā i ka wā i wili ai ka wai o Kawainui i ka hi'u kinikini o ka 'anae. Aia ka pono 'o ka hānai 'ia 'ana o ka 'āina e kona kaikaina—ho'oulu 'ia e ke poho o kona lima; mele a mo'olelo 'ia e kona waha a me kāna maka peni; kūpale 'ia e kona aupuni; a kāko'o 'ia e ke dālā o kāna pāisi.

'Oko'a ke ao a kākou e noho nei; 'oko'a ho'i ke ao a kākou e wānana a kūlia nei, 'o ia ho'i ke ao e ho'i ai ka waiwai i ka 'āina, a e ho'i ai nō ke ea i ka lāhui. Nui nō ka loli a kakou e 'imi nei, ma ke aupuni, nā 'oihana, nā loina o ka lehulehu, a me nā hana ma'amau e kō aku i kēlā me kēia lā. 'O ka maka mua na'e o ia 'ano loli o ke au a me ka hana a kānaka, aia nō i ka loli 'ana o ka no'ono'o, a me nā pō'aiapili e no'ono'o 'ia ai nā māhele o ko kākou ola, e la'a ka 'ai. E like me kā Laiana Wong i kākau ai no ke a'o 'ōlelo 'ana:

> The most difficult aspect here is imagining new ways of speaking that do not exist in the default repertoire. The default repertoire, although it does not limit the ideas we are able to conceive, does have a profound influence on them. An English speaker might never imagine the existence of certain Hawaiian ways of pointing unless prompted by exposure to them. Even upon recognizing such ways of speaking as important aspects of Hawaiian worldview, it is not easy to incorporate them into one's repertoire without a full understanding of the appropriate environment for their use. (160)

Pēlā ka mahu'i 'ana i nā 'ano 'oko'a o ka 'ōlelo 'ana; pēlā nō ho'i ka mahu'i 'ana i nā 'ano 'oko'a o ka noho 'ana. Ma o kēia 'ano mele na'e e 'ike le'a 'ia ai ka nohona i wali i nā kūpuna o kākou, ke kuana'ike i lilo i kahua no ke ola pono 'ana o ko lākou 'āina a me kā lākou papa'aina, a me ke ea mau 'ana a lākou i kūpa'a ai. He mo'olelo nō ia e mau aku nei, i ola no ka 'aipōhaku.

KUHIA O HOPE

1. Penei au e kapa aku ai i kēia mau mele i haku 'ia no ka le'ale'a, ke aloha, ka 'ikena a me ka mana'o o ka haku mele, a pēlā aku. 'A'ole ia he mele lāhui a mele kū'ē paha, akā, e like me kā Leilani Basham i ho'ākāka maila, he "leo nahenahe" nō ho'i ko ke mele lāhui, i 'upu a'e ai a ulu ke aloha i loko o kākou pākahi, a lana ai ho'i ka mana'o o loko i ka lōkahi 'ana mai o ka lāhui Kanaka Maoli. No laila, he pilina nō ko kēia mau mele, i kuhi 'ia paha e kēia hua 'ōlelo ho'okahi.

2. He ala nihinihi kai hele 'ia i ke kapa 'ana aku i kēia mau lāhui mele. 'O kekahi, e like me ke mele māka'ika'i, ua pa'a ka inoa i ka po'e pa'a mele o ka wā ma mua. 'O kekahi na'e, e like me kēia mau mele i haku 'ia no ka 'ai 'ana, ka pā'ina 'ana, a pēlā aku, 'a'ole i loa'a kahi inoa i ma'a iā kākou. 'Ano 'ē ke kani o ka inoa "mele 'ai" a i 'ole "mele 'aina" i ku'u pepeiao, a 'oko'a iki nā pahuhopu o kēlā me kēia mele i ho'ohui 'ia i kēia lāhui mele nei. No laila, 'oiai 'o ka hō'ike 'ana i ka nui o ka 'ai a me ka nui o ka mea 'ai kahi mea e pili ai nā mele a pau, e kapa 'ia ana nō he mau "mele ho'onu'u" i kēia mokuna.

3. Ma o kēia inoa ho'i e 'ike 'ia ai ka waiwai o nā 'ano hana li'ili'i i ho'okō 'ia i kēlā me

kēia lā, i mau ai nā loina o nā ʻōiwi, a i mau ai hoʻi ka pilina o ke kanaka ʻōiwi me ua mau loina nei, me kona lāhui kanaka, a me kona ʻaina kulāiwi.

4. Naʻu ke kālele ʻōlelo.

5. ʻAʻole i loaʻa iaʻu ka makahiki i haku ʻia ai kēia mele, akā ma nā nūpepa Hawaiʻi kahiko, ʻike ʻia ko Kauwē hala ʻana ma ka makahiki 1922, a me ka nui o kāna hana ʻahamele a puʻukani hoʻi ma waena o nā makahiki 1917–1922. Ke kuhi nei au, ua haku ʻia ma kahi o ka makahiki 1920.

6. Helu ʻia e Ortone he ʻumikūmālua puʻukani, na lākou he ʻumikūmāhā pāleo, i hoʻopaʻa i nei mele mai ka makahiki 1970 a i ka 1999. Helu ʻia he ʻewalu hou aku e Amazon, mai ka 2001 a i ka 2018. A hō mai ʻo iTunes he ʻelua i koe, mai ka makahiki 2006 a i ka 2012.

7. ʻO ke mele hoʻokahi i kūʻē i kēia hiʻohiʻona kūmau, ʻo ia hoʻi ʻo "Nā ʻOno o ka ʻĀina." ʻO ka pahuhopu nō naʻe o ia mele, ʻo ia hoʻi ke mele ʻana mai i kekahi mau ʻano o ke kalo: ʻo ka lehua ʻoe, ʻo ka manaulu ʻoe, a pēlā wale aku, a me ka hoʻoikaika ʻana i ka pilina o ke kanaka me ke kalo ma o ua mele nei. He iʻa naʻe ka ʻono maʻamau o ke mele ʻana mai.

8. ʻO kā Liliʻu "He ʻAi na ka Lani" ka mea i ʻokoʻa. ʻO ke mele hoʻokahi ia i kaulike loa ai ka ʻai a me ka iʻa—hoʻopuka ʻia ʻelua ʻano ʻai a me ka ʻelua ʻano iʻa. ʻOiai he mele ia no ke aliʻi, no ka ʻahaʻaina hoʻomana, a pēlā aku, he kūpono nō paha kēia kaulike o uka me kai, ka ʻai a me ka iʻa, a he mea koʻikoʻi paha ia no ka haku mele.

9. Stromberg, p. 1.

10. E hoʻomaopopo ʻia: helu ʻia nō ka pōpolo ma kēia puke, akā ʻaʻole i wehewehe ʻia kona ʻano e like me nā iʻa ʻē aʻe o luna nei. ʻAʻohe wahi ʻōlelo no ia mea he nahawele.

11. Helu ʻia e Titcomb ʻehiku ʻano ʻokoʻa no ka ʻai ʻana i ke kala, a ʻano like ia me ka hoʻomākaukau ʻana i nā iʻa like ʻole i wehewehe ʻia ma kā ia nei puke (85).

12. Wehewehe ʻia penei e Pukui mā: "Cooked and compressed sweet potatoes allowed to ferment slightly and used as a substitute for poi when poi was scarce" ("paʻi ʻuala," Pukui and Elbert).

PAPA HELU KŪMOLE

Alama, Sam. "ʻAmaʻama" (April 17, 2018). Performed by Johnny Noble and His Hawaiian Music, featuring Sam Alama. https://www.youtube.com/watch?v=EwEDpRX2DjM.

Asing, Blayne. *Young, Old Soul*. CD Baby, 2015.

Basham, Leilani. *I Mau ke Ea o ka ʻĀina I Ka Pono: He Puke Mele Lāhui no ka Lāhui Hawaiʻi*. 2007. University of Hawaiʻi at Mānoa, PhD dissertation. ProQuest Dissertations & Theses Global.

Beamer, Helen Desha. "Mahaiʻula." Performed by Robert Cazimero. *Robert Cazimero*, Mountain Apple MAC 1001, 1978.

Berger, John. "Sovereignty Songs." *Hawaiian Music and Musicians: An Encyclopedic History*, edited by Dr. George S. Kanahele, and revised and updated by John Berger. Mutual, 2012, pp. 774–787.

Corntassel, Jeff, and Cheryl Bryce. "Practicing Sustainable Self-Determination: Indigenous Approaches to Cultural Restoration and Revitalization." *The Brown Journal of World Affairs*, vol. 18, no. 2, 2012, pp. 151–162.

de Silva, Kīhei. (March 29, 2018). *He ʻAi na ka Lani: An Essay*. Waihona Mele. http://halaumohalailima.com/HMI/He_Ai_na_Kalani.html.

"DLNR, Army Corps of Engineers Break Ground for Kawainui Marsh Environmental

Restoration Project." (May 19, 2019). *US Army Corps of Engineers Headquarters*. https://www.usace.army.mil/Media/News-Archive/Story-Article-View/Article/477879/dlnr-army-corps-of-engineers-break-ground-for-kawainui-marsh-environmental-rest/.

Goodyear-Kaʻōpua, Noelani. Introduction. *A Nation Rising: Hawaiian Movements for Life, Land, and Sovereignty*, edited by Noelani Goodyear-Kaʻōpua, Ikaika Hussey, and Erin Kahunawaikaʻala Wright. Duke UP, 2014, pp. 1–33.

Handy, E. S. Craighill, and Mary Kawena Pukui. *The Polynesian Family System in Ka-ʻu, Hawaiʻi*. 1950. Charles E. Tuttle, 1972.

Hikaʻalani at Ulupō. (May 20, 2019). http://www.hikaalani.website/at-ulup333-nui.html.

Ichimura, Matilda Kauwē. "Me ka Miki Poi." Performed by the Kihei Brown Trio. *Right-On Keia*, Hula Records, HS-550.

Imada, Adria L. *Aloha America: Hula Circuits Through the U.S. Empire*. Duke UP, 2012.

Kamae, Eddie. *Eddie Kamae Presents the Sons of Hawaii*. Hawaii Sons HSC 1001, 1973.

Kamakahi, Dennis. *ʻOhana*. Dancing Cat 08022-38043-2, 1999.

Kanahele, Dr. George S., updated by John Berger. "Liliʻuokalani." *Hawaiian Music and Musicians: An Encyclopedic History*, edited by Dr. George S. Kanahele, and revised and updated by John Berger, 2012, pp. 504–507.

Kaulia, James Keauiluna. "Haiolelo a James Keauiluna Kaulia, Peresidena Nui o na Ahahui Aloha Aina." *Ke Aloha Aina*, 11 September 1897, pp. 4–5.

Kauluakalana. *Our Mission*. (January 4, 2021). https://www.kauluakalana.org.

Kauwē, Lot. "Aloha ka Manini." *He Mele Aloha: A Hawaiian Songbook*, compiled by Carol Wilcox. ʻOliʻOli Productions, L.L.C., 2003, p. 15.

"Kawainui Environmental Restoration Project: Draft Supplemental Environmental Assessment." (May 20, 2019). http://oeqc2.doh.hawaii.gov/EA_EIS_Library/2008-02-08-OA-DEA-Kawainui-Marsh-Restoration.pdf.

Kawainui Marsh Wetland Restoration and Habitat Enhancement Plan. (May 20, 2019). http://dlnr.hawaii.gov/wildlife/files/2013/10/knm_chapter-3-mar2011.pdf, 3-2.

"Ke Aloha Aina; Heaha ia?" *Ke Aloha Aina*, vol. 1, no. 1, 25 May 1895, p. 7.

King, Lisa, Rose Gubele, and Joyce Rain Anderson. "Introduction—Careful with the Stories We Tell: Naming Survivance, Sovereignty, *and* Story." *Survivance, Sovereignty, and Story: Teaching American Indian Rhetorics*, edited by King, Gubele, and Anderson. Utah State UP, 2015, pp. 3–16.

Kinney, Clarence. "Nā ʻAi ʻOno." Performed by Eddie Kamae and the Sons of Hawaii, *This is Eddie Kamae*. Hula Records HS-512, 1966.

Liliʻuokalani. "He ʻAi Na Ka Lani." *The Queen's Songbook*, edited by Barbara Barnard Smith. Hui Hānai, 1999, pp. 118–120.

Mossman, Bina. "He ʻOno." *Nā Mele o Hawaiʻi Nei: 101 Hawaiian Songs*, edited by Samuel Elbert and Noelani Māhoe. U of Hawaiʻi P, 1970, pp. 48–49.

Nelson, Melissa. "Getting Dirty: The Eco-Eroticism of Women in Indigenous Oral Literatures." *Critically Sovereign: Indigenous Gender, Sexuality, and Feminist Studies*, edited by Joanne Barker. Duke UP, 2017, pp. 229–260.

Oliveira, Katrina-Ann R. Kapāʻanaokalāokeola Nākoa. *Ancestral Places: Understanding Kanaka Geographies*. Oregon State UP, 2014.

Ortone, Brett C., ed. *The Island Music Source Book*. Brett C. Ortone, 1999, p. 10; amazon. com (April 13, 2018); iTunes Library (April 13, 2018).

"Pipi Kaula." Performed by The Alice Fredlund Serenaders, *Alice, Linda, and Sybil*. Tradewinds Records TR-109.

Pukui, Mary Kawena, and Samuel Elbert. *Hawaiian Dictionary*, rev. and enlarged ed. U of Hawaiʻi P, 1986.

Pukui, Mary Kawena, E. W. Haertig, and Catherine A. Lee. *Nānā I Ke Kumu (Look to the Source)*, vol. 1. Hui Hānai, 1972.

Pukui, Mary Kawena, and E. S. Craighill Handy. *The Polynesian Family System in Ka-ʻu, Hawaiʻi*. See Handy.

Salmón, Enrique. *Eating the Landscape: American Indian Stories of Food, Identity, and Resilience*. First Peoples: New Directions in Indigenous Studies, U of Arizona P, 2012.

Silva, Noenoe K. *Aloha Betrayed: Native Hawaiian Resistance to American Colonialism*. Duke UP, 2004.

Stromberg, Ernest. "Rhetoric and American Indians: An Introduction." *American Indian Rhetorics and Survivance: Word Medicine, Word Magic*, edited by Ernest Stromberg. U of Pittsburgh P, 2006, pp. 1–12.

Tatar, Elizabeth, updated by John Berger. "Introduction: What Is Hawaiian Music?" *Hawaiian Music and Musicians: An Encyclopedic History*, edited by Dr. George S. Kanahele, and revised and updated by John Berger, 2012, pp. xli–xlix.

Titcomb, Margaret. *Native Use of Fish in Hawaii*. U of Hawaiʻi P, 1972.

Vizenor, Gerald. "Aesthetics of Survivance: Literary Theory and Practice." *Survivance: Narratives of Native Presence*, edited by Gerald Vizenor. U of Nebraska P, 2008, pp. 1–23.

Wong, K. Laiana. "Hawaiian Methodologies of Indirection: Point-less vs. Pointless." *Critical Qualitative Research in Second Language Studies: Agency and Advocacy*, edited by Kathryn A. Davis. Information Age, 2011, pp. 151–170.

Wong, Kaleomanuiwa. Interview. Conducted by Kahikina de Silva. November 2018.

Kahikina de Silva is a kupa of Kaʻōhao, Oʻahu—a place awkwardly renamed "Lanikai" during its development as a residential neighborhood in the early 1900s. Growing up in a place whose true name was once all-but-forgotten, and witnessing its slow but steady inundation by waves of commerce, tourism, and Kanaka Maoli displacement has had a significant effect on her life. She is continually reminded of the need to ʻauʻa—to hold fast to that which sustains us as a people—and to hoʻomau—to persist, by occupying our native lands, continuing our cultural practices, speaking our mother tongue, and making sure our children do the same. She is a practicing Kumu Hula, and an Assistant Professor of Hawaiian Language at the University of Hawaiʻi Mānoa, where she earned her BA in Hawaiian Language (2000), her MA in English, with a focus on Asia-Pacific Literature (2005), and her PhD in Indigenous Politics (2018). She lives in Kaʻōhao, in the house she grew up in, cultivating the next generation of ʻAipōhaku.

The moʻolelo of a people are their foundation;
moʻolelo anchors kānaka to their people and
to themselves in all facets of life.

7

Nā Mele Koʻokoʻo

How Mele Serve as the Koʻokoʻo of Moʻolelo

Kaipulaumakaniolono Baker

As the carriers of a vast history of an intricate trans-pacific society, the oral histories of the Hawaiian people, Kānaka Maoli, played a prominent and consequential role in the establishment and lifestyle that became Kanaka Maoli culture. Moʻolelo, history or tradition, has been and continues to be the collective moʻokūʻauhau, genealogy, of Kānaka Maoli, carrying the mana, divine power, and mauli, seat of life or life-force, of each and every member of Kanaka Maoli society. The moʻolelo of a people are their foundation; moʻolelo anchors kānaka to their people and to themselves in all facets of life. Individual stories within the greater moʻolelo of the people not only collect essential information for primitive survival but also behavioral codes of conduct for what was a stringent society built upon numerous kapu or taboos meant to keep order and rank appropriately pono, prosperous, and balanced. Oftentimes an accurate understanding of moʻolelo, especially in situations requiring exact protocol, is the difference between life and death, and it is for this reason that Paʻa Moʻolelo, the keepers of moʻolelo, were held in such high esteem.[1]

Paʻa Moʻolelo were often trained from youth to memorize moʻolelo exactly as they were told to them (Pukui, "How"). Mary Kawena Pukui, renowned as the keeper of the Hawaiian language, recalls a moʻolelo that her grandmother once taught her. She describes sitting, with her grandmother retelling the story over and over again, ensuring that Pukui would say it exactly as her ancestors, kūpuna, said it before her (4). The rigid training of Paʻa Moʻolelo reflected the rigors and sophistication of Kanaka Maoli society. A forgotten detail in a moʻolelo is mana lost, and mana loss has consequences not only for the Paʻa Moʻolelo themselves but also the communities and greater lāhui which they represent—the collective of all Kānaka Maoli.

Maintenance of the mana and mauli of the lāhui is a primary focus of Paʻa Moʻolelo, but many will question the source of this mana and mauli. From what does mana and mauli derive in a moʻolelo? Is it in the presentation and oratorical capacity of the Paʻa Moʻolelo? Surely this played a vital role; however, from the narrative presented by Mrs. Pukui, one can deduce that most presentations would be very similar, passed on through the generations, with variations only coming from the different hālau aʻo, schools of knowledge, which have different perspectives on the events that took place. From the different hālau we find the variations, or mana, of moʻolelo. The more mana of a moʻolelo that exist, surely the more mana that the moʻolelo carries itself.

For example, the *Moʻolelo Kaʻao o Hiʻiakaikapoliopele* has at least thirteen mana moʻolelo published in the old Hawaiian Language Nūpepa, newspapers (hoʻomanawanui xxiv). Clearly this moʻolelo has a lot of mana (variations) and mana (divine power) as passed throughout Kanaka Maoli society in both kahiko and modern times. From a brief analysis of what brings mana to moʻolelo, it is clear that numbers and volume matter—the more mana big and small of a moʻolelo, the more mana the moʻolelo holds. This holds weight. Each mana provides new information, and the more ways a story is told, the more ways it can also be applied and used in living contexts. Just as a coconut, niu, is not to be used solely for its water and thrown out, the many mana of a moʻolelo allow us to dig deeper into the meat of the niu, to husk the niu, and to braid from it sennit cordage. The fronds of the kumu niu (tree) can also be harvested to weave baskets, and should that kumu fall, a pahu drum can be carved of its trunk. Like the niu, a moʻolelo not only hydrates, but feeds, fastens, and secures, and entertains the collective lāhui.

Because the extensive information held within moʻolelo gives them mana, memorization was the Paʻa Moʻolelo's key ability to bring mana to their own practice. Mele, chants, and songs are the most prevalent means by which ʻike is stored and transferred.[2] Mele are often in themselves a moʻolelo, either straight-forwardly or in their subtext (Lopes), and therefore contain the haʻawina, lessons, of the various undertones that the greater moʻolelo carries. "Ka Moʻolelo Kaʻao o Hiʻiakaikapoliopele," published by Joseph Poepoe in the newspaper *Kuokoa Home Rula* from 1908 to 1911, is renowned for having over 270 kau, which are variations of mele pule, prayerful mele. Many of the mele differ in the various mana moʻolelo of Hiʻiakaikapoliopele, thus adding to the mana of each mele within each moʻolelo. To do proper justice to the moʻolelo, the Paʻa Moʻolelo would need to accurately recite each mana of the moʻolelo along with the appropriate mele and/or kau. Once accomplished, this would maintain and advance the mana and mauli of the people.

The mana of mele is within its application. A popular mele from the saga of Hiʻiakaikapoliopele expresses her heartbreak at leaving a lover by the name of Kaʻanahau, from Kailua, Oʻahu (Hoʻoulumāhiehie 156). In the mele " ʻIno Koʻolau" Hiʻiaka reflects on and laments the famous rain of the Koʻolau mountain range, as it fuels her heartbreak and contributes to the flow of water down her cheeks while she turns back to see him in the distance. The lyrics are as follows:

'Ino Ko'olau ē! 'Ino Ko'olau!!	Stormy is Ko'olau, oh! Stormy Ko'olau!!
'Aikena ana i ka ua o Ko'olau	How wearying, the rains of Ko'olau
Ke ua maila i Māʻeliʻeli	It rains there at Māʻeliʻeli
Ke hoʻokawewe aʻela i Heʻeia	Clattering down there at Heʻeia
Ke kupākupā maila ka ua i ke kai	The rain scoops craters in the sea
Haʻa hula leʻa ka ua i ʻĀhulimanu	The showers dance delightedly at ʻĀhulimanu
Ka ua Pōʻaihale ma uka o Kahaluʻu ē	The encircling Pōʻaihale rain inland of Kahaluʻu
Luʻuluʻu ē	Burdened down, oh
Kuʻu luʻuluʻu	This burden is for me to bear
Luʻuluʻu au i kō aloha ē	I am weighed down by your love
Pūʻolo waimaka a ka ʻōnohi.	Bringing a deluge of tears.
	(Hoʻoulumāhiehie 156)

The mele has been immortalized as a reflection of heartbreak and is often quoted when someone is experiencing the grief of a lost lover. In and of itself, the phrase " 'Ino Ko'olau, 'aikena i ka ua" has become an ʻōlelo noʻeau, a proverbial saying, recalling the mele without a full recitation, but allowing the connotations, otherwise known as kaona, to speak for themselves. Each time the words " 'Ino Ko'olau" are said, those who know the moʻolelo will recall the greater context and haʻawina that lie within, giving mana to that moʻolelo and all those connected to it. And because the story of Hiʻiakaikapoliopele is a story of travel, all people of Hawaiʻi garner mana from the recollection and recital of any part of the moʻolelo.

Mele themselves are very much conduits of mana. They carry moʻolelo, which in turn carry mana and mauli, each feeding off and giving life to one another, each essential to another's existence. This is why mele are not limited to moʻolelo of old. They are a crucial component of the documentation and giving of mana to everyday life. Every great movement in Hawaiʻi's history has been accompanied and recorded by mele. Mele give life, hoʻōla, and give mana, hoʻomana, to life as a Kanaka Maoli. Mele are the quintessential instrument, performing the pulse of Kānaka Maoli.

During the unification of the Hawaiian archipelago by Kamehameha Paiʻea, his warriors composed "Hole Waimea," a mele to honor and rally themselves. In his analysis of the mele, Kīhei de Silva uncovers the poetry that likens the might of Kamehameha's army to the harsh and shivering Kīpuʻupuʻu rain of Waimea:

Hole Waimea i ka ihe a ka makani,
Hao mai nā ʻale a ke kīpuʻupuʻu
Waimea is tousled with the shafts of the wind
While the kīpuʻupuʻu puffs and gusts

The mele was complemented by a haʻa. Each movement in the dance correlated directly with movements of Kanaka martial arts, lua, thus inspiring the warriors to perform with excellence in battle. As the mele hoʻomana the warriors, it hoʻōla Kamehameha's vision of conquest. Upon the arrival of the missionaries and foreign instruments, it was instantly choralized and modernized to be a mele sung as well as chanted, and turned into hula, the haʻa complemented and reflected the transition.

Kānaka Maoli themselves seamlessly integrated modern instruments into their mele tradition and began to use the newfound sounds as new waʻa to carry their moʻolelo, mana, and mauli. The Aliʻi, chiefly class, became prolific composers, penning, composing, and arranging many masterful mele that are still sung throughout Hawaiʻi. Two of the most exceptionally talented Aliʻi were Mōʻī Kalākaua and Mōʻī Liliʻuokalani, the last two reigning monarchs of the Hawaiian Kingdom prior to the illegal overthrow. Both Aliʻi possessed impressive resumes as musicians, with hundreds of compositions to boast of collectively. Their mele persist and continue to be played at gatherings ranging from formal paid performances by modern Hawaiian musicians to a backyard impromptu "jam sesh." These mele continue to hoʻōla and hoʻomana our people.

It was only natural, therefore, that upon the illegal overthrow of the Kingdom of Hawaiʻi, thousands of mele were composed and published in the newspapers as rally cries. New mele are rediscovered on a day-to-day basis as the over 100-year-old nūpepa are digitized and uploaded into the various databases. But as is natural, one mele rose above all others in its call to all Kānaka across the pae ʻāina, archipelago. In January of 1893, American Marines landed on the shores of Oʻahu at the invitation of the Committee of Safety, led by Sanford B. Dole and other white traitors of the Hawaiian Kingdom. With loaded cannons pointed at ʻIolani Palace, they forced Queen Liliʻuokalani to "yield [her] authority until such a time that the Government of the United States shall…undo the actions of its representatives" (James H. Blount). Just after hearing the news, Mrs. Ellen Kekoaohiwaikalani Wright Prendergast turned to the medium which carried her people into power from time immemorial. She composed the "Mele ʻAi Pōhaku," Rock Eating Song, more commonly referred to today by its first line, "Kaulana nā Pua." Here is the mele:

Kaulana nā pua aʻo Hawaiʻi	Famous are the children of Hawaiʻi
Kūpaʻa ma hope o ka ʻāina	Immovably faithful to this ʻāina
Hiki mai ka ʻelele o ka loko ʻino	Malevolent messengers arrive
Palapala ʻānunu me ka pākaha	With greedy documents of extortion
Pane mai Hawaiʻi moku o Keawe	Hawaiʻi, land of Keawe answers
Kōkua nā Hono aʻo Piʻilani	Piʻilani's bays help
Kākoʻo mai Kauaʻi o Mano	Mano's Kauaʻi lends support
Paʻapū me ke one Kākuhihewa	Impervious by the sands of Kākuhihewa
ʻAʻole aʻe kau i ka pūlima	No one will fix a signature
Ma luna o ka pepa o ka ʻēnemi	To the paper of the enemy
Hoʻohui ʻāina kūʻai hewa	False annexation sellout
I ka pono sivila aʻo ke kanaka	Of our native civil rights
ʻAʻole mākou aʻe minamina	We will not regret
I ka puʻu kālā o ke aupuni	The government's sums of money
Ua lawa mākou i ka pōhaku	The stones are ample, we will suffice
I ka ʻai kamahaʻo o ka ʻāina	With the marvelous food of the ʻāina
Ma hope mākou o Liliʻulani	We will enforce the will of Liliʻuokalani
A loaʻa ē ka pono o ka ʻāina	Until morality is restored to the ʻāina
Haʻina ʻia mai ana ka puana	Let our story be pronounced
Ka poʻe i aloha i ka ʻāina	Of the people who love their land[3]
	(Prendergast)

The mele clearly displays the displeasure of Kānaka Maoli with the wrongdo-ings of the White Traitors and their American delegates. "Mele ʻAi Pōhaku" in-stantly became a staple of the Hawaiian push for the reinstatement of the rightful Queen Liliʻuokalani, and continues to be sung at Kanaka rallies across the pae ʻāina in the twenty-first century. Along with "Kaulana Nā Pua," many mele aloha ʻāina came and went as dire straits were encountered and pushed through, but "Kaulana Nā Pua" has persisted since the beginning of the politicization of Aloha ʻĀina—that is, the natural love of the land.

A love of land and country is what has and what always will drive the creation of mele. In her analysis of mele, Noenoe K. Silva confirms what many kānaka have already held true: that the use of place names and geographical features is a key component which drives the mele aesthetic (77), and that the beauty of the land is a beauty that resonates with all. Even in the stripping of the native tongue of Kānaka (de Silva, *Iwiwkuamoʻo*), the people continued to create, haku, mele in awe of and in love with the land. Amazingly, even in the foreign and imposed English language, Kānaka maintained the composition style and techniques of their kūpuna (Osorio). In his Hawaiian Studies 107 course, Dean of Hawaiʻinuiākea School of Hawaiian Knowledge Jonathan Kay Kamakawiwoʻole Osorio provides several examples of this. One is "The Beauty of Maunakea," composed by Keola Beamer, a mele expressing the awe of Kānaka at the beauty of one of Hawaiʻi's most sacred peaks. As an elegant mele aloha ʻāina, "The Beauty of Maunakea" tells the moʻolelo of a kanaka who leaves home but is forever anchored to the pulchritudinous Maunakea. The anchoring magnetic attraction that Kānaka Maoli share with the land is best summarized by Joseph K. Nāwahīokalaniopuʻu, a staunch aloha ʻāina patriot during the time of the overthrow, who in 1895 proclaimed, "O ke Aloha Aina, oia ka Ume Mageneti i loko o ka puuwai o ka Lahui" (7).

With this perspective in mind, it was only a matter of time before Kānaka confronted the mismanagement and outright desecration of the ʻāina in the years following the illegal overthrow. In the late 1960s and early '70s, Kānaka began to return to the spirit of Nāwahīokalaniopuʻu, questioning their predicament and displacement due to colonialism as they saw high-rises raised, water stolen, and lāhui dismembered. In the battle for Kahoʻolawe, a sacred island off of Maui that was used as a bombing range, along with other lands of sanctuary and ʻāina kapu, Kānaka Maoli remembered that ʻāina is paramount. They then returned to mele to hoʻōla and hoʻomana their moʻolelo via the art of haku mele, providing clear documentation and valid testimony of the Hawaiian experience.

With Kānaka being evicted from their agricultural land in Kalama Valley and Nānākuli in favor of multimillion-dollar homes and hotels, while water was stolen directly from the streams of Waiakāne and Waiāhole, the people of the land began to resist, as documented by Kapuaʻala Sproat (203). From massive protests and political rallies on the capitol and ʻIolani Palace grounds, to steadfast human walls blocking the roads to Waiakāne, Kānaka were united by the mana of aloha ʻāina that was carried via the voice of the people. That voice was a rally of mele, not only channeling the frustrations of the people but the mana and mauli of their moʻolelo. This return to mele as a capturing of experience was the return of Kānaka to their ancestral practice of Paʻa Moʻolelo.

Liko Martin and Thor Wold composed a mele to testify to the displacement and dismemberment of their beloved homeland, Nānākuli. In the "progress" around them, they saw an overwhelming abandonment of their lāhui, as it became more and more impossible to subsist as a Hawaiian. In the chorus they lament, "The beaches they sell to build their hotels, / My fathers and I once knew," the tone soft, as they sing "Nanakuli Blues." Mele declaratively invoking what used to be became a popular theme in Hawai'i's music during the "Hawaiian Renaissance" of the 1970s, and no song articulates more clearly reminiscing about younger days than "Ku'u Home o Kahalu'u." Composed by Jerry Santos of the band Olomana, the mele tells the mo'olelo of many, if not all, Kānaka of Hawai'i—a story of dispossession from one's own homeland. "I remember days when we were younger / We used to catch 'o'opu in the mountain stream" (Santos), implying that "we" could not be able to catch 'o'opu now as "we" once did, due either to the development and canalization of the streams and riverbeds, or to the unmitigated taking and redistributing of the water from the sources deep in the ahupua'a watershed. (For a discussion of the effects of redirecting water sources, see Sproat.) Regardless of the reasons for the change, Jerry Santos channels the adamantly felt message of the people. *This is not okay.*

In that period of mo'olelo revitalization through mele, the mana and mauli were returned to the people. Kānaka Maoli began to take more command of local affairs, new Kanaka-friendly legislation was introduced (Sproat), 'Ōlelo Hawai'i was revitalized and reinstituted in the educational systems via the Pūnana Leo preschools and the University of Hawai'i at Mānoa, the bombing of Kaho'olawe was ended and the island put in trust for a "future Native Hawaiian sovereign entity" (Kaho'olawe Island Reserve Commission), and overall, Kanaka Maoli wellness and consciousness began to return and flourish. Once again, mele propelled the mo'olelo of the people forward, giving all individuals connected to that mo'olelo more mana and mauli to sustain and inspire themselves. From then until now, Kānaka are proud to say that the collective lāhui has continued to document the Kanaka experience, especially in times of need. Even as it addresses the pressing issues of today, the lāhui has found new anthems in the battle against the Thirty Meter Telescope atop Maunakea. Kumu Hinaleimoana Wong of Hālau Lōkahi composed a rallying cry for all Kānaka Maoli, commanding everyone to "Kū Ha'aheo!" [Stand Proud!]. In her first verse, she captures the tumultuous beginnings of civilization in the metaphor of rough seas and the stabbed and bleeding wound of colonization, ending with "Auē ke aloha 'ole a ka malihini!" [Alas! Woeful indeed are the heartless foreigners.] The mele details through kaona the history of Hawai'i's battle against colonialism, with the chorus reminding between each segment of the mo'olelo to "Kū ha'aheo" and to be "māmakakaua"—to band together as warriors. "Kū Ha'aheo," as it is commonly known, became an instant staple atop Maunakea and throughout our community, as hundreds flocked to the mountain to sing their songs of liberation and validate their rights as the Indigenous people of Hawai'i.

To be able to contribute to this moʻokūʻauhau, legacy and genealogy, of haku mele is an honor in and of itself that brings mana and mauli to yourself and your family, but above all to whom or what the mele is composed for. So at the beginning of the Spring 2017 semester, when Professor Kāwika Tengan offered a half joke of sorts about a mele needing to be written for a course, I made sure to keep a journal. Ethnic Studies 455c and its extension 496c summer course were titled "Hawaiian Sovereignty in a Pacific Context." These courses had a simple objective: to create informed Kanaka Maoli leaders and engage them in critical thought in order for them to determine what their "Ea" is. Ea is a word unparalleled in English, articulating and connoting all of the different meanings of life. As defined by Pukui and Elbert, Ea is "1. n. Sovereignty, rule, independence . . . 2. n. Life, air, breath, respiration, vapor, gas; fumes, as of tobacco; breeze, spirit . . . 3. vi. To rise, go up, raise, become erect . . . 4. vi. To smell." This is a very abbreviated list of the various meanings of Ea; to completely understand its many layers of kaona would be a thesis paper on its own. Yet in one simple utterance of the word, the speaker and audience must recognize and understand the full magnitude of Ea. In many ways, the ultimate objective of Kumu Kāwika in this class was to give Ea (breath, life, rising) to the Ea (independence, sovereignty) of each student.

I was enrolled in both the ES455c and ES496c courses, and quite frankly, it is the reason I am writing this essay. Throughout the semester we explored the different connotative and literal meanings of Ea through readings, discussion, and community engagement. The overarching metaphor that Kumu Kāwika presented and impressed on us to be was "Nā Koʻokoʻo," or "The Walking Sticks." A koʻo is also a staff that can be used as a weapon, or as a crutch for those in need of assistance. The idea behind the metaphor was that those who graduated from the course would eventually become koʻokoʻo for the greater lāhui. Kumu Kāwika began to drive this point home by bringing in ʻōlohe lua, master of lua, and cultural specialist ʻUmi Kai to help us in crafting our own koʻokoʻo to koʻo us throughout the semester. This physical manifestation of the koʻokoʻo ultimately led to our better application of the kaona of the metaphor.

The rigorous Nā Koʻokoʻo course forced us, the students, to find a way to koʻo one another. A multitude of readings were due each class, with intense and meaningful discussion expected from each student. Naturally, study groups and friendships began to flourish as we met up after school to discuss how we would tackle the next assignments, and who would be in charge of what reading. Ultimately, this led us to find our roles, however large or small, in the Ea of the class, which translated nicely into our roles in the Ea of our communities. Nā Koʻokoʻo allowed us to find ourselves in each other.

Our community engagement as Nā Koʻokoʻo began in February during our class retreat at the Kamehameha Schools house in Punaluʻu. The first night we had an ʻawa ceremony to consecrate our commitment to each other and to the ea of Nā Koʻokoʻo with the sacred drink of the gods Kāne and Kanaloa. With that spiritual vow, our mauli was thus intertwined in the ea of the course and the mana of each individual present. We were therefore forced into accountability, not only to our classmates, but to our kūpuna as well. That was the beginning of our moʻolelo.

The following day we went to Ka Papa Loʻi o Punaluʻu to work in the loʻi, taro patches, of Punaluʻu. There the workers told us a moʻolelo of accountability—the moʻolelo of Kāneloa, a giant god who liked to peek at others' business. He was often found straddling the ridge of Mauna Pīʻei (literally "Peering Mountain") that runs adjacent to the east side of Ka Papa Loʻi. As he looked down upon the taro farmers and their loʻi he would laugh, because the rows were often planted crooked. This drove deeper into us the demand for excellence: to be the best koʻokoʻo that we could be for each other, and to plant straight rows for our lāhui.

Towards the end of the semester, we embarked on a harsh and physically demanding trek to the island of Kahoʻolawe that turned into a spiritual pilgrimage. On Kahoʻolawe, weather determines everything from the activities we do, to the geographical accessibility of sites, and whether or not we even go. The week we went, a large cloud loomed over Haleakalā and covered Molokaʻi and Lānaʻi, the island of Kanaloa. Kahoʻolawe was in the realm of Kāne—Kāne i ke ao uliuli, i ke ao ʻeleʻele, i ke ao panopano, i ke ao pōpolohua mea a Kāne lā ē. Not to be overlooked, however, is that Kāne is the god of life, Kāne ke akua ola, and in his houpo, his bosom, did we, Nā Koʻokoʻo, ola as koʻo for one another. Upon our hike to the summit, Kāne descended upon us in an ʻawa, a shivering mist, unlike any other. As Kāne's wai ola soaked into our clothes and sunk into the soil, we permeated into each other and steeped our mana and mauli in the enveloping waters of Kāne. It was almost as if we had entered into another ʻawa ceremony, but it was the gods and ʻāina who mixed, strained, and consumed us, consecrating the mana of our moʻolelo, almost as if they were affirming us to be what we set out to be, koʻo for our lāhui.

As Nā Koʻokoʻo, it was only natural that we have a koʻo of our own collective group, something to hoʻopaʻa our mana, our mauli, and our moʻolelo. That opportunity came when Kumu Kāwika approached me after the final week of the semester. I had mentioned to him earlier that I had ideas for a mele, which I kept in both my personal and our class for-credit journal. For the summer, he asked me if I could teach it to the class. With respect, I asked him to take a look at it and see what else he thought should be woven in. We arranged a meeting and he gave some manaʻo. We added a few more place names and allusions to the connections we had made throughout the semester, and included everyone's name, except for those who did not have a Hawaiian name. I characterized them through metaphors. After having Kumu Kāwika's approval, I felt confident enough to present our Mele Inoa, mele of naming, to the class. Here is the mele, along with its analysis, as presented to my fellow Koʻokoʻo:

Kau mai ka noe i ka mālie,
Māʻawe ka lau ahe a ka makani,
Niau ka oeoe hone a nā manu kuahiwi,
Hiwahiwa wale nei ʻāina e hiu nei,
Hei ʻia ka wao o ka naʻauao i ola nā kama,
Lana ka manaʻo, kū wīkani Nā Koʻokoʻo i ka nani aʻo Punaluʻu
Lei ana ka ʻanoʻi pua i ulu makoa,
Kēhau ka Nāulu o Moaʻula,
Lūlū mai ke ahe,
Lau aʻe ka manaʻo,
Aloha wale ʻoe e ka lāhui!
Auē e ka ʻiliʻili e puehu ala,
E ala e ka ʻĪ, ka Mahi, ka Palena,
Nauē pū mai ka ʻōiwi, i ola!
E hū e ka wai mānalo i ʻīnaʻi i oʻu maka,
Ola ka lāhui i ka laukanaka koʻokoʻo
E koʻo ē!
Ā pala lau hala.
E ala e Nā Koʻokoʻo o Mānoa ē!

As mentioned earlier, a love of the land and its unparalleled magnificence and beauty is an essential component to any mele. This one is no exception, as it begins with natural imagery. When we went to gather the waiwī in the uplands of Kahana Valley during our February retreat, there was a soft noe, mist, that uhi, covered, us in the calm of morning. As the ʻĀhiu wind that circumvents the valley wisped by us, the birds awoke and chirped in greeting the new day. The line "Niau ka oeoe hone a nā manu kuahiwi" is where I began to lay the kaona on thick. "Niau" and "oeoe" are situationally specific/exclusive words to describe the silky siren-like sound that echoes off of the pahu drum and its counterpart, the pūniu. These terms are used extensively in the story of Hiʻiakaikapoliopele to describe the voices of Pele's lover, Lohiʻauipo, and his aikāne, Kauakahiapaoa, through their drumming and chanting. They were both very handsome men, praised as the premier hula dancers in all of Hawaiʻi. The words "niau" and "oeoe" have come to represent excellence in voice and sound, in this instance, in the voice of the manu. Manu, birds, also commonly refer metaphorically to people (Silva 66). The "manu kuahiwi," "manu who traverse the uplands," could also be interpreted as us, Nā Koʻokoʻo, as we traveled into the uplands, first asking permission via an oli komo before entering the realm of the gods.

In the aforementioned noe that settled so mālie, we found acceptance by the forces of nature as it awoke and rose around and above us. That is what prompted the next line. "Hiwahiwa wale nei ʻāina e hiu nei" was a natural proclamation. "Hiwahiwa," meaning precious, was also a part of the name of a dear friend of mine in Nā Koʻokoʻo, and "hiu," meaning active or elevated, was an allusion to the ʻĀhiu wind of the area mentioned before. In that captivating moment of revelation, I wanted to ensure that we put mana into the idea of us capturing the knowledge that Kumu Kāwika was generously passing on to us. The word for snaring in Hawaiian is "hei," which brings the imagery of nets, string, and cordage to mind. All were heavy allusions to ʻŌlohe Umi Kai, who worked with us extensively throughout the courses, very often with nets, strings, and cords in weaving and braiding. The line "Hei ʻia ka wao o ka naʻauao i ola nā kama" reminds us of the reason we snare the age of enlightenment: so that the "kama," the offspring, may live. It puts our work in perspective as to what is expected, that is, for the future generations to thrive and prosper.

For these future generations we have high hopes, "lana ka manaʻo." We want them to thrive because we "kū wīkani," stand rigid, in our mana, our mauli, and our moʻolelo, so that they may learn from us and be better. But, more literally, the line "Lana ka manaʻo, kū wīkani Nā Koʻokoʻo i ka nani aʻo Punaluʻu" is the image of us standing strong in Punaluʻu as we first bonded together with hopes for a brighter future. On another note, "Ka Wīkani" and "Kū Wīkani" later came to be a nickname of sorts for Kumu Kāwika, as he stood strong and carried us along the course of our sail. I will elaborate more on this later.

In "Lei ana ka ʻanoʻi pua i ulu makoa," I manage to squeeze in five people's names in eight words—aided by the fact that two people were named Pua, but never mind that. Lei, Kaʻanoʻi, Pua, and Makoa were all students in the course, so the line is actually symbolic of the joining of people. It is to say that we, the ʻanoʻi pua, were strung as a lei together by our ancestors to grow together to be makoa, which is to be brave and warrior-esque. Yet within the imagery in the mele, makoa takes on a different meaning—being wet. The idea of becoming soaked in rain became a running theme and joke amongst our hui. We were literally covered by the ʻawa and kēhau Nāulu of Kahoʻolawe, ending up wearing 3 Mil trash bags to keep us from freezing in the high winds and endless rain of Kahoʻolawe. Now whenever we meet up, if there is even the slightest drizzle, someone will call for the 3 Mil bags. Due to this lasting impression, we make a reference to the kēhau Nāulu of Moaʻula, the highest point of elevation on the island of Kahoʻolawe. Nāulu is also recognized as a lei of clouds and rain that joins Maui, Kahoʻolawe, Molokaʻi, and Lanaʻi. A story often told to me during my years of going to Kahoʻolawe is of ceremonies being held simultaneously on each island, calling for the Lei Nāulu to embrace and give life to the islands. This mele gives mana to that moʻolelo in our reference to the Nāulu.

Many moʻolelo concerning the akua lay out protocols for how humans may approach them. Often the protocol is quite simply not to approach them—to steer clear of them at all costs. In some cases, such as the moʻolelo of Lāʻieikawai (Haleole) and modern-day encounters with Madam Pele, there is a detailed protocol and some overlap. One such overlap stressed hard in both cases is to approach "ma ka lulu," from the opposite way from which the wind blows. My best guess is this is to hoʻohaʻahaʻa, make humble—the lesser kanaka meeting with the greater akua. "Lūlū mai ke ahe" came to mind in recalling our approach to the Koʻa Nāulu on top of Moaʻula. The wind blew against a small group of us as we approached the sacred altar. During our ceremony the ʻawa only grew thicker, as Kāne heard our prayers. Some offered wai from where they were from, and others offered mele that they felt were appropriate. As a Moʻolono in training in the Makahiki practice on Kahoʻolawe, I opened and closed the space, acknowledging the blessings that enveloped us and those yet to come, while also recognizing that our manaʻo had "Lau aʻe" due to the mana and mauli which Kahoʻolawe had restored within us. "Lau aʻe ka manaʻo" is a play on the idea of "lana ka manaʻo" which is to be hopeful, but "Lau aʻe" is a reference to the wind, since "ka lau makani" is a popular term for the multitude of winds, just as "lau ahe" is in the second line. Lauaʻe is also a popular indigenous fern in Hawaiʻi that grows really fast, just as our pilgrimage to Kahoʻolawe had forced us to koʻo really fast.

Through the growth we shared, we wanted to ensure that we always act with aloha and in an effort to koʻo the collective lāhui. "Aloha wale ʻoe e ka lāhui" is a call to arms, just as Kumu Larry Kauanoe Kimura's "Ke Au Hawaiʻi" calls to our people. It is for that reason that I paraphrased his oli in the two lines, "Auē ka ʻiliʻili e puehu ala / E ala e ka ʻĪ, ka Mahi, ka Palena." His oli begins with the line, "Auē nā aliʻi ē o ke au i hala," as he, like nā haku mele a "Kuʻu Home o Kahaluʻu," "Nanakuli Blues," a me "The Beauty of Maunakea," reminisces about and laments the ages and kūpuna that have passed (Silva xiii). Kumu Kauanoe's oli also refers to a kahua, a base or platform, that is unstable. He talks about the ʻiliʻili being gusted by the winds, and he encourages us to "paepae hou" or rebuild our kahua so that we may "hoʻolulu" or sow our seeds. He then calls on all factions of Kamehameha's former army, the families ʻĪ, Mahi, and Palena, whom he symbolically summons as all people of the lāhui. This is the mana that I was looking to summon in those lines, with the addition of one more family, "Nauē pū mai ka ʻōiwi i ola," inviting all Indigenous peoples into our collective battle against colonialism.

We then call upon the fresh waters to burst from the earth and give life to our vision. "E hū e ka wai mānalo i ʻīnaʻi i oʻu maka." Makainai and Mānalo are the last names of two koʻokoʻo, and the imagery here of fresh water to the face, for me, represents the best way to wake up. In the awakening of the lāhui, we must koʻo each other.

Ola ka lāhui i ka laukanaka koʻokoʻo
E koʻo ē
Ā pala lau hala
E ala e Nā Koʻokoʻo o Mānoa ē!

This is a very straightforward call to our people to support one another until we perish, or as the esteemed aloha ʻāina of the late nineteenth century James Keauiluna Kaulia put it, "a hiki i ke aloha aina hope loa" (5).

After Nā Koʻokoʻo learned the oli, we used it everywhere we went—on our visit to the ʻIolani Palace and to Hanakēhau Farms, and to greet and mahalo our various guest speakers. It was an honor to compose such a mele for such a powerful group of individuals whom I shared numerous connections and a lifetime of aloha with. To be able to immortalize our moʻolelo, solidifying the mana and mauli of our connections, is the highlight of being a Koʻokoʻo for me. Carrying on the legacy of Paʻa Moʻolelo through the "Mele Koʻokoʻo," we repatriate our mana and mauli as Kānaka with our own moʻolelo in the twenty-first century. During the last week of our official time together during the summer, I began to reflect on all of our experiences, especially those which I shared intimately with Kumu Kāwika. I came to a realization that he was truly the greatest kumu, ka heke o nā kumu, and I felt like he deserved to be recognized as such. To be able to orchestrate the logistics of the course, with two guest speakers a month during the Spring semester, along with many events on the weekends! Then during the summer, when we had three speakers a week, along with a full afternoon itinerary of events to engage with the community, and then camping on the weekends! The madness never ended. And after making sure that everyone was where they were supposed to be, he then made it all make sense, ensuring that the knowledge spread into the air by guest speakers became ʻike that was paʻa in our naʻau.

Kumu Kāwika Tengan is a man of extraordinary character and fortitude. He carried this course like no other could. He enabled us to become a moʻolelo, in that we grew mana and mauli. We were cut down, stripped of our bark, sanded, stained, oiled, and strapped to become Koʻokoʻo, all by the hands of Ka Wīkani, the greater Koʻokoʻo of us all. With that in mind, during our final presentations, I along with a two of my fellow Koʻokoʻo, Kaleihiwahiwaokalani Kaʻapuni and Kamaliʻi McShane-Padilla, wanted to present him with a mele and hula. I composed the mele and they arranged the hula, and we performed it for him in front of all of the distinguished guests that came to our final Hōʻike, so that all recognized him as ka heke o nā kumu.

I will end this brief essay with his mele inoa, as a mahalo to him for providing us with this incredible opportunity.

He aloha ʻoe e Ka Wīkani,
Ka heke nō ʻoe o nā kumu

Kū nō i ka pali kūhōhō
O ke awāwa o Kahana

ʻO ka hana nō ia a ke koʻokoʻo
I paʻa pono ke kahua hoʻolūlū

Nou nō ke koʻo kū ā holo
I ke au wili ahi aʻo Kanaloa

Loa nō ke ala a ka Mua
A he alahula kā ka moʻopuna

Nākolokolo e ka lani hākuʻi
ʻO ke awa haki ʻole i uhi maila

Puana ka mana, eō mai ʻoe
E Ka Wīkani, ka heke o nā kumu

Haʻina hou ʻia me ke aloha
E ola Ka Wīkani ā mau loa

He inoa no Ka Wīkani

NOTES

1. For a discussion of mana and its maintenance, see Krug in this collection.
2. For further discussion, see Lopes in this collection.
3. Translation by author.

WORKS CONSULTED

Beamer, Keola. "The Beauty of Maunakea." *Hawaiian Slack Key Guitar in the Real Old Style.* The Mountain Apple Company, January 1, 1972.

Blount, James H. "Report of U.S. Special Commissioner James H. Blount to U.S. Secretary of State Walter Q. Gresham Concerning the Hawaiian Kingdom Investigation." Honolulu, 17 July 1893.

de Silva, Kahikina K. *Iwiwkuamoʻo o ka Lāhui: Nā Manaʻo Aloha ʻĀina i nā Mele Nahenahe o ka Lāhui Hawaiʻi.* 2018. University of Hawaiʻi at Mānoa, PhD dissertation.

de Silva, Kīhei. "Hole Waimea." [Haku Mele: The Warriors of the Kīpuʻupuʻu.] Kaʻiwakī-

loumoku: Hawaiian Cultural Center. Kamehameha Schools. https://kaiwakiloumoku
.ksbe.edu/article/mele-hole-waimea.

Goodyear-Kaʻōpua, Noelani, Ikaika Hussey, and Erin Kahunawaikaʻala Wright. *A Nation Rising: Hawaiian Movements for Life, Land, and Sovereignty.* Duke UP, 2014.

Haleole, S. N. *Ke Kaao o Laieikawai, Ka Hiwahiwa o Paliuli, Kawahineokaliula.* Henry M. Whitney, 1863.

Hoʻomanawanui, Kuʻualoha. *Voices of Fire: Reweaving the Literary Lei of Pele and Hiʻiaka.* First Peoples: New Directions in Indigenous Studies, U of Minnesota P, 2014.

Hoʻoulumāhiehie. *Ka Moʻolelo o Hiʻiakaikapoliopele. Ka Wahine i ka hikina a ka lā, ka uʻi pale-koki uila o Halemaʻumaʻu.* Unuhi ʻia a paʻi hou ʻia mai e, modernized and translated by M. Puakea Nogelmeier. Awaiaulu, 2006.

Kahoʻolawe Island Reserve Commission. *Kūkulu ke Ea a Kanaloa Kahoʻolawe.* The KIRC Team, 2017.

Kaulia, James Keauiluna. "Haiolelo a James Keauiluna Kaulia." *Ke Aloha Aina,* vol. 3, no. 37, 11 September 1897, pp. 4–5.

Kimura, Larry Kauanoe. "Ke Au Hawaiʻi." In *The Power of the Steel-Tipped Pen: Recon-structing Native Hawaiian Intellectual History,* by Noenoe K. Silva. Duke UP, 2017, p. xiii.

Lopes, Robert Keawe, Jr. *Ka Waihona a ke Aloha: Ka Papahana Hoʻoheno Mele: An interactive resource center for the promotion, preservation and perpetuation of mele and mele practitio-ners.* Hawaiian Pacific Collection, Hamilton Library, University of Hawaiʻi at Mānoa, 2010.

Martin, Liko, and Thor Wold. "Nānākuli Blues." *Surfin' Bay Blues.* Performed by Liko Martin and Friends. Self-produced, 2014. CD.

[Nāwahīokalaniopuʻu, Joseph.] "Ke Aloha Aina; Heaha ia?" *Ke Aloha Aina,* vol. 1, no. 1, 25 May 1895, p. 7.

Osorio, Jonathan Kay Kamakawiwoʻole. "Haku Mele as Poetry." Hawaiian Studies 107. University of Hawaiʻi at Mānoa. Fall 2016. Lecture.

Poepoe, Joseph M. "Ka Moolelo Kaao o Hiiaka-i-ka-Poli-o-Pele." *Kuokoa Home Rula,* vol. 6, no. 2, 10 January 1908 to vol. 9, no. 3, 20 January 1911.

Prendergast, Ellen Kehoʻohiwaokalani Wright. "Kaulana Nā Pua" [Famous are the Flowers]. *Huapala: Hawaiian Music and Hula Archives.* https://www.huapala.org/Kau/Kaulana_Na_Pua.html.

Pukui, Mary Kawena. "How Legends Were Taught." *Hawaiian Ethnographic Notes,* vol. 1, 1602–1606. Bishop Museum Archives, pp. 1–5. http://kumukahi-online.net/haku-olelo -331/na-kumu-ike/mokuna-iv---moolelo-kaao/pukui---how-legends-were.pdf.

Pukui, Mary Kawena, and Samuel H. Elbert. *Hawaiian Dictionary, Hawaiian-English, English-Hawaiian,* rev. and enlarged ed. U of Hawaiʻi P, 1986.

Santos, Jerry. "Kuʻu Home ʻo Kahaluʻu." *Like a Seabird in the Wind.* Seabird Sound Inc., 1976.

Silva, Noenoe K. *The Power of the Steel-Tipped Pen: Reconstructing Native Hawaiian Intel-lectual History.* Duke UP, 2017.

Sproat, D. Kapuaʻala. "A Question of Wai: Seeking Justice Through Law for Hawaiʻi's

Streams and Communities." In *A Nation Rising: Hawaiian Movements for Life, Land, and Sovereignty*, edited by Noelani Goodyear-Kaʻōpua, Ikaika Hussey, and Erin Kahunawaikaʻala Wright. Duke UP, 2014, pp. 199–219.

Wong, Hinaleimoana. "Kū Haʻaheo E Kuʻu Hawaiʻi." *Kumu Hina—Ku Haʻaheo on Mauna Kea*. YouTube, April 10, 2015. https://www.youtube.com/watch?v=q-UB3XwiPzs.

Kaipulaumakaniolono, MFA, hails from the Pali Hāuliuli o ke Koʻolau, the verdant Kahaluʻu, Oʻahu in the center of the Hawaiʻi archipelago. His studies in the MFA for Hawaiian Theatre program at UH Mānoa culminated in staging his thesis production *He Leo Aloha* (2021), which garnered eight national awards by the Kennedy Center American Theatre Festival and has been invited to play at both the *Reflections of Native Voices* and *Hana Keaka* theatre festivals in New York and Hilo, respectively. Kaipu is a practicing Moʻolono of the Makahiki practice on Kanaloa with the Protect Kahoʻolawe ʻOhana. His current research centers around the ideological development of aloha ʻāina and the function of Hoʻomana (Hawaiian religious practices) as a subjectivizing apparatus that interpellates and posits Kānaka into substantial subjectivities that allow them to divorce themselves from the chaotic "being-for-self" Noa of occupation. In addition to his academic work, Kaipu composes Hawaiian chant and poetry. His vocal talents were featured at the *Art of the Chanter* (2017) and his latest compositions are available on Nā Palapalai's *Back to the Patch* (2019) and Ikaakamai's *I Kuanoʻo* (2020).

'Auʻa ʻia calls on us to learn, preserve, and retain our moʻolelo, mele, oli, hula, ʻōlelo, and ʻāina, for these are the foundation and source of our identity as Kānaka Maoli.

8

Hana Keaka

Staging Moʻolelo as a Political Statement

Tammy Hailiʻōpua Baker

Aia Lāʻieikawai
I ka uka wale lā o Paliuli
ʻO ka nani, ʻo ka nani,
Helu ʻekahi o ia uka.

Hui: E nanea e walea ana paha,
I ka leo nahenahe o nā manu,
E nanea, e walea ana paha,
I ka leo nahenahe o na manu.

Kau mai Lāʻieikawai,
I ka ʻēheu lā o nā manu,
ʻO ka nani, ʻo ka nani,
Helu ʻekahi o Paliuli.

Ua lohe paha i ka hone mai,
ʻO ka pū lauʻī o Maliʻo,
Honehone, honehone,
Helu ʻekahi o Hōpoe. (Meheʻula 131)

Theatre: A Tool for Storytelling

Historically the theatre has been a place for storytelling. Steeped in ritual practices and seasonal celebrations, traditional theatre performances around the world served as social institutions for their nations. Early Greek and Roman theatre festivals were tied to religious rituals that honored particular gods through the performance of drama, chant, dance, and song (Wilson and Goldfarb 19). The Japanese form of Nō drama derives from Shinto religious practices that when performed honor the gods and ancestral stories through dramatization. This form of theatre combines mime, dance, poetry, and song, each form transcending the others in turn "to produce…an experience of profundity and almost religious exhilaration" for the audience (Rimer and Masakazu xvii). In India, Sanskrit dramas are linked to rituals and mythology informed by cultural aesthetics and Hindu beliefs (Brockett and Hildy 607–608). African theatre considers language, song, and story as the pillars of its form. Ngũgĩ Wa Thiong'o, Kenyan activist, scholar, and playwright, asserts that the performance of African stories in their language is an act of decolonization and Indigenous community empowerment.

In America, individual Native American tribal communities establish the standards of their traditional drama (Huntsman x–xii). The performance of Native American creation stories communicates religious beliefs, ethics, and proper behavior while honoring ancestors. Chicano theatre, as exemplified by El Teatro Campesino, draws from the oral tradition of storytelling. When dramatized, these stories "personify culture-bound relationships reflecting fundamental concepts of mankind, god, and the universe" (Broyles-González 89). And in the Pacific, storytelling is a common practice and pastime, often accompanied by song and dance. Performing or retelling traditional stories is the root of Pacific theatre praxis (Baker, Looser, and Maser). In *Remaking Pacific Pasts: History, Memory, and Identity in Contemporary Theatre from Oceania*, Diana Looser writes:

> Communicating stories of the past in many different forms has always been a way for communities to educate, to entertain, and to remember; to maintain and reinvent cultural heritage; to produce, perpetuate, and challenge cultural norms; and to guide future behavior. (13)

Theatre therefore fulfills a significant civic and social function. Though varied iterations of dramatic form may exist throughout the world, the central component embraced by all is the communication of story or myth. The theatre is a tool for storytelling that may be employed to educate the masses or simply entertain the populace. The theatre has also been employed as an apparatus to promote a political agenda, to sway public opinion, or to present cultural values and worldview.

The medium or language of a particular performance also undoubtedly determines its audience, making a clear statement about intention and identity. Aboriginal playwright and novelist Tomson Highway notes that to be heard by a large audience, Native playwrights tend to write in English. He believes, however, that his language, Cree, which he prefers to write in, "is so completely different and the world view that the language engenders and expresses is so completely different," that a distinct theatrical experience results (2). Since language or the medium of a production speaks so strongly about the playwright's intentions, it is especially worthy of analysis in certain political and social contexts—most notably for me, in Indigenous nations colonized by the west. Later in this essay, the function and intention of performance in Hawai'i at the end of the nineteenth century will be revisited by taking a closer look at a particular Hawaiian theatrical production of that time.

Haʻi Moʻolelo: Hawaiian Storytelling

The term haʻi moʻolelo or haʻi kaʻao identifies the particular forms of storytelling in Hawaiʻi. Moʻolelo are the historical, factual stories, whereas kaʻao, though based on historical events, may add a fanciful flair or embellishments to the retelling of those kinds of stories (Baker, "Constructing" 122). Esteemed Hawaiian elder and scholar Mary Kawena Pukui describes the training for a paʻa moʻolelo (storyteller) in her ʻohana (family) as an arduous task that involved intense focus and impeccable memorization ("How" 2–3). This training traditionally began at an early age. For Mrs. Pukui, her grandmother would tell her a story, and then she would need to recite exactly what she heard. There were consequences for leaving details out or getting something wrong, because moʻolelo carry the history of one's moʻokūʻauhau (genealogy), one's ʻāina (land), one's aliʻi (chief), one's akua (god), and ultimately one's lāhui (nation, race, tribe, people, nationality). As a cultural informant and scholar at the Bishop Museum, Mrs. Pukui also recorded interviews with kūpuna who practiced haʻi moʻolelo. These interviews and Mrs. Pukui's recitation of moʻolelo and kaʻao give us glimpses into the practice of haʻi moʻolelo in times past. Paʻa moʻolelo were known for their ability to recite historical events, genealogies, and epic chants. These individuals were well-respected orators, or kākāʻōlelo, in Hawaiian society.

Written accounts by Kānaka Maoli such as those of John Papa ʻĪʻī, an influential member in the aloaliʻi (royal court) of Kauikeaouli, Kamehemeha III, are another resource that aids our understanding of pre-western contact performance of storytelling. ʻĪʻī mentions frequent gatherings on Oʻahu referred to as Lōkū, nights of entertainment that existed prior to 1810. These Lōkū included "hula dances, chants, the recitation of narratives in chant form, and the telling of legends" (64). A common thread in haʻi moʻolelo, found in ʻĪʻī's accounts and Pukui's documentation of this performance form, is the inclusion of oli (chant) and mele (song) to communicate particular elements of a story. Often animated in its presentation, haʻi moʻolelo may also incorporate other traditional performance forms to communicate a story.

The following is a list of traditional Hawaiian performance forms, ritual and secular, practiced here in the Hawaiian archipelago prior to western contact:

| Haʻa | A dance with bent knees; dancing; called hula after the mid-1800s |
| Haʻi Moʻolelo/ Kaʻao | Storytelling |

Ho'opāpā	Oratory; a contest in wit (such as riddling) or strength
Hula	Dance driven by lyrics, often accompanied by instruments
Hula Ki'i	Dance of images by performers, or with wooden puppets similar to marionettes; Hawaiian puppetry
Lua	Hawaiian martial arts
Mele	Song, anthem, lyrics, or chant of any kind; poem, poetry; to sing
Oli	Chant that was not danced to; especially with prolonged phrases chanted in one breath, often with a trill ('i'i) at the end of each phrase; to chant thus
Pule	Prayer, magic spell, incantation, blessing, grace; to pray, worship, say grace, to ask for a blessing

With varying degrees of fluency, these forms continue to be practiced today in the Hawaiian community. I will further assert that these forms, often in combination, are the foundations of an Indigenous Hawaiian theatre aesthetic. At the turn of the twentieth century, Nathaniel B. Emerson, son of Protestant missionary Reverend John S. Emerson, wrote a text on Hawaiian performance entitled *Unwritten Literature of Hawaii*. Primarily focused on hula, this book is the earliest, and still one of the most comprehensive looks at Hawaiian performance. Emerson writes that "The hula ki'i was, perhaps, the nearest approximation made by the Hawaiians to a genuine dramatic performance" (92). But he never mentions ha'i mo'olelo or the dramatization of mo'olelo that would align with the typical presentational western theatre he would have known. Perhaps he was not exposed to these performance forms.

Hana Keaka: The Development of Hawaiian Theatre

Hana keaka is the Hawaiian term for theatre. The concept may or may not be an Indigenous Hawaiian form—an issue to be debated in a future publication. But the form exists, and that is what will be explored here. The goal of this section is to establish an historical account of the practice of hana keaka by Kānaka Maoli or Native Hawaiians. There is currently a dearth of research and scholarship about hana keaka. Most modern-day publications pertaining to theatre in Hawai'i draw from English language resources, resulting in a limited view of what actually existed. For this chapter, I draw from the wealth of knowledge printed in the Hawaiian language newspapers from 1834 to 1948—a repository virtually unexplored regarding the practice of hana keaka.

During the time period referred to as the "monarchy period"—from 1810 to the turn of the nineteenth century—ʻŌlelo Hawaiʻi (Hawaiian language) was the primary medium of communication amongst citizens living here. Hawaiians and many Hawaiian nationals were fluent in the language. ʻŌlelo Hawaiʻi was the language of business, politics, law, church, scholarly activities, and so on. The official status of the Hawaiian language in the judicial, legislative, and cultural activities of the time is confirmed by legal documents, land surveys, and the multitude of newspapers. The many Hawaiian language newspapers eventually created a repository of over 125,000 closely printed pages (Nogelmeier 64). The language was thriving and so were the arts. From 1834 into the early 1900s, the Hawaiian language newspapers document a variety of performance forms from all over the world, presented in outdoor venues and in the theatres located in downtown Honolulu. The first permanent theatre, The Thespian, was built in 1847, with a royal box for Kauikeaouli, Kamehameha III (Angell 9). Over the next fifty years, five more mainstream theatres were built in Honolulu. Most were constructed near ʻIolani Palace and in the area now known as downtown Honolulu.

The newspapers regularly advertised a wide range of hana keaka presented in Hawaiʻi. Articles and letters to the editors further substantiate the presence of a theatre community and drama connoisseurs. The performance forms documented included Keaka Pākē (Chinese theatre), Keaka Kepanī (Japanese theatre), Keaka hololio (equestrian shows), Keaka Farani (French theatre), Keaka mele Ikalia (Italian opera), and numerous touring hana keaka companies from America, Britain, New Zealand, and Australia. Occasionally, these productions even toured to the neighbor islands of Maui and Kauaʻi. These performances had varying degrees of success. An article published in *Ka Makaainana* on 13 May 1895 states:

> Aia ma alanui Maunakea, kokoke ia alanui Beritania, he hale keaka Kepani. E ikeia no ia wahi e na hae lole waihooluu loloa e kuuwelu ana i ka makani. Na kekahi Kepani me kekahi pahu e hookani ai, a e paa ana he laau ohe loihi me ka lepa e welo ana me na huapalapala, oia ka hoike a me ka hoolaha no ka hana keaka. Aole ka i holopono loa na hoohanaia ana iho nei, nolaila, ua hoopau a paniia. (3)

> [On Maunakea street, near Beritania, there's a Japanese theatre. This place can be recognized by the long colorful flags dangling in the wind. A Japanese individual plays a drum, and a long bamboo with a banner flutters with the words advertising the details for the play. Nonetheless, it was not successful, so it is done, the theatre has been closed.]

Apparently the advertisements, though bold and creative, did not entice enough patrons: that particular Japanese theatre failed. It seems however that other theatres were thriving in Honolulu, even if they too were not always appealing to the ears of some. Later that same year, several individuals write in to *Ka Makaainana*, complaining about the loud noise coming from the Chinese theatre on ʻAʻala Street. Some letters detail the ruckus near River Street at length; others are short and to the point:

> Nui loa ka uluhua o ka poe e noho nei ma Aala no ka hana kuli mau o na mea kani o ka hale keaka Pake i na po a pau. Aohe io aku la no e nele. ("Kela me Keia" 8)

> [Many who live in ʻAʻala are extremely frustrated by the obnoxious deafening sounds of the Chinese theatre each and every night. Truly no shortage (of noise).]

Clearly, Hawaiians and the citizens of Hawaiʻi were familiar with a variety of performing arts during the monarchy period. At least two Asian forms had their own theatres, adding to the landscape of production that the western theatre establishments offered in Honolulu. It seems reasonable to assume that Kānaka Maoli ventured into these theatrical spaces, contributing to the tapestry of theatre that evolved here, and in fact, abundant evidence shows that this was indeed the case. Kānaka Maoli participated in, and more importantly, created their own plays and musical productions, called hana keaka. These events occurred even as the traditional forms of performance Indigenous to Hawaiʻi continued to be performed, providing a foundation for the development of hana keaka.

The following excerpt from *Nupepa Kuokoa* in 1902 not only confirms the participation of Kānaka Maoli in theatre, but also describes the kinds of stories that they chose to dramatize. The headline reads, "Na Keaka mai na moolelo kahiko mai" (Plays/theatre from the stories of old), followed by "Ke hoomakaukau nei kekahi mau keiki Hawaii no ke keaka ana mai" (Hawaiian youths are rehearsing/preparing for a theatrical presentation). The author of this article records the joy and support of the Hawaiian community for the efforts of these enthusiastic young thespians:

> Ke hauoli nei makou i ka ike ana i keia mau keiki Hawaii e hooikaika ana e hana i keia hana, oiai he hana ia e mau ai ka hoomanao ia ana o kekahi o na moolelo maikai o kakou mai kahiko mai e like me Laieikawai, ka Moolelo nohoi o Kapena Kuke, Lohiau, ame Kaala. ("Na Keaka" 1)

[We are overjoyed to see these Hawaiian youths committing to endeavor in this kind of work, since it's a way to maintain the recollection of some of the great stories of our past like Laieikawai, the story of Captain Cook, Lohiau, and Kaala.]

This excerpt mentions four different hana keaka in the Kanaka Maoli theatrical repertoire of the time. I am confident that with more research other hana keaka will surface.

These Kānaka Maoli selected particular moʻolelo at particular times to serve a purpose. In her book *Aloha Betrayed: Native Hawaiian Resistance to American Colonialism*, Kanaka Maoli scholar Noenoe K. Silva talks about the establishing of Hawaiian written, edited, and published newspapers as a form of "anticolonial resistance" (55). By publishing traditional moʻolelo, songs, and incantations in the newspapers that Kānaka Maoli read widely during this period, Hawaiian identity is firmly asserted. Dr. Silva's research leads me to ponder the selection and intention of a specific moʻolelo produced as a hana keaka in 1893. Three months after the overthrow of our Aupuni Mōʻī, Hawaiian Kingdom, the Hui Keaka Hawaii Ponoi produces a hana keaka for Laieikawai at the Hale Mele Hou, or New Opera House, makai of ʻIolani Palace on King Street.

The production ran for five weeks, and was the subject of many advertisements and articles in both *Ka Leo o ka Lahui* and *Ka Makaainana* newspapers. *Ka Leo o ka Lahui* published a very positive article on April 24, 1893, with many accolades for the accomplishments of the Hawaiian theatre troupe:

> Maikai ka hana Keaka o ka Poaono nei, maloko o ka Hale Mele Hou, Ua pii ka makaukau o ka Puali Keaka Hawaiʻi Ponoi, a ua kuupau ia mai ka nani o na hana a ka wahine o ka Liula. Mahalo a nui ia oukou a ka Hui Keaka Hawaii, i ko oukou holomua ma keia hana e hoomau aku ma keia Alanui. ("Nuhou" 3)

> [The play this Saturday was excellent, at the New Opera House, the Hawaiian thespian warriors have increased their skill, performed with no inhibitions the beauty of the woman of twilight. Much gratitude to the Hawaiian theatre company, thank you for the progress you've made in this field, continue on this path.]

In *Nupepa Puka La Kuokoa*, someone writes that the house was filled to capacity to see a production composed and performed by "na Hawaii Maoli," or authentic Hawaiians, and although the story line wasn't seamless, the audience never complained because of the impressive performance by the cast ("Na Poe" 3). Given the context of newspaper politics, the comments in this paper are

HOIKEIKE NUI.

MA KA

HALE MELE HOU.

I Keia Ahiahi

POAONO,

E

Haawi Mua Loa ai ka
HUI HANA KEAKA
HAWAII PONOI.

Ka Hiona Nani Lua Ole

O KE

Kaikamahine Ui

O

PALIULI

O

LAIEIKAWAI.

Iluna o ka Eheu o na
Manu, ka mea hoi
i Oleloia ua like

Kona Ui me ka
LIULA o ke Ahiahi.

Kahauokapaka

A ME

Malaekahana,

Na Luani o ka Ui
Laieikawai a
me ko Laua
Hale.

AIWOHIKIPUA,

E Hee ana i ka Nalu o Puna, a
me Kona mau kaikuahine
MAILE

A ME

KAHALAOMAPUANA

Poliahu,

Ka Wahine Noho
Kuahiwi

Maunakea,

Hooko o kona aapa hau
Kaomohiokala.

Ka Ui o Kealohilani

I hai malule ai ka puuwai o na
Kaikamahine Ui oia mau la.

Hauailiki,

KE KAEAEA O KA AINA
KAILI LA.

He Nanea Welehia iloko o na La o
Noho Alii
ANA O

Kauakahialii

A ME

Kana Aliiwahine

Kaililauokekoa.

Na Kii Pena ia o na Wahi Kaulana
o keia Poe i noho ai—Ka Hale o
ka Makua o

Laieikawai,

Ka Poe Mua ana mai
O

KAPENA KUKE

A ME

Kona Make Ana.

Ma Maisekahana, Koolauloa—Ka
Puu Kaulana o Kauwiki, a me
ka Heiau ma Hana—Kiowai o
Waiapuka kahi i huna ia ai o
Laieikawai ma Laie.

Kiowai kapu o Palinli iloko o ka
Mokulehua o Panaewa.

Ke kuahiwi o Maunakea ka Home
noho o ka Eheu

Poliahu.

He Nani na hana a pau e hoike ia
mai ana.

O KA UKU KOMO HE $0.50, $0.75, A
ME $1.00.

apr5 4ted.

NA LETA.

Aole o makou makomake e lawe i ke
kokoi o na hala no na manao i hoopuka
iwaenakio o keia poe e ka makou poe
kakau manao.

HE HOOHUOI.

Heaha, a no keaha ke kumu o
ka hoohuoi? wahi a ka mea ninau. Eia: O na wahi inoa o makou i kakau ai ma ka buke, iloko
o na makahiki i hala, ua ke ano,
he mea hoa a he mau lala hoi no
ka hui hoole waiona a libine holu
hoi. Eia aku nei ia ihea ua mau
inoa nei o makou? Eia ae no pa-
lia i na Peresidena mikanele a makou, i ole, ua helo pu aku nei paha i Wasinetona me W. R. Kakela
ma i ka hoohui nina?

Oia ke kumu o ka hoohuoi la,
ulu ae nei, a haluuape i ko'u hou-

po; wahi a kekahi hoa o ka libine
boia, a laia hoi o ka hui hoole waiona.

Ae, he kumu maikai no kena e
ka hoohuoi, aoa; wahi hoi a ka ninau. Aka, ua hele anei oe e ninau
ke oukou Peresidena, no ua buke
inoa nei o kakou, kahi a oukou i
haawi makapo, naaupo ai i na inoa
o oukou?

Aole au i hele e ninau, wahi a ka
pane.

E hele hoole hoi ha oe e ninau,
maopopole mai ka oiaio; malia
aia no ke moe malie la na inoa o
oukou iloko o ka pahu hao Sekotia,
alaila, nohe olelo ana, he hooliuu
wale no. A ina e hoolulau ia mai
ena ea, alaila e manao iho oe, ua
hao ia a ka Inuwai o Lehua na ne-
ne o oukou, aia ke pili ka ma'alo o
ke poo, hoohui aupuni. He haupa
wale no nae hoi keia.

O ka mea e pau loa ai keia hoohuoi e ka lehulehu; o kahea keia
a me keia la o ka hui hoole waiona
a pau, o halawai lakou, a e laweia
mai ka buke inoa o oukou, kahi a
oukou i kakau ai, a e nana pono
iho na maka.

Heaua la? Nawai hoi ka hewa
o ka mea maikai, e hoopuiia ai ke
na olepu hoole waino.

HOOLE WAIONA.

Hilo, Hawaii.

HAALELE KA POE LAWE I
KE KUOKOA.

Ma ke ku ana mai o ka moku
ahi Kinau, me ke kakahiaka o
Poakolu nei, ua loaa mai ia ko mau
Leta mai Hawaii mai a me Maui;
eia na manao ano nui.

Mr. Luna Hooponopono, o ka
Nupepa Ka "OIAIO," a me "KA LEO
O KA LAHUI" Aloha oe:—

E noi aku ana makou i kou oluolu, ina e hiki ke hana ia pela, oia
hoi, e hoouui ia a'e ke kino o ka
Nupepa Oiaio, nona ka auhau elua
dala o ka makahiki.

Oiai hoi, o ka poe e lawe nei i ka
Nupepa Kuokoa, ua pau loa i ka
haalele, aole he hoinoi, a i ka ike
ana i ka Nupepa ka "OIAIO," ua
nui ka hauoli, a o ka lakou noi
wale no ia, ke hiki mae, i pau pono
ai ua mea apau i hoopuka ia iloko
o ka "Leo."

Ma keia mau Leta a na makamaka, ua ike makou i ke ohohia o
ka lahui mai o a o o ka Aina.

Aka, e na' makamaka a me na
hoa'loha, o ko oukou leo nonoi i ka
Luna Hooponopono o KA "LEO" a
me KA "OIAIO," no ka hoomahua-
bua ana a'e i ke kino o ka kakou
hiwahiwa, e hooo ia ana no, ke loaa
ka wa pono.

Oiai hoi, eia la ua le'i kakou,
ka, ua laua ko makou manao e
hiki ana no ke hooko ia.

Nolaila, inui ke aho, a hiki mai
ke kupu lai.

E au aua ipu aloha o Ka OIAIO, a
me KA LEO, ke iki waie no keia la,
he nui ko Lehuua i ke kau pun ke
moni aku, a ka hookeikei puhala
a'e keia a'e ia, he olohaka aloko
pehea laia, e ua hoa'loha nei?

NUHOU KULOKO.

Na ka Hana Lahui e kokua ana i
ka Hui Keaka Laieikawai.

Nui ka aihue o keia mau la o
hele nei, kai no hoi e meemaoo ana
ia mea ma a'e nei e liki nei.

Ua haawiia mai nei ka Papa Ola
he $4.50 e ka paona no na paona
Opiuma i hoe e waiho nei iloko o
ka Halewai.

Ua lohe mai makou o ka Poai
Puhi Oho Hawaii ponoi ke liki ai
ana me ka Hana Keaka a ka Hoi
Hana Keaka Hawaii ma keia ahi
ahi Poaono, ma ka Hale Mele Hou

Ua hoike mai nei o Mr. Bele o
Waimea Hawaii ia makou no ka
hoaa ole ana aku o ka Nupepa Kuokoa i lakou ala i ka pule i hala,
a na manao wale ia, na inoi loa aku
nei paha ia Kakina ma i Amerika.

Nui ka umhalo o na keaaka ;
kahi welu Kuokoa puka ia, no ka
hoolawa pono ana' aku i ka lakou
mau wahi keena hooleina me kona
mau papalina palupala. E aho ia
loaa ka mea nana e hoiahelu mai.

Ua lohe ia mai ua papa aku nei
ka Papa Kinaiahi o Honolulu nei
i na hoa a pau o ka Ohana Kinaiahi aole 'e kau i kekahi hooiloiloo
Aloha Aina maluno o lakou. E hoo-
manawanui e na hoa iloko o keia
mau hana hoopilikua.

O Mr. J. A. Magoon kai pani
aku ia ma kahi o ka Loio Kuhina
ma ke aoe he Hope Loio Kuhina
no ke Aupuni imua o kau Kiure o
Kau, no ka Loio Kuhina Gardner Wilder ke
kumu o kona hiki ole ana.

Ke haawi aku nei ka "Oiaio" i
kona mahalo ia oe o Mr. Geo, Bell,
ke keiki a kaua Kipuupuu o Waimea, no kou eleu i na hoeana ana
mai i kou ola oia na poke hau
pua o Maunakea, no lakou ka huina Eono poohina. Owai hou ae.

Ma ke ahiahi Poaono o keia pule
Aperila 8 e haawi mua loa mai ai
ka Hui Hawaii Hana Keaka ma
ka Hale Mele Hou i ka lakou mau
hana hoohiua puuwai e pili ana i
ka hoolelo o ka wahine ui o Paliuli
Laieikawai, e hele kino ae i pai
kuhihewa.

He olo pihe kumakena ko ka
home o kekahi Luna Hooponopono
Nupepa ma Alanui Paipalapala i
ka Poaono i hala. O ke kumu ka,
no ka hoki ia ana o ka hae Amerika ilaio, a welo haehao hou aela ka
hae Hawaii aloha i ka makaui.
Aloha ino no ka hoi ka poe i kaeua
ae, aole he mea nana e huki iho i
ka hae Amerika ilaio.

Ua hoike ae kahi nupepa hoohui
aina a Iosepa ua, ke kokua nei i
Iosepa Kahunapule o Hana, i ka
poe kini. Nu hou no hoi ea o J. K.
Hanuna i ka oleha i ko oukou
Kahunapule e hike pu pela, aoi i o
hoi no oukou aku ia pomaikai ke
lilo ae oia i Peresidena, a i ole i
Kuhina nui paha.

Na Leta e Waiho nei Maloko o
ka Halelela a hiki i Maraki 31, 1893.

KAWAIAHAO.

M. A. Nalwi
Tknole
Kalehmameaa
Kawaihoa
Keaia
J. Kaiama
L. Kuakoa
S. Kauhola
Makakathonaa
Keai
H. Kahoomana

MANA.
Kekaio
J. Kaniane

KAMANUWAI.
M. Lakea
Haliaka
Penikaina
P. Kaili

KAPUUKOLO.
D. K. Napunoa ?
Kapeua
N. Noiku

KALIHI.
D. M. Makaholo
Kapa 2
S. K. Kapole
L. Maniela
J. H. Paaniaulu
Maraan
S. W. Hoopilaina

KAMAKELA.
Maaloka
Caimana
K. Richard

KEPOHONI.
K. Kaonaana
S. Pakes

NIOLOPA.
Liila

KAOPUAUA.
Auikaiia
Pilahi

KAHEHUPA.
Apoi

MANAMANA.
K. Naipo

KAULUWELA.
K. Howahewa
S. Kemiehandane
D. P. Kikolao
Kawaihuaaa
M. Palenapa
Hookohekei

MOANALUA.
Naloha
J. Kanae 4
Na Leta i hoihoi ia mai na Mo-
kupuni mai.
Kaluholo-Hilli
Pailikani

HONOLULU.
Kamakela 2
K. Uilama
S. D. Naahiwa
O ka poe na lakou ua Leta maluna ae
e nanea mai ma na Leta i Honlahuia.

WALTER HILL,
Luna Leta Nui.
aprd 1wk-8v.

KAUKA
Yong Kam Pung
[APANA.]

Helu 81 Alanui Maunakea.

KAUKALOEA OKAAINAPUA

Ua hiki ke hoola ia kela a me
keia ano ma'i, mai ko na kane, wahine a me ko na keiki lillii. O na
ma'i ha-ho a me na ma'i e pili ana
i'ka maka, pau pu ia i ke ola. Oiai
ma'i koko inoino a me ka hoouka
na maalaha. Pela me oe ma' ko'i
koko maloo, ua hiki ke hoola ia ma
ke oki ole. Ke hoike ia aku nei wake ola nanei ma ka oluolu pu o kanaka ma'i, a na'u oukou e hooluolu
aku.

E KIPA mai e ka poi
hooluuluuu me ua hanuina pilikua
ka ma'i, a na'u oukou e hooluolu
aku.

KAUKA YONG KAM PUNG,
mar.29—2mousd

particularly striking. *Nupepa Puka La Kuokoa* was owned by the *Hawaiian Gazette*, a major pro-American entity attempting to consolidate the new white power in Hawai'i. This paper refused to print Queen Lili'uokalani's protest against the overthrow, and immediately began referring to her as Hawai'i's ex-queen. In fact, two columns over from the very article mentioned above, a letter to the newspaper claimed that the queen could not and would never be restored to her throne. The author of the letter, Hawaii Oiwi, writes that "Ua make loa kela mana aupuni, a he hookahi wale no mea hiki, o ke kaniaku aku" (That power of the monarchy is completely deceased; there's but one thing to do, lament). It is very likely, then, that those publishing the newspaper were monitoring the Kanaka Maoli activities of the day, and especially public presentations such as a hana keaka.

Is it possible that the staging of this hana keaka about Lā'ieikawai was part of a political protest? Why select her story from all the mo'olelo available? And why was it important to tell her story in April of 1893? The story of Lā'ieikawai is about resilient wāhine Hawai'i who in dire times overcome hopeless odds. Through publication and performance, it has resurfaced every twenty years or so over the last century and a half. S. N. Hale'ole authored the first published version, serialized in the Hawaiian language newspaper *Ka Nupepa Kuokoa* from September 4, 1862, to October 23, 1863, and published as a book in 1863. In 1888, Sol Mehe'ula and Jas. Henry Bolster published the story in a series of Hawaiian literary texts. Including Hale'ole's, at least three serializations appeared in the Hawaiian language newspapers—in 1862–1863, 1888, and 1926.

The titles of the installments vary: "Ke Kaao no Laieikawai: Ka hiwahiwa o Paliuli, ka wahine o ka liula" (The legend of Laieikawai: The beloved one of Paliuli. The Lady of the Twilight), "Ka Moolelo o Laieikawai, ka mea i kapa ia ka wahine o ka liula" (The story of Laieikawai, the one that was called the woman of twilight), and "Moolelo no Laieikawai: ka U'i helu akahi o Paliuli i ka uka o Puna" (A story for Laieikawai: The number one beauty of Paliuli inland of Puna). This list is not comprehensive; as more pages of Hawaiian language newspapers become available on such digital repositories as the Papakilo database and nupepa.org, we will likely discover more versions of Lā'ieikawai.

English texts of the story of Lā'ieikawai are also widely available. Martha Warren Beckwith's 1917 translation of Hale'ole's original text was the first published English version. Reprinted in 1997, it was long the most widely used English version of the story. In 2006, Richard Hamasaki, Dennis Kawaharada, and Esther Mookini prepared a revised translation for today's generation. This text is currently used in literature classes throughout Hawai'i.

As for the hana keaka, the scene chart printed in the 1893 newspaper shows that the performance opened with the birth of the kapu ali'i wahine Lā'ieikawai, follwed by a scene with her suitor 'Aiwohikupua, ali'i nui from Kaua'i, and his sisters, Maileha'iwale, Mailekaluhea, Mailelauli'i, Mailepākaha, and the youngest favorite sister, Kahalaomāpuana. Subsequent scenes cover 'Aiwohikupua's relationship with Poli'ahu; the failure of another suitor from Kaua'i, Haua'ilikī; and the seeking of Ka'ōnohiokalā, the eventual husband of Lā'ieikawai. Specific examples of female strength include the survival of 'Aiwohikupua's sisters in a distant and unfamiliar land after he abandons them, and the sisterhood bond established between the sisters and Lā'ieikawai that provides strength, solidarity, and solace in times of despair. The women take on one another's luhi, or burdensome pains, throughout the story, navigating the many trials and tribulations in the journey of life. There is also Kahalaomāpuana's perilous journey to Kūkulu o Kahiki to restore Lā'ieikawai's mana and status as an ali'i. The women in this story are triumphant in their battles, and eventually become the governors of the islands. These women were survivors, known to be fair leaders loved by their people. Lā'ieikawai is eventually deified, and honored by Kānaka Maoli as Ka wahine o ka li'ulā, the woman of twilight.

The themes in this story powerfully resonate with the trials and turmoil the Hawaiian nation was experiencing in 1893. This hana keaka is performed shortly after Lili'uokalani had been deposed from her throne. Was this performance for her, for our beloved queen? Perhaps the hana keaka of Lā'ieikawai was intended to give our queen hope that like Kahalaomāpuana and the sisters in the mo'olelo, she too would prevail in the devastating situation the Hawaiian nation was currently facing. Was it a conscious decision by the Hui Keaka Hawaii Ponoi to retell this story because of the kaona, or hidden meaning, that Kānaka Maoli would have recognized? I cannot help but speculate about the true intention of this production.

Plays are always written with intent. William Shakespeare often used the stage to address political and social problems of his time. His plays addressed a wide variety of themes, and skillfully commented on the crown without directly mentioning Queen Elizabeth. Playwrights employ this tool today, and through their artistic choices, directors highlight the playwrights' social or political content. The first two questions a director often asks when selecting a play are "Why this play?" "And why now?" The question of relevance for a particular community at a specific time is paramount: audiences must somehow identify with the world of the play. Impactful theatre has varying degrees. The theatre of the oppressed as conceived by Augusto Boal is a high-impact theatrical experience. Other impactful forms include theatre for social change, theatre for rebuilding community, and what Richard Schechner has called environmental theatre.

A performance studies lens can help us analyze the impact and affect that a particular mode of presentation may have on the performers, audience members, and community, and the 1893 production of Laieikawai provides us with an excellent subject. The collective of Kānaka Maoli who produced that performance made a significant contribution to the political landscape of 1893. This particular treasured story would have resonated with the lāhui, speaking to the Kānaka populace on multiple levels. Like the kaona embedded in mele (Pukui, "Songs"), hana keaka would have been infused with messages and layers of meaning. Kanaka Maoli Scholar Brandy Nālani McDougall describes kaona this way:

> Inclusive of allusion, symbolism, punning, and metaphor, kaona draws on the collective knowledges and experiences of Hawaiians, recognizing these knowledges and experiences as unique, while also recognizing the range and contexts within which we must inhabit, learn, and access knowledge in its many forms. ("Putting" 3)

To the undiscerning eye, the function of this hana keaka might seem to have been purely to entertain audiences, but it is highly probable, and indeed certain, that it offered a range of coded messages for the lāhui Kanaka Maoli. The printed moʻolelo of Lāʻieikawai already contained embedded teachings of cultural values, religious practices, and proper protocol. Richard Hamasaki argues that when originally published by S. N. Haleʻole in 1862, the story served as an allegory for Hawaiʻi's leadership as it responded to the influx of new ways in Hawaiʻi (ix–x).

Understanding this content can inform our speculations about the reasons for mounting this 1893 hana keaka production. First, there's the choice of a moʻolelo with a female protagonist surrounded by a supporting cast of other females—not unlike Liliʻuokalani and her court. Second, there's the concept of losing one's birthright of mana. This would have been a salient point for Kānaka Maoli and Hawaiian Nationalists alike, since their queen had been deposed less than three months before. Next, the story appeals to traditional ways and the akua of old. The story's characters perform incantations to family gods, summoning these ʻaumākua to aid in their battles and fulfill their requests. Finally, the theme of allegiance or loyalty is explored in this moʻolelo's familial relationships. It is therefore highly probable that by presenting this moʻolelo as a theatrical performance, the director and actors were expressing their loyalty to the queen, and inspiring their audiences to stand in solidarity against the illegal acts of the provisional government.

As the cast was preparing for the final performance in April 1893, the theatre Hale Mele Hou was raided. According to an article in the *Hawaii Holomua* newspaper:

> Ua lohe mai makou, ma ke ahiahi Poaha nei, oiai ke Keaka Laieikawai e makaukau ana e hoike i ka lakou mau *ai* i ao ai, ua hoike ia aku la ka lohe i ka Alihikaua Nui Mr. J. H. Soper, aia he mau pu raifela he lehu-lehu iloko o ka Hale Mele Hou, na ka Hui Keaka Hawaii, a ua manao

ia he wahi ia e hoomoana ai ka poe kue i keia aupuni, a lele kaua aku
paha! ("Maka'u" 2)

[We heard, on Thursday evening, while the Laieikawai performers were
rehearsing their blocking/movement, Commander-in-chief Mr. Soper
was notified that there were numerous firearms stored in the New
Opera House belonging to the Hui Keaka Hawaii. It was also speculated
that the theatre was a place where the resistance party (those who stood
against the new government) was camping out, and that they may incite
a rebellion!] (Translation by author)

How much of a coincidence is it that the location of the hana keaka is also the
alleged hideout for the Kanaka Maoli resistance party? Otherwise known as
Royalists, the resistance movement had a track record of meeting at the Hale
Mele Hou. The day before what President Grover Cleveland later referred to as
the illegal act of war by American and American-affiliated businessmen (Cleveland; *Act of War*), an announcement in the *Hawaii Holomua* on the 16th of January
1893 calls for a gathering of Kānaka Hawai'i to support the kingdom and Queen
Lili'uokalani:

> Halawai Makaainana Nui
> E na kanaka Hawaii a me ka poe a pau i aloha io i ka aina a makee
> i ka pono a me ke kaulike–ke kono ia aku nei oukou e hele ae ma ka
> halawai a ka [*sic*] Kanaka aloha aina a makee maluhia e malama ia
> ana ma ke Kuea mamua iho o ka Hale Mele Hou i ka hora 2 o keia
> auaina la Poakahi, Ianuri 16. E hele ae kane, wahine me keiki, a e
> akoakoa ae i mau tausani. (2)

> [Huge Citizen's Assembly
> Hawaiians and all those who truly love the land and treasure good-
> ness and justice—you are all invited to attend the meeting of peace-
> loving patriots, which will be held in the Square directly in front of
> the New Opera House at 2:00 pm this Monday, January 16. Men,
> women, and children should all go, and gather by the thousands.]
> (Translation by M. Puakea Nogelmeier)

This announcement and others like it suggest that the Hale Mele Hou was a
gathering place for the patriots of the Hawaiian nation. With regard to the gun
raid at the theatre, a phone call convinced the commander-in-chief of the provisional government, who must have already had suspicions about the activities
at the Hale Mele Hou, to act. That the thespians were harboring Royalists, or

were Royalists themselves, is an exciting revelation. And if the members of the Hui Keaka Hawaii Ponoi were not just actors but also activists, perhaps the performance of *Laieikawai* was part of a Royalist campaign to unite for social change, and to protest the unfair treatment of their queen and the treacherous establishment of the provisional government.

The police officers and military who searched the theatre turned up one gun: a stage prop for a play about Captain Cook in the troupe's repertoire. Annoyed by the ordeal, and sympathetic to the Hui Hana Keaka, the editor of *Hawaii Holomua* closed the article this way: "a aohe hoi o na haneri, tausani, miliona, a keliliona o na pu a ka wahahee nui wale. Ma-tau!" (and there weren't hundreds of guns, thousands, millions, or trillions as indicated, such exaggerated lies. Frightening/dangerous!) ("Maka'u"). This article provides evidence that Kanaka Maoli activities were strictly observed by the provisional government, which clearly feared an uprising, and also helps us to understand the social and political climate for Kānaka Maoli and Hawaiian National Royalists alike. I would suggest that the Hui Hana Keaka Hawaii Ponoi cleverly performed a mo'olelo at the Hale Mele Hou that would have resonated with the Royalist party, and inspired those staging political protests following the overthrow.

It is also interesting to note that three months after this hana keaka production of *Laieikawai*, an 'aha mele or concert featured a tableaux of six scenes from the story of Lā'ieikawai and Lā'ielohelohe interspersed between dramatized historical events, such as the story of Kamehameha. The newspapers report that this performance appealed to a large audience, and was very successful ("Hale Mele Hou!"). At a time of great upheaval, then, hana keaka provided a venue for Kānaka Maoli to articulate their voices, recount historical events, and promote Hawaiian epistemology, ontology, cultural values, and practices.

Modern-Day Hana Keaka and Its Functions

Modern-day hana keaka's core values and practices are analogous to those of African and other Indigenous theatre forms. In its current incarnation, hana keaka recounts traditional myths and historical events typically classified as mo'olelo. The stories represented are drawn from oral tradition and literary texts often extracted from the Hawaiian language newspapers, published from 1834 through 1948. Hana keaka therefore depends on traditional mo'olelo dealing with ancestors and historical figures. Frequently those involved with the production are genealogically connected to the characters portrayed, which creates a sense of responsibility and accountability in the cast members, artistic team, and playwright to present accurate and authentic representations of the mo'olelo adapted for the stage. Hana keaka also interweaves hula (dance), oli (chant), and mele (song/poetry) with the dialogue and dramatic action. These performance forms serve as dramatic structural devices already possessing an Indigenously Hawaiian aesthetic.

"One of Oceania's most prominent vernacular theater ensembles," since 1995, Ka Hālau Hanakeaka has led the way in presenting this modern form of Hawaiian theatre (Looser 52). By performing for immersion schoolchildren and developing curriculum, this Hālau has contributed to the Hawaiian language revitalization movement. Since its inception, Ka Hālau Hanakeaka has taken its productions to schools across the pae 'āina of Hawai'i. Travel grants and fundraising allow rural Hawaiian communities to experience Hawaiian medium theatre. *Kamapua'a* (hog-child), the longest running Ka Hālau Hanakeaka production, toured the Hawaiian archipelago and internationally (2004–2007). This full-length two-act play with twenty-three scenes chronicles the hero's exploits and challenges in life. Kamapua'a searches for the love of his mother Hina, who renounces and abandons him at birth, under the impression that he is stillborn. The source literature states that Kamapua'a is a kaula (rope/cord) at birth. Scene one ends with his grandmother, Kamaunuaniho, taking the kaula to a religious altar, where she breathes life into her grandson through prayer. Raised by his grandmother, Kamapua'a takes the form of a pua'a (hog) in his youth and matures into a man. The play depicts the various transformative events in Kamapua'a's life, telling the less known stories revealing his compassionate side and leadership in the communities he served. In this and its other productions, besides entertaining audiences in the medium of Hawaiian language, Ka Hālau Hanakeaka holds steadfast to the values of education, knowledge transmission, ancestral knowledge, cultural practices, and the socialization of our people. Each production has honored 'āina, perpetuated 'Ōlelo Hawai'i, helped to raise the level of language fluency in the community, and strengthened Hawaiian identity and nationalism.

I would be remiss if I did not mention other Hawaiian theatre productions performed in Hawai'i since the rise of the cultural renaissance. In the late 1970s, traditional performance forms such as *hula* (dance) and *mele* (song/poetry) resurfaced in public arenas, as a resurgence of Indigenous cultural practices echoed the political uprisings and protests of the time. Hawaiian chant, music, and dance performances coupled with traditional ceremonial practices provided a framework of solidarity amongst Kānaka Maoli at cultural events and protests. A distinguished hālau hula, Hālau o Kekuhi, recognizes eight generations of kumu hula in its lineage. Internationally recognized for its artistic contributions, Hālau o Kekuhi has produced eight theatrical productions based in the Pele, goddess of volcanism, lineage of their kumu. Since 1995 its productions have formalized the genre of Hawaiian dance theatre, a form deeply rooted in hula genealogy. Employing primarily dance and chant, each performance is a recitation of the travels, challenges, and triumphs of an ancestor or ancestral hula deity. The result is therefore a personal expression of ancestral knowledge recreated through ancestral memory. When members of the Kanaka'ole family perform their Pele tradition, they invoke their ancestors and honor their mana (spiritual power). Administered through the Edith Kanaka'ole Foundation, Hālau o Kekuhi is recognized as the foremost hālau to produce this kind of work.

Its first production, *Holo Mai Pele* (Pele travels), recounted the travels of Pelehonuamea, another of her many names, her youngest sister Hi'iakaikapoliopele, Hi'iaka-in-the-bosom-of Pele, and their family clan from Kahiki, the South Pacific ancestral homeland for many Polynesians. Crossing the south Pacific Ocean, the Pele clan brought their religious practices and idols with them in search of a new home. After visiting and paying respects to their family members on the islands of Kaua'i, O'ahu, and Maui, they made their home at Halema'uma'u on the island of Hawai'i. The epic story continues with Hi'iakaikapoliopele's journey to fetch Pele's lover Lohi'au on the island of Kaua'i. The many dances and chants in this production revealed Pele's supernatural abilities as a creator of land, and her ascent to be the matriarch of her clan. Also significant is Hi'iaka's role as a healer and a source of inspiration. *Holo Mai Pele* offered "a basic yet sophisticated understanding of the primary functions and powers of women and the female Earth... both the human family aspects of the story and the relationship of elemental forms are recognized" (Kanahele, *Holo* 6). Hawaiian dance theatre recounts and celebrates traditional stories through hula and mele performance.

Another dance theatre form that incorporates song, Hawaiian language, and contemporary dance informs the works of Tau Dance Theater. Founder and artistic director Peter Rockford Espiritu has created two productions in particular that drew from mo'olelo and employed the Hawaiian language for narration and dialogue. The first production, *Naupaka*, told the story of two lovers who were forbidden to be together. From this came the naupaka flower, one half of which resides in the mountains, while the other half can be found seaside. Tau Dance Theater's other production based in mo'olelo was *Poli'ahu*, the goddess of Mauna Kea. Billed as "a Hawaiian dance opera that blends traditional hula with modern European elements such as ballet," this production explored the relationship of Kānaka and the snow goddess Poli'ahu (Keany).

From the island of Maui, Nākinimakalehua, under the direction of kumu hula Hokulani Holt-Padilla, has produced original theatrical productions since the 1980s. *Kahekilinui'ahumanu* is likely the most well-known of them all. This production chronicled the life of Maui's great chief Kahekili. The pageant-like performance included original hula, mele, and oli compositions from a number of kumu hula on Maui. This production, and the company's most recent production, *Kūlanihāko'i*, have toured internationally. On the island of Hawai'i, productions by the students of Ke Kula 'o Nāwahīokalani'ōpu'u, a Hawaiian immersion charter school, have integrated hana keaka into the curriculum. *Hoʻoulu*, their most recent production, focused on the use of traditional Hawaiian plants and the relationship between mele and the featured mea kanu (plants). The performance weaved tableaux-like scenes with original hula and chant. *Hoʻoulu* was performed at the inaugural *Keaka: Hawaiian Theatre Festival* at the University of Hawaiʻi at Hilo in June 2016. Also featured were the students from Kamehameha Keaʻau campus, who shared an original Hawaiian opera entitled *Hāʻupu*. Each of these productions mentioned adapts moʻolelo for the stage. It is an innately Kanaka practice to perpetuate the stories of our ancestors. The collective efforts of the hālau, dance companies, and schools referred to here have maintained the practice of haʻi moʻolelo in the various forms of performance.

The most recent achievement in advancing the teaching and practice of hana keaka has been its institutionalization at the University of Hawaiʻi at Mānoa. In the fall of 2014 the Department of Theatre and Dance established the new Hawaiian Theatre Program, including a graduate degree, a Masters of Fine Arts in Hawaiian Theatre. The only Indigenous graduate degree of its kind in the world, program course work includes the history of theatre in Hawaiʻi, the study and analysis of Indigenous Hawaiian theatre, and training in both traditional and contemporary Hawaiian performance forms. Students now can learn the art form of hana keaka and participate in original Hawaiian medium productions on the Kennedy mainstage that reflect and honor the language, traditions, history, and values of the Hawaiian community. The Hawaiian Theatre Program furthermore ensures the regular staging of hana keaka productions for the larger Hawaiʻi community.

Three hana keaka have been produced since the establishment of the program: *Lāʻieikawai* in 2015, *Nā Kau a Hiʻiaka* in 2017, and *ʻAuʻa ʻIa: Holding On* in 2019. *Nā Kau a Hiʻiaka* was the first Hawaiian Theatre MFA Thesis production of the new program. Each hana keaka presented traditional moʻolelo with themes highly relevant to today's world, evoking strong emotions from audience members. Staging these plays in ʻŌlelo Hawaiʻi is a political statement in itself, and presenting these moʻolelo lays claim not only to the stories themselves, but also to the dramatic space for retelling them in a modern context. There was some controversy about the inaugural Hana Keaka production at Kennedy Theatre being performed solely in ʻŌlelo Hawaiʻi. Faculty members in the Department of Theatre and Dance were concerned that the production would marginalize the audience, and argued for projected English subtitles. This sentiment was coupled with questions during the department and production meetings during the season planning, such as "Do Hawaiians go to the theatre?" Clearly some were skeptical that the production could attract a large audience, since over the past fifty years Kennedy Theatre had not staged a Hawaiian, let alone a Hawaiian language, production as a part of its advertised season. As the playwright and

Cast photo, Lā'ieikawai. Author's image.

director of *Lā'ieikawai*, I stood firm in my conviction that our program should and would produce our hana keaka in our language.

Reviews in the local newspapers commended the production, calling it "A cultural and linguistic triumph" (Reyes 1). Non-Hawaiian speaking reviewers such as Eleanor Svaton, Features Editor for *Hitting the Stage*, also shared their appreciation: "Watching *Lā'ieikawai* made me want to know Hawaiian—from the language to the stories and the history—to learn the culture of this place I call my home." Many audience members attended the production *because* of the language and the story. The Hawaiian community and supporters of 'Ōlelo Hawai'i came out in droves over two weekends in February 2015. Kennedy Theatre staff did not expect a response of this magnitude. The front of house was not able to process tickets quickly enough, so a line of patrons extended down East-West Road for nearly an hour before showtime. Seven of the eight shows sold out, with potential audience members turned away at the door on the second weekend (*Kennedy*). Approximately 4,000 people experienced the production of *Lā'ieikawai* at Kennedy Theatre, and the positive community response dispelled the previous skepticism of my colleagues. The impact of relevant hana keaka such as *Lā'ieikawai* and *Nā Kau a Hi'iaka* and most recently *'Au'a 'Ia: Holding On* is undeniable. Such productions elevate the community, honor our mo'olelo, our language, and ultimately, our mo'okū'auhau, or kūpuna. The

Hawaiian Theatre Program will continue to celebrate moʻolelo, with each future production nurturing a puʻuhonua Ōlelo Hawaiʻi, a place of refuge and safety for the language and culture, within the academy.

This essay has focused on productions of Lāʻieikawai; however, the Fall 2019 production of ʻAuʻa ʻIa: Holding On is worth mentioning here as an illustration of political theatre. A contemporary exploration of archival materials for a class assignment carries the four main characters, students at the University of Hawaiʻi at Mānoa, into encounters with the actual historical events. By activating a link to their ancestors and the spiritual realm by reciting mele and passages from the nineteenth-century newspapers, the time-traveling students engage with kupuna, as their personal journeys of self-discovery unfold. Kaʻihi, Ala, ʻĀina, and Ola seek to understand their identity, place, and mana as Kānaka Maoli in 2019. They witness and eventually participate in protests against the annexation of Hawaiʻi to the U.S., the bombing of Kahoʻolawe, and the desecration of Mauna Kea. As these scenes unfolded, the reenactment of these significant moments in time evoked a visceral response from the audience members, who raised their voices in song and chant with the cast. Columnist Lee Cataluna wrote about her experience at the closing performance:

> The play ran three hours. Still, when it was over, the audience wouldn't leave. They wanted more. So they sang—the audience and the huge cast, together—song after song, until finally settling on "Hawaii Aloha," which brought enough of a feeling of closure so that people could, slowly, reluctantly, start to move toward the exits.

The audience's engagement with the cast and content of the play demonstrates the significant impact that socially conscious theatre can produce. This type of experience goes beyond the passive watching of a show. ʻAuʻa ʻIa: Holding On incited a response, invigorating the audience and calling them to action. At the beginning of Act II, for instance, actors portraying Kuaihelani Campbell and Emma Nāwahī, leaders of the Hui Aloha ʻĀina o Nā Wāhine, entered the house with anti-annexation petitions, asking audience members to sign the Palapala Kūʻē Hoʻohui ʻĀina. On more than one occasion, members of the audience called to the women, asking them to bring the palapala over so that they could sign and stand in opposition to American annexation, as their kūpuna had in 1897. This act of signing the petition was a way to confront and reclaim that history. This was an act of empowerment. The concept of ʻauʻa ʻia, to hold steadfast, resonated with our community. ʻAuʻa ʻia calls on us to learn, preserve, and retain our moʻolelo, mele, oli, hula, ʻōlelo, and ʻāina, for these are the foundation and source of our identity as Kānaka Maoli. This production deserves to be the sole subject of a future publication dedicated to production methodology, process, and analysis. For now, I invoke the famous words of our kūpuna when recounting moʻolelo in the newspapers, "Aole i pau."

Haʻina ʻia mai ana ka puana

The stage is a tool for storytelling, a vehicle for enlightenment, and a platform for political statements. Historically, Kānaka Maoli have adapted the theatre to perpetuate the practice of haʻi moʻolelo, developing a modern means to express the experiences of our kūpuna, our environment, and our own personal journeys. Together with our kūpuna, we've moved forward into a new phase of Kanaka Maoli expression. Just as the words in the mele *Aia Lāʻieikawai* retain intricate details about the moʻolelo of Lāʻieikawai, so too do the hana keaka produced by Kānaka Maoli.

Kau mai Lāʻieikawai,	Lāʻieikawai rests/rides,
I ka ʻēheu lā o nā manu,	On the wings of birds,
ʻO ka nani, ʻo ka nani,	Oh what beauty, beauty indeed,
Helu ʻekahi o Paliuli.	The favored one of Paliuli.

Lāʻieikawai, the favored beauty of Paliuli, was upheld and cared for. We do the same for our moʻolelo. Recognizing their beauty and value, we are the kahu manu, carrying our cherished moʻolelo forth collectively on our wings, delivering the stories from one generation to the next.

E nanea, e walea ana paha,	Relax at ease, enjoy, perhaps delight,
I ka leo nahenahe o nā manu.	In the sweet, gentle, melodious voices of the birds.

Presenting hana keaka beckons our people to relax, listen, experience, and enjoy the retelling of our moʻolelo. The sweet and gentle words spoken and sung by our pūali hana keaka, our troupe of actors, reconnect today's audience with the adventures of our ancestors. Hana keaka is one of many cherished vessels for retaining our heritage, remembering our moʻolelo, and strengthening our fluency in culture and language. E ola mau nā moʻolelo o nā kūpuna.

WORKS CONSULTED

Act of War—The Overthrow of the Hawaiian Nation. Produced by Puhipau and Joan Lander, Nā Maka o ka ʻĀina, 1991.

Angell, Lowell. *Theatres of Hawaiʻi.* Images of America, Arcadia Publishing, 2011.

Baker, Christopher K. "Constructing Kanaka Maoli Identity through Narrative: A Glimpse into Native Hawaiian Narratives." In *Narrative and Identity Construction in the Pacific Islands*, edited by Farzana Gounder. John Benjamins Publishing Company, 2015, pp. 119–134.

Baker, Tammy Haili'ōpua, Diana Looser, and Sharon Mazer. " 'The Vessel Will Embrace Us': Contemporary Pacific Voyaging in Oceanic Theatre." *Performance Research: A Journal of the Performing Arts*, vol. 21, no. 2, 2016, pp. 40–49.

Beckwith, Martha Warren, trans. *The Hawaiian romance of Laieikawai, with introduction and translation by Martha Warren Beckwith.* By S. N. Haleole. *Reprinted from the Thirty-third annual report of the Bureau of American Ethnology.* Government Printing Office, 1918.

Boal, Augusto. *Theatre of the Oppressed.* Theatre Communications Group, 1985.

Brockett, Oscar G., and Franklin J. Hildy. *History of the Theatre*, 10th ed. Pearson, 2007.

Broyles-González, Yolanda. *El Teatro Campesino: Theater in the Chicano Movement.* U of Texas P, 1994.

Cataluna, Lee. "Epic theater piece became rallying moment." *Honolulu Star-Advertiser*, October 9, 2019. https://www.staradvertiser.com/2019/10/09/hawaii-news/lee-cataluna/cataluna-epic-theater-piece-became-rallying-moment/.

Cleveland, Grover. "President Cleveland's message about Hawaii, December 18, 1893." American History: From Revolution to Reconstruction and Beyond. http://www.let.rug.nl/usa/documents/1876-1900/president-clevelands-message-about-hawaii-december-18-1893.php.

"E Ao Kanaka mai Kakou." *Ka Nupepa Puka La Kuokoa*, Buke 1, Helu 46, 11 April 1893, p. 3.

Emerson, Nathaniel B. *Unwritten Literature of Hawai'i: The Sacred Songs of the Hula.* Bureau of American Ethnology Bulletin, Smithsonian Institution. Government Printing Office, 1909.

"Halawai Makaainana Nui." *Hawaii Holomua*, Buke 3, Helu 140, 16 January 1893, p. 2.

"Hale Mele Hou!" *Hawaii Holomua*, Buke 3, Helu 256, 5 July 1893, p. 3.

Hale'ole, S. N. "Ka Moolelo o Laieikawai." *Ka Hoku o Ka Pakipika*, 4 September 1862–23 October 1863.

———. *Ke Kaao o Laieikawai, Ka Hiwahiwa o Paliuli, Kawahineokaliula.* Henry M. Whitney, 1863.

Hamasaki, Richard. "Introduction." In *Lā'ieikawai*, by S. N. Hale'ole, edited by Richard Hamasaki, Dennis Kawaharada, and Esther Mo'okini. Kalamakū Press, 2006, pp. ix–x.

Hawaiian Gazette. http://chroniclingamerica.loc.gov/lccn/sn83025121/.

Highway, Tomson. "On Native Mythology." 1987. In *Aboriginal Drama and Theatre: Critical Perspectives on Canadian Theatre in English*, vol. 1, edited by Robert Appleford. Playwrights Canada Press, 2005, pp. 1–3.

"Hoikeike Nui, Ma ka Hale Melu Hou…" *Ka Leo o Ka Lahui*, Buke 2, Helu 679, 7 April 1893, p. 3.

Huntsman, Jeffrey. Introduction. *New Native American Drama: Three Plays by Hanay Geiogamah.* U of Oklahoma P, 1980.

ʻĪʻī, John Papa. *Fragments of Hawaiian History*. Bishop Museum Press, 1959.

Ka Makaainana, Buke 3, Helu 10, 13 May 1895, p. 3.

Kanahele, Pualani Kanakaʻole. *Holo Mai Pele Educator's Guide*. Pacific Islanders in Communications, 2001.

———. *Ka Honua Ola, ʻEliʻeli Kau Mai* (The Living Earth: Descend, Deepen the Revelation). Kamehameha Publishing, 2011.

Kawaikaumaiikamakaokaopua, Z. P. K. "Moolelo no Laieikawai ka Uʻi Helu Akahi o Paliuli i ka Uka o Puna. *Ka Nupepa Kuokoa*, Buke 65, Helu 12 (mokuna 4), 25 March 1926–24 February 1927.

Keany, Michael. "Tau Dance Theater." *Honolulu*, October 5, 2010. https://www.honolulumagazine.com/tau-dance-theater/.

"Ke Kaao o Laieikawai, Ka Hiwahiwa o Paliuli, Kawahineokaliula." *Ka Nupepa Kuokoa*, 4 September 1862–23 October 1863.

"Kela me Keia." *Ka Makaainana*, Buke 4, Helu 6, 5 August 1895, p. 8.

Kennedy Theatre Season 2014–2015 Box Office Report. University of Hawaiʻi at Mānoa, 2015.

Looser, Diana. *Remaking Pacific Pasts: History, Memory, and Identity in Contemporary Theater from Oceania*. U of Hawaiʻi P, 2014.

"Makaʻu Paha i ke A-ka o Laieikawai e!!" *Hawaii Holomua*, Buke 3, Helu 17, 22 April 1893, p. 2.

McDougall, Brandy Nālani. *Finding Meaning: Kaona and Contemporary Hawaiian Literature*. U of Arizona P, 2016.

———. "Putting Feathers on Our Words: Kaona as a Decolonial Aesthetic Practice in Hawaiian Literature." *Decolonization: Indigeneity, Education & Society*, vol. 3, no. 1, 2014, pp. 1–22.

Meheʻula, Sol, and Jas. H Bolster, nā luna hoʻoponopono. *Ka moolelo o Laieikawai; a o ka mea i kapa ia Kawahineikaliula*. Papa Pai Mahu "Bulletin," 1888. http://hdl.handle.net/10524/35937.

"Na Keaka mai na Moolelo Kahiko mai." *Ka Nupepa Kuokoa*, Buke 40, Helu 9, 28 February 1902, p. 1.

"Na Poe Hana Keaka Hawaii." *Nupepa Puka La Kuokoa*, Buke 1, Helu 46, 11 April 1893, p. 3.

Ngũgĩ wa Thiong'o. *Decolonising the Mind, The Politics of Language in African Literature*. James Currey, 1986.

Nogelmeier, M. Puakea. *Mai Paʻa I Ka Leo: Historical Voice in Hawaiian Primary Materials, Looking Forward and Listening Back*. Bishop Museum Press and Awaiaulu, 2010.

"Nuhou Kuloko." *Ka Leo o ka Lahui*, Buke 2, Helu 690, 24 April 1893, p. 3.

Pukui, Mary Kawena. "How Legends Were Taught." *Hawaiian Ethnographic Notes*, vol. 1, 1602–1606. Bishop Museum Archives, pp. 1–5. http://kumukahi-online.net/haku-olelo-331/na-kumu-ike/mokuna-iv---moolelo-kaao/pukui---how-legends-were.pdf.

———. "Songs (Meles) of Old Kaʻu, Hawaiʻi." *Journal of American Folklore*, vol. 62, no. 245, 1949, pp. 247–258.

Reyes, Daniella. "'Lā'ieikawai' a Cultural and Linguistic Triumph." *Ka Leo o Hawai'i*. University of Hawai'i at Mānoa, February 23, 2015, p. 28.

Rimer, J. Thomas, and Yamazaki Masakazu, trans. *On the Art of Nō Drama: The Major Treaties of Zeami*. Princeton UP, 1984.

Schechner, Richard *Environmental Theater*. Applause Theater and Cinema Books, 1994.

Silva, Noenoe K. *Aloha Betrayed: Native Hawaiian Resistance to American Colonialism*. Duke UP, 2004.

Svaton, Eleanor. "SPOTLIGHT on Language—The Power of Immersion?" *Hitting the Stage*, March 3, 2015. Web. August 20, 2015. http://hittingthestagearchive.site/uhms-kennedy-theatre-presents-laieikawai/3.

Wilson, Edwin, and Alvin Goldfarb. *Living Theatre: An Introduction to Theatre History*. 7th ed. McGraw-Hill, 2017.

Tammy Haili'ōpua Baker is an Associate Professor in the Department of Theatre and Dance at the University of Hawai'i at Mānoa. As a Director/Playwright/Theatre Educator/Scholar, her work centers on the development of an Indigenous Hawaiian theatre aesthetic and form, language revitalization, and the empowerment of cultural identity and consciousness through stage performance. Baker is the artistic director of Ka Hālau Hanakeaka, a Hawaiian-medium theatre troupe based on O'ahu. Originally from Kapa'a, Kaua'i, she now resides in Kahalu'u, Ko'olaupoko, O'ahu with her 'ohana.

here is a gendered interrelationship between ʻāina, art, and activism expressed through moʻolelo, representing each in words, iconography, other images, techniques, and styles.

9

The Art of Moʻolelo
Mana Wahine, Aloha ʻĀina, and Social Justice

kuʻualoha hoʻomanawanui

Moʻolelo is a broad term that encompasses all genres of story and history, connected narratives that begin in ancient oral traditions classified in English as myths, tales, legends, and folklore. Expanding in the nineteenth century with the advent of writing, the concept of moʻolelo was applied to literature and all other forms of writing. Other modes of expression of moʻolelo include performance through storytelling, mele (songs), hula (dance), puppetry, drama, and later opera and theater. It also includes stories told and represented through visual art. Kiʻi is a Hawaiian word for image that includes drawings, illustrations, and visual artwork. Thus, kiʻi is a medium for representing moʻolelo visually. Traditionally, this includes images carved from natural materials such as wood and stone, kākau (tattooing), and kapa cloth designs. Visual telling of moʻolelo continues through traditional media as well as through new ones, including painting, photography, and sculpture.

Hawaiian nationalist, poet, and scholar Haunani-Kay Trask argues that "art is a fluid political medium, as politics is metaphorical and artistic" (18). Nineteenth-century Maui writer and editor Moses Manu recognized the political aspect of moʻolelo when he described the first epic-length publication of a Pele and Hiʻiaka moʻolelo (*Ka Hoku o ka Pakipika*, 1861–1862) by M. J. Kapihenui as a "moʻolelo kālaiʻāina" (political narrative) (4). This recognition by Kanaka Maoli (Native Hawaiian) thinkers was a form of literary activism intended to remind Kānaka Maoli of their intellectual history, to hāliʻaliʻa (positively remember) their identity as a lāhui (people, nation) rooted in ʻōlelo Hawaiʻi (Hawaiian language), moʻokūʻauhau (genealogy), and aloha ʻāina (land and culturally based nationalism), and to resist Americanization. Read this way, traditional moʻolelo, such as the Pele and Hiʻiaka moʻolelo of 1860–1928, inform Hawaiian nationalism and literary production today, which continue to weave new moʻolelo of the poʻe aloha ʻāina (cultural and political nationalists, literally people who love the land) into our intellectual moʻokūʻauhau handed down mai ka pō mai (from the beginning of time), mai nā kūpuna mai (from the ancestors).

The "new moʻolelo" I refer to include visual arts, which through kaona (metaphor) often depict or reference traditional moʻolelo—both story and history—and contain resolute messages of kālaiʻāina through their inclusion of ʻōlelo Hawaiʻi, moʻokūʻauhau, and aloha ʻāina.

As numerous scholars have acknowledged in different contexts, visual and other arts have always played an integral role in revolutionary movements and social justice advocacy. Within a cultural context, Kanaka Maoli women's contemporary visual art is a kind of moʻolelo kālaiʻāina, a strand of cultural and social activism that contributes to aloha ʻāina advocacy. As Trask has noted,

> You cannot just dance hula and go to Hawaiian language class at night and think you're going to get a land base. You can't do that. Cultural people need to become political. . . . Our culture can't just be ornamental and recreational. . . . Our culture has to be the core of our resistance, the core of our anger, the core of our mana [power]. That's what culture is for. (*Hoʻokūʻokoʻa*)

I've previously published on Kanaka Maoli women's writing as both expression and embodiment of mana wahine (women's power, and by extension, activism). This project focusing on Kanaka Maoli women's visual art as moʻolelo kālaiʻāina continues that work. While some critics overly evoke the tropes of Hawaiian activism and resistance as victimization, I'd like to suggest instead that our arts reflect kūpaʻa—steadfastness, affirmation, and celebration—of who we are as Native people, drawing from our Indigenous economies of abundance. Our arts are also kūʻē—resistance to settler colonial hegemony and its insistence on assimilation and denial of Indigenous peoples, cultures, and kinship to ʻāina (land). Thus, there is a gendered interrelationship between ʻāina, art, and activism expressed through moʻolelo, representing each in words, iconography, other images, techniques, and styles.

Pacific Studies scholar Teresia Teaiwa has written about the importance of recognizing and studying the systematic visual culture of Indigenous Pacific peoples, as "throughout the Pacific, complex visual symbol systems [are] found [everywhere]. . . . The proliferation (and elaboration) of visual and material culture in [traditional] Pacific societies indicates a sophisticated understanding of the visual," which has influenced contemporary artists (734).

Kanaka Maoli arts and politics go hand in hand from ancient times, bound together in moʻokūʻauhau, our collective lineage that links us to our ʻāina. Cultural expert, hula master, and scholar Pualani Kanahele has written that "I have two convictions in my life. One . . . is that I am Hawaiian. The other . . . is that I am this land, and this land is me" (23). Through earth mother Papahānaumoku and sky father Wākea, Kanaka Maoli descend from our ʻāina. This relationship is implicit through the birth of Hāloanakalaukapalili (literally long breath quivering leaf), the first kalo (taro) plant, and his younger brother Hāloa, the first

Kanaka Maoli. Thus, our identity is rooted in our land and embodied in our language, which is reflected in our arts.

Even prior to the 1893 illegal and unwarranted overthrow of the Hawaiian kingdom, Hawai'i was contested ground, and its ongoing disenfranchisement by settler society and the dispossession of Hawaiian 'āina continue to harm and erode our lāhui. The representation of Hawai'i, Kānaka Maoli, and our culture in the imaginations of artists and audiences in and outside of our homeland, and especially the theft and appropriation of our traditional knowledge and intellectual property, are also sites of struggle.

Some important themes in Kanaka Maoli women's art that reflect aloha 'āina nationalism and represent kūpa'a and kū'ē include:

- Mo'okū'auhau—Kinship, identity, and critique of blood quantum
- Dispossession from 'āina
- Reclaiming 'āina, celebrating wahi pana, protesting U.S. military occupation
- Defending sacred lands and practices
- Protecting environment, 'āina, and ancestors
- Remembering ancestors and reaffirming kūpa'a and kū'ē
- Cultural affirmations of health and wellness, healing of 'āina and kānaka (people)

Selected examples of each theme will be analyzed, followed by a discussion of the community inclusivity and focus of the art and artists. The artists discussed represent different islands and mo'okū'auhau, and reflect multiple generations, artistic media, and genres. In this way, I will explore the visual and creative diversity of contemporary Kanaka Maoli women artists in conveying mo'olelo through the medium of ki'i, with an eye towards social justice and culturally informed aesthetics.

Mo'okū'auhau: Kinship, Identity, and Blood Quantum

Lili'u Tomasello's "Koko" (blood) critiques the issue of settler-imposed blood quantum qualifications and Kanaka Maoli ethnic identity. Since the Hawaiian Home Lands Act was enacted by Congress in 1921, U.S. federal laws, later followed by Hawai'i state law, define "native Hawaiian" as having fifty percent or higher blood quantum. Hawaiians with less than fifty percent blood quantum are considered "part Hawaiian." Native Hawaiians are eligible for federal entitlements, such as Hawaiian Home Lands, that part Hawaiians are not. Since the 1920s, this settler colonial-imposed definition of 'Ōiwi identity and ancestry has artificially divided Kanaka families and communities. Kānaka Maoli have responded by more insistently asserting kinship ties through Indigenous cultural practices such as moʻokūʻauhau, and by using identifying terms in our own language, such as Kanaka Maoli, Kanaka ʻŌiwi, and Kanaka Hawaiʻi, which have no such legally divisive problems.

As suggested by the name of the piece, Tomasello's image is shaped as a drop of blood. The word koko is repeated throughout, and the color is red, a sacred color in Hawaiian culture as well as the color of blood. At the top of the blood drop, the word koko is set close together, suggesting an abundance or "purity" of Maoli koko. But as the word is repeated, it slowly breaks apart into non-words—"okokok," "kokko," "kokok." These nonsensical pairings of the letters k and o suggest the confusion that accompanies the mixing of Hawaiian koko with other ethnicities. The letters that spell out koko as well as the lines between are spaced further apart, appearing dissolved and weakened in strength and meaning. The word koko only appears in its whole and unadulterated form five times in the bottom half of the image, and is rendered a few more times in a broken form, "ko ko," which then transforms into "ko," an allusion to half blood, indicated by half a word. It also alludes to the slang acronym for "knocked out," indicating defeat. The diluted blood suggests fractured identity, and the multiple issues it raises. But "koko" also transforms into "ok," perhaps indicating a normalcy of mixed blood identity. As each successive generation of Kanaka moves forward through time, fewer and fewer full-blooded Kānaka survive. The current projection is that by the year 2040, no full-blooded Kānaka will remain.

Tomasello's "Koko" is a visual moʻolelo telling a layered narrative of Kanaka Maoli moʻokūʻauhau and identity. It can be read as a lament of the loss of koko, as the blood drop shape evokes a teardrop, suggesting tears of sorrow. It can also be read as a celebration of Kanaka identity via an assertion of moʻokūʻauhau, in that one drop of Hawaiian koko, as presented here, carries Kanaka Maoli genealogy, the DNA and ancestral memory of kūpuna (ancestors). In this way, it is also a defiant expression of kūʻē against settler colonial legislation of Kanaka identity via blood quantum, turning the "one drop rule" of ancestry on its head. Historically in the U.S., "one drop" of sub-Saharan African blood made one "black" and subject to racial subjugation. But here, "one drop" of

Koko. Liliʻu Tomasello, 2010. Used with permission.

Kanaka Maoli blood connects one to one's ancestors through genealogy, a kūʻē to identity politics based on phenotype markers such as skin color ("you don't *look* Hawaiian").

"At its heart," Tomasello writes,

> "Koko" is a reflection of my experiences and the stories of my kūpuna. These stories of strength and cultural perseverance, as told to me by my mother and tūtū, are stories that have become a part of me. It is my hope that in my journey as a writer, I can continue to honor their memory by sharing their stories with the world. (160)

Tomasello's moʻolelo of moʻokūʻauhau and identity, of remembering her ancestors, therefore reflects her personal, and by extension, the collective moʻolelo of the lāhui as we continue to assert our own moʻolelo of ancestry and identity and counter false racist settler colonial narratives that continue to redefine us in ways that disconnect us from our ʻāina and ancestors.

Dispossession from ʻĀina: Kanaka Maoli Houselessness

Homelessness has been a huge problem in Hawaiʻi, and Kānaka Maoli, dispossessed from our own ʻāina, have been disproportionately affected. Multimedia artist Bernice Akamine's response to Kanaka Maoli houselessness began in the 1990s with visits to camps, many at beach parks around the island of Oʻahu (Waimānalo, Mokuleʻia, Mākua), where houseless Kānaka lived, and where Akamine recorded the experiences of the people she met.

Between 1997 and 2000, Akamine's "Kuʻu One Hānau" was included in a larger installation called "The Houseless Project," sponsored by a consortium of Hawaiian churches and non-profit organizations. "Kuʻu One Hānau" is inspired by an anonymous Kanaka's words she incorporates into the artwork, "We are not homeless. We are houseless. Hawaiʻi is our home."

While Akamine witnessed evidence of problems that often accompany homelessness (drug and alcohol abuse, mental illness), she also saw among Kānaka Maoli "a desire to reconnect with the land and their Hawaiian culture," with many expressing "a sense of pride in their ability to fish or gather limu [seaweed] from the ocean or to grow their own edible plants, even if [only] in tin cans." Akamine also noted "a layer of normalcy in the everyday rhythm of life on the beach," which was undercut by the constant "threat of being evicted from the beach parks" and the stigma of being homeless. Akamine has described her project as demonstrating "the similarities of living [houseless] in the beach parks, [compared with] . . . what we consider normal everyday life. . . . The only difference [being] the tools or methods used to complete these tasks and where the families were living."

A traveling exhibit, "Ku'u One Hānau" has been installed at multiple locations; two important Hawaiian institutions, Kamakakūokalani Center for Hawaiian Studies at the University of Hawai'i at Mānoa and Kaumakapili Church in Kalihi, O'ahu. Both locations are significant Hawaiian institutions, the first representing the highest level of formal institutionalized Hawaiian education; the second is one of the oldest Hawaiian Christian churches, located in the heart of a longtime working-class urban center with a high population of Kānaka Maoli, though more recently, primarily Asian and Pacific Islander immigrants. Since its founding in 1837, Kaumakapili has been considered the church of the common person, as working-class Hawaiians [maka'āinana] felt the need for a place of worship where they could be treated with 'equality,' " something lacking at the already established Kawaiaha'o Church, where ali'i (chiefs, royalty) such as Queen Lili'uokalani worshiped ("History"). However, the Queen was regularly involved in activities at Kaumakapili, including the laying of a cornerstone on her birthday in 1881, and hosting an 'aha'aina (feast) there in 1887. When Queen Lili'uokalani and her government were overthrown in 1893, Kawaiaha'o Church turned on her, and she was mocked from the pulpit, thus deepening the connection between Kaumaka-pili Church and caring for the people, and making it a more appropriate site for Akamine's installation. Kalihi also was and remains a predominantly working-class neighborhood, with a higher number of Kanaka Maoli families, making the installation more accessible to the people it represents.

"The Houseless Project" was also installed at Kea'au Beach Park on the Wai-'anae coast, a well-known houseless campsite primarily populated by Kanaka Maoli families, "during the week of Thanksgiving because the City and County

Ku'u One Hānau. Bernice Akamine, 1997–2000. Used with permission.

had served the houseless population on the beach with eviction notices, which meant they could come in at any time to remove the families."

The use of giant Hawaiian flags as tent tarps evokes the kaona (implied, hidden, metaphoric meaning) of what the flags represent: the traditional kuleana, or roles and expectation of aliʻi to protect and care for the people. Traditional aliʻi hōʻailona (symbols), such as ʻahu ʻula (feather cloaks and capes) and mahiole (feather helmets) would be too sacred and personal to evoke the communal care and protection of the makaʻāinana as effectively as the Hawaiian kingdom flag. First adopted by Kamehameha I, this flag intentionally emulated the flag of Great Britain because it represented the most powerful nation of his time. Akemine's incorporating the flag adopted by Kamehameha is, I argue, a kaona-laden reference to Kamehameha's Kānāwai Māmalahoe (Law of the Splintered Paddle), enacted in 1797, which guaranteed protection to "every elder, woman, and child to lie safely alongside the roadways" without harassment or fear. Widely acknowledged as a precept of human rights laws in Hawaiʻi, it is incorporated into the Hawaiʻi state constitution, article 9, section 10, which addresses public safety (Constitution). As such, it is often cited by advocates for the homeless in Hawaiʻi when lobbying the state and local governments to provide more support for the homeless populations, and to stop harassing and evicting them, especially from public (state) lands, which themselves are ceded (or illegally obtained) Hawaiian kingdom lands transferred to the U.S. federal government after the illegal annexation of Hawaiʻi. Because some of these were transferred to the state government after statehood in 1959, while makaʻāinana and other kānaka would have found shelter and respite on aliʻi and kingdom lands prior to annexation, certainly since statehood, the state and federal governments have aggressively continued to dispossess and evict Kānaka Maoli and others from public lands.

A critique of the state is implied in Akemine's use of the flags as well. Although it has appropriated such symbols of the overthrown kingdom as the flag and the Kānāwai Māmalahoe, the state does not do enough (if anything) to protect the people overall, let alone those most vulnerable. And while these symbols are a source of pride in Kanaka Maoli cultural practice and political sovereignty and history, the state's appropriation of such important symbols through settler colonialism has opened itself up to the inherent critique embedded in Akemine's project. "Kuʻu One Hānau" (literally, my beloved birth sands), deepens the connection between kanaka and ʻāina, which is both homeland and home, the place where one lives. Hence the insistence on houselessness, not homelessness. "Kuʻu One Hānau" evokes a beloved mele, "Hawaiʻi Aloha," which begins, "E Hawaiʻi e kuʻu one hānau ē" (O Hawaiʻi, my beloved home), which also demonstrates aloha ʻāina, love for the land, or Hawaiian nationalism. The title also alludes to poetic compositions much earlier in Hawaiian history that recognize Hawaiʻi as kanaka ancestor as much as place, solidifying a reference to the intertwining of human and non-human ancestors in Kanaka Maoli moʻokūʻauhau.

Quotes from houseless Hawaiians interviewed by Akamine adorn the inside of the tents, representing their experiences by inscribing their words within the flag "walls." One of the long-standing Kanaka Maoli houseless populations represented by Akamine's "Kuʻu One Hānau," and Kēhaulani Watson's photography, is located at Mākua Beach. Some have lived and camped there for decades. Periodic evictions from the 1960s to the present have occurred. Mākua resident Sparky Rodrigues has shared that the U.S. Army

> bombed the houses in the 1940s and took over the entire valley. The [U.S.] government moved all of the residents out and said after the war, you can move back—and then they used the houses for target practice. The families tell stories that the military came with guns and said, "Here's $300, thank you," and "You've got to move." Those people remain without their houses, and for years, many lived on the beaches in Mākua, watching the bombing of their land. (LaDuke)

As environmentalist and writer Winona LaDuke notes in an article, "Homeless in Hawaiʻi," there is "More Land for the [U.S.] Military than for [Native] Hawaiians."

The U.S. Army has occupied Mākua since 1942, with a tenuous claim to the land. Hawaiian genealogies, however, indicate Mākua was continuously occupied for thirty-five generations, or roughly 800 years. In 1992, the Army once again attempted to get the state to evict Hawaiians, calling them squatters and claiming unsanitary conditions posed a threat to health and the environment. Yet across the centuries of Hawaiian occupation, the water was clean, the fish abundant, the soil productive, and the natural resources healthy. Critics have pointed out that the Army's own activities in Mākua have had a far greater negative impact on the health of people and the environment. In the half-century of Army use, the natural and cultural resources of the site have been wantonly abused to the point that many may never be retrieved, however many dollars the Army might plow back into environmental studies, biological assessments, cultural and archaeological surveys, or remedial actions.

Watson's "Not Homeless" photo expands upon Akamine's "Houseless Project" work, and the understanding that Kānaka Maoli are not homeless in the homeland, but houseless. The photo shows a male kupuna (elder) sweeping his "home" under the sheltering branches of a tree. The Hawaiian word for shade, malu, also means protection and shelter—the functions of a house. The couple's meager possessions are carefully tended in their home, which includes a garden. A kalo

Not Homeless. Kēhaulani Watson, 2010. Used with permission.

plant, representing the kinship connection between ʻāina and kanaka through
Hāloa, is planted in the sunny area on the left of the photo.

Like Akamine, Watson uses a flag to critique the lack of settler colonial concern
for or care of Kānaka Maoli, including the houseless. But Watson's critique is not
leveled against the state of Hawaiʻi; rather, it is leveled against the U.S.
government.

In "Lawe Hae Hawaiʻi" (To carry off the Hawaiian flag), Watson depicts the
meager possessions of a houseless Mākua Beach ʻohana (family) in the back of
an old truck, draped with a tattered and faded American flag. Both the Ameri-
can-made automobile (Ford), and the American flag represent the promise of
"life, liberty, and the pursuit of happiness," an idealized trope of the American
Dream. But the broken down, rusting, late model truck and the faded flag more
accurately represent the limitations and failures of settler colonialism and a U.S.
occupied Hawaiʻi, which has not brought freedom, justice, or prosperity for
Kānaka Maoli dispossessed from their land base and nation.

The possessions in the truck may be junk, collected for scrap by the truck
owner to make a living. Or all of it may be possessions seized by Kānaka evicted
from their homes or houseless campsites. Finally, they may suggest the environmental destruction faced by Kānaka Maoli and the environment at Mākua.

Through their art pieces on Kanaka Maoli houselessness, Akamine and
Watson offer a moʻolelo kālaiʻāina that both celebrates and remembers Kanaka
Maoli connections to specific ʻāina. This moʻolelo is laden with multiple levels of

Lawe Hae Hawaiʻi. Kēhaulani Watson, 2010. Used with permission.

kaona, evoking safety, care, nourishment and abundance, as well as continued kūpaʻa, alluding to "kūpaʻa mākou ma hope o ka ʻāina" (we [Kānaka Maoli] stand firm behind the land), in one line, and "ma hope mākou o Liliʻulani" (we stand firm behind Liliʻu[oka]lani) in another, of the famous lines of Ellen Kekoaohi-waikalani Prendergast's renowned overthrow and anti-annexation protest anthem, "Mele ʻAi Pōhaku" (Rock-eating song). Simultaneously, these artists critique the settler moʻolelo that Hawaiʻi's transition from sovereign kingdom to fiftieth state has been both benign and beneficial for Hawaiʻi and its people, making it a "patriotic paradise" of military strength and tourist respite, the twin economic engines for the state's economy, with little attention paid to Kanaka Maoli dispossession.

Reclaiming ʻĀina, Celebrating Wahi Pana, Protesting U.S. Military Occupation

Meleanna Meyer's "Mākua: Two Panels" is a moʻolelo that visualizes the U.S. military's environmental and cultural destruction at Mākua as described by an *Environment Hawaiʻi* report in October 1992:

> There are the fires that the Army continues to set...which burn up the valley sides and threaten endangered native plants and animals. There are the open burns and open detonations of munitions and other chemicals, including some that are known to cause cancer in humans.

There is the matter of unexploded munitions having been scattered everywhere into this once productive valley, making it unsuitable for any human activity other than the training of soldiers for combat. There are the once forested valley walls laid bare and eroding thanks to years of shelling; the diversity of plant life reduced to stands of [foreign] molasses grass; the sites of Hawaiian habitation and worship, both ancient and modern, trashed. . . .

When unserviceable munitions from military installations on Oʻahu need to be destroyed, they are brought to Makua Valley where they are burned or blown up. To do this, the Army must have a permit from the Environmental Protection Agency.

But when the Army burns or blows up unserviceable munitions brought to Makua Valley for training purposes, it claims (without argument) that this activity is exempt from EPA regulation. . . . ("Editorial")

The destruction described above does not even include the endangered native flora and fauna and their habitat in Mākua valley; some are found nowhere else in the islands or the world.

The Mākua panels were part of a 2008 MaMo (Maoli Arts Month) exhibition, "The Art of Resistance: Art and Resistance in Hawaiʻi," which explored "a number of struggles to protect Hawaiian land, waters, and culture through the eyes of contemporary artist/activists and their work" on contested spaces and places with an eye towards shaping the future ("About").

The left panel shows a verdant green profile of Mākua valley walls splattered with blood. Because of the violent nature of the blood splatter and the military's use of the land, violent death through acts of war are clearly implied. The Kanaka kinship to ʻāina through Papahānaumoku is also implied and perhaps even more violent, as ʻāina is rarely personified to the point of bleeding in the same manner as humans do. The second panel also depicts the violence of war through the shattering of the ʻāina by penetrating projectiles, symbols of settler colonial heteropatriarchy-induced violence, here enacting the rape and death of the epitome of the Indigenous female body, the earth mother Papahānaumoku, the primordial maternal makua (parent), and the abundance she provides.

Together, the different art projects of Akamine, Watson, and Meyer create a symphonic moʻolelo that critiques settler colonialism's disastrous effects on Kānaka Maoli and ʻāina. Akamine and Watson both address houselessness. Meyer's "Mākua: Two Panels" bears witness to and critiques the U.S. military's destruction of Mākua, and its erasure of Kanaka Maoli moʻolelo and connection to ʻāina.

In Haley Kailiehu's visual depiction of moʻolelo of Mākua, she reinscribes, remembers, and reasserts Kanaka Maoli history and story as kūpaʻa and kūʻē through a community mural project, "Mālama Mākua" (care for Mākua). In 2014,

Mālama Mākua. Haley Kailiehu, 2014. Used with permission.

Kailiehu led a group of volunteer artists comprised of Waiʻanae community members, Nā Pua Noʻeau (Center for Gifted and Talented Native Hawaiian Children), and students from Hawaiʻinuiākea School of Hawaiian Knowledge at the University of Hawaiʻi at Mānoa.

The mural depicts the moʻolelo of Hiʻiakaikapoliopele, the youngest and most favorite sister of Pele, the Hawaiian volcano goddess, who travels from Kīlauea, Hawaiʻi to Hāʻena, Kauaʻi to fetch Pele's dream lover, the aliʻi Lohiʻau. This is a well-known and important oral tradition first recorded in writing in nineteenth-century Hawaiian language newspapers.

On her return from Kauaʻi, Hiʻiaka saves the life of a young woman of Mākua. As Hiʻiaka and her companions Wahineʻōmaʻo and Lohiʻau arrive off the west coast of Oʻahu, Hiʻiaka is so struck by the beauty of the land that she asks for the canoe to land at Keawaʻula, so she may walk down the coastline. She performs a series of chants, offering her aloha (greetings, affection), and praising the beauty of the ʻāina. When she arrives at Mākua, a giant rock, Pōhakuloa, has covered a favorite spot to jump in the ocean from the low cliffs. A young woman arrives from the uplands and doesn't see Pōhakuloa, so when she leaps into the water, she hits the rock instead and dies. As her family begins to mourn her, Hiʻiaka retrieves the woman's body and restores her life through a combination of prayers, sharing of breath, and the application of medicinal plants from the ʻāina. Explaining the meaning of the moʻolelo on her website, Kailiehu writes,

> The story speaks of the natural resources and cultural practices found within the ahupuaʻa of Mākua, and the surrounding areas of Koʻiahi and Kahanahāiki—which include resources for lei making, medicinal

plants, places for lele pali (cliff diving), and plants that could bring restoration from illness (of land or body). ("Mālama")

Therefore, the mural is an example of how "place holds memory for people who share an intimate relationship with their environment...[as] all memories are embodied and grounded in place." Hawaiian geographer and Hawaiian language professor Kapā Oliveira asserts that "even people who leave their birthplace often retain vivid memories...later in life" (66). But as Kailiehu's community-based mural project demonstrates, remembering places through ancestral stories is a powerful way of remembering and connecting to ʻāina, even when one is not born there. Hiʻiaka utilizes ancestral knowledge and connection to familial akua (deities) to assist her in drawing upon the resources of the ʻāina she visits, in order to restore life to the ʻāina and the kamaʻāina (natives) of various locations "that have experienced unhealthy shifts in land use." In this way, "it is a moʻolelo that teaches us the value of reviving our relationships with our ʻāina, in part, through genealogical practices."

Meyer's art represents and critiques the violence of the U.S. abuse of Mākua. Watson's photo reveals the maintained connection to ʻāina by Kanaka families displaced from their family lands by U.S. military occupation. And Kailiehu's community mural is an act of hulihia, an overturning of the history of settler colonial violence upon the land by a reassertion (remembering) through Hiʻiaka and her moʻolelo of abundance, nurturing, and caring of the ʻāina.

Kanaka Maoli women's art is multivocal; one strand of what Dakota scholar Waziyatawin calls "Indigenous truth-telling" that speaks back to power. It is decolonization and an assertion of cultural memory. Through recalling traditional relationships with ʻāina, it remaps and reimagines our presence, even when displaced and expelled from our lands by colonial force, because as Patrick Wolfe solemnly reminds us, the goal of settler colonialism is "the elimination of the native" (387). A key agent of Native elimination is military power, and the U.S. military is considered the highest symbol of an aggressive power that has been instrumental in the elimination and subjugation of Native peoples in many places across the globe, and particularly the Native people of North America. Hawaiʻi has been increasingly militarized since 1893. It is currently the most militarized state in the U.S., which has a long, contentious military history here, particularly with Kānaka Maoli. Speaking back to the power of the U.S. military is an important theme of Kanaka Maoli women's art and activism.

Protecting ʻĀina and Ancestors: ʻAʻole GMO

In 2008, Kānaka Maoli grappled with the issue of genetic modification of kalo. Our Indigenous cultural beliefs and practices surrounding kalo, described in mo'olelo as the first ancestor and staple crop, dramatically clashed with settler colonial systems of Big Science, capitalism politics, and law. The University of Hawai'i's College of Tropical Agriculture and Human Resources (CTAHR) has led efforts to genetically modify and patent kalo in Hawai'i, arguing for preservation and better marketing (and marketability) of kalo for local and foreign markets while downplaying cultural, scientific, and other concerns. While GMO proponents claimed they were wanting to preserve heritage kalo varieties, GMOs are also patentable, and thus a potential money-maker for the patent holder (the University of Hawai'i, not Kānaka Maoli). Thus, GMO is a tangent of settler colonialism that colonizes Kānaka Maoli on multiple levels. Senate Bill 958 proposed a ten-year moratorium on the development, testing, propagating, cultivation, growing, and raising of genetically modified taro, and on the patenting of taro plant varieties in Hawai'i. Over 1,500 pages of testimony in support of the bill were submitted, and it ultimately passed and became effective on July 1, 2008, with a five-year moratorium. Kānaka Maoli responded with visual art during testimonies and in other venues, many of which reference traditional mo'olelo for images of Hāloanakalaukapalili, first kalo, and his younger sibling Hāloa, the first human ancestor.

Maui artist Abigail Romanchak's "Kumu" (source) was part of the MaMo 2008 "Makawalu" (multiple perspectives) exhibit at Nu'uanu Gallery and Marks Garage in downtown Honolulu. "Kumu" features a kalo corm with rootlets attached, suggesting the rootedness of the people. The word kumu is a kaona reference to the narrative of the Hāloa siblings, the first kalo plant and his younger brother, the progenitor of the Hawaiian people. In Romanchak's visual mo'olelo, the kalo corm is framed by the letters "G M O" (genetically modified organism), which directly represent western science and the settler desire to genetically modify indigenous plant crops through Big Science and Corporate Agriculture—another strand of the settler colonial narrative focused on Native annihilation. But Romanchak reasserts an indigenous mo'olelo that literally centers the root of Hāloanakalaukapalili—the physical and metaphorical core of Hāloa and his kanaka descendants, as the center of our world, our very existence dependent upon it. On one hand, then the kalo is framed or surrounded by settler colonialism, represented by the repetitive "G M O" sequence of letters. But on the other hand, it is also repelling and resisting that threat, maintaining its place in the piko (center) of the image, and by extension, maintaining our integrity and connection to the center of our ancestry.

Regarding her work, Romanchak writes that

> I see my prints as a way to empower and assert a Hawaiian sense of identity and to perpetuate Hawaiian culture through art. I believe that native cultures are jeopardized once they stop speaking to people

in the present day. As an artist, I seek to perpetuate traditional culture not through traditional means, but contemporary ones, so that it may endure for generations to come. ("About")

Contemporary Maoli artists are inspired by both traditions (practices, materials, concepts, and tools, for example), as well as contemporary experiences, which Romanchek has acknowledged with her own art. "Kumu" is one such work, eloquently making such an important statement through the moʻolelo it narrates and remembers.

In 2008, one of the MaMo art installations at Marks Garage in Honolulu focused on the theme "Invasive Species." Curated by Kanaka Maoli artist and Hawaiian Studies professor Maile Andrade, invited Kanaka Maoli artists were asked to share works that reflected the theme. While artists could use any media of their choice, there was one stipulation—only black and white could be used.

For "GMO=Kalocide," I chose a black background to reflect pō, the Hawaiian night and period of the gods, nature, and creative forces of the universe in the Kumulipo, a koʻihonua or cosmic genealogy composed of 2,108 lines of poetry recounting the creation of the Hawaiian universe. The image of kalo/Hāloa outlined in white alludes to ghosts and iwi (bones), both of which represent death or what remains after death for Hāloa, and by extension, Kānaka Maoli, because of the genetics-altering process. The face image in the main kalo leaf suggests Expressionist painter Edvard Munch's series of paintings dubbed "The Scream." The most well-known was painted in 1893, the year the Hawaiian kingdom was overthrown, so it's a hidden kaona—the kalo's face isn't painted to replicate a German Expressionist style per se, but to reference the date of another horror and tragedy faced by our people. A quote from nineteenth-century Kanaka Maoli writer Kepelino is handwritten around the kalo leaves:

> He mea maikai loa ka mahiai kalo ma na aina maloo. He hoaloha oluolu loa ia ano, a he kumu paipai mau i ka puuwai o kanaka. He ea ala ka lau, ka ha, ka pua ma na kihapai kalo. He mea aloha, a he mea makemake maoli, ke ike aku i ke ulu a ke kalo, a me na ano huli he nui wale, ke noho oe, a hoomaha paha iloko o na puepue kalo.
>
> I ka wa kahiko, he mea ue na ka poe mahiai ka hana, ke loohia ko lakou mau kino i ka mai; nolaila, ue maoli lakou i ka minamina i ka hana, a me ke aloha i na mea kanu. "He keiki aloha na mea kanu," wahi a ka poe mahiai. (155)

> [Kalo planted on dry lands is an excellent thing. [Kalo is] an affable companion and one pleasing to the hearts of the people. The leaves, stems, and blossoms have a pleasant scent in the patch. It is a lovely

GMO. kuʻualoha hoʻomanawanui, 2008.

sight, really delightful, to see the different varieties of kalo growing
when one sits down to rest amongst the mounds of kalo plants.

In the past the farmers wept when they became disabled from
work, because they loved their plants. "Plants are beloved children,"
said the farmers.] (My translation).

Kepelino's quote supports the kinship connection between kalo/Hāloa as the
ancestor who provides for and feeds the people with his body. Kalo is a domestic
plant that must be tended, and therefore it becomes the beloved child of the taro
farmers, taking on a dual role of ancestor/child, connecting ʻāina, kanaka, and
multiple generations of kānaka sustained by the abundance of the land.

Kalo. Bernice Akamine, 2016. Used with permission.

Because kalo holds such an important place in Hawaiian history and culture, it is not surprising that it is evoked in any number of moʻolelo kalaiʻāina. Another visual art piece that evokes kalo is Bernice Akamine's "KALO." "KALO" is a mixed media installation that uses maps of the islands and signature pages from the 1897–1898 Hui Aloha ʻĀina Anti-Annexation Petitions to create the leaves and stems of kalo plants, attached to "corms" fashioned from pōhaku (stones). As such, it is a visual remembrance of ancestors, as well as a reaffirmation of a collective moʻokūʻauhau maoli of kūpaʻa and kūʻē.

The leaves were initially colored, but the color was removed in the 2016 installation, "to keep the focus of the artwork on the original intent of the Petition and the signors." Akamine describes "KALO" as "an artistic interpretation of the importance of the historical document, the *Anti-Annexation Petition,* both as a statement of support of Queen Liliʻuokalani and as a symbol of lōkahi [unity] and haʻaheo [pride]." Thus, it is a visual retelling of an important moʻolelo kālaiʻāina that in the modern, historical era both commemorates, and helps us to remember the thoughts, actions, and presence of our kūpuna who fought annexation of Hawaiʻi to the U.S. This critical moʻolelo kālaiʻāina refutes the settler colonial narrative of Hawaiʻi's gentle, uncontested acquisition by the U.S. as a territory and state—a false narrative that continues to be regurgitated in colonial institutions ranging from education to tourism, despite ample evidence to the contrary.

Akamine originally chose her own pōhaku, but later decided to accept donations from "anyone who wished to support the original signers of the Petition," thus transforming the KALO exhibit into "a piece about creating community in the present, while also connecting with the past and … the ancestors" (Earlier). Pōhaku from all the islands represented by signers in the petition were included. The art piece has been installed in several locations, including the Wailoa Center in Hilo, and most recently at the Mānoa Commons Gallery at the University of Hawai'i at Mānoa. There are eighty-seven kalo plants, which Akamine plans to donate to Hawaiian culture and community groups, such as Hawaiian immersion schools or civic clubs, who can care for the kalo, with the intent to create a connection from the past through the present for the future.

Media used include pōhaku from Kaua'i, O'ahu, Maui, and Hawai'i; all of the pages of the Hui Aloha 'Āina Anti-Annexation Petitions (1897–1898), and maps of Kaua'i, O'ahu, Moloka'i, Maui, and Hawai'i. Thus far, pōhaku have been donated by sixty-five people from four islands. Some contributors donated pōhaku in memory of other family members, deepening the community and generational ties. In describing the donation of pōhaku for the project, Akamine has shared that "many … [come with] touching stories attached to them. [Some] pōhaku … come from a place significant to the donor and some have a deep connection between the donor and a loved one. Some of the pōhaku represent the descendants of the original signers of the Petition." One example is from the great-granddaughter of Kahula Ha'ae, the first signer of the petition, who also donated a pōhaku. To expand the community connection, Akamine reached out not only to descendants of petition signers, but "to those who have not found their ancestors' signatures … as a way to create a larger sense of community and inclusiveness." For all of the artists, community engagement and activism are important parts of their art, with multiple connections to the lāhui.

Defending Sacred Lands and Practices:
Protecting Mauna a Wākea against the Thirty Meter Telescope (TMT)

Since 2014, the protection of Mauna Kea from the Thirty Meter Telescope (TMT) and further development is the most visible political and cultural issue in Hawai'i. It isn't the first, last, or only fight to protect Hawaiian lands and the right to practice our culture, and it isn't going to be resolved any time soon. There are legal avenues, scholarly and intellectual debates, and deep discussions around moral and ethical issues. What's sacred? What's expendable? What's not? Whose culture, whose lifestyle? And the artists continue to contribute ho'okupu (offerings) of kū'ē and kūpa'a. As mentioned earlier, mele is an important medium for relating mo'olelo. One of the most important roles of mele is the mana i ka leo—the power of the voice that touches the naʻau (guts) and not just the intellect, a critical path for reaching out and moving people. Mauna Kea is the highest point in Oceania, and thus the water that emanates from its summit, from the Hawaiian deity Poliʻahu's snowfall, is the purest, most sacred water in all of Oceania, making it an important symbol not only for Native Hawaiians, but for Indigenous peoples throughout Oceania.

Kailiehu's Mauna a Wākea community mural was painted as part of the Ka Leo Arts Festival, October 12–13, 2015, on a temporary construction fence that was meant to come down. A graduate student at UH Mānoa at the time, Kailiehu was also a member of HauMANA, the student section of the Hawaiian independence hui (group) MANA (Movement for Aloha No ka ʻĀina). Dozens of people, including students, faculty, and community members from keiki (children) to kūpuna (elders) representing different islands participated.

What was not expected was the backlash by some in the UH community, including students (Ka Leo newspaper staff) and administration. The mural depicts the moʻolelo of Kamiki. While Mauna a Wākea is not known for perpetual stream flow, fresh water (snowmelt), with Lake Waiʻau also a source, streams down the mountain. As English professor and community activist Candace Fujikane writes, the mural moʻolelo "map[s] the abundance of the people and the kalo plants fed by Mauna a Wākea . . . the aquifer for all of Hawaiʻi Island, and the genealogical path of the life-sustaining waters of Kāneikawaiola . . . where it feeds several springs that extend out across the plains of Pōhakuloa" ("Cartographies" 6). In the mural, kānaka are rendered as kalo, feet planted in the nourishing ʻāina, with bodies as kalo corms, arms raised to the sky transformed into kalo stems and leaves, remembering the moʻolelo of Hāloa that represents a direct kinship connection between kānaka and ʻāina. Placed in front of Mauna a Wākea, the image includes the mountain as part of Hāloa's moʻokūʻauhau. As Fujikane writes,

Mauna a Wākea. Haley Kailiehu, 2015. Used with permission.

the mural shows us the water streaming down the mountain, "feeding the Kānaka as kalo people, siblings of the kalo, their leafy arms outstretched to Wākea, Sky Father." At the center of the mural is Papahānaumoku and Wākea.

> To the right of them is their daughter, Hoʻohōkūkalani, holding a baby in her arms. Her first child by Wākea was born as an unformed fetus and, when buried, grew into the kalo plant Hāloanakalaukapalili, whose leaves tremble in the wind. The second child she carries in her arms is Hāloa the aliʻi, the younger sibling to the kalo and also to Mauna a Wākea. These ancestors fill the land in the mural, reminding us of the genealogical descent of Mauna a Wākea, of kalo, and of Kānaka from Papa and Wākea, all fed by the life-giving waters of Kāne at Waiau. The mural is a map that restores the land to its embeddedness in the moʻolelo, oli, and mele of abundance and the kuleana given to Kānaka to care for their elder siblings. (*Mapping* 112–113)

Lake Waiau is placed above these ancestors in the center of a large kalo leaf. It is painted in red, a symbolic color of blood, royalty, life, the heart (emotions and center) of the lāhui, and the color of sap of certain varieties of kalo, such as lehua. Lehua (*Metreosideros maropus*) is also a native tree closely associated with Hawaiʻi Island. Kaona references to lehua include "a warrior, beloved friend or relative, sweetheart, expert," all of which are suggested in the kalo people as kūpuna, kū kiaʻi mauna (mountain protectors), and poʻe aloha ʻāina.

Chalkboard paint around the central image extended an invitation for students to contribute messages, a critical part of the mural for community contribution, and because words have mana. But *Ka Leo* staff members objected to the "political" messages, and they were painted over without consultation. Settler colonial hegemony is so prevalent within the inherent anti-Indigenous structure of the university that Kailiehu responded, "Not even a painting of our Mauna a Wākea can exist on the UHM campus." The moʻolelo kālaiʻaina Kailiehu envisioned had widespread repercussions of kūpaʻa and kūʻe, demonstrating the power of moʻolelo. Fujikane writes, "When the mural was censored, the gathering of hundreds of students to protest that censorship attests to the power of this decolonial map" as a kiʻi visually depicting moʻolelo "that restores people to the map in a way that suggests a crisis in capitalist attempts to manufacture scarcity and an alternative economy for a decolonial future. In many other ways, the struggle to protect Mauna Kea has been one of restoring the abundance of the lāhui." The community mural supports other efforts of aloha ʻāina activism for Mauna a Wākea and beyond, as "The activism of the protectors have inspired people across the islands to grow the lāhui through building networks that connect us and organizing their own communities to stand for Mauna Kea" ("Cartographies" 6).

Kailiehu shares,

> What I have come to understand through my community-inclusive murals is that the image is only as powerful as the people who truly understand the meaning and moʻolelo behind it. The Mauna a Wākea Mural we did at UH, I knew at some point would be taken down, if not by someone who thoroughly disagreed with the moʻolelo, it would eventually be disassembled by the construction crew. The experience of painting was important because it allowed us time to talk with the community that showed up to educate them about the moʻolelo and thus the importance of Mauna ā Wākea and our genealogical connection to that place, and why we have kuleana, as Kanaka Maoli to protect it.

In May 2015, Kanaka Maoli scholar, activist, and educator Noelani Goodyear-Kaʻōpua participated in a zine workshop organized by Maui graduate student and poet Noʻukahauʻoli Revilla. The purpose was to create art and poetry to affirm aloha ʻāina and speak back to a pro-TMT settler colonial political cartoon by Dave Swann. Goodyear-Kaʻōpua's mixed media collage protesting the TMT telescope on Mauna Kea is captioned with the phrase "They tried to bury us, but they didn't know we are seeds." The words are neatly handwritten across a white mantle of Poliʻahu's snow cloaking Mauna Kea's summit. The mountain is presented in three colors—dark gray, bright orange, and deep red—set against a black sky. These three colors representing the mountain can be viewed in multiple ways: as an outer, middle, and inner core of the mountain; different altitude ranges of the mauna, the highest in the Pacific; or as different puʻu (hills) that give a three-dimensional breadth to the mauna. The colors also represent different layers of earth and elements comprising the soil. They suggest the volcanic nature of the mountain, and a (once) molten core to a hardened surface. The black sky represents the sacred element of Pō, night, from whence all life unfolds genealogically in the Kumulipo. Night is the time of the gods and elements of nature, both flora and fauna, from whom Kānaka descend.

At first glance, the image is simple: six colors, large, basic shapes (circles, ovals, triangles). But the minimalist image is richly imbued with multiple layers of kaona. Goodyear-Kaʻōpua employs the traditional Hawaiian poetic device of helu (listing, to recount). Rain names are encapsulated in white ovals emanating from the snow-caption: Kiʻowao, Pōpōkapa, Lililehua, Poʻolipilipi, Tuahine, Leikokoʻula, Waʻahia, and Makahuna. These rains are actively falling on a half-dozen or so kiaʻi "seeds" firmly planted in the nurturing soil-body of the ancestral earth mother Papahānaumoku, represented by Mauna a Wākea. The layers of the mauna also suggest the kiaʻi seeds are widely scattered across the ʻāina, ready to sprout and flourish at any moment. Goodyear-Kaʻōpua's image reflects the intimate and loving relationship between Kānaka and our ʻāina. As with the moʻolelo of Hāloa, our ʻāina nurtures us, and we, in turn, nurture and protect (kiaʻi) it as well.

Rain is an important metaphor in Hawaiian culture that carries myriad levels of kaona. The quality of rain can indicate passion, joy, sorrow, or love. Combined with other elements such as wind or surf, times of trouble or intense grief may be indicated. Rain, fresh water, and drenching also refer to sweethearts. The more obvious meanings of water and rain are life, fertility, growth, grief, and hardships. Hawaiians love the rain and know that the beauty of their islands is due to rain, as expressed in the saying, "Uē ka lani, ola ka honua" (the heavens weep, the earth lives).

Named rains contain other layers of kaona, such as associations with aliʻi. Names of kānaka, akua, and ʻāina encapsulate stories and connections between people, places, and shared history or characteristics. Names are "poetic devices that contain history and story." Where haole see a nameless element, Kānaka see kino lau (body forms) of deities and ancestors, a physical dimension of poetic expression. As Leimomi Akana so eloquently notes,

> Rain names are a convergence of past, present, and future, and in using them, we will summon the knowledge of our kūpuna, joining them in calling out to the lands on which the rains reside, calling on ourselves to rise to a higher consciousness, and calling to the future, where new life will continue to be born. (xx)

The rain names listed are from different islands, connecting the sacred waters of Mauna a Wākea's summit snowfall as the source of all rain. The listing also connects the kiaʻi symbolically, as coming from all islands across the Hawaiian archipelago, and asserts that all our ʻāina nurtures and sustains us, and thus our kuleana (responsibility) is to be kūʻē and kūpaʻa in our protection of it. The listing also invokes Prendergast's call to the kānaka of each island to join together ma hope o ka ʻāina, to stand steadfastly behind the land, which they do. It is a communal and interactive nurturing and blossoming of the kiaʻi seeds/pua (flowers, offspring) rooted—literally and figuratively—in the ʻāina.

The personified rains in the image cleverly evoke kaona. Several of the rain names are found on Oʻahu and Hawaiʻi: Pōpōkapa (Nuʻuanu, Hilo), Poʻolipilipi (Kalihi, Hilo), and Waʻahia (alternately Waʻahila) (Kaimukī, Hilo), demonstrating traditional connections between these places that are also now connected through the activism of nā kiaʻi, who hail from all islands (Akana 118, 240, 271). The names also reference the personal genealogical connections of the mele's creator to these islands. Still others are associated with specific aliʻi, referencing their sacred nature, as well as the period of Hawaiian independence before the overthrow, evoking other historical moʻolelo. Kiʻowao, a cool mountain rain of Kamaoha, Oʻahu, is found in a mele for Prince Albert composed by his father Kamehameha IV, while Leikokoʻula, a rain of Waimea, Hawaiʻi, is referenced in both a political mele for Queen Emma, in a kanikau (lament) for her husband, Kamehameha IV, and in a name chant for Queen Liliʻuokalani (74). Thus, their naming reinforces the sacredness of Mauna a Wākea, a child named in the genealogy of the deities Papahānaumoku and Wākea, who are also the ancestors of Kānaka.

The rain names reference important qualities that elicit such connections: the Leikokoʻula is literally a "lei of red color or a rainbow hued lei." The color red is both a sacred and royal color. Moreover, this rain is described in one mele as falling, "Me he ʻahuʻula i luna o ka lāʻau" (Like a feather cape above the trees) ("Hana Waimea"). The ʻahuʻula is a specific garment often composed with red feathers, worn only by the highest ranking aliʻi. Another example is the Poʻolipilipi rain, which is included in a wind chant to the people of Hilo to get up and prepare to sail (be alert, be ready, and follow the command or face the consequences). The name means "adze head," which supports the metaphoric warning—an adze is an important tool to shape canoes, its sharp head fashioned from the hardest, densest stone, the best quarry of which is located on the summit of Mauna a Wākea (92, 104, 148–149, 195). Goodyear-Kaʻōpua is from Oʻahu, living and working in the areas represented by the rains Lililehua (Pālolo), Makahuna (Pālolo, Waikīkī), Tuahine (Mānoa), and Waʻahia (Kaimukī) rains, all within the same ahupuaʻa.

"They tried to bury us," the phrase Goodyear-Kaʻōpua uses as the theme for her image, has been popularly referred to as a Mexican proverb of resistance associated with the Zapatista movement. More recently, it has been credited to Greek poet Dinos Christianopoulos, who was speaking back to the mainstream literary community that marginalized LGBTQ writers. Thus, there are multiple layers of kūʻē and kūpaʻa inherent in the saying that speak to multiple activist communities. What perhaps resonates the most with aloha ʻāina nationalism is the metaphor of ʻāina. But in the cross-fertilization of inspiration between Indigenous movements replicating kūpaʻa and kūʻē, the inspiring phrase also points to Goodyear-Kaʻōpua's first book, *The Seeds We Planted*, and her experiences as a Kanaka Maoli educator and the creation of Hālau Kū Māna, one of the first New Century Charter schools in Hawaiʻi.

To deepen the connection, the book begins with lines from a mele composed by students Kuʻulei Freed, Shari Kapua Chock, Kaleialiʻi Baldwin, and Kaʻapuni Asaivao called "Seventh Generation." The title references the Iroquois ethic to consider the impact and effect of decisions not only on current communities, but also the impact seven generations into the future.

After evoking the 1893 overthrow and imprisonment of Queen Liliʻuokalani, the refrain states,

> As the seventh generation, we must all become a nation.
> Keep the land prosperous, rise above, above all the rest.
> We won't take it for granted, ʻcuz that is the seed you planted.
> We will not take it for granted, ʻcuz that is the seed we planted. (1)

The last two lines of the stanza subtly shift from being a recipient of knowledge ("that is the seed *you* planted"), the perspective of student to teacher, or younger to older generation who is responsible to teach and guide, to being a protector, nurturer, and source of knowledge ("that is the seed *we* planted"), as well as co-creators and collaborators of the knowledge, reflecting the positive collaborative ethic valued in ʻŌiwi culture, as it is the responsibility of all of us working together for the benefit of all. Kalo does not grow from seeds per se, but the connection between planting knowledge to educate and uplift, and planting kalo to feed and nourish, is metaphoric, represented in the abundance of art, mele, and moʻolelo celebrating kalo, Hāloa, and even our chief kalo product, poi.

In all of these examples of Kanaka Maoli women's storytelling through various media of kiʻi telling visual moʻolelo, remembering and honoring our ancestors, genealogies, and lands demonstrate kūpaʻa, even when ridiculed and denigrated in mainstream settler society. As I've written,

> The scientific and economic discourses of settler colonialism scoff at indigenous relationships with nature. In public hearings throughout the islands, the visible sneers of politicians and developers are barely contained as culture and aloha ʻāina are evoked to argue against development. Yet as such cultural practices as long-distance voyaging remind us, there is also a practical side to knowledge about wind, one from which metaphoric references in Hawaiian moʻolelo are woven. ("He Lei" 66)

Similarly, intimate knowledge and relationships with other elements such as rain are just as vital. In an article discussing the importance of knowledge of wind in Hawaiian culture, as described in a moʻolelo of Pele recalling the winds of Kauaʻi in a chant, Noenoe Silva references Sydney Iaukea's "*makani* (wind) discourse" that "invites us to consider 'reorienting ourselves ideologically' toward 'a Hawaiian sense of place' through recuperating the worldview of our kūpuna, for whom 'there is no separation between nature and self'" (244, quoting Iaukea 50). How might orienting ourselves to other aspects of our cultural knowledge—ua (rain) discourse, voyaging discourse, Makahiki and traditional divisions of the year discourse, planting loʻi or fishing with net discourse, pōhaku discourse—help us remember and reimagine our relationships with our ʻāina and each other into the future?

Haʻina ʻia mai ana ka Puana (Conclusion)

The political resonance of art, particularly in response to and within the context of settler colonialism, is well documented. Trask's recognition of all art being political affirms African American writer Toni Morrison's observation, applying it to an Indigenous Pacific context. More recently, Cherokee scholar Daniel Heath Justice also affirms this perspective in relation to Native American literatures. He writes that his work on Indigenous literatures in North America and Hawaiʻi "affirms the fundamental rights of Indigenous peoples to the responsible exercise and expression of our political, intellectual, geographic and artistic self-determination.... Politics without art moves quickly toward efficient dehumanization and intellectual myopia; art without politics descends swiftly into self-referential irrelevance." Justice quotes the Menominee poet Chrystos, who asserts that "poetry without politics is narcissistic & not useful to us...everything is political—there is no neutral, safe place we can hide out in waiting for the brutality [of settler colonialism] to go away." Indigenous writing, to paraphrase Justice, must therefore engage in political struggle to confront, challenge, and overturn "centuries of representational oppression" (xix–xx, citing Chrystos 129).

Thus, the Native-centered, decolonial trajectory of contemporary Hawaiian culture and arts informs acts of kūʻē against colonial repression and representations of Kānaka Maoli, resisting what Chimamanda Adichie identifies as "the danger of a single story"; in this case, the constructed myths of colonization and settler colonialism perpetuated through corporate tourism, increasing militarization, and the settler myth of the U.S. being a nation comprised solely of immigrants where "all lives matter." These are also acts of kūpaʻa affirming and reflecting who we are, celebrating our land, culture, heritage, and experiences.

Kanaka Maoli arts demonstrate our resilience and resistance, engaging and solidifying our connections to ʻāina. They demonstrate the resilience of Indigenous epistemologies, despite settler efforts to destroy them. Our moʻolelo do many things, such as connect Kānaka to ʻāina, and to each other across space and time, through the interweaving of ʻāina, genealogy, memory, and symbolic, visual representation. Memory is an important social organizer of Hawaiian epistemologies, and performance inscribes such knowledge into our bodies. In Hawaiian thinking, ʻāina is a familial part of our moʻokūʻauhau, not a commodity. It is an extension of the body and nā akua (the gods), which reflects spiritual and emotional attachments. For Kānaka Maoli, our arts are an extension and celebration of the relationship. Our art is essential, a necessary response to settler colonial imposed systems of power, a necessary, gendered response by Native women to settler colonial men in power, and, I would add, a necessary response for Indigenous women to the settler colonial patriarchal system of power. It is through interweaving our art with our activism that we reweave moʻolelo, and more specifically, moʻolelo kālaiʻāina, that speak truth to power on behalf of our lāhui, and with our lāhui, and enact our path of freedom. It is a path to remembering, reconnecting, and honoring our connections to our lands, to love and cherish and protect them. In discussing the organization of the Aloha ʻĀina Zine Workshop responding to Swann, Revilla writes,

> [Why respond to Swann?] Because I need to respond to it. Because I am a Kanaka Maoli woman who is not dead or dying or destined to be out-futured. Because the way I see change is decolonial, do-it-ourselves, do-it-now, do it tomorrow, doing it and doing it. Because I have found a new way to respond. A new way that is not new at all but linked to an extensive and vibrant history of independent, radical, and imaginative makers of change. ("Do-It-Ourselves")

Revilla is not just talking about one man's portrayal of a telescope, or a singular mocking of one group of people. She is describing the need to resist the colonial desire of the Noble Savage transformed into defeated Dying Native, of the White Male Gaze incapable of seeing Polynesian women as anything but the topless, voiceless, languorous dusky maiden with averted eyes and a bright tropical flower tucked behind an ear. We are the mothers and grandmothers, aunties, cousins, and sisters who nurture and give birth to the nation, and, like our Native American sisters who are Idle No More, the urgency to act and reinvigorate the nation not just to survive, but to thrive in the abundance of our lands, our culture, and each other, is upon us. We are compelled from within to kūpaʻa and kūʻē. Kanaka Maoli women's bodies are instrumental in the continuity of the lāhui, birthing, nurturing, and raising the next generations. Together with our kāne, our bloodlines are interwoven stories and histories of our people that connect us back to our gods and land, and through our children, to our collective future. Kanaka Maoli women's intellect and creativity are critical strands of discourse deftly woven into the larger fabric of kūpaʻa and kūʻē that provide collective strength, resilience, and inspiration. Our art and activism reflect our traditional occupations as weavers and artisans. This is part of the community focus echoed by all of the Kanaka Maoli women artists, who work tirelessly not only in creating their own art, but working with and within our communities across the archipelago. Teaiwa has pointed out that in other parts of Oceania, "the most penetrating analysis of Pacific symbology is emerging, not from academics, but from...artist[s] and cultural practitioner[s]." This move is reflected in Hawaiʻi as well (734). Kanaka Maoli women and men did not stop fighting for nationhood after the overthrow or annexation. As Kauʻi Goodhue reminds us, he ʻo ia mau nō—we continue on, participating in politics and culture in support and defense of our lāhui (36). We continue our activism for political and social justice, employing myriad methods of advocacy, including visual arts.

WORKS CONSULTED

"About." *The Art of Resistance: Art and Activism in Hawaiʻi,* 2008. https://artofresistanceshow .wordpress.com/about/.

Adichie, Chimamanda. "The Danger of a Single Story." Ted Global, 2009.

Akamine, Bernice. "KALO." *Bernice Akamine.* https://www.bernice-akamine.com/kalo.

———. Earlier website—source of many references. No longer accessible. http:// berniceakamine.com/kalo-an-art-installation.php (no longer available online), accessed March 18, 2016.

Akana, Collette Leimomi. *Hānau ka Ua, Hawaiian Rain Names.* Kamehameha Publishing, 2015.

Basham, Leilani. *I Mau ke Eo o ka ʻĀina i ka Pono: He Puke Mele Lāhui no ka Lāhui Hawaiʻi.* 2007. University of Hawaiʻi at Mānoa, PhD dissertation.

Chrystos. "Gathering Words." *Fire Power.* Press Gang, 1995.

The Constitution of the State of Hawaii. https://lrb.hawaii.gov/constitution.

Elbert, Samuel H., and Noelani Māhoe. *Nā Mele Hawaiʻi Nei, 101 Hawaiian Songs.* U of Hawaiʻi P, 1970.

"Editorial: Army Lays Waste Riches of Makua Valley." *Environment Hawaiʻi: A Monthly Newsletter,* November 1992. https://www.environment-hawaii.org/?p=3902.

Freed, Kuʻulei, Shari Kapua Chock, Kaleialiʻi Baldwin, and Kaʻapuni Asaivao. "Seventh Generation." In Noelani Goodyear-Kaʻōpua, *The Seeds We Planted.* Minneapolis: U of Minnesota P, 2013, p. 1.

Fujikane, Candace. "Cartographies of Abundance: Mapping the Movement to Protect Mauna a Wākea." 8th Annual Meeting of the Native American & Indigenous Studies Association. Honolulu, May 21, 2016. Unpublished paper.

———. *Mapping Abundance for a Planetary Future: Kanaka Maoli and Critical Settler Cartography in Hawaiʻi.* Duke UP, 2021.

Goodhue, Kauʻi P. "We Are Who We Were: From Resistance to Affirmation." *ʻŌiwi: A Native Hawaiian Journal,* vol. 1, 1998, pp. 36–39.

Goodyear-Kaʻōpua, Noelani. "They Tried to Bury Us." Zine, 2015.

"Hana Waimea." Digital Collections. *Kaʻiwakīloumoku: Pacific Indigenous Institute.* https:// kaiwakiloumoku.ksbe.edu/article/mele-hana-waimea.

"History of Kaumakapili Church." *Kaumakapili Church.* www.kaumakapili.org/about -us/history.html, accessed October 31, 2020.

hoʻomanawanui, kuʻualoha. "From Captain Cook to Captain Kirk, or, From Colonial Exploration to Indigenous Exploitation: Issues of Hawaiian Land, Identity, and Nationhood in a 'Post Ethnic' World." In *Transnational Crossroads, Remapping the Americas and the Pacific,* edited by Camilla Fojas and Rudy Guevarra. U of Nebraska P, 2012, pp. 229–268.

———. "GMO=Kalocide." Invasive Species. Exhibition curated by Maile Andrade. MaMo (Maoli Arts Month). Nuʻuanu Gallery and Marks Garage. Honolulu, 2008.

———. "He Lei Hoʻoheno no nā Kau a Kau: Language, Performance and Form in Hawaiian Poetry." *The Contemporary Pacific,* vol. 17, 2005, pp. 29–82.

———. "Mana Wahine: Feminism and Nationalism in Hawaiian Literature." *Anglistica,* vol. 14, no. 2, 2010, pp. 27–43.

———. *Voices of Fire, Reweaving the Literary Lei of Pele and Hiʻiaka.* Minneapolis: U of Minnesota P, 2014.

"Hoonoho ana i ka Pohaku Kumu o ke Kihi o Kaumakapili." *Ko Hawaii Pae Aina,* vol. 4, no. 36, 3 September 1881, p. 2.

Iaukea, S. L. "Land agendas vis-à-vis wind discourse: Deconstructing space/place political agendas in Hawaiʻi and the Pacific." *Pacific Studies,* vol. 32, no. 1, 2009, pp. 48–72.

Justice, Daniel Heath. *Why Indigenous Literatures Matter.* Wilfred Laurier UP, 2018.

Kailiehu, Haley. "Mālama Mākua" *Haley Kailiehu.* https://www.haleykailiehu.com/community-art.html.

Kanahele, Pualani. "I Am This Land, and This Land Is Me." *Hūlili, Multidisciplinary Research on Hawaiian Well-Being,* vol. 2, no. 1, 2005, pp. 21–30.

Kapihenui, M. J. "Ka Mooolelo no Hiiakaikapoliopele." *Ka Hoku o ka Pakipika,* 26 December 1861–17 July 1862.

Kauanui, J. Kēhaulani. *Hawaiian Blood: Colonialism and the Politics of Sovereignty and Indigeneity.* Duke UP, 2008.

Kepelino. *Kepelino's Traditions of Hawaii.* 1932. Bernice P. Bishop Museum Bulletin 95. Edited by Martha Warren Beckwith. Bishop Museum Press, 2007.

LaDuke, Winona. "Homeless in Hawaii: More Land for Military than for Hawaiians." *Indian Country Today,* July 28, 2004. Also Rense.com, https://rense.com//general56/homesles.htm.

Manu, Moses. "Ke Kaua Nui Weliweli mawaena o Pele-keahialoa a me Waka-Keakaikawai." *Ka Loea Kalaiaina,* vol. 3, no. 18, 13 May 1899, p. 4.

Maoli Arts Month (MaMo) blog. "The Art of Resistance: Art and Resistance in Hawaiʻi." https://artofresistanceshow.wordpress.com/.

McPhee, Josh. "Four Questions for Anarchist Art." *Perspectives in Anarchist Theory.* 2005. https://backspace.com/notes/2006/02/four-questions-for-anarchist-art.php.

Meyer, Meleanna. "Mākua: Two Panels." *The Art of Resistance: Art and Resistance in Hawaiʻi.* 2008. https://artofresistanceshow.wordpress.com/about/.

Oliveira, Katrina-Ann Kapāʻanaokalāokeola Nākoa. *Ancestral Places: Understanding Kanaka Geographies.* Oregon State UP, 2014.

Prendergast, Ellen Kekoahiwaokalani [Kekoaohiwaikalani]. "Mele ʻAi Pōhaku" ["Mele Aloha Aina. Ai-Pohaku"]. *Buke Mele Lahui,* Buke 1, edited by F. J. Testa. Halepai Makaainana, 1895, p. 1.

Pukui, Mary Kawena, and Samuel H. Elbert. *Hawaiian Dictionary*, rev. and enlarged ed. U of Hawai'i P, 1986.

Revilla, No'ukahau'oli. "Do-It-Ourselves, Do-It-Now: Zines & Aloha 'Āina." *Ke Ka'upu Hehi 'Ale*, May 26, 2015. https://hehiale.wordpress.com/2015/05/26/do-it-ourselves -do-it-now-zines-aloha-%ca%bbaina/.

Romanchak, Abigail. "About Abigail." https://www.abigailromanchak.com/.

———. "Kumu." "Makawalu" (multiple perspectives) exhibit. MaMo (Maoli Arts Month). Nu'uanu Gallery and Marks Garage. Honolulu, 2008.

Silva, Noenoe K. "E Lawe i ke Ō: An Analysis of Joseph Mokuohai Poepoe's Account of Pele Calling the Winds." *Hūlili, Multidisciplinary Research on Hawaiian Well-Being*, vol. 6, 2010, pp. 237–266. http://kamehamehapublishing.org/_assets/publishing/hulili/ Hulili_Vol6_11.pdf.

Stillman, Amy Ku'uleialoha. "'Aloha 'Āina': New Perspectives on 'Kaulana nā Pua.'" *Hawaiian Journal of History*, vol. 33, 1999, pp. 83–99.

"Students Rally against Censorship of Mauna Kea Message." *Hawaii Independent*, October 15, 2013.

Swann, Dave. "Views and Voices Cartoon." *Honolulu Star Advertiser*, April 19, 2015. https://www.staradvertiser.com/2015/04/19/editorial/views-and-voices-comic/ views-and-voices-cartoon-165/.

Teaiwa, Teresia. "What Remains to Be Seen: Reclaiming the Visual Roots of Pacific Literature." *PMLA*, vol. 125, no. 3, 2010, pp. 730–736.

Tomasello, Lili'u. "Koko." *'Ōiwi: A Native Hawaiian Journal*, vol. 4, 2010, pp. 160–161.

Trask, Haunani-Kay. *Ho'okū'oko'a 1985*. Conference on Hawaiian Sovereignty. Kamehameha Schools, Honolulu, recorded November 30, 1985. Nā Maka o ka 'Āina, producers. Video.

———"Writing in Captivity: Poetry in a Time of Decolonization." In *Inside Out: Literature, Cultural Politics, and Identity in the New Pacific*, edited by Rob Wilson and Vilsoni Hereniko. Rowman and Littlefield, 1999, pp. 17–26.

Untitled article. *Ko Hawaii Pae Aina*, 15 January 1887, Buke 10, Helu 3, p. 4.

Utt, Jamie. "From Truth Telling to Land Return: 4 Ways White People Can Work for Indigenous Justice," *Everyday Feminism*, January 31, 2015. https://everydayfeminism .com/2015/01/truth-telling-land-return/.

Vecsey, Christopher, and Robert W. Venables, eds. "An Iroquois Perspective." *American Indian Environments: Ecological Issues in Native American History*. Syracuse UP, 1980.

Watson, Kehaulani. "Lawe Hae Hawai'i." Photograph. *'Ōiwi: A Native Hawaiian Journal*, vol. 4, 2010, p. 41.

———. "Not Homeless." Photograph. *'Ōiwi: A Native Hawaiian Journal*, vol. 4, 2010, p. 267.

Waziyatawin. *What Does Justice Look Like? The Struggle for Liberation in Dakota Homeland*. Living Justice Press, 2008. Quotation also available in "Maka Cokaya Kin (The Center of the Earth): From the Clay We Rise," University of Hawai'i at Mānoa ScholarSpace, p. 18

Wolfe, Patrick. "Settler Colonialism and the Elimination of the Native." *Journal of Genocide Research*, vol. 15, no. 4, 2006, pp. 387–409.

kuʻualoha hoʻomanawanui is a Kanaka Maoli scholar, poet, artist, and mālama ʻāina advocate. She is a professor of Hawaiian literature in the English Department at the University of Hawaiʻi at Mānoa. Her research and teaching specialties are Native Hawaiian and Pacific literatures; her current research and writing focuses on Native Hawaiian poetics, rhetorics, and aesthetics. She is the founding and current chief editor of *ʻŌiwi: A Native Hawaiian Journal*. Her first book, *Voices of Fire—Reweaving the Lei of Pele and Hiʻiaka Literature* (2014) won honorable mention in the 2014–2015 MLA (Modern Language Association) Prize for Studies in Native American Literatures, Cultures, and Languages. She is currently directing Ka Ipu o Lono, a Native Hawaiian literature digital humanities archive and database, through DAHI, the University of Hawaiʻi's Digital Arts and Humanities Initiative.

The past is our foundation, and when it's built on our mo'olelo,
not the idea of loss, we have solid and stable ground
to stand on, to live on, to plant on, to grow on.

10
Three Mana of a Moʻolelo about Translation

Bryan Kamaoli Kuwada

When someone asks us to translate the word "ea," we are often answering with multiple words that get at different facets of meaning. Life, breath, rising, sovereignty. The same goes for "aloha." Love, affection, kindness, mercy, connection. No single word is sufficient, and even taking the sum of all of those words only gets a few shades of meaning. Imagine what happens when you add another word to them. ʻĀina, lāhui, mau, kanaka. And then add a hundred more words to them. This points to the interpretive nature of translation, and also its impossibility. Yet this is what happens anytime we try to communicate. Miscommunications abound. We can never communicate perfectly, but we can often communicate successfully. And the same goes for translation.

What is important is to realize what is happening. The Spanish philosopher José Ortega y Gasset once remarked, "Since I said before that a repetition of a work is impossible and that the translation is only an apparatus that carries us to it, it stands to reason that diverse translations are fitting for the same text" (62). With this in mind, I present three versions of what I am trying to say about translation. They are all linked, and they all come from the same source, but each gets at a slightly different understanding. On the surface, one calls for translation to make itself more useful, the second proposes a new model of translation for our community I have called "embedded translation," and the third talks about the price and promise of translation. Yet each overlaps as well, reiterating and rephrasing and retranslating what the others have said.

Mana I: Eh, Go Make Yourself Useful: Thoughts on Contemporary Translation

On a relatively unremarkable day in 2014, the Hawaiʻi State Legislature was in session. It was a staid session, with none of the tense arguments that accompanied the passage of the Hawaiʻi Marriage Equality Act the previous year, or the hushed tones that accompanied their discussions of ethics violations by senators. It was just a Tuesday in March when they were going about their business, discussing a bill to protect lifeguards from liability (Hofschneider). Representative Sharon Har, from the Kapolei district, a suburb outside of Honolulu, gave her testimony, and all was going smoothly until the House Speaker, John Mizuno, called on Faye Hanohano, the Representative from Puna, a district on the island of Hawaiʻi known for its connections to our volcano goddess and a fierce sense of Hawaiian pride.

When Mizuno invited her comment on the bill, the sixty-one-year-old former prison guard, wearing a flower over her right ear and a fuzzy blue sweater with white sequined embroidery around the edge, said: "Mahalo, luna hoʻomalu ʻōlelo. Kākoʻo loa. Makemake au i ka haʻi ʻōlelo o ka luna makaʻāinana mai Kapolei mai e komo i loko o ka puke hale luna makaʻāinana." An irritated but indulgent Mizuno responded, "Rep. Hanohano, could you please translate for the members?" To which Hanohano replied, " ʻAʻole au e makemake e unuhi. I don't want to translate. Mahalo."

Mizuno, clearly irritated, called for an immediate recess, banging the gavel and tossing it down. When he returned, he announced indignantly that "Rule 60.1 provides members should conduct themselves in a respectful manner." A normally outspoken critic of Hanohano's jumped to her defense, reminding the Speaker that Hawaiʻi has two official languages, and that the Representative from Puna was well within her rights to speak Hawaiian on the House floor. Mizuno then asserted that it was not the fact that she spoke in Hawaiian that was disrespectful, but that she refused to translate.

When the story broke, all the people I saw on my Facebook feed posting the story prefaced it with comments of support for Rep. Hanohano, or for the enduring nature of the Hawaiian language—which was to be expected, since most of them who posted are dedicated to fighting for Hawaiian rights or are language students or teachers.

But once I stepped out of the comfortable and supportive bubble that is my circle of friends and colleagues, the opinions expressed were very different. Hanohano was already a relatively controversial figure, so her refusal to translate set off a flurry of media coverage and outraged responses from critics in the legislature and among the general population. News articles and televised reports investigated the issue, some calling for Hanohano to be censured and dismissed, while the more tolerant news outlets called for the state to hire Hawaiian-language translators for the legislative sessions.

Despite over three decades of language revitalization and increasing numbers of Hawaiian-language speakers of all ages, the assumption that Hawaiian was only to be used in important capacities as a vehicle for English is so ingrained that not a single article or news report called for the legislators to learn Hawaiian. Some of the online comments on these news stories were even more damning. It would be foolish to equate the online comment section of any site to an accurate summary of the community-at-large's opinions on any matter, but the sheer number and regularity of these kind of comments about Hanohano and Hawaiians in general, and the fact that these commentators are not obvious trolls, at least show the kind of feelings the community has towards Hawaiians, and concerns about cultural- and language-related matters.

The majority of the comments centered around the perceived practical, economic, and etiquette value of Hawaiian-language use. Many commenters felt that Hanohano's use of Hawaiian was somehow ineffective, as evinced by Cindy G. Jenness's comment:

> if she has something important to say shouldn't it be said in a language that everyone else is understanding? ... otherwise just sitting there and listening does not help move what ever she had said forward ... so what was the point?

Jenness puts the onus of understanding on the speaker, very clearly basing her comments on the idea that the minority must make themselves intelligible, while the majority group is under no requirement to try to understand.

A commenter with the screen name jusanopinion101 angrily denounced Hanohano as follows:

> General practice when speaking to a group of people is to utilize the more common language the majority understands. This B S of acting out like a little child isn't in the best interest of "We the People" she is supposed to be representing.

Jusanopinion101 reiterates Jenness's call for respecting the mores of the majority, and goes on to infantilize Hanohano's stance as that of a petulant child, reminiscent of the way that Hawai'i, Puerto Rico, Cuba, and other nations were portrayed in political cartoons at the turn of the twentieth century (Silva, *Aloha* 107). Jusanopinion101's use of "we the people" also invokes the majority rules vision of democracy, in which all minority groups must be assimilated into the whole.

Joshua Ka'mea'lanakila [*sic*] Tabag echoes both Jenness's and jusanopinion101's comments, with an interesting addition:

> Brilliant idea, but poor in practice. How can you expect a person to know your points if they can't understand you? You're better off speaking simlish at that point, because at least then other people can chime in. Now if she said it in Hawaiian first then english second ... yea.

Tabag's assertion that Hanohano would have been more effective had she been speaking in Simlish, a made-up nonsense language developed for *The Sims* series of video games, is also interesting, in that he seems to imagine a rather large speaking population for Simlish (larger than Hawaiian at the very least), an idea likely undergirded by the modernity of the media through which one interacts with *The Sims*'s world. Tabag further relegates the Hawaiian language to the past, implying that more utility would be gained from speaking a language that actually has a place in the modern world.

Although the Speak American movement had its heyday here in Hawaiʻi in the 1940s, we can hear the remnants of that ideology running throughout these comments. Mixed in with the usual bits of misogyny, odd punctuation and grammar, historical inaccuracy, and casual racism, we see the recurring sentiment that if you want to speak in Hawaiian, you *must* translate. *We* must make ourselves intelligible to *them*. Hawaiian is fine for Zippy's or other places where nothing of real import is going on, but it is not for the serious business of government.

Here, let me use a tactic often found in our nineteenth-century moʻolelo, and copy people like Kamakau, ʻĪʻī, Kānepuʻu, and Hoʻoulumāhiehie, who would often interrupt their stories to say "Oh, dear reader, this reminds me of a mele!" And while these authors would usually then go on to relate lines of traditional or contemporary Hawaiian mele, I would like to present a few lālani mele from a poem called "The Bridge Poem" by the feminist African-American poet Donna Kate Rushin:

> I must be the bridge to nowhere
> But my true self
> And then
> I will be useful

This is not to claim that Rushin's poem speaks directly to Representative Hanohano's motivations, especially as we must be careful about removing this poem from Rushin's intended context and identity as a radical Black lesbian poet, but I think that those of us who have experienced this kind of translation fatigue will identify with at least some of the marginalization Rushin is describing here. Leading up to this "bridge to nowhere," Rushin talks about the demand that she translate herself for the benefit of everyone else, "filling in your gaps," as she calls it early on in the poem. "Forget it / I'm sick of it," she states, a refrain that echoes several times through the poem, expressing the labor that is demanded of marginalized populations so that they may be legible to the majority. Forget it. What she is calling for is the need to translate in ways that are not just for the benefit of others, but in ways that allow us to grow, that allow us to be empowered. Rushin is further saying that we truly become useful when it is *we* who decide where the bridge goes. Or if there even is a bridge. Sometimes that means we translate for a particular, limited audience. Sometimes that means that we do not translate at all.

This unquestioned expectation for translation, particularly in the rabidly monolingual United States, is something that we as native peoples must face any time our language crosses from our own communities into the public eye. Now, though I have become ambivalent over the last two decades about how much translation we as a lāhui actually need, I am a translator who truly believes in the power of translation for effecting positive change, so it might seem weird that I am offended by the demand to translate. But what upsets me is that this demand does not come from our community, or our friends and allies. This demand comes from people who see us as artifacts of the past, who see us as potholes and speed bumps on the road to progress. This demand presumes that all aspects of our people and our culture should be open and accessible for *their* perusal and consumption—like so many goods on a Wal-Mart shelf. This demand does not recognize the damaging history of translation here in Hawaiʻi and other places affected by colonialism. In fact, this demand is merely a continuance of that history, wherein once the translation is made, there is no longer a need for the original.

Though Hawaiians employed translation in a number of ways throughout our history for disseminating and empowering our voices and our moʻolelo, translation was and is one of the most-used tools in the colonizer's toolbox. In fact, Eric Cheyfitz, in his book *The Poetics of Imperialism: Translation and Colonization from The Tempest to Tarzan*, states that "translation was, and still is, the central act of European colonization and imperialism in the Americas" (104). Tejaswini Niranjana goes a step further than Cheyfitz, and characterizes translation as a tool for colonial situations in general, one that is used for the "containment" of the colonized:

> By employing certain modes of representing the other—which it thereby also brings into being—translation reinforces hegemonic versions of the colonized, helping them acquire the status of what Edward Said calls representations, or objects without history. (3)

In this manner, colonized and indigenous peoples are represented and produced through translation in a way that justifies their further dispossession, subjugation, and oppression.

We in Hawaiʻi are still dealing with that legacy today, with reordered and misleading translations, highly skilled Hawaiian nineteenth-century authors cast as mere "native informants" who did nothing more than record what they heard of the oral tradition, cultural practices relegated to the past with the sweep of an editorial pen, and decontextualized stories presented as quaint artifacts of a vanishing people. These kinds of translations have enabled those who read them to mischaracterize us and to appropriate our stories and traditions for their own use, creating structures of oppression based on these misunderstandings of our history and culture. It is no wonder that people in our community are leery of translation.

I am too.

But, as longtime translation scholar and activist Mona Baker says:

> undermining existing patterns of domination cannot be achieved with concrete forms of activism alone (such as demonstrations, sit-ins, and civil disobedience) but must involve a direct challenge to the stories that sustain these patterns. (30)

To directly challenge the stories that sustain these patterns of domination, however, we must refuse to see translation as the only worthy goal for Hawaiian-language texts, and when we do decide to translate, we cannot continue to translate using the same model that has been followed for so long (something that I deal with in the next mana of this moʻolelo). As Rushin points out in her poem, we must build the bridges to our own power. We must reevaluate how translations have been produced here, almost without exception, for over a hundred years.

Despite translation's painful history in Hawaiʻi, it can also provide the opportunity to create positive change, and translators-as-activists are well-suited for challenging the stories that sustain these patterns of domination, oppression, denigration, and violence by reintroducing, reawakening, and remembering our own stories, especially in Hawaiʻi and other indigenous places.

By focusing on a particular text, Frances N. Frazier's translation of *The True Story of Kaluaikoolau*, I would like to demonstrate that if a translator engages with a text on strictly linguistic terrain, without also coming to terms with the ethical and political implications and necessities of responsibly retelling someone else's story, she runs the risk of not only isolating the story from its context, but also of diminishing the potential for positive change that may have been inherent in such texts. I would also like to show how changing our understandings and expectations of translation can result in translations that are more empowering for our community, more culturally and historically nuanced, and to echo Rushin again, just more useful.

Several years ago, one of my Hawaiian-language teachers told me that Kahikina Kelekona's account of Koʻolau, Piʻilani, and Kaleimanu was an amazing story and definitely worth reading, but that I should read the Hawaiian version, which was included with Frazier's translation. Being in second year Hawaiian at the time, I attempted to read the first few pages and realized that it was way past my meager Hawaiian-language abilities. I decided I would cheat and read the English translation, figuring that it would be pretty much the equivalent of reading the Hawaiian. I read it in one sitting, as it was only forty pages or so, while I waited in a parking lot for friends to finish class and ended up being a little disappointed when I was done because it was not the amazing experience that my teacher had promised. I enjoyed the story itself, but I just was not as impressed with it as my teacher had been. A couple of years later, when I was finally able to work my way through Kelekona's beautifully dense and image-laden Hawaiian—which by the way was inexplicably thirty pages longer than the English translation—and I began researching a little bit more, I realized how much I had missed by relying on the translation to tell me the story.

Before we jump into the analysis of Frazier's translation, a little background, both on the events of the story and how the story came to be told in ensuing decades. In June of 1893, soon after the overthrow of the Hawaiian monarchy, a number of articles in the Hawaiian-language newspapers about a family of three from Kaua'i caught the attention of the entire Hawaiian nation. Ko'olau, the father, was a cowboy from Kaua'i who was diagnosed with Hansen's disease—what was then known as "leprosy." When he found out that the newly established Provisional Government had decreed that his wife Pi'ilani and son Kaleimanu would not be allowed to accompany him to the "leper colony" on Moloka'i, something that had often been allowed under the monarchy, he refused to be separated from them. He and his family fled into the rugged Kalalau Valley with several others afflicted with the disease, and Ko'olau ended up shooting and killing a deputy sheriff in order to protect one of them. In response, the Provisional Government sent a detachment of police and soldiers equipped with a howitzer to Kalalau in order to bring them all back, dead or alive. Using a single rifle, Ko'olau held off the P.G. soldiers until they were forced to retreat and return to O'ahu. Ko'olau and his son later succumbed to the disease, but Pi'ilani stayed in the forest for three and a half years before returning to live in the town of Kekaha.

Ko'olau, Pi'ilani, and Kaleimanu became huge symbols of resistance for the supporters of ka lāhui Hawai'i, because they were ordinary Hawaiians who stood up to the forces of the Provisional Government. When the steamer 'Iwalani returned to Honolulu bringing home the unsuccessful P.G. soldiers, it was met by a crowd of over one thousand people, who cheered wildly when they got the news that Ko'olau and his family had escaped ("Hoi"). A flurry of newspaper articles appeared across four Hawaiian-language newspapers. Numerous mele and editorials were written, Pi'ilani mā were compared to the three hundred Spartans at Thermopylae ("Hoole"), and one paper even published a ka'ao about an ancestor of Ko'olau, also named Ko'olau, who was responsible for all the Ko'olau names on the island, had met with Pele, had his surfboard towed out to the break by owls, caught a thirty-foot 'ulua, and when ali'i from O'ahu came to invade his home on Kaua'i, threw a net over them and cast them into the sea ("He Moolelo").

A decade after Piʻilani returned to Kekaha, with Hawaiʻi as a newly minted territory of the United States and English the medium of instruction in all its schools, staunch Hawaiian nationalist and newspaper editor Kahikina Kelekona (also known as John Sheldon) published a book in 1906 based on interviews with Piʻilani. Kelekona's story was a highly political Hawaiian-language text reminding his readers about the importance of resistance and familial relationships to the land and each other. It told the story of a brave and tight-knit family using their knowledge of and connection to the land to survive the threats made by the Provisional Government forces, who symbolized foreign encroachment on Hawaiian sovereignty and values. When the themes of family coming together to resist outside encroachment became particularly relevant again in the wake of the Massie Case in 1932, Kelekona's version was reprinted in the newspapers. But for anyone other than the relative few who had linguistic or even physical access to it, Kelekona's book remained rather obscure throughout the majority of the twentieth century, until it was translated by Frances Frazier in the early 1970s.

Over the last few decades, Frazier's translation has gained in popularity, going through a number of printings. It now appears regularly in Hawaiian and local literature classes, often taught by teachers and professors who wish to support the cultural revitalization movement, and interrogate or challenge colonial history and literature. This is a good outcome of the translation. It is important that more people are getting to know this beautiful story about standing up against oppression and fighting for your family in the face of insurmountable odds. The problem is that Frazier's translation does not give readers enough to really understand this story.

Now, it must be taken as a given that all translation is interpretation, and that there is no such thing as a completely literal translation, so my analysis is not meant to quibble with the particular word choices Frazier made, except for one example that's coming up later. What I want to focus on is her presentation of the translation, which, more than the translation itself, hugely transformed Kelekona's story about Koʻolau and Piʻilani.

For one thing, some of you who have read the translation are probably wondering why I keep calling it Kelekona's story and not Piʻilani's. If you look at the Library of Congress information for the book, you will see that Piʻilani Kaluaikoʻolau is listed as author and Frazier is listed as translator. Kelekona's name does not appear anywhere in the list of people associated with the book. But then, wasn't he just the reporter who wrote down what Piʻilani said, and published it in 1906? That's how Frazier described him ("Battle of Kalalau" 108). But while she does note that he was the son of Henry Sheldon, who had been editor of the *Pacific Commercial Advertiser* for several years, and was a well-regarded translator in his own right, John, also known as Kahikina, was more than just a reporter. A staunchly royalist newspaper editor himself, he was also one of the most talented Hawaiian authors of his time, writing everything from scathingly political poetry in English to spy stories and Edgar Allan Poe–ish tales of horror in Hawaiian. In *Hawaiian Grammar,* Samuel Elbert and Mary Kawena Pukui characterize Kelekona's writing as "Victorian, almost Dickensian, with a vocabulary of astonishing richness and complexity" (xiii–xiv). He is even referenced in the Pukui and Elbert Hawaiian dictionary in the definition for "kipona," which notes that "translations vary greatly and depend on context; very common in Kelekona."

But even though this fantastically skilled writer and rabble-rouser has already been demoted to mere reporter in Frazier's account, that doesn't automatically mean that he should be given credit for writing the story. What does indicate that Kelekona should get credit for authorship, besides his strikingly distinctive style of writing, is that on page seven of the original Hawaiian text, he writes: "na'u ponoi i kakau, hooponopono a i hookele hoi ma ka oihana pa'i a me ka humu buke" (I personally wrote, edited, and directed the printing and binding (of this book) (*Kaluaikoolau*)). And if that's not enough to convince you, two sworn and notarized statements printed right after the story ends clearly record that Pi'ilani told the events of the story to Kelekona, while Kelekona himself wrote the story. Frazier's text does not include these statements, and her simplified English representation of Kelekona's distinctive literary Hawaiian allows Pi'ilani's authorship to go unquestioned.

The highly interpretive nature of translation renders a lot of specific critiques of word choice obsolete, and Frazier's stripped-down translation style actually works well to allow readers, particularly students, to get more easily into the story rather than having to slog through some of the obstacles that a closer translation of Kelekona's highly stylistic prose would entail. What I will focus on, however, is one particular instance where she clearly translated something incorrectly. I point this out not to criticize her translation abilities, but to continue my call for a different approach to translation and even the production of Hawaiian-language texts.

There is a part of the story that takes place after Ko'olau publicly vows that he will not go to Kalawao without his wife, and everyone is waiting anxiously for the deputy sheriff Lui Stolz to come and arrest him. When Ko'olau hears that Stolz has landed with armed police, he proclaims, "Yes, they think that I shall be imprisoned by the sickness, but marriage is the only thing that keeps this body a prisoner!" (Kelekona 17). While some people might identify with the idea of being a prisoner to marriage, this declaration struck me oddly in a story that talks so much about the strength of Pi'ilani and Ko'olau's marriage and how that connection was what really allowed them to persevere throughout all their tribulations. The reason for the oddness in the translation becomes clear when we refer to the original Hawaiian: "Ae; ua hiki no ia i ko lakou manao; ua lilo au he pio na ka maʻi, aka, o ka *make* wale no ka mea nana e lawe pio i keia kino" [emphasis added]. Frazier has misread "make" (death) as "male" (marriage), so her translation should have read: "Death is the only thing that will make this body a prisoner"!

I point this mistake out not to make fun of Frances Frazier. We all make mistakes. I once accidentally translated "father" as "grandfather" on an old land deed and didn't realize until a lawyer called me about it. The reason I'm pointing it out is that it shows that we cannot view translation as a solitary process. When we analyze historical translations, we have to realize that there were editors, and publishers, and financial backers involved in these processes, making often unseen decisions about the presentation and content of these texts. And when we think of contemporary translations like this one, we have to ensure that there are editors, indexers, designers, and others who are skilled in Hawaiian language and culture who can assist translators and authors and academics in catching these kinds of errors.

This community-centered translation, what I refer to as embedded translation, can also better envision the possibilities enabled by working with Hawaiian-language materials, and help present these texts to the public in appropriate and high-quality ways. That mistake in Frazier's translation has gone for nearly forty years without ever being corrected. Just as I think that there need to be more qualified people around the translator to enable her or him to do a better job, I think that there also needs to be more material around the translation to help it do its job. The translation of text alone has proven insufficient for our efforts at cultural and historical revival. When we leave out sociopolitical context, mainly in the form of what we call paratexts—introductions, translator's notes, appendices, and the like—important themes that were highly relevant during the publication of the original text go unnoticed in subsequent readings of these translations.

Paratexts have been called "the fringe [of a book] that in reality controls the whole reading" that assures its reception and its consumption (Lejeune, qtd. in Genette 261; Lejeune, 45). As Donald Haase explains, "because they have a public impact on how readers understand, respond to, and evaluate written cultural artifacts, authorial and editorial paratexts have a social, cultural, and political role" (66). In this case, Frazier's slim paratexts, consisting only of a two-page foreword and a two-and-a-half-page introduction, speak almost exclusively of the situation with Hansen's disease at the end of the nineteenth century, and characterize the moʻolelo as only a Kauaʻi-based love story. In contrast, and with an acute understanding of the importance of paratexts in directing the reading, the highly nationalistic Kelekona included twenty-seven pages of "supplementary" material not included in Frazier's translation, including a series of newspaper articles and anecdotes about Koʻolau's prowess as a paniolo. These anecdotes provide semi-fantastic descriptions of Koʻolau using his rifle to pick coconuts, capturing a wild bull with nothing but a rope, and shooting a goat through the ear from across the valley while it was amidst an entire herd (Kelekona, *Koolau* 78–85). Besides providing entertaining "tall tales," these stories further establish Koʻolau's heroic and legendary reputation, making him even more worthy as a role model for Hawaiians of the day. There are also a number of articles from the newspaper *Kuokoa,* which outline the events of June 1893 and the reactions of the populace. Kelekona also included the mele "Ai Manu Koʻolau" and "Ka Uwalo Poloʻai Aloha," by Piʻilani herself. Frazier removed all of this historical and cultural thickness from Sheldon's story by leaving the majority of the Hawaiian-language paratexts Kelekona included in the book untranslated. By removing the fringe that Kelekona selected to direct the reading of his own text, she moved the narrative away from its avowedly political purpose towards that of a less threatening love story.

As I bring this mana to a close, let me reiterate that I am not trying to single out Frances Frazier as a bad or irresponsible translator, because I feel that these critiques can be made of numerous translated moʻolelo, including ones that I've had a hand in producing. But I do want to show how rethinking our approach to translation and our responsibilities as translators can positively transform how our moʻolelo are presented and understood. We translators must not be satisfied with the role of good-hearted linguistic technician. We are not Google Translate, robotically switching out Hawaiian words for their most proximate English synonyms. We translators must be, among other things, sympathetic listeners, diligent editors, concerned community members, careful historians, keen observers, tenacious researchers, staunch activists, critical theorists, and responsible readers. If we do all of these things, then maybe, just maybe, we can be useful.

Mana II: ʻOni a paʻa: Being Useful through Embedded Translation

Though we place so much value on our ʻōlelo, we are often admonished that talk is cheap and actions speak louder than words. And it is true. With the Hawaiʻi community dealing with colonial legacies in education, government, and economics, and increasing threats to our lands and culture, we need more than empty promises from our politicians and administrators, who throw around buzzwords like "sustainability" and "mālama ʻāina" as they try to sell off public lands and build on our sacred sites. Telling stories, continuing our traditions in the loʻi and on the sea, performing oratory, teaching literature, and performing creative pieces are important activist works, and translation should be counted among them rather than just being seen as a mechanical, derivative, and secondary act.

Here in Hawai'i, translation as a process—from choosing the text, to the act of translation, to the publication and dissemination of the finished product—often goes unremarked or unexamined. And while we have a vibrant and ever-growing contemporary literary scene here in Hawai'i, our connections to our mo'olelo, by which I mean very broadly our stories and histories, have grown very tenuous. Thus, even though translation has had a very painful and damaging history in many Indigenous contexts, it also provides the opportunity to create positive change, and translators-as-activists, what I am calling embedded translators, are well-suited for challenging the stories that sustain these patterns of domination, oppression, denigration, and violence by reintroducing, reawakening, and remembering (re-membering) our own stories, especially in Hawai'i and other Indigenous places.

Translation is often posed as being the opposite of language revival, and if you abstract this comparison to a high enough level, it's true. Translation carries the reader *away* from Hawaiian, while language learning carries the reader *towards* it. When you add context and history back into the equation, however, particular kinds of translation more clearly present opportunities for intervention, complementing language revitalization efforts as we strive to achieve our various sovereignties. All sorts of economic and social factors hinder the process of learning Hawaiian to the fluency necessary to enjoy and deeply understand these stories. Until access to learning Hawaiian is more widespread, we need to do something for the generations of people who have not been fortunate enough to learn Hawaiian. I cannot bring myself to espouse the belief that these people, our people, can be left to the wayside, merely "opportunity costs" or "collateral damage" in our struggle to reclaim our language, culture, and sovereignty (Wong and Maaka 10–11). Yes, we must push ahead in our language, breaking boundaries and making our 'ōlelo ring out in places that do not always welcome it. Yet I think that we can do that while still making room for those who were unable to learn our language. For many of us, language classes are easier to access (economically and ideologically), social attitudes towards learning Hawaiian have shifted, and we learned it at a time in our lives when we didn't have to worry about providing for our families or taking care of our children, all things our parents' and grandparents' generations simply didn't have. This is not to dismiss all of the hard work and sacrifices that our generations have put into learning Hawaiian and making it a large part of our lives, but merely to point out that the older generations created these opportunities for us, but didn't get to enjoy them themselves.

Though most Hawaiians have at least some mo'olelo that are passed down through our families or people we know, a lot of people in our community have very limited access to these mo'olelo and traditions, and they feel the loss. They know something is missing, and they try to seek these stories out. They yearn for these stories with a thirst that is almost palpable, and some are lucky enough that they are able to slake their thirst with the wai maoli, the fresh water, moʻolelo that have been responsibly produced or even translated. Others are not so lucky. Too many Hawaiians or people who want to understand Hawaiians turn to what is easily accessible: books written by casual historians like Sarah Vowell, or New Age–inflected websites on "huna." And sometimes, they even resort to making up stories and histories on their own.

An example of this last category is the spread of the red, yellow, and green "Kānaka Maoli" flag, which is often seen proudly flying at rallies and adorning cars, T-shirts, posters, and surf shorts. The story goes that the Kānaka Maoli flag was the original flag of the Hawaiian kingdom, and in 1843, when the British naval captain Lord George Paulet occupied the Hawaiian Islands, he ordered all the Kānaka Maoli flags he could find lowered and destroyed, raising the British flag in its place. Several months later, when Admiral Thomas, Paulet's commanding officer, ended the occupation, the British flag was lowered and the flag we know today as the Hawaiian kingdom flag (the white, red, and blue one with the Union Jack in the corner) was raised in place of the red, yellow, and green flag that had been destroyed. This original "Kānaka Maoli" flag had been hidden away for almost one hundred and fifty years before it was resurrected in 1999, after a descendant of Lord Paulet was said to have alerted us to its existence. This story of the Kānaka Maoli flag is stirring and inspiring, because it shows a lineage of resistance to colonial domination that has continued to the present day. Under the colonial aegis of Great Britain, Lord Paulet tried to stamp out and destroy the very symbol of our nationhood and sovereignty, but it was secretly preserved for all this time, a conspiracy so thorough that no one in our history ever, ever, mentioned it. *Ever.*

As might be clear from my tone, the problem is that this story is made up. None of the very detailed historical accounts of the Paulet Affair, in English or Hawaiian, make mention of Paulet's bait and switch, and both John William Norie's book *Plates Descriptive of the Maritime Flags of All Nations* (1838) and the missionary William Ellis's journals, which were published nearly two decades before the Paulet Affair, contain images of the red, blue, and white kingdom flag. While five months can seem like a relatively long time, it is highly likely that someone would have noticed if Admiral Thomas had raised a completely different colored flag with a completely different design than the one that had been taken down. Disputing the origins of the Kānaka Maoli flag is really quite easy, and though I have dedicated some space to doing just that, disproving its origins is *not* why I brought it up. I used to get irritated every time I saw that flag flying from the back of someone's truck, or stuck onto their notebook in class, and lament how little we knew of our own history and how sheep-like our people had become, accepting and even celebrating this flag so uncritically. But I now see it as a symbol of how much our people are crying out for a history and literature that they can be proud of.

This example makes clear that our people desperately want to connect to our moʻolelo, our history, and our stories. We don't *want* to believe the accepted histories that were often written and translated by outsiders, histories that said we were pulled from the darkness of our traditions and shepherded towards enlightenment like good little children. We *want* to believe that we stood up to America and Britain. We *want* to believe that there is more to our history than what we've been told. We *need* to believe that something that we thought was destroyed and lost over one hundred and fifty years ago can resurface and live again today. And the amazing thing is that all of these things that seem to be missing from our histories, the stories of insistence and survivance, are all there, and by re-figuring and re-membering our moʻolelo through language learning and translation and other modes of recovery, we can refigure and remember ourselves.

In a January 9, 1906, article entitled "Ka Moolelo o Kou Aina Oiwi" [The Moʻolelo of Your Native Land], Joseph Poepoe—an important language advocate, translator, newspaper editor, schoolteacher, historian, lawyer, politician, and public intellectual (Silva, *Power*)—speaks to the importance of knowing our own moʻolelo and putting them to contemporary use:

> [O] ka makaukau ma na Moolelo o kou Aina Makuahine ke keehina ike mua ma ke Kalaiaina e hiki ai ke paio no ka pono o ka Nohoʻna Aupuni ana.
>
> A o ka paa o na moolelo o na Aupuni like ole, oia no auanei ka makaukau paio naauao ana maluna o na kumuhana pili kanawai no ka pono o kou lahui....
>
> E ka lahui, pehea la e hiki ai ia kakou ke ninau i ka aoao maikai, ke ole e paa ia kakou ka moolelo kahiko o ko kakou Aina Aloha. [?]
>
> [Being well-versed in the histories of your motherland is the first important political step to take that would allow us to fight for the benefit of our Nationhood.
>
> And as for having a firm grasp of the histories of all nations, that is the enlightened skill that is more important than knowledge of the law in the fight for the benefit of your nation....
>
> O my people, how indeed will we be able to ask "which way is for the best?" if we do not know the old stories of our beloved land?]

While it is important to note that reconnecting with our moʻolelo is but a single step in a much longer process that includes language revitalization and political activation, Poepoe reminds us that even though our histories have not been free from pain and heartache, no matter how many times we are told that it's better to forget the past and move on, the past is not a burden that we have to get rid of. The past is our foundation, and when it's built on our moʻolelo, not the idea of loss, we have solid and stable ground to stand on, to live on, to plant on, to grow on.

Recovering our foundation reminds us of our possibilities, but it also reminds us how heavy the kuleana is that comes with this work. To put it mildly, our experiences with translation in Hawaiʻi for the last two hundred years have not been too positive, and I think that we would be justified in being critical and vigilant about any and all translation projects, because once something is made accessible to more people, *it is made accessible to more people*. These moʻolelo and everything described within them are opened up for people to be inspired and moved by them, but they are then also subject to misunderstanding and appropriation in dangerous ways, ways that would not be open if these texts were left in Hawaiian.

Only a small percentage of the Hawaiian community is able to speak Hawaiian, with the rest of them thirsting for a way to connect to their culture and place. Because harmful misrepresentations of Hawaiian history and culture shape our current political and social realities, I feel like we *must* take that risk. I am not saying that we should translate the entire body of the Hawaiian-language archive into English, because I think that would create its own problems. Nor am I saying that translation is the way, the truth, and the light. What I am saying is that I think if we do decide that we are going to translate (a decision not to be taken lightly), we should practice a particular kind of provisional, community-based translation, something I am calling "embedded translation."

This idea of embedded translation is meant more as a philosophy than a strict model to follow, as each text and context is going to require a different approach. The first aspect of embedded translation I want to discuss is that of the translator's position. All too often, translators are thought of as being *between* two languages, unconstrained, and translation is seen as a neutral "carrying across" that is somehow outside of both the source and target languages, usually involving a text from a foreign country or culture that is domesticated through translation. This understanding of translation really breaks down here in Hawaiʻi, as both the "foreign" language to be translated out of and the "domestic" language to be translated into belong to the same group of people. While the bulk of translations outside of Hawaiʻi are carried out explicitly for audiences other than whom the text was originally intended for, here we translate these texts for us. In Indigenous contexts, where each translation is a politically charged and potentially activist act, the expectations and responsibilities for translators must be radically different.

We have heard "i ka ʻōlelo nō ke ola, i ka ʻōlelo nō ka make" (in language there is life, in language there is death) enough times that we know that there is a lot at stake every time we translate and change the language of a text. We as translators cannot afford to view ourselves as somehow outside of the fray, in the neutral third space between languages, between communities, and not responsible for that life and death. We need to embed ourselves in the Hawaiian language and the Hawaiian community, and make our allegiances clear to all involved, planting ourselves in the community, being nourished by the community, but also and always feeding the community. In this community, we also need to honor and recognize the work that goes into translation and the toll that it takes on translators and other cultural workers when they go unnoticed and unsupported. The more we allow this invisibility of translators to continue, the more we are sabotaging our own recovery efforts, relegating some of our most dedicated and prolific translators to the obscurity of working without pay and health insurance, much less publication or institutional support. How can we create more engaged and embedded translators when we often see translation as merely a technical process of substitution that can be done by machines or outsourced to Cambodia?

Another thing that being an embedded translator demands is having the Hawaiian community and their allies be our primary audience for our translations. Translations have for too long been *about* us, and never *for* us. And while the main audience *has* to be the Hawaiian community, I think it is clear as well that the second audience is people of other ancestries—our friends, family members, other supporters, and hell, sometimes even our enemies—because these stories provide them too with the shared foundation upon which to stand, so that they may support us in our struggles for sovereignty.

The term embedded translation is a bit of an oxymoron, so I think it's only fitting that I use another oxymoron to help explain it, and that oxymoron is ʻonipaʻa, best known as the motto of our beloved queen, Liliʻuokalani. It is most commonly translated as "steadfast," something that she truly was. As you might imagine, however, though that word conveys some of the same things that ʻonipaʻa does, they are not equivalent. "ʻOni" refers to movement, motion, and shifting, while "paʻa" means to be fixed, solid, rooted, and/or complete. The range of meaning and movement here is much greater than the fixity and lack of forward motion implied by "steadfast," and can be seen in the fact that in English "steadfast" is descriptor of a thing, while in Hawaiian "ʻonipaʻa" is much more active and filled with motion, something you can do/be. When Hawaiians are ʻonipaʻa, then, it implies that we are moving and taking action while still being embedded in our culture, our community, and our beliefs.

This explanation of ʻonipaʻa undergirding the idea of being embedded should also serve as an example of the kind of translation I am calling for. Translation has to be undertaken with an understanding of the weight these words carry, and while we must always keep the larger text in mind, sometimes *every, single, word* has the possibility of transformation embedded within it, and we need to be able to open that up for our readers. For an embedded translator, this means no more romantic ideas about the lone translator cloistered away from the world, working diligently on a text for the sheer intellectual challenge of it. It has to become more of a social and interactive process. Translation has to be useful. Being embedded and being ʻonipaʻa come down to the idea that we translators need to listen—to our community, our ancestors, and ourselves, which is not always easy. It will be an overwhelming cacophony of voices, at once full of love and compassion, but also streaked with anger, hatred, and dismissal. Maybe these voices will tell us that they don't want us to translate what we're thinking of translating, or maybe they won't say anything because we should have already known better. In any case, we have to pay attention and find out how to build the bridge that leads to our own power.

We can't be marionettes pulled by a thousand strings, but we can attend to our people's concerns and misgivings. In my experience, when you're working with these Hawaiian texts and trying to make them more accessible, it's pretty easy to find a lot of voices in support of what you're doing, but we also have to engage in building what translation theorist S. Shankar has called a "culture of translation," by focusing more closely on the material practice of translation and by ensuring that translations are not produced transparently, meaning that the translator and their role in the act of translation remain invisible. By doing so, members of the community become more cognizant of translation debates beyond whether to translate or not, and can discuss and debate the translation process in useful ways, even if that debate leads us to say that a particular text should not be translated.

Sometimes being embedded just means being around other Hawaiians, taking the time to find out what they want and need. Just because they want these stories doesn't mean that they want the story as a 400-page book that costs $40. Maybe they want graphic novels, or 3D animated shorts, or free interactive texts online, or speculative steampunk alternate history webisodes. We need to think outside of the book. We also have to put in the effort to get the community involved in the process of translation from the earliest stages, and be brave enough to subject ourselves and our work to community scrutiny, and the chance that we're going to get scolded by our kumu and kūpuna.

When I was little, if one of us kids did anything wrong, my grandma would spank everyone, even if they had just happened to be in the area, because they should have stopped the wrongdoer from doing what they did. That is what being embedded and acknowledging your kuleana to the community really entails—looking out for each other, paying attention to each other, learning from each other, and when it really comes down to it, being on the hook for getting spankings from the kūpuna.

Mana III:
The Decoy Uhu, or How to Tell Someone a Story When They're Not Listening

The founder of our *nation*, Kamehameha I, died two hundred years ago, but his legacy is alive and well. Here are some of the popular stories about him that are alive today. The *state* celebrates Kamehameha Day—since 1871, according to their website. They use the flag he helped design in 1816 as the state flag. His kānāwai māmalahoa, often translated as "the law of the splintered paddle," is in Article IX, section 10, of the state's constitution, and the Honolulu Police Department makes symbolic reference to his law on its badges. They call him "Makua lani" in the state anthem. He is even on the Hawai'i state quarter, proclaiming the state motto: "Ua mau ke ea o ka aina i ka pono," just 1.75 mm away from the face of George Washington portrayed on the other side. I read on a website that a "fun fact" about the Hawai'i quarter is that it's the only state quarter to feature royalty! And if you ask almost anyone on the street about Kamehameha, they'll tell you that he conquered and unified the Hawaiian Islands, that he was a great warrior, that he was seven feet tall, and that he lifted the big rock that's in front of the Hilo Library.

Most of us can already see how problematic some of these stories are. We can see the gaps in the popular understanding of history that allow the state of Hawai'i and the federal government to proudly celebrate their occupation of the Hawaiian Islands by using the image of someone who in all likelihood would have fought tooth and nail against the very thought of them ruling over Hawai'i. We know that some other stories are missing: how Kamehameha's highly advanced skills of statecraft allowed him to outmaneuver foreign diplomats and ship captains, how he would use foreign manners or technologies, but only in ways that fulfilled Hawaiian aims, or how when you translate "Ka Na'i Aupuni" as "The Conqueror of the Nation," you leave out that "na'i" also means to strive, reminding us that Kamehameha was always striving for the nation, the aupuni. So what is the point in bringing up this legacy and these stories? It is not necessarily to talk about how Hawaiian stories came to be so marginalized, as many of us already understand this marginalization very deeply. What I would like to focus on is how we can repopulate our 'āina with our stories.

We sometimes forget the importance of our stories when we are engaged in land and water struggles, fighting for social justice, and protesting the further militarization of the islands. These actions can all seem much more immediately urgent than ensuring that people know that you can translate a word like "na'i" in more than one way. But, as Thomas King says, "Stories are wondrous things. And they are dangerous" (9). Our kūpuna knew this well. Yet too many of us nowadays don't know or refuse to accept these stories that enable us to ask "which way is for the best?" as the Poepoe quote in the previous mana calls for.

All too often, the stories that we do know are the ones that maintain the narrative of Hawaiians as semi-reformed savages who have become happy but unhealthy little consumers of the American Way. The ease with which we accept this damaging story becomes a problem because the Hawaiian word for a version of a story or a retelling of a mo'olelo is "mana," recognizing the fact that the more a story gets told and retold, the more it gains in mana. And while this may be hard to believe coming in a book about mo'olelo like this, these damaging narratives are the stories that often have the most mana.

How strong these stories must be today, for people who have heard or passed them on to still think that corporate interests trump all, and that the bones and bodies of our ancestors are not worthy of reverence and respect. How powerful these stories must be, to make people think that man has dominion over the earth, and that the tops of mountains are only good for telescopes. These stories are told and retold every minute of every day, through books, movies, advertisements, laws, T-shirts, and verbal declarations that together construct tales in which we are not the main characters, merely the backdrop.

Over the years, we have produced or recovered many stories that we throw against this narrative flood, and these are what other scholars have called the "momi," the pearls, the big guns. *The Queen's Songbook*, bam! Contemporary performance of the Kumulipo, bam! "Mele 'Ai Pōhaku," bam! $1500 version of the Hi'iaka, bam! And we as a community are enriched by these stories, *if* we have access to them through language, affiliation, or economics. But because these stories are so clearly powerful, and so often express our dissatisfaction with the status quo, we began to scare people. And rightly so. As Thomas King said, "Stories are wondrous things. And they are dangerous" (9). We also began to scare some of our own people too. For some of them, these mo'olelo were too cultural, too political, too "sovereign." They are more comfortable with *Lilo and Stitch* and criticizing *Hawai'i 5-0* for having the characters turn right on Kalākaua and end up in Ka'a'awa two minutes later.

And as for the people we actually *wanted* to scare—well, now they knew what to look for and avoid. Judging by things I have heard in casual conversation, or in public forums, or in the comments section of the newspaper, a lot of the people standing in opposition to or rejecting participation in Hawaiian struggles refuse to even consider any stories that include the words "overthrow" or "U.S. imperialism," or begin with the phrase, "If we look at Hawaiian history...." When confronted by the problem of people not listening to our stories, it is easy to think, "Well, forget about them," and stop sharing. As a translator and teacher, I worry when we say that if people want to read our stories, the only way is to learn Hawaiian. I very much agree that to fully appreciate the beauty and humor of mo'olelo originally written in Hawaiian, you really do have to read it in Hawaiian, and I think we should demand this of people who are going to take on the kuleana of working closely with our stories, whether as scholars or as tellers of mo'olelo. But the fact remains that 95 to 98 percent of our people are not privileged enough to speak Hawaiian for a whole host of reasons that often have to do with the legacy of colonialism, and with the problems that our community faces with literacy and education; for some, the biggest stumbling block is not that the text is in Hawaiian but that *it's in a book*. I do not think we can rightfully demand that they learn Hawaiian for several years just to partake of the legacy our ancestors left for all of us. If we are going to write off the vast majority of our own people as collateral damage in the fight to recover our language and our sovereignty, I think we're on the wrong path.

I am taking it as a given that to continue to fuel the language revitalization movement, we *must* continue to produce books in our own language, whether they be re-presentations of older mo'olelo and mele, or new compositions. But what do we do when people won't or can't listen to these mo'olelo? Well, that's where the uhu pākali, the decoy uhu, comes in. Uhu are notoriously difficult to catch on a hook and line, and sometimes if the water is clear enough you can even see uhu swimming indifferently past your bait while you're sitting there sweating in the sun. And even if you finally hooked one, you'd likely only get the one, as the rest would scatter into their holes and stay there. But what traditional fishermen would do is catch one, however they could, and rig it up like a live bait and put it back in the water. Then the uhu would struggle and swim around, and the other uhu watching from their holes would get curious as to what the uhu pākali was doing. And as these other uhu would get closer to the decoy, the fisherman would slowly by slowly pull the decoy towards the mouth of the net, and the other uhu would follow and follow, still curious, until...

A bunch of uhu with one scoop.

And this is how I propose we should try to scoop all the uhu that are afraid of or antagonistic towards our stories. Let's trick them. Let's make them think that these powerful stories we are telling them are no more threatening than, say, watching the Food Network. For instance, many of us know some of the basic problems of translation, in terms of translators' unspoken biases and how they secretly transmit Western values through the way they translate certain things, and so on and so forth. So why can't we do the same thing back, and use tools like translation to secretly transmit our own Hawaiian values and culture to our readers? For example, a group of us finished translating *Ka Moolelo o Kamehameha I* a couple of years ago, and though it hasn't yet been published, I think that a text like this is the perfect opportunity to send our mo'olelo creeping into people's brains. *Everyone* loves Kamehameha—well, maybe not Kaua'i people, but mostly everyone else. For a large percentage of the population of Hawai'i, I think it is safe to say that Kamehameha is the quintessential symbol of Hawai'i. His statue has a spear in one hand, but he seems to be welcoming you with the other. He is at once dangerous, but safe because he is of the past. He is exotic, larger than life, romantic, yet seems totally harmless. Even the most dyed-in-the-wool ardent American patriots here in Hawai'i think Kamehameha is neat.

All of this is to say that there is a willing audience for our translation of *Ka Moolelo o Kamehameha I*. People want to read about the warrior king, and we want to give them what they want. Are they going to get the story about him lifting the big rock in front of the Hilo library? Yes. But are they also going to get the story about him deflecting so many spears as his canoe is arriving near Papawai Point on Maui that he can walk to shore on the discarded weapons? Yes. Are they also going to get the story of how he appropriated Western technologies and used them in Hawaiian ways to achieve Hawaiian goals? Yes. Are they also going to get the story of the man who fought on the battlefield and in the political arena to ensure Hawaiian sovereignty? Hell, yes.

This is not to say that we have to sanitize our translations and meekly produce texts only fit for a general audience. This is to say that *Ka Moolelo o Kamehameha I* is a stirring story, and stirring stories pull the reader in, sometimes against our will. And while the readers are enthralled by the descriptions of Kamehameha tearing people in half with his bare hands, or of how beautiful Ka'ahumanu is, we're re-visioning their understanding of history and slipping them doses of Hawaiian nationalism.

Who's to say that we can't take a page from hegemonic Western culture's playbook, and use its own sneaky tricks against it? For the people opposing the Hawaiian movement, the foundational stories that they often unconsciously rely on to make their decisions are not Indigenous stories. I am not so naive as to believe that once these people are tricked into hearing *our* stories as told by us that they will automatically see the error of their ways and repent, but as the journalist, writer, and cultural critic Eduardo Galeano once said in relation to writing (and I think it holds true for stories as well): "To claim that [writing] on its own is going to change reality would be an act of madness or arrogance. It seems to me no less foolish to deny that it can aid in making this change" (177). So even if it takes a lot of time and effort, I think it is worth it to sneak our stories past the defenses of those who stubbornly oppose our lāhui, replacing or revising their stories so that the narrative that they turn to when making their decisions is one that we've had a hand in crafting. So that when they try to make statements dismissing the value that Hawaiians place on the bones of our ancestors, they have the story of Hoapili hiding Kamehameha's bones whispering in their ear. When they talk about making huge wind farms on the outer islands to feed O'ahu's unrestrained energy consumption, they will have Kūapaka'a telling them that the wind is not theirs to control. When they say that our language has no place, no power, the keiki ho'opāpā Kalapana will be shouting at them, "Mō ke kī lā make!" Whenever they are making decisions about anything, even what to eat for dinner, I want them to feel one of our stories looming behind them, peeking over their shoulders, unable to be dismissed.

Now, letting our big scary moʻolelo hide under the beds of people who oppose us is one thing, but what about those Hawaiians and others who want to know these stories, but are intimidated by the kind of leap it takes to commit to learning some of our cultural heavy-hitters? Engaging with the Pele tradition is not for day-trippers, nor is just reading the almost 500-page, 5-pound beast of a book that our translation of *Ka Moʻolelo o Hiʻiakaikapoliopele* became. There were a a lot of young Hawaiians and local students in the 100- and 200-level English classes that I taught before I began at Hawaiian Studies, and a very high number of them came in having been taught that reading is a punishment, that reading is for and about haole people, that what they like to read is not considered "real" reading. Well, the uhu pākali comes in handy here again. Some people believe that certain colored decoy uhu would only let you catch other uhu of that color. Fine, let's take well-researched stories based on Hawaiian-language sources of all different colors and genres, rig them up like live bait, and have them draw the rest of these uhu into our net.

Four-hundred-page-plus book about Kamehameha too much for you? Here's a mural in which the placement of every line and figure tells a story and represents our genealogies and voyaging pasts. Too complicated? Here's a Young Adult fantasy romance about when Hina was kidnapped and taken to Molokaʻi by Kaupeʻepeʻe, yet ended up falling in love with the charming bandit. Romance not your thing? Here's a stop-motion animated recreation of the overthrow using *Star Wars* action figures, with Darth Vader playing Lorrin Thurston. Too crazy? Here's a comic about a war that took place in Puʻuloa between man-eating sharks and the ones led by Kaʻahupāhau. And on and on and on.

As trite as this sounds, I think the world would be a better place if the land and sea were repopulated with our stories. Living and breathing stories. This is why I don't refer to our moʻolelo as "momi," or pearls. It's not because I don't treasure them, or don't think that they are a precious legacy from our ancestors. It's because pearls sit in boxes, hidden away. Pearls are not made to be worn every day. I want our stories to be a part of our daily lives, told and retold and changed and remade. And if they just sit in a drawer in the dark, they won't catch any fish.

E kuʻu hoa heluhelu, I have just given you three mana of my moʻolelo on translation. You may have liked all three, or one more than the other. Or you may have even hated them all. But now you have engaged with this story, engaged with the idea of translation as one of our many tools for change. For me, this story was about freeing our moʻolelo, letting them loose on the ʻāina again, allowing us to stand on their firm foundation. Learning and speaking ʻōlelo Hawaiʻi is one way to do that. Dancing hula is as well. Retelling our moʻolelo in new forms is another.

Translation is another. What I will leave you with, e ke hoa, is that we have many useful paths to follow, and each of them will give us more mana.

('A'ole i pau.)

WORKS CITED

Baker, Mona. "Translation and Activism: Emerging Patterns of Narrative Community." In *Translation, Resistance, Activism,* edited by Maria Tymoczko. U of Massachusetts P, 2010, pp. 23–41.

Cheyfitz, Eric. *The Poetics of Imperialism: Translation and Colonization from The Tempest to Tarzan.* U of Pennsylvania P, 1997.

Elbert, Samuel H., and Mary Kawena Pukui. *Hawaiian Grammar.* U of Hawai'i P, 1979.

Ellis, William. *Journal of William Ellis: Narrative of a Tour of Hawaii, or Owhyhee: with remarks on the history, traditions, manners, customs and language of the inhabitants of the Sandwich Islands.* 1827.

Frazier, N. Frances. "The 'Battle of Kalalau,' as Reported in the Newspaper *Kuokoa*." *Hawaiian Journal of History,* vol. 23, no. 1, 1989, pp. 108–118.

———. *The True Story of Kaluaikoolau, as Told by His Wife, Pi'ilani. Translated from the Hawaiian Language by Frances N. Frazier.* Kauai Historical Society, 2001. But see Kelekona.

Galeano, Eduardo. "In Defense of the Word." *Days and Nights of Love and War.* Monthly Review Press, 2000, pp. 167–178.

Genette, Gérard, and Marie Maclean. "Introduction to the Paratext." *New Literary History,* vol. 22, no. 2, 1991, pp. 261–272.

Haase, Donald. "Framing the Brothers Grimm: Paratexts and Intercultural Transmission in Postwar English-Language Editions of the *Kinder- und Hausmärchen*." *Fabula,* vol. 44, 2003, pp. 55–69.

Hofschneider, Anita. "'I Don't Want to Translate': Rep. Hanohano's Use of Hawaiian Leads to Tension on House Floor." *Civil Beat,* March 4, 2014. http://www.civilbeat.org/2014/03/i-dont-want-to-translate-rep-hanohanos-use-of/. Accessed December 4, 2020.

"Hoi Nele i ke One o Hanakahi." *Hawaii Holomua,* vol. 3, no. 262, 14 July 1893, p. 2.

"Ua Hoole Mai o Koolau." *Ka Leo o ka Lahui,* vol. 2, no. 722, 10 July 1893, p. 2.

Jenness, Cindy G. Comment on "Smooth Passage for Most Bills at Hawaii Legislature," by Chad Blair and Anita Hofschneider. *Civil Beat,* March 5, 2014. https://www.civilbeat.org/2014/03/21373-smooth-passage-for-most-bills-at-hawaii-legislature/. Accessed July 5, 2014.

jusanopinion101. Comment on "Rep Hanohano Prevails in Language Flap," by Web Staff. KITV, March 6, 2014. http://www.kitv.com/news/hawaii/rep-hanohano-prevails-in-language-flap/24839996#comments. Accessed July 5, 2014.

Kelekona, Kahikina. *Kaluaikoolau, ke kaeaea o na Pali Kalalau a me na Kahei O Ahi o Kamaile: Piilani, ka wahine i molia i ke ola, ke kiu alo ehu poka : Kaleimanu, ka hua o ko laua puhaka, ka opio haokila iloko o na inea : he moolelo oiaio i piha me na haawina o ke aloha walohia.* Honolulu: Gazette Print, 1906.

[Kelekona, Kahikina]. *The True Story of Kaluaikoolau, as told by his wife, Piilani.* Translated by Frances N. Frazier. U of Hawai'i P, 2001. Attributed to Frazier.

King, Thomas. *The Truth about Stories: A Native Narrative.* U of Minnesota P, 2004.

Lejeune, Philippe. *Le Pacte Autobiographique.* Seuil, 1975.

"He Moolelo Kaao no Koolau, ke Kaeaea o na Pali Nihoniho o Kalalau, ka Weli o Kauai o Manokalanipo." *Ka Leo o ka Lahui,* vol. 2, nos. 723–730, 11–20 July 1893.

Niranjana, Tejaswini. *Siting Translation: History, Post-Structuralism, and the Colonial Context.* U of California P, 1992.

Norie, John William. *Plates Descriptive of the Maritime Flags of All Nations.* J. W. Norie and Co., 1838.

Ortega y Gasset, Jose. "The Misery and the Splendor of Translation." In *The Translation Studies Reader,* edited by Lawrence Venuti. Routledge, 2000, pp. 49-64.

Poepoe, Joseph. "Ka Moolelo o Kou Aina Oiwi." *Ka Na'i Aupuni,* vol. 1, no. 37, 9 January 1906, p. 2.

Pukui, Mary Kawena, and Samuel H. Elbert. *Hawaiian Dictionary. Hawaiian-English, English-Hawaiian.* Rev. and enlarged ed. U of Hawai'i P, 1986.

Rushin, Donna Kate. "The Bridge Poem." In *This Bridge Called My Back: Writings by Radical Women of Color,* edited by Cherríe Moraga and Gloria E. Anzaldúa. Persephone Press, 1981, pp. xxi–xxii.

Shankar, S. *Flesh and Fish Blood: Post-Colonialism, Translation, and the Vernacular.* U of California P, 2012.

Silva, Noenoe K. *Aloha Betrayed: Native Hawaiian Resitance to American Colonialism.* Duke UP, 2004.

———. *The Power of the Steel-Tipped Pen: Reconstructing Native Hawaiian Intellectual History.* Duke UP, 2017.

Tabag, Joshua Ka'mea'lanakila [*sic*]. Comment on "Smooth Passage for Most Bills at Hawaii Legislature," by Chad Blair and Anita Hofschneider. *Civil Beat,* March 5, 2014. https://www.civilbeat.org/2014/03/21373-smooth-passage-for-most-bills-at-hawaii-legislature/. Accessed July 5, 2014.

Vowell, Sarah. *Unfamiliar Fishes.* Riverhead Books, 2011.

Wong, Laina, and Margaret Maaka. "Foreword." *AlterNative,* vol. 5, no. 2, 2009, pp. 6–13.

Bryan Kamaoli Kuwada is a tiny part of a beautiful beloved community that fights every day for breath, for ea, for connection, for sovereignty. He is sometimes called tree, bear, Morris, hoa, Uncle Jacket, and more. He is also sometimes an academic (publishing on comics, Bluebeard, translation, and life writing, all in the context of Hawai'i and 'ōlelo Hawai'i), editor (*Hūlili: Multidisciplinary Research on Hawaiian Wellbeing,* and co-editor with Aiko Yamashiro and No'u Revilla on issues of *Marvels and Tales* and *Biography: An Interdisciplinary Quarterly*), translator, blogger (hehiale.wordpress.com), poet (*The Offing, American Quarterly,*

Yellow Medicine Review), writer of dorky sci-fi and speculative fiction stories set in Hawai'i (*Black Marks on the White Page, Pacific Monsters, Hawai'i Review, The Dark*), photographer, and/or videographer. What he mostly does is cook too much food and surf with his mother and a crew of fierce activist poet wāhine who tease (and teach) him mercilessly.

The importance of moʻolelo to Kanaka Maoli knowledge goes beyond the understanding of content in a narrative; it provides a platform to base claims.

11

Pragmatic and Discourse Analysis of *A*-class Selection

Moʻolelo as Empirical Data

C. M. Kaliko Baker

Introduction

Given that the overarching purpose of this book is to illustrate the importance of moʻolelo in modern Kanaka Maoli research, the purpose of this chapter is to illustrate how using moʻolelo in linguistic analysis is critical to understanding discourse and pragmatic factors in the selection process of certain linguistic forms within particular linguistic contexts. The analysis will be focused on *a*-class selection in connection to subjects of nominalization and relative clause constructions. It will become clear that a linguistic analysis inclusive of discourse and pragmatic data which contextualizes the assertions is a more complete and comprehensive one, which aims to include why a speaker chooses a certain form for a particular context to linguistically illustrate a specific meaning.

Before moving forward, let's provide some background on the linguist construction that we'll be considering here, and then move on to what discourse and pragmatic analysis entail. The so-called Hawaiian possessive has two distinct classes and functions in Hawaiian. The classes are determined by the first vowel in the possessive, that is, *koʻu* is an *o*-class possessive and *kaʻu* is an *a*-class one. However, when we consider the function of these so-called possessives, we must first question if possessive is the correct classification for the category. One function is as a true possessive and the other is as a subject marker of nominalizations and relative clauses. This is true for the two major "possessive" types in Hawaiian, that is, the *k*- and *n*-forms (for a discussion on possessive forms in Hawaiian, see Elbert and Pukui 115–119). The term possessive seems obscure here because now possessive refers to both a morphological category and one of two functions within the category. A better term for the so-called possessive in Hawaiian is the morphological category known as genitive. Thus, the term "genitive" will be used henceforth to mean the morphological category generally known as possessive in Hawaiian. For this chapter, we'll be considering genitive marked subjects (GS henceforth) of nominalizations and relative clauses.

Let's examine some examples to illustrate what's meant by a GS. Consider the phrase *koʻu hele ʻana* "my going." This is a nominalization construction. The determiner *koʻu* is a *k*-form first-person singular genitive, similar to "my"; *hele* is "go"; and *ʻana* is a gerund marker which essentially marks *koʻu hele* as an event and not a thing; for example, the difference between "my going" with *ʻana* and "my path" without. Now consider *ka hale aʻu i hele ai* "the house that I went to." This noun phrase contains a relative clause; that is, *aʻu i hele ai* "that I went to." The word *aʻu* is a *k*-less first-person singular genitive. This form is a GS. I've argued elsewhere that genitives similar to those found in these examples are GSs (A-*class*).

We'll now move into discussing pragmatics. Pragmatics and discourse are where human interactive needs meet their grammars. Chandler writes that language is a semiotic system, and semioticians generally view language as the semiotic system most central to human existence. Chandler credits Saussure for proposing that language has two basic systems, langue and parole. Langue refers to the system of rules that preexists individual speakers. Parole refers to the use of language by speakers. Discussions in my earlier work (A-*class*) concerning *a*- and *o*-class GS distribution and selection have made attempts to illustrate the langue properties of Hawaiian GS distribution. Wilson (1976) focused heavily on langue properties in his analysis of the distribution of *a*- and *o*-class in Hawaiian. My 2012 work begins by discussing GSs as independent of speaker use and/or intention, and therefore considered nearly exclusively the langue properties, and not parole properties. Later in that same work, I considered discourse and pragmatic parole factors in the analysis. In this essay, we will focus on the parole properties in a speaker's linguistic selection because we want to address the question of why and/or how Hawaiian speakers use these linguistic phenomena, that is, *a*- and *o*-class GSs, in the context of narrative discourse. That is, looking at examples in the context within which the examples occurred will provide us with more information for interpreting the pragmatic and discourse factors in selecting either an *a*- or *o*-class GS.

Pragmatics and Discourse

This section will establish a methodological framework through which we will analyze *a*- and *o*-class GS selection using pragmatics and discourse. As a basis for approaching pragmatic and discourse grammar, we will use Preferred Argument Structure (Du Bois, "Discourse" and "Argument"). According to Du Bois:

> Preferred Argument Structure is simply a description of a statistical preference for certain patterns in the realization of argument tokens in a discourse.... Preferred Argument Structure can be seen to carry im-

plications for, among other things, strategies for information management, the discourse basis for ergativity, discourse profiles of verb classes and constructions, argument realization, and the grammaticization of the system of argument structure.... What Preferred Argument Structure shows in some detail is how particular cognitive-pragmatic functions are regularly associated with certain syntactic roles, to the exclusion of others. From the perspective of grammar in use, argument structures are resources for speakers to exploit, for cognitive-pragmatic as well as semantic functions. ("Argument" 40)

Preferred Argument Structure uses statistical preferences to reach conclusions about grammatical patterning. Elsewhere I have used statistics to propose and base claims about Hawaiian GS class selection (A-*class*). In this essay we will qualitatively analyze data and draw conclusions.

To analyze discourse grammar is to analyze how a language functions. DeLancey describes a functionalist description as one that

links structures at all levels with their semantic and pragmatic functions. A functional theory is one in which grammatical structures and the relations among them are motivated by...their semantic and pragmatic functions and the relations among them.... (289)

This analysis of GS selection in Hawaiian nominalization and relative clause structures will now be done through discourse from which they were extracted. We will look specifically at the function of *a*-class marked GSs in narrative discourse. Syntactic analysis is confined to the sentence and its boundaries. Semantics at its simplest is the study of meaning in human languages (Palmer, Allan). Discourse analysis places sentences and utterances within their linguistic context. Hence, it looks beyond the sentence to understand why certain forms are used (and/or not used) in a given context.

By default, a discourse analysis requires a pragmatic analysis, because pragmatics is the study of meaning beyond semantics. According to Levinson, "Pragmatics is the study of deixis (at least in part), implicature, presupposition, speech acts, and aspects of discourse structure" (27). Renkema states that pragmatics is concerned with signs and "deals with questions about how signs function" (36). Yule provides another definition: "Pragmatics is the study of relationships between linguistic forms and the users of those forms" (4). From Yule's perspective, pragmatics is primarily concerned with what a speaker intends by an utterance rather than the actual utterance itself. Huang contrasts semantics and pragmatics by saying that semantics is concerned with the "conventional aspects of meaning" and "pragmatics is concerned with the non-conventional aspects of meaning" (174). The analyses provided below indeed step away from conventional aspects of meaning and focus on the non-conventional. Pragmatics will, thus, be used to analyze speaker intention in using an *a*-class GS as a discourse grammatical tool.

Consider the Hawaiian utterance *ka'u ali'i* "my chief." Possession of ali'i is normally expressed with *o*-class, for example, *ko'u ali'i* "my chief." When however an individual chooses a new *ali'i* to reside under, the possession of this new *ali'i* is expressed with an *a*-class possessive. Hence, the use of *a*-class in *ka'u ali'i* shows the perspective of the speaker. This sort of *a*-class usage might be used by a speaker with the intent of showing that his/her previous *ali'i* was abusive and, therefore, s/he sought another *ali'i*. The act of communicating non-overtly expressed messages as such is known as an illocutionary act. Illocutionary acts have illocutionary effects. An addressee who heard such an utterance as *ka'u ali'i* may have thought that by using the *a*-class possessive the speaker was trying to communicate that the previous *ali'i* had died and that is why the speaker sought out a new *ali'i*. A perlocutionary act resulting from the addressee perceiving that the *ali'i* has died (e.g., the illocutionary effect) could be the addressee crying and attempting to comfort the speaker because of his/her loss. How *a*-class is used to create context is beyond the scope of syntax and semantics. Inquiries in locution, illocution, and perlocution are focused on the question of why a certain form is used in a certain way and/or in a certain context as well as the interpretations thereof. Inquiries of this nature are subsumed under the field of pragmatics. (See Duranti, Renkema, Huang, and others for discussions on inquiries involving locutions.)

Pragmatics provides a means for linguists to investigate why speakers say what they say, how they intend people to interpret it, and how people interpret differently on their own what is said. Because pragmatics assumes a position of knowing what is going on in peoples' heads (Yule), native or native-like fluency is necessary to provide insight into what a speaker and/or addressee may, or may not, have been thinking in connection to some utterance. This is where my years of being a Native Hawaiian autoethnographer—learning, studying, analyzing, and using Hawaiian as a Native Hawaiian—come into play. (See Adams et al. for discussions on autoethnographic studies.) That is, to understand Hawaiian pragmatics, it is imperative for one to be socialized as a Hawaiian; that is, know how a Hawaiian thinks, acts, and negotiates his/her linguistic world. Autoethnography is a means by which such an understanding is achieved and discussed by non-native speakers such as myself. Thus, my years of autoethnographic study of the Hawaiian worldview provides me with insight into how my people, the Hawaiian people, used Hawaiian forms to convey their mana'o "thoughts, views, options, etc." in their own pragmatic way(s).

It is my contention that pragmatics is the missing link to a fuller understanding of GS class selection in Hawaiian. A pragmatic analysis allowed us to analyze

the *ka'u ali'i* example and ask why a speaker uses an *a*-class genitive in a possessive construction in conjunction with a noun like *ali'i* that is normally possessed
with *o*-class. That is, a speaker produces the locution (i.e., utterance) *ka'u ali'i* as
an illocutionary act to illustrate that his/her *ali'i* is one that s/he chose and/or is
new, that is, not the same chief as before. Pragmatics also allows us the means
to analyze how an addressee understands and/or reacts to what was said by the
speaker, that is, the perlocutionary effects. In connection to GS class selection,
speaker intent becomes central to pragmatically analyzing the question of why
one form and not another is used in a discourse.

According to Du Bois ("Argument"), the study of discourse is the study of
language, that is, grammatical phenomena, particularly syntactic phenomena,
in use, meaning that discourse analysis begins where syntax ends, at the sentence boundary. Contextualization of the data provides insight into the illocutionary properties of the specific utterances. Discourse analysis will be used
here to provide contextual evidence to support new claims about why certain
GSs are chosen by speakers to be *a*-class and others not.

Combining Pragmatics and Discourse: Perspective and Saliency

The combination of pragmatics and discourse analysis is very natural. Pragmatic
analysis requires insight into why speakers utter certain phrases at certain times,
how they intend them to be received, and how they are actually received. Discourse analysis looks at linguistic forms in context and asks why a certain pattern
(syntactic or otherwise) of language is used in a certain context. The two approaches complement each other through reciprocity. That is, a discourse context
establishes the means for a speaker to make pragmatically informed linguistic
choices, and pragmatic information concerning content and the flow thereof influences discourse choices by a speaker.

Fillmore ("The Case") demonstrates that perspective, a discourse-pragmatic
issue, is what motivates which agent in a multi-agent scenario is to be selected
as the grammatical subject in English. In connection with Fillmore's perspective
analysis, Du Bois states that "it becomes difficult to escape the need for referen-
tial pragmatics in argument selection" ("Argument" 26). Therefore, in analyzing
speaker intention through what a speaker says, we are best served with a holistic
view of discourse context in combination with pragmatics.

Basing his work on Fillmore's saliency hierarchy ("Topics"), Du Bois provides
a hierarchical feature system by which subjects are selected.[1] These features are
provided in rank order in Table 1. In connection to *a*- and *o*-class GS selection in
Hawaiian, a working hypothesis in this essay is that the more salient an actor
GS is in a discourse, the more viable a candidate it is to be marked with *a*-class.
That is, in terms of Table 1, the more outranking features listed on the left side a

GS has, for example, active, causal, etc., the more likely the GS will be marked with *a*-class than with the non-specific, unmarked form *o*-class.

Discourse saliency is imperative to foreground information. Because foreground information is normally salient, the saliency hierarchy is relevant to understanding what information is foregrounded and what is not. My hypothesis is that GSs in foregrounded narrative contexts when marked with *a*-class indicate that the referent of the GS affected the progression of the narrative.

To define foreground versus background information, we will begin by using Carlota Smith's properties of such information. Narrative foreground information is to be understood as information concerned with affecting the flow of discourse, while background information provides supporting and descriptive information for the foreground information. Foreground information "presents the main, sequential events of a narrative" (35). Background information is subsidiary and does not affect the progression of a narrative. According to Hopper and Thompson, foreground information in discourse is the information that "supplies the main points of the discourse" and background information is "that part of a discourse which does not immediately and crucially contribute to the speaker's goal, but which merely assists, amplifies, or comments on it" (280).

Hopper and Thompson found that 78 percent of all foregrounding information in the discourse examples they examined had defining properties of transitivity, as opposed to only 39 percent of backgrounding information (288). Foregrounding is therefore associated with transitivity because in supplying the main points of a discourse, transitive clauses including their agents move the discourse along temporal lines. That is, narrative progression is generally orchestrated by acts of volition within the context of the story world. Therefore, agentive GSs should frequently occur in foregrounded narrative contexts. In my dissertation, I found that the GS category that contained the highest token counts of *a*-class GS in both corpora of nominalizations and relative clauses was the agent class of transitive clauses. The proposal here is that *a*-class GSs are used by authors of Hawaiian narratives to indicate that the referent of the *a*-class marked GS affected the flow of discourse.

Table 1. Saliency Hierarchy (as found in Du Bois, "Argument" 26)

active	outranks	inactive
causal	outranks	experiencer
experiencer	outranks	non-experiencer
changed	outranks	non-changed
complete/individuated	outranks	part
figure	outranks	ground
definite	outranks	indefinite

Four properties that indicate foreground as opposed to background information are provided in Table 2. These properties are influenced/derived from the foreground/background properties as described in Hopper and Thompson, Smith, and to some extent from Fillmore's saliency hierarchy ("Topics") as discussed by Du Bois ("Argument"). The categories provided in Table 2 are continuous, that is, not discrete. For example, between the categories agentive and patientive are what is known as experiencer subjects; for example, subjects of lexical items such as *lohe* "hear," *'ike* "see, feel, know, meet," etc. For the purposes of this essay, there is no need to distinguish experiencers versus non-experiencers as categories because within the agentive–patientive continuum experiencer subjects are accounted for.

This approach is in line with Dowty's approach, which I discuss at length in my previous work (A-*class*). Dowty proposed that there are essentially two semantic roles, namely Proto-Agent and Proto-Patient. More agentive subjects have the following properties: volitional involvement, sentience, causal, and movement. They are also likely to exist independently of the event. Less agentive subjects are more patientive, and have the following properties: undergo a change of state, have an incremental theme, are causally affected by another participant, stationary, do not exist independently of the event, or even not at all. As I have argued before, in theory, the more agentive a GS is, the more likely it will be marked with *a*-class, and the more patientive a GS is, the more likely it will not be marked with *a*-class. When we apply Dowty's properties, we find this is true, which led to my proposal of the following GS class selection continuum (A-*class* 156).

A narrative event inclusive of its entities that affects the narrative progression occurs in the discourse foreground. A narrative event inclusive of its entities that prefaces and/or subsidizes essential foreground information is non-affecting, because its contents do not alter the narrative progression. The assumption here is that authors (and/or speakers) use particular linguistic tools, be they lexemes, grammatical patterns, etc., to affect narrative information flow. Information inclusive of these types of linguistic tools is referred to here as being affecting. Authors (and/or speakers) also use linguistic tools to either minimize affect or be ineffective in moving the narrative forward along temporal lines. Information of this type is referred to here as non-effecting.

Table 2. Properties Used in Qualifying Foreground Information

affecting	outranks	non-affecting
agentive	outranks	patientive
independent	outranks	part
definite	outranks	indefinite

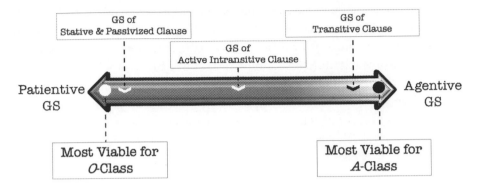

Genitive Subject Class Selection Continuum. Author's image.

An extension of the meaning of *agentive* here is that a discourse entity's action affected (i.e., caused a change) the progression of some narrative context. A foreground discourse actor acting in the story world causes the narrative to progress along the temporal line(s) that the author intends. Connecting back to Hopper and Thompson, transitivity is therefore associated with foreground information because transitive clauses are more likely than intransitive clauses to contain subjects whose referents act. As for patientive, it is the property of some narrative entity that does not affect the progression of the narrative along temporal lines, and is thus associated with background information.

Being independent is one of Dowty's Proto-Agent properties. Independent means that the information is distinct from other information and is not part of the background. In connection to agentive GSs that qualify to be marked with *a*-class within foreground information, independent agents of transitive and intransitive clauses perform actions that are intended to individuate them within the narrative. These independent actors are in part responsible for the progression of the narrative, and thus often occur in foregrounded information.

Definiteness is also important to narrative foregrounding and is defined here in terms of discourse saliency. That is, it must be clear to the addressee (a) who (or what) the narrative entity is, and/or (b) what the culturally important and relevant details about the narrative entity are. For example, in the narratives about Kamapuaʻa used for this analysis, if not already familiar with Kamapuaʻa beforehand, by the time the addressee has finished reading the title and the first paragraph, the reader of the original moʻolelo knows or is made aware of critical iconic cultural and contextual information about him in the sub-heading. Therefore, Kamapuaʻa is salient throughout the narrative and is often part of foreground information, and often triggers *a*-class GS.

The proposal for understanding *a*-class usage is that an *a*-class GS is a linguistic tool used by speakers of Hawaiian to indicate that the GS is (a) specified as an essential actor, and (b) marked as foregrounded in a narrative and therefore as affecting the progression of the story line. Hence, *a*-class GSs are used by authors/speakers to mark an actor in a narrative context as an individuated, normally definite, essential actor in the narrative foreground.

Pragmatic and Discourse Factors in GS Class Selection in Hawaiian Nominalizations

We will begin our testing of the hypotheses proposed above by analyzing nominalization constructions in Hawaiian. The findings in this section illustrate that in nominalizations *a*-class GSs are used when the GS is minimally an actor within the event scenario and the GS is involved in an event that is essential to the progression of the story and/or the reader's comprehension of it. *O*-class GSs are defined as unspecified as actors that are essential to the progression of the narrative, hence a neutral category.

For the purposes of the study, nominalization constructions are defined as and limited to those phrases that contain the gerund marker *'ana*. The data were further limited to those that contain a full possessive genitive phrase understood as the subject of the nominalization. As Elbert and Pukui write, "the combination of verb + 'ana usually represents an ongoing process, frequently translated into English by the present participle" (80). The presence of 'ana turns what seems to be a thing into an event. For example, *kāu hele* "your move (in a board game)" is different from *kāu hele 'ana* "your moving/going" (Baker, *A-class* 33–34). The corpus data in my dissertation consisted of 865 total tokens of nominalization constructions. Of the 865 tokens, 728, or 84 percent, contained *o*-class GS. This data quantification, however, tells us only that *o*-class is the norm. It does not tell us when and/or why to use *a*-class.

The data in example (1) below are provided to illustrate a context in which *o*-class is used to mark backgrounding GSs and *a*-class is not used. If it were, an *a*-class GS would be at best strange (i.e., infelicitous). The portion of the narrative context found in (1) occurred immediately prior to the narrative context provided in (2) below. The square bracketed portions—[...]—in the free translations are provided to give insight into the meaning that the author encoded through how the text was written.

Example (1c) contains the specific data that we want to analyze. The GS in (1c) is the preposed non-pronominal GS complex; for example, *ko ke ali'i a me ko nā kānaka* "the chief's and the people's." The two GSs are coordinated by *a me* "and," and the genitive markers in both are *ko*, which we recognize as *o*-class.[2]

1. **I ke ala ana ae o na kanaka kiai mai ko lakou hiamoe ana**, no ka mea, ua kiekie loa ae la ka la.

Ua ike koke ae la lakou i na mea i hana ia, ua pau loa ka ai a me ka ia i ka ai ia, a ua piha pu hoi ka hale i ka hana lepo o ua puaa nei, a ua ku no hoi i ke ino ke ea o ka hanalepo o ua puaa nei.

I ko ke alii a me ko na kanaka ike ana i keia mau hana hoonaaikola, ua ninau aku la oia i kona mau kanaka.

("He Moolelo," 29 July 1891, 4)

a. **I ke ala ʻana aʻe o nā kānaka kiaʻi** mai ko lākou hiamoe ʻana, no ka mea, ua kiʻekiʻe loa aʻela ka lā, ua ʻike koke aʻela lākou i nā mea i hana ʻia, ua pau loa ka ʻai a me ka iʻa i ka ʻai ʻia, a ua piha pū hoʻi ka hale i ka hana lepo o ua puaʻa nei, a ua kū nō hoʻi i ke ʻino ke ea o ka hana-lepo o ua puaʻa nei.
I ko ke aliʻi a me ko nā kānaka ʻike ʻana i kēia mau hana hoʻonaʻaikola, ua nīnau akula ʻo ia i kōna mau kānaka....

When the guards rose up from their resting, because the sun was high above, they quickly saw what was done, all the food and fish were eaten, and the house was also full with the excrement of this [focalized, e.g., *ua ... nei*] pig, and the air [smell] of the excrement of this [focalized] pig was rancid.
Upon the chief's and the people's seeing these contemptuous acts, he [the chief] asked his people....

b. I   ke   ala   ʻana   aʻe   o   nā   kānaka   kiaʻi
Loc   the   awake   ʻANA   up   ø-Gen-o   the+pl   people   guard
When the guards woke up

c. I   ko   ke   aliʻi   a   me   ko   nā   kānaka   ʻike   ʻana
Loc   Gen-o   the   chief   and   with   Gen-o   the+pl   person   see   ʻANA
i   kēia   mau   hana   hoʻonaʻaikola,
Acc   this   pl   work contemptuous
Upon the chief's and the people's seeing these contemptuous acts,

d. ua   nīnau   akula   ʻo   ia   i   kōna   mau kānaka
Prf   ask   thither-ø=Centr.   Nom 3sg   Acc   3sg=Gen-o   pl   people
he (the chief) then asked his people...

The data in (1c) are background information because the information was given in the first paragraph (1a). The information in (1c) seems to be emerging into the foreground. However, the sentence in the first paragraph that reads *ua ʻike koke aʻela lākou i nā mea i hana ʻia* "they quickly saw what was done" illustrates that the author mentioned prior to the phrase in (1c) that the *aliʻi* "chief" and the *kānaka* "people" witnessed these *hana hoʻonaʻaikola* "contemptuous acts."[3] Moreover, the use of *kēia* "this" in (1c) in the phrase *kēia mau hana hoʻonaʻaikola* "these contemptuous acts" suggests that the O argument of this *'ike* "see" event is what is focused upon, not the event nor the agents.

As mentioned above, a property of narrative background information is description, and the use of statives is one way to describe the landscape. For example, in (1) the lexical item *ki'eki'e* "high" and its subject *ka lā* "the sun" are used to describe the time of day, the lexical item *pau* "finished" is used to describe the state of the character's elders' food,[4] the lexical item *piha* "full" is used to describe the state of the characters' *hale* "house," and the lexical item *kū* "full; resemble" is used to describe the state of the smell of the characters' *hale*. Moreover, the lexical item *'ike* in (1) implies that the characters not only "saw" the "contemptuous acts" of Kamapua'a, but also experienced the effects of bearing witness to them because *'ike* not only translates as "see," but also as "feel" and "experience" too. Thus, the narrative content in (1c) is provided as subsidiary information. As such, the information maintains the scene for the following sentence in (1d) as well as the subsequent narrative context that followed, leading to the text found in (2) below, that will be argued to be foregrounded information.

Example (1) begins with the nominalization repeated in (1a), which is also background information that establishes the scene (i.e., the ground) for the clause *ua 'ike koke a'ela lākou*... "they soon saw (i.e., realized)...," which was marked with *ua*, a perfective/inceptive marker. Elbert and Pukui explain that *ua* indicates a lexeme as being both a perfective and inceptive marker (58). The way that *ua* is used as an inceptive marker in a narrative context indicates that verbs and nouns, that is, predicates or phrasal heads, are either new and/or important information, essential to the speaker's communicating of the content and for the addressee's understanding of what the speaker is communicating. Thus, the *ali'i* and the *maka'āinana* seeing what happened is foreground information that was subsidized by the nominalization found in (1b). Whereas subsidiary information is background information, the GS found in (1b) is therefore *o*-class.

The data found in (1c) establish the context for (1d) which affects the progression of the discourse. (1d) is foreground information, as evidenced by the use of the inceptive marker *ua* and the narrative affect it possesses in moving the narrative toward the subsequent dialogue, part of which was provided in (1) above.

The data in (2) below contain a quote attributed to a character, a *maka'āinana* "commoner," who is addressing his *ali'i* "chief." The data in (2a) repeat the beginning of (2), which is provided to contextualize (2b). The nominalization in (2b) is *kā kou luna'ikehala 'ike 'ana he pono* "what your conscience sees as right." The GS of the nominalization is a preposed *a*-class GS. Moreover, the head noun of the GS is *luna'ikehala* "conscience," a common noun.

2. A he nani hoi na e ke alii, ke huli mai nei oe a ninau ia makou, i kou mau
   hulu lepo makaainana, he mea pono no nau no e ke alii e koho e like me
   ka kou lunaikehala ike ana he pono.
   ("He Moolelo," 29 July 1891, 4)

   a. A he nani ho'i nā   e   ke ali'i,
      and a pretty indeed Dem Add the chief
      And that (which you have done (cf. *nā*)), chief, is wonderful,

      ke huli mai nei 'oe a   nīnau iā   mākou,
      Imp turn hither near 2sg and ask   Acc 3pl=excl
      you are turning and asking us,

      i   kou   mau hulu lepo maka'āinana,
      Acc 2sg=Gen-o pl   feather dirt commoner
      your humble common people

   b. he mea pono nō   nāu   nō   e   ke ali'i e koho
      a thing right indeed 2sg=*n*-Gen-a indeed Voc the chief Imp chose
      it's indeed best that you, chief, be the one to choose

      e   like me **kā** **kou**   **luna'ikehala** '**ike** '**ana** he pono.
      Imp like with Gen-a 2sg=Gen-o conscience   see 'ANA a   right
      according to what your conscience sees as right.

The GS of '*ike* "see, know, feel" in the nominalization corpus used for my dissertation were *o*-class in 42 of 44 tokens, or a rate of 96 percent. Therefore, the data set given in (2b) represents a highly unusual use of *a*-class. To address this issue, we must turn to the narrative, or the mo'olelo, from which the data were extracted. The data in (2) were extracted from a mo'olelo about Kamapua'a, a famed Hawaiian hero who was eventually deified.[5] This particular portion of data was part of a dialogue between an *ali'i*, Pueonuiokōna, and his *maka'āinana*. In this particular section of the mo'olelo, Kamapua'a was coming to kill Pueonuiokōna and his *maka'āinana* for conspiring with other chiefs and *maka'āinana* against what Kamapua'a thought was *pono* "right." Since (2) contains part of a dialogue between two characters in the context of the mo'olelo, there are certain ways of communicating that the author used to illustrate authentic locutions between a *maka'āinana* and his *ali'i*. The use of *a*-class is an indicator that the *ali'i* possesses the power to be essential in the decision-making process that will determine the faith of the *maka'āinana*. This locution expressed in form selection, that is, including the *a*-class GS, thus exemplifies an illocutionary act by the author illustrating the *maka'āinana*'s intent that the *ali'i*'s will is essential and affective in the context.

The *ali'i* in the context of (2) was being asked by the character assigned the text/speech to make a decision on behalf of the people. The *ali'i* previously stated in the narrative that there was no way that they could defeat Kamapua'a because Kamapua'a has *kino lau* "many bodies." That is, he is a shape-shifter who on land could change into a *pua'a* "pig" or multiply into thousands of *pua'a*. Thus, the *maka'āinana* is pleading with the *ali'i* to follow his *luna'ikehala* "conscience"; that is, to not engage with Kamapua'a, and to do what is *pono*, that is, avoid getting everyone killed.

The author chose the preposed non-pronominal *a*-class GS in the context from which (2) was extracted to specify that the *maka'āinana* perceived the chief's conscience (*luna'ikehala*) as being an essential actor in the *'ike* event. In specifying this, the *maka'āinana* is saying to the *ali'i* that his conscience can, and will, willfully and affectively act in an essential manner in the scheme of the larger context that the characters are facing in the story world. Therefore, the GS in (2b) affects the narrative progression by putting the faith of the *maka'āinana* in the choice, or *koho*, of the *ali'i*'s *luna'ikehala*. Moreover, the *ali'i*'s *luna'ikehala* is independent and definite in the narrative context, where it seems the *luna'ikehala* is distinctly acting under its own volition to affect the decision-making process, although we know that the *luna'ikehala* is associated through metonymy and/or contiguity to the possessor of it.

To summarize the discussion of (2), the author used the *a*-class GS in (2b) to explicitly specify that the action to be performed by the referent of the GS was essential, causal, and intrinsic to how the narrative would progress. Because the event described in (2b) is therefore foregrounded in the narrative context, moving the narrative forward along temporal lines, the author used an *a*-class GS in this particular context to communicate to his reader that the action of this *luna'ikehala* could or will affect the narrative flow.

Demonstratives are also key indicators of where elements lie within the scheme of discourse foreground and background. The demonstrative *kēia* "this" is used to mark a discourse element as central and in the foreground. Elbert and Pukui (141–142) provide an interesting example that contains *kēia* and an *a*-class GS of a nominalization, which is provided in (3) below, cited from its original source.

3. O ke kumu o keia kii ana mai ia Kawelo, o **ke pai ana o Aikanaka i na makua o Kawelo** mai Hanamaulu ae. Ma **keia pai ana a Aikanaka i na makua**, lawe ia ae la ka ai a me ka ia, a me na pono a pau loa, a noho wale iho la lakou aohe ai, hookahi ai o ka uku a me ka lia o ke poo. (Fornander 16)

'O ke kumu o kēia ki'i 'ana mai iā Kawelo, 'o **ke pa'i 'ana o 'Aikanaka i nā mākua o Kawelo** mai Hanama'ulu a'e. **Ma kēia pa'i 'ana a 'Aikanaka** i nā mākua, lawe 'ia a'ela ka 'ai a me ka i'a, a me nā pono a pau loa, a noho wale ihola lākou 'a'ohe 'ai, ho'okahi 'ai 'o ka 'uku a me ka lia o ke po'o.

As for the reason of this fetching of Kawelo, it was because of **the eviction of 'Aikanaka of the parents of Kawelo** from Hanama'ulu. In **this eviction by 'Aikanaka of the parents**, the starches (i.e., taro, etc.) and the fish (i.e., fleshy-foods) were taken, and (as well as) all necessities, and they lived with no food, the only food (they had) were the lice and nits of the (their) heads.

a. ke   pa'i   'ana o   'Aikanaka i   nā   mākua
   the eviction 'ANA ø-Gen-o. 'Aikanaka Acc the(pl) parent
   the eviction of 'Aikanaka (agent) of the parents (undergoers)

b. kēia pa'i   'ana a   'Aikanaka i   nā   mākua
   this eviction. ANA. ø-Gen-a 'Aikanaka Acc the(pl) parent
   this eviction of 'Aikanaka (agent) of the parents (undergoers)

Notice that the lexical predicate *pa'i* is nominalized twice in (3). The reason that the first *pa'i* "evict, punish" token (repeated in 3a) contains an *o*-class GS is because the *pa'i* event was background information. The latter *pa'i* mention (repeated in 3b) is preceded by *kēia*, the centrality-marking demonstrative determiner. Hence, the reason that the later *pa'i* mention has an *a*-class GS is because the *pa'i* event has been foregrounded and focalized in the narrative context.

Elbert and Pukui noticed that the only formal difference between the two *pa'i* tokens is the determiners, for example, *ke* "the" and *kēia* "this." Because the phrasal elements in the two *pa'i* nominalizations in (3a) and (3b) are identical except for the determiners and the GS classes, the two examples are minimal pairs (or couplets). In connection to what is listed here as (3b), Elbert and Pukui comment that,"Perhaps *a* here indicates greater deliberateness and control; it makes the eviction more forceful. The preceding *kēia* 'this' makes the act more specific and less general" (142). These suggested possible reasons for *a*-class selection are plausible to me and I agree with them here. The more specific a reference is, however, the more salient it is within the narrative context, and as we have seen in connection to the other *a*-class GS tokens above, greater saliency makes a more viable candidate for *a*-class GS selection. The use of *kēia* in (3b) indicates that the nominalization is focalized and foregrounded. When the GS strategy is employed and the GS is perceivably an actor, the theory presented here is that a GS will more likely be *a*-class when an action is more affective, as seen in (3b), and is important in affecting the narrative progression.

Prior to discussing the specifics found in (4), we will first briefly describe the moʻolelo, the story surrounding the (4) data set. (4) is an example of character dialogue. The character and his/her group were being attacked by Kamapuaʻa. Because many people in the story world (i.e., characters) were being killed at the time, there was a lot of tension, anxiety, and fear for safety among those being attacked. In (4) below, we find ʻai "eat." ʻAi events contain subjects that have Proto-Agent properties. The subjects of ʻai generally are volitional, sentient, and cause an affect and/or movement. Agentive subjects were by far the most represented amongst the *a*-class tokens in the corpora.

4. E—papapau kakou e ke alii i ka make i ka puaa e—... Aohe ahailono o
   keia ai ana a ua puaa nei, i ke alii Olopana me kona makaainana
   ("He Molelo," 29 June 1891)

   E   papapau   kākou   e   ke aliʻi i   ka make
   Imp   destroyed 1pl=incl   Voc   the chief Loc the dead
   We'll all be killed, chief

   i   ka puaʻa ē
   Loc   the pig   Voc
   by the pig

   ʻAʻohe ʻāhaʻilono o   **kēia ʻai ʻana a   ua puaʻa nei**
   zero   survivor ø-Gen-o.   this eat ʻANA ø-Gen-a. Prf pig Cntr
   There will be no survivors of this eating by this (focalized) pig

   i   ke aliʻi Olopana me   kōna makaʻāinana
   Loc   the chief Olopana and his   commoner
   of chief Olopana and his people

Found in (4) above is the nominalization *kēia ʻai ʻana a ua puaʻa nei* "this eating by this pig." The determiner of the larger NP is the centrality-marking demonstrative *kēia*. The determiner in the GS phrase is *ua*. As mentioned above, when *ua* is used as a demonstrative determiner, it indicates an NP is (a) previously mentioned and (b) focalized in the narrative. The *nei* that is postposed to the noun *puaʻa* "pig" is another centrality demonstrative. Therefore, the NP is indexed as being foreground information by these markers.

By using *kēia* and *ua...nei*, the author is performing an illocutionary act by (metaphorically speaking) placing the narrative information immediately before the eyes of the reader. The author created an elevated sense of discourse saliency through the combination of the lexeme *ʻai* "eat" and its syntactic-semantic features; that is, having an agentive subject complement and the pragmatic and discourse markers found in foreground information, for example, *kēia* and *ua...nei*. Because the narrative context is foreground, we find an *a*-class GS in (4). Again, by using the *a*-class GS as well as the other linguistic tools in reciting moʻolelo, the author is indicating that the *ʻai* event of the GS is affective in moving the discourse forward.

We will now consider a nominalization containing the demonstrative *kēlā* "that" in conjunction with the lexical predicate *noho* "dwell." The subject of *noho* does not possess the same Proto-Agent properties as lexemes such as *paʻi* above. The lexeme *paʻi* has a subject that is volitional, sentient, and causes motion. The lexeme *noho*, on the other hand, has a subject that is not necessarily volitional, nor in motion at all. The only Proto-Agent property that the subject of a *noho* event has is sentience. Hence, there are two types of subject arguments here, one that is volitional and/ or in motion and another that is neither. Forty-four tokens of the lexeme *noho* occurred in the nominalization corpus; of these, only five were *a*-class. In (5) below, we find a nominalization of non-volitional nor in motion *noho* with an *a*-class GS in combination with *kēlā*. The data in (5) are thus statistically unique.

5. A ma **kela noho ana a Kamapuaa** ma kela ana, ua kapaia iho la ua ana nei o Keanapuaa a hiki i keia wa.
   ("He Moolelo," 20 July 1891, 4)

   A   ma **kēlā noho ʻana a**   **Kamapuaʻa** ma kēlā ana,
   and Loc that dwell ʻANA ø-Gen-a. Kamapuaʻa Loc that cave
   And in (i.e., by way of) that dwelling of Kamapuaʻa in that cave,

   ua kapa ʻia ihola   ua ana nei ʻo   Keanapuaʻa
   Prf name Pass dir+ø-Cntr Prf cave Cntr Nom Keanapuaʻa
   this (focalized) cave was (since) named Keanapuaʻa

   ā   hiki i   kēia wā.
   until arrive loc this time
   until today

In comparing *kēia* "this," or what was termed above a centrality-marking determiner, and *kēlā*, we find that both are demonstratives. *Kēia* specifies and/or marks narrative entities and events that are central to the current narrative story line. In the context provided in (5), *kēlā* is not part of the major story line, although it is relevant. Hence, *kēlā* is a non-centrality-marker, which in narrative discourse grammar means that the information is peripheral and/or not central to the progression of the current narrative.

The data in (5) refer to the event that is the cause of the naming event of the following clause, for example, *ua kapa ʻia ihola ua ana nei...* "this (focalized) cave was (since) named" and is thus important information. This nominalization is different from the nominalizations in (1) that have *o*-class GSs, because the nominalizations in (1) are backgrounding phrases that provided subsidiary and/or scenic information for their respective clauses and did not affect the progression of the narrative. The nominalization in (5) contains information that is essential to the naming event, that is, it effectively moves this narrative to the next informational clause, and thus is foreground in the discourse context. That is why the GS is *a*-class.

To summarize, specifying that Kamapuaʻa is essential to the context surrounding the *noho* event described in (5) impresses on the reader that if it were not for Kamapuaʻa's dwelling there, that cave would not have the name Keanapuaʻa, or "the pig-cave." Such an implication is an issue of pragmatics, and in a narrative context, so is *a*-class usage. The pragmatic implicature offered by the *a*-class GS in (5) is therefore governed by the moʻolelo, or narrative context, and not by the syntax, semantics, or any combination thereof.

Summary of GS Class Selection in Nominalizations

We have seen that *a*-class GSs are used in narrative contexts that are foreground, while *o*-class GS occur in background contexts. It has not been illustrated yet that all foreground GSs are *a*-class. In the discussion above we saw that in connection to discourse grammar, predicates referencing events are part of a story's context. Because *a*-class GSs mark an event as essential in the narrative, they are understood as indicating important information that helps progress the story line forward by essentializing the agentivity of the actors.

Other foreground marking tools were apparent in the examples above. One is *kēia*, a centrality-marking demonstrative determiner, and another is the combination of the inceptive marker *ua* with the postposed centrality-marking demonstrative *nei*. These centrality markers were used to indicate the information as foreground and to focus the attention of the reader on the NP and its importance to the progression of the narrative story line. As a reminder, see (4) above, where we saw the combination of both *kēia* and *ua . . . nei* with an *a*-class GS in a single nominalization, the result of this combination was that the content is understood as significant narrative content relative to the progression of the story line.[6]

Pragmatic and Discourse Factors in GS Class Selection in Hawaiian Relative Clauses

In this section, we will analyze *a*- and *o*-class GS use in Hawaiian relative clauses in their narrative or story context. Proposed in my dissertation were Maxims, or broad generalizations found in the data.[7]

The lexeme *noho* "dwell" as discussed above has a subject that normally is of low agentivity, unlike that of *pa'i* and *'ai*. Example (6) presents a paragraph of narrative within which the lexeme *noho* is the predicate in two relative clauses that both have *a*-class GSs. (6a) contains the first relative clause and (6b) contains the other. Example (6) begins with the sentential predicate *ua pae maila* "came ashore." The predicate is marked by *ua*, the perfective/inceptive marker. As noted above, authors and speakers of Hawaiian use *ua* to mark information as new and/or important. Thus, the mo'olelo context found in (6) is foregrounding information intended to be salient to the reader and to affect the progression of the narrative.

6. **Ua pae mai la na waa ma kahi a Kamapuaa e noho aku nei**, no ke kai maloo, malaila lakou e moe ai a hiki i ke kai pii o ka wanaao, alaila lakou **holo no Kou, kahi a na alii kane e noho mai la**, o Kou i oleloia o Honolulu no ia i keia manawa.
("He Moolelo," 20 July 1891, 4)

Ua pae maila nā wa'a ma kahi a Kamapua'a e noho aku nei, no ke kai malo'o, ma laila lākou e moe ai ā hiki i ke kai pi'i o ka wana'ao, **a laila lākou holo no Kou, kahi a nā ali'i kāne e noho maila**, 'o Kou, i 'ōlelo 'ia, 'o Honolulu nō ia i kēia manawa.	**The canoes landed near where Kamapua'a was staying**, because of the low tide, there they would sleep until the high tide of the morning, and then they sail for Kou, **where** as it is said, this is indeed Honolulu now.

a. Ua pae mai   -la   nā   wa'a
   Prf land hither -ø-Cntr the.pl canoe
   The canoes came ashore

   ma kahi   a   Kamapua'a e   noho aku   nei
   Loc he.place. ø-Gen-a. Kamapua'a Imp dwell thither Cntr
   near where Kamapua'a was staying

b. a   laila   lākou holo no Kou,
   and then 3pl   sail for Kou,
   and then they sail for Kou,

   kahi   a   nā   ali'i kāne e   noho maila
   the.place ø-Gen-a the.pl. chief male Imp dwell hither-ø-Cntr
   where the male chiefs were staying

The directional following the predicate head *pae* is *mai* "hither." The directional *mai* is used in Hawaiian to mean that some event is moving toward the center. (For a discussion of directionals in Hawaiian, see Elbert and Pukui 91–95). In speaker-listener speech events, *mai* is used in combination with events moving toward the speaker. In mo'olelo, *mai* is used in combination with events moving toward the deictic center. The directional *mai* in (6a) indicates that the *pae* "land, come ashore" event is moving toward the deictic center of the story. The prepositional phrase *ma kahi a Kamapua'a e noho aku nei* "near where Kamapua'a was staying" is also understood as the place near to where the canoes came ashore. Therefore, where Kamapua'a was staying is in the deictic center of the narrative because the *pae* event moved *hither* toward the place Kamapua'a was at. Attached to *mai* in the matrix clause of (6a) is the suffix *-la*, an allomorph of *ala*, which is a demonstrative postposed to the directional that is non-specific in connection to the centrality of its head within a narrative. The suffix *-la* indicates that the predicate is not specified as occurring and/or originating in the deictic center. The combination of *mai* and *-la* in (6a) means that the predicate is moving toward the deictic center (e.g., *mai*) yet originated elsewhere (e.g., *-la*).

The directional following the relative clause predicate *noho* in (6a) is *aku* "thither." The reason that the directional in the relative clause is *aku* could be because *aku* seems to be the most neutral of directionals, resulting in *aku* not carrying much meaning at all in the mo'olelo. However, the author used the postposed centrality marker *nei* after *aku* to specify that the preceding narrative context, that is, Kamapua'a's *noho* event, is central and in the deictic center of the narrative. The centrality of Kamapua'a and his dwelling event should thus be apparent to the informed reader, who knows from the first directional *mai* on the sentential predicate and the *nei* in the relative clause that Kamapua'a's story space is foregrounded in the mo'olelo. Therefore, Kamapua'a's space, inclusive of what goes on within, is charged with a sense of essentiality, as indicated by the grammar used to describe what happens in that space being composed through linguistic tools that specify narrative centrality and foreground. This is why, amongst other discourse centrality markers, an *a*-class GS is used in (6a).

In (6b), another relative clause predicated by *noho* contains an *a*-class GS. Example (6b) occurs in an appositive phrase that clarifies why Kou, the place to which the canoes were heading the next day, is important to the story. The appositive creates another *mental space* (Fauconnier, *Mental* and *Mappings*). According to Fauconnier, mental spaces are "partial structures that proliferate when we think and talk, allowing a fine-grained partitioning of our discourse and knowledge structures" (*Mappings* 11). Mental spaces have their own essential elements, and new mental spaces are built off or out of base mental spaces. A story can therefore have multiple mental spaces in effect at any given time. The canoe landing near Kamapua'a, who is in the deictic center of the story, is one mental space, and the goal destination of the canoe, namely Kou, the place where the *ali'i* "chiefs" were dwelling, is another, for example.

Moreover, Kamapua'a was pursuing the *ali'i* referred to in the GS *a nā ali'i* "ø-Gen-a the chiefs" to kill them for their presumptuous reign over O'ahu, the island that Kamapua'a conquered earlier in the mo'olelo, as well as their outcasting of his beloved grandmother, Kamaunuaniho. Because Kamapua'a was pursuing the *ali'i* referred to in (6b), and we as readers now know where the *ali'i* are because of this relative clause that is part of this appositive phrase that has created another mental space for us, the author used an *a*-class GS to indicate that the *ali'i* and where they were staying are essential to the discourse and pragmatic implications of the expression.

Example (7) is provided below to illustrate an example of the lexeme *noho* used in a relative clause in conjunction with an *o*-class GS. This example contains a dialogue between the primary character of the narrative, Kamapua'a, and his antagonist Makali'i, who is also family to Kamapua'a—a paternal uncle of sorts. At this point, Kamapua'a has spared Makali'i's life, and Kamapua'a is telling Makali'i where he will live. Makali'i rejects all but Kamapua'a's last proposition. For Makali'i's rejection of Kamapua'a, the author uses a relative clause in one instance, where Makali'i is requesting where he shall live. This instance is repeated in (7a).

7. Pane aku la o Makalii ia Kamapuaa, e, i hea wau e noho ai? I Kahiki io Koea la, hoole aku la o Makalii, aohe wau e ola ilaila, he nui na kai a'u e hele aku ai i wahi no'u e noho ai. I Hawaii me Pele, he aina maikai, he nui o Puna, he paia ala, he nui no hoi o Kau a me Hilo, a me Hamakua, a me Kona a me Kohala, ka moku haaheo, o hoi a me Pele, noho.

   Hoole aku la no o Makalii, aohe wau e ola ilaila, i wahi no'u e noho ai. I Maui hoi ha, i ka aina o Kapo, aohe no wau e ola ilaila, imi ia mai ua wahi o'u e noho ai. I Molokai, i ka moku o Hina, aohe wau e ola ilaila. I Oahu, i ke one hanau, hoi no a me Kekeleiaiku a me Kamauluaniho, kupunawahine o'u nei la; noho pu, aohe no wau e ola ilaila. Pane aku la o Kamapuaa, iuka hoi ha oe o ke kuahiwi, (i manelenele) i kahi nui o ka ai, he nui ke ki, he nui ka hapuu, he nui ka hoi, hoi alaila noho me kou poe kanaka, ae mai la o Makalii, ka hoi aku la no ia me kona poe a pau. (Kahiolo)

   Pane akula 'o Makali'i iā Kamapua'a, "Ē, i hea wau e noho ai?" "I Kahiki i o Koea lā." Hō'ole akula 'o Makali'i, " 'A'ohe wau e ola i laila. He nui nā kai a'u e hele aku ai." "I Hawai'i me Pele, he 'āina maika'i. He nui 'o Puna, he paia 'ala. He nui nō ho'i 'o Ka'ū a me Hilo a me Hāmākua a me Kona a me Kohala, ka moku ha'aheo. O ho'i a, me Pele, noho."

   Makali'i responded to Kamapua'a, "Hey, where shall I live?" "In Kahiki, near Koea." Makali'i refused, "I shall not survive there. There are many oceans that I will travel through." "On Hawai'i, with Pele, it is a good land. Puna is large, it has a fragrant bower of forest. Ka'ū and Hilo and Hāmākua and Kona and Kohala, the proud district, is also large. Best you go, with Pele, live.

Hōʻole akula nō ʻo Makaliʻi, "ʻAʻohe wau e ola i laila, i wahi noʻu e noho ai." "I Maui hoʻi hā, i ka ʻāina o Kapo." "ʻAʻohe wau e ola i laila. ʻImi ʻia mai ua wahi oʻu e noho ai." "I Molokaʻi, i ka moku o Hina." "ʻAʻohe au e ola i laila." "I Oʻahu i ke one hānau, hoʻi nō a me Kekeleiʻaikū a me Kamauluaniho, kupuna wahine oʻu nei lā, noho pū."

Makaliʻi denied indeed, "I will not survive there, (give me) a place to live." "On Maui then, the land of Kapo." "I will not survive there. Search out this (focalized) place that I will live." "On Molokaʻi, the island of Hina." "I will not survive there." "On Oʻahu, the birth sands, go home, with Kekeleiʻaikū and Kamaulu-aniho, a grandmother of mine, live together.

"ʻAʻohe nō wau e ola i laila." ʻImi ʻia mai **ua wahi oʻu e noho ai**." Pane akula ʻo Kamapuaʻa, "I uka hoʻi hā ʻoe o ke kuahiki (i Mānelenele) i kahi nui o ka ʻai. He nui ke kī, he nui ka hāpuʻu, he nui ka hoi. Hoʻi a laila, noho me kou poʻe kānaka." ʻAe maila ʻo Makaliʻi, ka hoʻi akula nō ia me kōna poʻe a pau.

"I will not survive there. Search out this place that I shall live." Kamapuaʻa responded, "Inland of the mountains (at Mānelenele), where there is plenty food. There is plenty tī, there is plenty *hāpuʻu* (fern), there is plenty bitter yam. Go unto there, live with your people." Makaliʻi agreed and immediately went off with his people.

a. ʻImi   ʻia   mai   ua   wahi oʻu   e   noho ai.
   search Pass hither Prf   place ø-Gen-o Imp dwell AI
   Search out this place that I shall live.

Makaliʻi has minimal control over where he will live in the data provided in (7). Thus, the author did not choose an *a*-class GS in (7a), because doing so would create an undue effectiveness for Makaliʻi, which is contrary to the moʻolelo. An *a*-class GS would mean that Makaliʻi is the essential (foreground) actor in the current narrative context, and thus affects the narrative progression, which is untrue because Kamapuaʻa is obviously in control. Moreover, an *a*-class GS in (7a) would somewhat reduce Kamapuaʻaʻs effectiveness in having the authority to order Makaliʻi to live at various places. If the author had chosen an *a*-class GS for (7a), rather than the *o*-class, the reader would interpret the author's text to mean that Makaliʻi was in control over where he would live, resulting in Makaliʻi being perceived as equal or superordinated in the narrative to Kamapuaʻa. It was obvious to me that the author was attempting to convey that Kamapuaʻa had the upper hand in this portion of the story, and Makaliʻi was a subordinate charac-ter. Therefore, the author chose an *o*-class GS in (7a) to help construct this notion through the discourse grammatical devices available, specifically here the *o*-class GS constructions. The context in which (7a) occurred also is foreground and it did move the story forward. Therefore, we cannot claim that being part of foregrounded information alone triggers *a*-class selection, because the GS is *o*-class in (7a). What this example does illustrate is that *o*-class is the unmarked form that can be used for all types of GSs, including GSs in foreground information.

Moreover, lexical items are assumed here to have meaning inclusive of their varying meanings; that is, the degree of agency of their agentive subjects, should those arguments be inherently agentive. As the data have illustrated to this point, meaning, that is, semantics, alone cannot account for *a*- and *o*-class selection. The semantics of the lexical item *noho* allows both *a*- and *o*-class GS selection—recall (1) and (5) above. Thus, the data illustrate that the semantics of *noho* in (7a) is not what triggers the *o*-class GS, nor did it trigger the *a*-class GS usage in (6) above. The narrative context and pragmatic needs of the author are what influenced the *o*-class GS selection in (7a), and (1) for that matter, as well as the distinctions discussed between *pa'i* with an *o*-class GS and one with an *a*-class one in (4). The conclusion drawn here is that pragmatic and discourse needs are what determine GS class selection.

S = O Ambitransitive: A Look at Waiho *"be Remaining"* *in Connection* A-Class GS Selection

There's an interesting phenomenon in Hawaiian: lexical items seem to not sit within a single valency category. That is, a single lexical item may be used in a canonical transitive construction or in an intransitive one, depending on the contextual needs. The relative clauses found in (8) and (9) below both contain the predicate *waiho* "left, remain" in their respective relative clauses. *Waiho* is translated by Pukui and Elbert as "to leave, lay or put down, . . . file, deposit. . . ." But these translations of *waiho* are all transitive notions. The *waiho* tokens in (8) and (9) are included here because they occur in intransitive clauses, where the subjects correspond to the patient arguments of would-be transitive uses of *waiho*. These intransitive usages of *waiho* are examples of ambitransitive uses. Dixon as well as Dixon and Aikhenvald refer to canonical transitives of this type that are used intransitively as S = O ambitransitive.

The text in (8) involves Kamapua'a, the focal character of the narrative, and his grandmother returning to their home at Pu'uokapolei. The backstory is that Kamapua'a's brother recently committed suicide and his corpse remained in a separate structure on their family's parcel. As soon as Kamapua'a arrives there, he immediately goes to the brother's corpse and laments. Restated in (8a) is the NP *ka hale o ke kaikua'ana i waiho ai* "the house in which the brother remained" which contains the *o*-class GS *o ke kaikua'ana* "ø-Gen-o the brother." The GS would seem to be more patient-like than agent-like, and therefore, an *o*-class GS is expected, given the findings in my prior work that all patient GSs are *o*-class, which was captured in Maxim 2: PAT GS Effect (Baker, *A-class* 144–147), which states that GSs that do not possess Proto-Agent properties are not allowed to be *a*-class, as well as the GS Class Selection Continuum provided above. Moreover, in the context of this chapter, the moʻolelo reader knows that the brother's body being left at the family's residence was previously mentioned as subsidiary information, and thus not foreground information that affected the narrative's progression. In (8) the phrases *kēia oli ʻana a ke kupuna wahine ona* "this chanting by his grandmother" and *ko ia nei hele akula nō kēia* "he immediately went" are both foreground information.

8. A pau kēia oli ʻana a ke kupuna wahine ōna, hiki lāua nei i ka hale i Puʻuokapolei, a kuʻu ka hāʻawe a ke kupuna wahine. Ko ia nei hele akula nō kēia a **ka hale o ke kaikuaʻana i waiho ai**. E waiho ana nō ke kino, lālau akula ʻo ia, a hāpai maila ā luna o kōna ʻūhā. Uē ihola ia, me kōna kaukau iho ma loko o ke oli penei:
(Kahiolo, Hale Kuamoʻo 52)

A pau kēia oli ʻana a ke kupuna wahine ōna, hiki lāua nei i ka hale i Puʻuokapolei, a kuʻu ka hāʻawe a ke kupuna wahine. Ko ia nei hele akula nō kēia ā **ka hale o ke kaikuaʻana i waiho ai**. E waiho ana nō ke kino, lālau akula ʻo ia, a hāpai maila ā luna o kōna ʻūhā. Uē ihola ia, me kōna kaukau iho ma loko o ke oli penei:

When this chanting by his grandmother was finished, they [focalized, foregrounded] reached the house in Puʻuokapolei, and dropped off the grandmother's sack. He immediately went unto the house where the older brother remained. The body was remaining; he grabbed him and lifted (him) upon his thighs. He cried, with his lamenting inside of the chant thus:

a. ka hale o   ke kaikuaʻana   i   waiho ai
   the house ø-Gen-o the older-sibling-same-sex. Prf leave   AI
   the house where the older brother was left (behind/alone)

The text in (9) is dialogue attributed to Kamapuaʻa in explaining to a grandfather of his, namely Kuolokele, that he saw the antagonist, an *ʻīlio* "dog," and the *ʻīlio* was indeed dead. Restated in (9a) is the NP *kahi a ua ʻīlio nei e waiho ana* "the place where this [focalized, foregrounded] dog was remaining" which contains the *a*-class GS *a ua ʻīlio nei* "ø-Gen-a this [focalized, foregrounded] dog." The text in (9a) is potentially the one counter example to Maxim 2. In my dissertation (152–154), I demonstrate that the subjects of intransitive clauses, or S arguments of S = O ambitransitive uses, differ from stative and *'ia* marked predicates, because the S arguments of S = O ambitransitives have agentive qualities unlike those of the S arguments of stative and *'ia* marked predicates. The reason is that when *waiho* "remain" is used intransitively, it is understood as an event of action in Hawaiian. Thus, the S argument could be interpreted as performing within the scenario, along similar semantic lines as to why *noho* has an agentive subject. Therefore, the S argument is qualified to be marked with an *a*-class GS, and this *waiho* token is not a counter example to Maxim 2: PAT GS Effect.

9. Nolaila, ua alualu aku nei wau mahope o ua ilio la, a hiki i ke kahawai o Kaukaonahua, a ua holo aku nei ua ilio la i ke kuahiwi me kona mama nui, aka, ua lilo nae ia mama ona i mea ole, mamuli o kona holo pupule loa, ua pau loa ia kona aho, ua holo oia a moe okoa i ke kula.

I ko'u hiki ana aku i **kahi a ua ilio nei e waiho ana**, ua ike koke iho la wau i ke ano o ka ilio, ua lele loa kona hanu hope loa mai iaia aku. ("He Moolelo," 21 August 1891, 3)

No laila, ua alualu aku nei wau ma hope o ua 'īlio lā, ā hiki i ke kahawai 'o Kaukaonāhua, a ua holo aku nei ua 'īlio lā i ke kuahiwi me kōna māmā nui, akā, ua lilo na'e ia māmā ōna i mea 'ole, ma muli o kōna holo pūpule loa, ua pau loa 'ia kōna aho, ua holo 'o ia a moe 'oko'a i ke kula.

I ko'u hiki 'ana aku i **kahi a ua 'īlio nei e waiho ana**, ua 'ike koke ihola wau i ke 'ano o ka 'īlio, ua lele loa kona hanu hope loa mai iā ia aku.

Therefore, I then chased after that [foreground] dog, until the stream named Kaukaonāhua, that [foreground] dog then ran to the mountain with his great speed, but this speed of his became nothing, because of his very crazy running, his breath was completely taken, he ran and laid exhausted in the fields.

Upon my arrival to **the place where this [focalized, foregrounded] dog was remaining**, I quickly noticed the status of the dog, his final breath departed from him.

a. kahi   a   ua 'īlio nei e   waiho   ana
the+place ø-Gen-a. Prf dog near Imp leave/remain Imp
the place where this [focalized, foregrounded] dog was remaining

As the data have illustrated thus far, *a*-class GSs generally occur in foreground information. Thus, we can explain the *a*-class GS in (9a) by illustrating that the context in which the text occurred was foreground information. We know that the information is foregrounded in (9) because Kamapua'a's coming upon this *'īlio* is the information crux that moves the narrative forward. That is, this event brings closure to Kuolokele's anguish discussed previously in this mo'olelo. The author also used other foreground information indices in the data set, *viz.*, the inceptive marker *ua* and the postposed centrality-marker demonstrative *nei*, in combination with the *a*-class GS.

To summarize (8) and (9), both GSs discussed were patientive (not necessarily true patients, however, like those of statives and *'ia* marked "passives") and both referred to corpses. However, because the narrative information in (9) is new information that specifically resolves an issue within the discourse, the GS is *a*-class.

Findings

A-class Usage

The findings above illustrate that *a*-class GSs occurred in foregrounded information that at times specifically move the narrative forward along temporal lines. *A*-class marked GSs indicate that the actions of the referent of the GS were essential to the success of the event, which means that the action of the referent of the GS somehow affected the narrative progression. The phrase *essential to the success of the event* therefore indicates that the agent's action was essential not only to the event itself, but also to the event's effectiveness in the context of the narrative.

Specifying agency is therefore a pragmatic and discourse issue in Hawaiian. The use of *a*-class in Hawaiian discourse narrative structure is determined by the speaker's need to implicate and/or indicate that some entity is acting in the foreground of the story, and that the *a*-class marked GS should be understood as having effect on the narrative's progression along temporal lines.

O-class Usage

A hypothesis put forward here is that *o*-class is the unmarked genitive class. The advantage that my claim has over Wilson's that "sufferers" and "non-controllers" are marked with *o*-class is that my hypothesis allows for *o*-class GS in all subject categories, whether the argument is agentive in foreground information or not. Moreover, Wilson was forced to claim in his discussion of *a*-class selection that a GS that should be *a*-class in his theory is "optionally replaced" by *o*-class in oblique relative clauses, without any reason as to why (119). The proposal that *o*-class is unmarked allows for *o*-class to be used with more than just sufferers, non-controllers, and locations. In this approach, we expect to find *o*-class GSs in all GS categories, and as we have seen, the data support this position.

Other Indices of Foreground Information

Three other indices of foregrounded information were discussed above: *ua, kēia,* and *nei. Ua* marks information as perfective and/or inceptive (Elbert and Pukui 58). *Ua* is both a verbal marker and a determiner.[8] In the discussion above, we claimed that *ua*, as an inceptive marker, marks new and/or essential information. The determiner *kēia* "this" is claimed to be a centrality-marking demonstrative as is *nei*, although *nei* is postposed to the phrasal head. We illustrated above that *kēia* and *nei* were used to indicate that the phrase is central and/or focalized, in the narrative context. Hence, these centrality markers are used in narrative discourse to indicate foreground narrative information, and are often found used in concert with *a*-class GSs.

Maxim 3: A-class Genitive Subject Effect

The data illustrate that *a*-class GSs are (a) minimally actors within some event scenario, and are (b) used by Hawaiian authors to mark essential actors that affect the progression of their respective narratives along temporal lines. In my dissertation work I therefore proposed the following:

> MAXIM 3: *A*-CLASS GS EFFECT: (A) AN *A*-CLASS GENITIVE IS USED TO REPRE-
> SENT THE AGENTIVE SUBJECT OF A SCENARIO AND/OR EVENT; AND (B) AN
> *A*-CLASS GENITIVE MARKED PHRASE IS UNDERSTOOD AS ESSENTIAL AND EF-
> FECTIVE INFORMATION IN A COMMUNICATIVE ACT. (228)

Conclusions

In the analyses provided above, the data illustrated that *a*-class GSs were used to indicate foreground information and *o*-class GSs were neutral occurring in both foreground and background information. The key defining properties for *a*-class GS selection in narratives are that the GS is (a) agentive, that is, has one or more Proto-Agent properties, and (b) affects the progression of the narrative. If these two properties are present, then *a*-class may be used to indicate that the action(s) of some GS is essential to the narrative progression. The data set provided in (9) illustrates that an *a*-class GS can also be used for GS of intransitive clauses in S = O ambitransitive instances, if the GS is part of the narrative foreground information and essential to the progression of the narrative discourse. We also saw in (7) that some *o*-class GSs occur in foreground contexts. This finding illustrates that *o*-class is the unmarked class, supporting the hypothesis that the Hawaiian genitive classes are not dichotomous, because *o*-class GSs occur in all GS categories, and *a*-class is far less likely to occur in all GS categories.

Applying Maxim 3 and the GS Class Selection Continuum to Genitive Possession

As Wilson explained in his 1976 master's thesis, *a*- and *o*-class selection in possessive constructions is more set and/or constant than that of genitive case subjects of nominalizations and relative clauses. Let us consider some data analyzed in Wilson's thesis under his control hypothesis and reanalyze them under the agentive hypothesis presented here. Wilson argues that the reason why the possessors in (10) through (13) are marked with *a*-class is because the possessors *control the initiation of the possessive relationship* in some way (81–82).

10. ka'u keiki   my child
11. ka'u mo'opuna   my grandchild
12. ka'u wahine   my wife
13. ka'u kāne   my husband

The claim presented here that *a*-class specifies agentiveness forces us to say that the possessors in the possessive relationships in (10) through (13) are agentive in some way. Again, agentive here is defined in terms of Proto-Agent properties as discussed above. If a possessor, for example, has causal effect on the possessed, then an *a*-class possessive is required. This is different, however, from Wilson's control hypothesis, because (a) agentive is not limited to initiating the possessive relationship, and (b) agentive is defined in terms of particular properties held by possessors that qualify entities as either agentive or not, as suggested by, but not limited to, Dowty.

All these relationships provided in (10) through (13) involve the possessors acting in a way that maximizes the success of these relationships. For example, (10) contains the phrase *ka'u keiki* "my child." The possessor is agentive in that the possessor is the caregiver of the child. Hawaiian grammaticizes this semantic aspect of the relationship by marking the possessor with *a*-class. The approach taken here is different from Wilson's notion that the individuals' *control* in making children is the reason why the possessive is *a*-class, because Wilson's hypothesis does not explain why *ka'u keiki hanauna* "my nephew" or *ka'u kaikamahine hanauna* "my niece" are *a*-class.[9] Wilson claims that through analogy with the lexical item *keiki*, *keiki hanauna* is possessed with *a*-class (92). However, as a *makua*, or a "parent, any relative of parents' generation" (Pukui and Elbert) of these *keiki hanauna* and *kaikamahine hanauna*, *makua* share the burden of rearing these children. Thus, because I am a *makua* to *ka'u mau keiki hanauna* "my nephews and nieces," I hold an essential agentive relationship in the development of these children, and this is why I possess them with *a*-class. As for spouses, for example, (12) and (13), spouses are possessed with *a*-class because spouses are supposed to care and provide for one another. Thus, each spouse holds agency in the relationship.

Parents, grandparents, and ancestors, in contrast to children, grandchildren, and descendants, are possessed with *o*-class because the possessors (i.e., the children, grandchildren, and descendants) are not responsible for rearing those who have come before. Consider (14) and (15) below. The possessors are *koʻu* "my, *o*-class" in both.

14. koʻu makua kāne   my father
15. koʻu kupuna kāne   my grandfather

Make "dead" is a stative verb in Hawaiian, which means that the subject holds a true patient semantic role. When the patientive argument possesses *make*, the possessive is always *o*-class, for example, (16) below. This generalization is captured above as Maxim 2: PAT GS Effect. However, when the possessor holds an agentive role in the *make* scenario, causing the state of *make*, the possessor is marked with *a*-class, for example, (17). Wilson accounts for these types of couplets in (16) and (17) by saying that the *manō* in (16) is a non-controller, but a controller in (17). When applying Maxim 3 to these data, the claim is that the possessive in (17) is *a*-class because the possessor is specified as agentive. Moreover, in the context of a narrative, a phrase similar to that in (17) would be interesting, ear/eye catching, and/or used to indicate that this information is important to the narrative's progression (i.e., Maxim 3, where essentialness is indicated by *a*-class GSs). Hence, when plotting (16) on the GS Class Selection Continuum, the plot would be more right on the background/patientive side, and when plotting (17) on the GS Class Selection Continuum, the plot would be more right toward the foreground/agentive side.[10]

16. ka make o ka manō   the death of the shark
17. ka make a ka manō   the death by the shark

As it is not the contention here to analyze genitive class selection in possessive uses, we can see that if we apply the concept of agency to *a*-class possessives, there seems to be hope for the hypothesis. In connection to kinship terms, there is no need to claim analogy amongst the lexical items *keiki* and *keiki hanauna*. Another advantage that Maxim 3 has over the control hypothesis is that there is also no need for Wilson's locational hypothesis. That is, my hypothesis that all *a*-class genitives must be minimally agentive eliminates Wilson's location hypothesis, because if *a*-class genitives must be in some way agentive, then genitive case possessors holding a locational relationship with the possessed, for example, *koʻu hale* "my house," do not qualify for *a*-class marking because locational relationships are inherently non-agentive ones. Furthermore, when we encounter the following, *kaʻu hale*, we must conclude that the possessor did something to that house, for example, built it, bought it, burned it down, etc. However, more research is needed in connection to the theory proposed here and possession.

Cultural Scripts

Cultural scripts are used as an attempt to explain what a scholar believes to be the rationale for the cultural phenomenon being described.[11] Provided here are cultural scripts for *a-* and *o-*class selection.

A Hawaiian Cultural Script for A-class Genitives

people think like this:

If I hear an *a*-class genitive,

It means that the referent of the genitive phrase is agentive and/or is essential to its scenario

because of this I interpret the *a*-class genitive in expressions like
  ➢ kaʻu keiki "my child"
    ○ to mean that the referent of the genitive, that is, myself, holds the role of caregiver, which entails that I provide essentialities, inclusive of my social beliefs of those essentialities as taught by my elders

because of this I interpret the *a*-class genitive in expressions such as
  ➢ ka make a ka manō "the one killed by the shark"
    ○ to mean that the referent of the genitive is agentive and thus played a volitional role in the event and caused the state of the head lexeme under its own volition

because of this I interpret the *a*-class genitive in expressions like
  ➢ ʻaʻohe aʻu hele "I did not go"
    ○ to mean that the event and its *a*-class marked agent represented in the genitive case is distinct, individuated, and/or not general

because of this I interpret the *a*-class genitive in expressions like
  ➢ ka hale aʻu i hele ai "the house that I went to"
    ○ to mean that the S of the relative clause is specified as having one or more of the following properties—control, causation, sentient, volition, and/or movement, that is, agentive—as well as perhaps be essential to the success of the event and/or its utterance as foreground information.

A Hawaiian Cultural Script for O-*class Genitives*
people think like this:
If I hear an *o*-class genitive,
It means that the referent of the genitive is not specified as agentive
    because of this I interpret the *o*-class genitive in expressions such as
        ➢ ko'u makuahine "my mother"
            ○ to mean that the referent of the genitive, that is, the speaker, is not specified as agentive, thus may be subordinated to the mother, not necessarily needing to provide the essentialities and the social beliefs entailed in those essentialities

    because of this I interpret the *o*-class genitive in expressions like
        ➢ ka make o ka manō "the shark's death"
            ○ to mean that the referent of the genitive is not specified as agentive, thus likely has causal telic effects as described by the head lexeme, with a minimal chance that the referent of the genitive is the causer (i.e., agent) of the head lexeme

    because of this I interpret the *o*-class genitive in expressions like
        ➢ 'a'ohe o'u hele' "I do not go"
            ○ to mean that the referent of the genitive is not specified as agentive, thus is general, not necessarily distinct or individuated

    because of this I interpret the *o*-class genitive in expressions like
        ➢ ka hale o'u i hele ai "the house that I went to"
            ○ to mean that the referent of the genitive is not specified as agentive, thus it can be interpreted as general, not necessarily distinct or individuated from the *hele* event, background to other foregrounded information

Aloha nō 'oe, e ku'u makamaka heluhelu. Eia nō kou mea kākau ua hele loa aku nei paha i Kalalau. Eia na'e, he 'āina uluwehiwehi 'o Kalalau. It may seem that this chapter strayed off course a bit. However, this chapter illustrates the importance of using mo'olelo in Hawaiian linguistic inquiry. The importance of mo'olelo to Kanaka Maoli knowledge goes beyond the understanding of content in a narrative; it provides a platform to base claims. Here, mo'olelo has provided the foundation for making lingustic claims, but mo'olelo offers necessary data and support for empirical research connected to Kanaka Maoli inquiry, no matter the discipline. We know not who we are without knowing who we were, and the only way for us Kānaka Maoli to know who we were is through our mo'olelo, a great majority of which remains in the language of our aboriginal ancestors, 'Ōlelo Hawai'i.

ABBREVIATIONS

A	agent or experiencer subject of a transitive clause
Acc	accusative marker; that is, *i* or *iā*
Add	addressee, preposition used to mark addressee; for example, *e*
Cntr	deictic center or central marker; for example, *nei*
Dat	dative
Dem	demonstrative
Det	determine
Dir	directional
Dub	dubitative
excl	exclusive
Gen	preposed genitive
Gen-a	preposed genitive in the *a*-class; for example, *kaʻu*- 1sg=Gen-a
Gen-n	preposed genitive neutral in class; for example, *kuʻu* "my" or *kō* "your"
Gen-o	preposed genitive in the *o*-class; for example, *koʻu*- 1sg=Gen-o
GS	genitive subject
Imp	imperfective
Incl	inclusive, as a pronoun
Int	intensifier
Loc	locative
n-Gen	genitive in the *n*-form; for example, *naʻu* "for me, mine," *a*-class, *no Kimo* "for Kimo," *o*-class
Neg	negative
Nom	nominative
NP	noun phrase
O	patient, or object, of a transitive clause
ø-Cntr	non-specific deictic marker; for example, *ala/-la* or *lā*
ø-Gen	postposed genitive
ø-Gen-a	postposed genitive in the *a*-class; for example, *aʻu*- 1sg=ø-Gen-a
ø-Gen-o	postposed genitive in the *o*-class; for example, *oʻu*- 1sg=ø-Gen-o
pl	plural
Poss	possessive
PP	prepositional phrase
Prf	perfective/inceptive aspect
RC	relative clause
S	lone complement of an intransitive clause
sg	singular
1	first person
2	second person
3	third person
=	a symbol connecting two semantic values of single morpheme or lexeme

NOTES

1. By subjects I mean the A or S argument of a transitive or intransitive clause, respectively (Dixon).

2. Of interest here is that the GS in (1c) take the determiner position and are coordinated by *a me*, as complete NPs are. This illustrates the phrase head and/or phrasal qualities that GS and determiners in general have in Hawaiian. This is an area in need of further inquiry. (Baker, A-*class*).

3. One might view foreground and background either as having a dichotomous relationship or as being on a continuum. Phrases similar to that found in (1d) may be classified as foregrounding, in that they move the narrative from background information to foreground information on a continuum. Hence, it seems that foreground and background information are indeed on a continuum.

4. See Kanahele in this collection for her use of *kupuna* over character in Hawaiian narratives.

5. The original title was "He Molelo Kaao no Kamapuaa." The term *ka'ao* indexes the *mo'olelo* as folklore (see Baker, "Ke Mele" and "Constructing," and ho'omanawanui for discussions of *mo'olelo* and *ka'ao*). This story ran in *Ka Leo o ka Lahui* from 22 June to 28 September of 1891. On 15 July 1891 the title changed without comment to "He Moolelo no Kamapuaa."

6. It should be noted that neither the kēia, nor the centrality-marking and focalizing nominal markers *ua...nei* have been fully explicated here. Centrality-marking focalizing in Hawaiian is in need of further inquiry.

7. First is Maxim 1: Object Relative Clause Effect (Baker, A-*class* 80–100), which asserts that relative clauses whose head nouns correspond to the object of the relative clause force an *a*-class selection when the GS strategy is used. Second is Maxim 2: Patient GS Effect (144–147), which states that genitive subjects that do not possess Proto-Agent properties are not allowed to be *a*-class. The data analyzed below are not subject to Maxims 1 or 2.

8. The verb marker and demonstrative determiner *ua* is polysemous. I classify *ua* as one morpheme used in two distinct syntactic ways, that is, as a verbal marker and as a determiner, because the pragmatic and discourse functions are similar in both VPs and NPs.

9. This analysis does not support that *a*-class = alienable analysis either as suggested for other languages of Polynesia (see Schütz, "Voices" 247).

10. The data in (17) is an example of an S = A ambitransitive.

11. "One of the key techniques for ethnopragmatic description...is the "cultural script." Essentially, this refers to a statement—framed largely or entirely within the non-ethnocentric metalanguage of semantic primes—of some particular attitude, evaluation, or assumption which is hypothesised to be widely known and shared among people of a given speech community" (Goddard 5).

WORKS CONSULTED

Adams, Tony E., Stacy Holman Jones, and Carolyn Ellis. *Autoethnography*. Understanding Qualitative Research Series, Oxford UP, 2014. *ProQuest Ebook Central*. https://ebookcentral.proquest.com/lib/uhm/detail.action?docID=1784095.

Allan, Keith. *Natural Language Semantics*. Blackwell, 2001.

Baker, C. M. Kaliko. *A-class Genitive Subject Effect: A Pragmatic and Discourse Grammar Approach to A- and O-class Genitive Subject Selection in Hawaiian*. 2012. University of Hawaiʻi at Mānoa, PhD dissertation.

———. "Constructing Kanaka Maoli Identity through Narrative: A Glimpse into Native Hawaiian Narratives." *Narrative and Identity Construction in the Pacific Islands*. Studies in Narrative, John Benjamins Publishing Company, 2015, pp. 119–134.

———. "Ke Mele ma ke Kaʻao." In *Ka Waihona a ke Aloha Monograph: E Mau ai ka Puana*, edited by R. Keawe Lopes Jr., Ka Waihona a ke Aloha, 2014, pp. 18–26.

Chandler, Daniel. *Semiotics: The Basics*. 2nd ed. Rutledge, 2007.

DeLancey, Scott. "Ergativity and the Cognitive Model of Event Structure in Lhasa Tibetan." *Cognitive Linguistics*, vol. 1, no. 3, 1990, pp. 289–321.

Dixon, R. M. W. *Basic Linguistic Theory: Grammatical Topics*. Oxford UP, 2010.

———. *Ergativity*. Cambridge UP, 1994.

Dixon, R. M. W., and Alexandra Y. Aikhenvald. Introduction. *Changing Valency: Case Studies in Transitivity*, edited by R. M. W. Dixon and Alexandra Y. Aikhenvald. Cambridge UP, 2000, pp. 1–23.

Dowty, David. "Thematic Proto-Roles and Argument Selection." *Language*, vol. 67, 1991, pp. 547–619.

Du Bois, John W. "Argument Structure: Grammar in Sse." In *Preferred Argument Structure: Grammar as Architecture for Function*, edited by J. Du Bois, L. Kumpf, and W. Ashby. John Benjamins Publishing Company, 2003, pp. 11–60.

———. "Discourse Basis for Ergativity." *Language*, vol. 63, 1987, pp. 805–855.

Duranti, Alessandro. *Linguistic Anthropology*. Cambridge UP, 1997.

Elbert, Samuel, and Mary K. Pukui. *Hawaiian Grammar*. U of Hawaiʻi P, 1979.

Fauconnier, Gilles. *Mappings in Thought and Language*. Cambridge UP, 1997.

———. *Mental Spaces*. MIT Press, 1985.

Fillmore, Charles J. "The Case for Case Reopened." *Syntax and Semantics*, vol. 8: *Grammatical Relations*, edited by P. Cole. Academic Press, 1977, pp. 59–81.

———. "Topics in Lexical Semantics" In *Current Issues in Linguistic Theory*, edited by R. Cole. Indiana UP, 1977, pp. 76–138.

Fornander, Abraham. *Hawaiian Antiquities and Folk-lore*. Bernice P. Bishop Museum Memoirs, vol. 5, 1918.

Goddard, Cliff. "Ethnopragmatics: A New Paradigm." In *Ethnopragmatics: Understanding Discourse in Cultural Context*, edited by Cliff Goddard. Mouton De Gruyter, 2006, pp. 1–30.

"He Molelo Kaao no Kampuaa...." *Ka Leo o ka Lahui*, vol. 2, nos. 220–236, 22 June–14 July

1891. Then "He Moolelo No Kamapuaa," vol. 2, nos. 237–290, 15 July–28 September 1891.

hoʻomanawanui, kuʻualoha. "He Ahu Moʻolelo: E Hoʻokahua i ka Paepae Moʻolelo Pala-pala Hawaiʻi: A Cairn of Stories: Establishing a Foundation of Hawaiian Literature." *Palapala*, vol. 1, 2017, pp. 51–100. https://scholarspace.manoa.hawaii.edu/bitstream/ 10125/43988/05_1hoomanawanui.pdf.

Hopper, Paul J., and Sandra A. Thompson. "Transitivity in Grammar and Discourse." *Language*, vol. 56, 1980, pp. 251–299.

Huang, Yan. *Pragmatics*. Oxford UP, 2015. ProQuest Ebook Central. https://ebookcentral .proquest.com/lib/uhm/detail.action?docID=5891914.

Kahiolo, G. W. "He Moʻolelo No Kamapuaʻa." Hale Kuamoʻo & Ka Haka ʻUla o Keʻelikō-lani. Hilo, Hawaiʻi, 1998.

———. "He Moolelo No Kamapuaa." *Ka Hae Hawaii*, vol. 6, no. 24, 11 September 1861, p. 96.

Levinson, Stephen C. *Pragmatics*. Cambridge UP, 1983.

Palmer, F. R. *Semantics*. 2nd ed. Cambridge UP, 1981.

Pukui, Mary Kawena, and Samuel H. Elbert. *Hawaiian Dictionary: Hawaiian-English, English-Hawaiian*. U of Hawaiʻi P, 1986.

Renkema, Jan. *Introduction to Discourse*. John Benjamins Publishing Company, 2004. ProQuest Ebook Central. https://ebookcentral.proquest.com/lib/uhm/detail.action ?docID=622714.

Schütz, Albert, Gary N. Kahāhoʻomalu Kanada, and Kenneth Cook. *Pocket Hawaiian Grammar*. Island Heritage, 2005.

Smith, Carlota. *Modes of Discourse*. Cambridge UP, 2003.

Wilson, William H. *The O and A Possessive Markers in Hawaiian*. 1976. University of Hawaiʻi at Mānoa M.A. thesis.

Yule, George. *Pragmatics*. Oxford UP, 1996.

Dr. C. M. Kaliko Baker's teaching focus is on Hawaiian grammar and world-view. His dissertation analyzed *a*- and *o*-class selection in grammatical subjects of events, that is, as subjects of nominalizations and relative clauses primarily. His analytical methodology in his research is based in discourse grammar and pragmatics. Generally speaking, by using corpora, he draws generalizations about specific structures and patterns in Hawaiian.

As President of Haleleʻa Arts Foundation, a 501(c)3, Kaliko works at support-ing, promoting, and publishing Hawaiian-medium media, for example, han-keaka ʻōlelo Hawaiʻi such as *Kaluaikoʻolau, Māuiakamalo, Kamapuaʻa,* and most recently *Lāʻieikawai* and *ʻAuʻa ʻIa: Holding On*. Within hanakeaka as a process, he serves as researcher, writer, editor, and dramaturge.

Kaliko has been a member of the Protect Kahoʻolawe ʻOhana (PKO) since 1993. His major contribution to the PKO has been leading the Makahiki ceremonies since 2003 and as a kōkua with all media endeavors. Recently, he has been leading huakaʻi ʻōlelo Hawaiʻi under the PKO to Kahoʻolawe during UH's Spring Break, during which the UH Mānoa and Hilo campuses connect and work on Kahoʻolawe using ʻōlelo Hawaiʻi as their means of communication. I mau ka ʻike a me ka ʻōlelo a nā kūpuna [So that the knowledge and language of the ancestors carry on].

*Ma ka hue ʻike kupuna i ʻaleʻale loa, aia nā haʻina nane
e ʻōʻili hou aʻe ai ke ʻano maoli o ka poʻe kanaka o Hawaiʻi.*

12
Kā i ka Mōlī a Uhia!
Ke aʻo ʻana i ke kākau uhi Hawaiʻi

Kalehua Krug

Hoʻolauna Mua

ʻAuhea ʻoukou e nā kumu akua, nā kumu aliʻi, a me nā wēlau aliʻi. He wawalo hōʻihi kēia na kahi leo kuolo o ke Kaiāulu. I ō nā kai ʻewalu, mai ka wai huna i Kīlauea a hiki loa aku nō i ka wai huna o Lehua, he kipona aloha kēia o ka iʻa lēkei i kuʻu lāhui aloha. Aloha kākou. Ua hele a lauaʻe a henoheno maoli ka ʻikena o nā kupa lehia o nei pae ʻo Hawaiʻi. He ʻike nō ia i laha a manana ma nā kihi ʻehā o ka honua. Ua lilo ia ʻikena i ʻike i hoʻohihi ʻia e ko ka honua poʻe lehulehu. Ma ka piko nei naʻe ʻo Hawaiʻi, he ʻikena ia e hōʻalo ʻia nei e ka hapanui o nā kānaka noho paʻa ma kēia ʻāina. Ma nā hanauna makule o koʻu ʻohana, ua ʻikea ko lākou hōʻalo pū ʻana me ke kukupaʻu loa ʻana. Kohu mea lā, ua piha lākou i ke ʻeʻehia. He haʻo wale hoʻi.

He mau kumuhana ko loko o nei palapala na ka ihu pani. I palapala ʻana kēia e ʻuwehe aʻe ai i nā hiʻohiʻona koʻikoʻi loa o ke aʻo ʻana i ke kākau uhi Hawaiʻi ma kona ʻano hoʻonaʻauao ponoʻī iho nō. I palapala pū nō hoʻi ia e huʻe ai i nā kumuhana koʻikoʻi e noʻonoʻo ai ma ke aʻo ʻana i kekahi ʻoihana Hawaiʻi. ʻO kekahi mea nui o kēia ʻuwehe a huʻe ʻana ka hōʻea ʻana o kākou a pau e komo nei i kēia palapala i ka pae like o ka noʻonoʻo ʻana no ia mea he ʻikena Hawaiʻi maoli. Eia naʻe, ʻaʻole e wehewehe ʻia a e kuhikuhi pono ʻia ia ʻano maoli o kekahi hana Hawaiʻi. He mau ala wale ana nō ko loko o nei palapala e kaupoana ai a e kālailai ai i ke aʻo ʻana i nā ʻoihana a kākou e kapa nei i kēia mau lā he Hawaiʻi.

Wela ka honua

Ma ka ʻakahi o koʻu aʻo ʻana, ko ka mea kākau aʻo ʻana, i ka ʻōlelo Hawaiʻi, ua hele nō koʻu ʻohana a hopohopo. Ua hoʻomau akula nō naʻe au i ke aʻo me ka haʻaheo loa. Ia wā, e hui ana au me kekahi poʻe i kākau uhi ʻia ma ke ʻano o i kapa ʻia ai he "kahiko." Ma koʻu ʻimi ʻana i ka inoa o ka mea nāna ia hana, puka maila ka inoa ʻo Keone Nunes. E ka mea heluhelu, he inoa koʻikoʻi loa kēia e hoʻomaopopo ai ʻoiai ʻo kēia kanaka ka mea nāna i hoʻoulu nui mai i ka mea kākau nei ma koʻu ʻimi ʻana i ka ʻikena Hawaiʻi. Aia hoʻi, ua kipa nō au i ke kanaka kākau. ʻAkahi hui ʻana nō, ʻakahi pū nō hoʻi kau ʻana o ka weli ma luna oʻu. Ua pākele akula nō au.

Lilo loa ihola koʻu noʻonoʻo i ke kumu o koʻu hopohopo i ke kākau ʻia ʻana oʻu. ʻAʻole nō au i hopohopo iki i koʻu kākau mua ʻia ʻana i ka mīkini kākau haole. Nūnē nui hou ihola au. Ma ia nūnē ʻana, komo loa akula au i ka heluhelu kuʻupau ʻana i nā moʻolelo Hawaiʻi i paʻa ma ka ʻōlelo Hawaiʻi, ʻo nā mea hoʻi i pili i ka ʻikena kupuna. ʻO koʻu ʻike akula nō ia i kekahi ʻano kuanaʻike ʻokoʻa i wehewehe ʻia e nā mea kākau o ia au. ʻIke pū akula au, ʻaʻole nō au i kūkulu piha i koʻu manaʻo no ia mea ʻo ka Hawaiʻi ʻana. Me ke kaʻulua ʻole, hoʻi akula au i mua o ke kanaka kākau ʻo Keone e hoʻāla aʻe ai i kēia mau manaʻo.

A hōʻea au i mua o kēia kanaka, e lelele ana ka houpo no nā manaʻo e kaʻa ana ma waena o māua. Ma ka hoʻomaka ʻana o kā māua ʻōlelo ʻana, e ō aku ana ka malani o nā kumuhana walaʻau. ʻAʻole ʻemo, ʻo kona nīnau pololei maila nō ia iaʻu me ke kāwala ʻole, "He aha ke kumu e kākau ʻia ai ʻoe?" ʻO ka pane akula nō ia, "No ka mea, ʻo ka hana ia a koʻu mau kūpuna." Ua komo akula māua i loko o kekahi wā kūkā lōʻihi a kūkonukonu no ka waiwai o ka pono kupuna Hawaiʻi. Mai ia wā kūkā o māua, ʻaʻohe poina iki o nā mea a māua i walaʻau iho ai. Ua lilo pū ia pane ʻana oʻu i mākia nui o ke ola o nei mea kākau.

Ea mai Hawaiʻinuiākea

Ma mua o ka holomua wale o kā kākou moʻolelo, e kū pōkole kākou e kūkā ai no ia mea ʻo ka ʻikena Hawaiʻi. Penei ko ka lāhui kanaka Hawaiʻi aʻoaʻo ʻia ʻana maila e Joseph Poepoe no ke ʻano o ia ʻikena penei:

> E hoomaopopoia, he lahui kakou me ko kakou Moolelo Kahiko, i ano like loa aku me ka moolelo kahiko o ka lahui o Helene; a he mau mele kahiko hoi ka ko kakou mau kupuna i like aku a i oi aku nohoi ko lakou hiwahiwa ame ke kilakila i ko na mele kaulana loa o ua lahui Helene nei.

He hoa like ke kūlana o ka lāhui Hawaiʻi me ko ka lāhui Helene. He mea nui ia lāhui Helene i nā moʻolelo kaulana o ke au nei. Na ka ʻikena o ia poʻe i hoʻokumu i ka nohona e laha nei i Hawaiʻi a me ke kahua o ko Amelika kuanaʻike e manana nei ma Hawaiʻi. Ma muli o kēia like ʻana, he kūlana kiʻekiʻe pū nō ko ka lāhui Hawaiʻi a me ko kākou ʻike lāhui.

I ke au nei, ua lilo ka hoʻohālikelike ʻana iā kākou iho me nā lāhui ʻē aʻe o Amelika i mea maʻamau iā kākou. ʻO ka hoʻohālikelike ʻana hoʻi kēia o ke kuanaʻike Amelika me ke kuanaʻike o nā kūpuna i noho ma Hawaiʻi ma mua o ko Kāpena Kuke ʻōʻili ʻana ma nei pae. Ma nei ʻano hoʻohālikelike ʻana naʻe e ʻāhewa ʻia ai kākou. He ʻāpono nō ia i ka naʻi ʻana o ko ke au nei mau manaʻo nui i ko ke au kūnewa akula. He ʻāpono nō hoʻi i ko kākou naʻi ʻia ʻana iho na kākou iho nō. Me ka manaʻo hoʻi, aia ke kūlana kilakila o ka lāhui Hawaiʻi a kū like ia me ka iwi hilo o ka lāhui nāna i pōā i ko kākou ʻāina a me ko kākou poʻe. Waiho maila ʻo Poepoe penei:

Ua piha ko kakou mau mele me na hoonupanupa ana a ia mea he aloha; piha me na keha ana no na hana koa a wiwo ole a ko kakou poe ikaika o ka wa kahiko; ka lakou mau hana kaulana; ko lakou ola ana ame ko lakou make ana. Aia ma loko o ko kakou Moolelo Kahiko na Mele a me na Pule Wanana, na mele ha'i-kupuna a kuauhau hoi.

Na nei 'ōlelo e kuhi mai i nā mea nui o nā kūpuna. Ma loko o kēia mau mo'olelo kahiko, kahi e loa'a mai ai 'o ka 'ike o nā pule, nā mele a me nā inoa 'āina a 'ohana ho'i. 'O nā ha'awina nō ho'i ia i a'o 'ia ai nā hanauna o ke au ma mua i ke 'ano o ko kākou lāhui a me nā loina e pono ai (Krug).

Ma ka hue 'ike kupuna i 'ale'ale loa, aia nā ha'ina nane e 'ō'ili hou a'e ai ke 'ano maoli o ka po'e kanaka o Hawai'i. I waihona 'ike nō ia e kū ho'okahi ai ka lāhui Hawai'i i lāhui hanohano a kū kilakila. Ma kēia palapala, e ka mea heluhelu, e kahe ai kēia 'ike a hālana me ka mana'o ē he 'ikena ia e ola ai nā hanauna e kūnewa a'e nei. I palapala kēia e ahuwale ai ke kū ho'okahi 'ana o ka 'ikena lāhui Hawai'i nona pono'ī iho. 'A'ole nō he hope e ho'i aku ai me ka hō'oia'i'o 'ana i ka waiwai o ko kākou 'ikena ma o ka ho'ohālikelike 'ana aku me ko ka haole. He au hou maila kēia no ka hanauna halehale loa nei e 'a'ahu ai i ka nani o ka 'ikena kupuna.

Kūkulu o Kahiki

He mo'olelo

E ka mea heluhelu ē, i ka pa'a 'ana o ka lā e kākau uhi 'ia ai ke alaniho ma ko'u wāwae hema, lu'u loa ihola au i loko o ka ho'omākaukau no ia lā. Nīnau hele akula kēia i ka'u mau kumu a pau no ka loina e pono ai kēia 'ano kākau 'ia 'ana. Ua hele a nui 'ino nā mana'o 'oko'a no ka loina e pono ai kēia 'ano 'aha kākau a'u e komo ana. Ma muli o ka nui mana'o o ka'u mau kumu, ua lilo ia i mea e 'oi aku ai ko'u huikau a me ka lo'ohia. Nīnau akula nō ho'i au i ke kanaka kākau uhi a wahi āna, 'a'ole e 'ai i ka pa'akai he nui. 'A'ole pū e puhi paka a inu lama i ka pō ma mua o ke kākau 'ia 'ana. Nīnau hou akula au penei, "he aha na'e ka loina kupuna e pono ai kēia 'aha?" Hene iki mai 'o ia, "nāu e koho i ka loina e pono ai 'oe."

He nani ia, na'u ka loina e koho aku, ua noi'i au ma nā mo'olelo a me nā nūpepa 'ōlelo Hawai'i e 'imi ai i nā 'ano loina e pono ai ke komo 'ana i ka 'aha kākau. Laua'e 'ia akula nō nā mana'o no ka Makahiki, ka hālau hula, nā loina kahuna a me ka ho'omana. 'A'ole na'e i aea mai kahi loina e pili ana i ke kākau uhi 'ana. He mea 'ē ka hopohopo i ka loa'a 'ole o kekahi ha'ina pa'a. Ia wā, mālama akula au i ka loina 'ohana i a'oa'o 'ia mai e ko'u Tūtū a 'o ko'u hele akula nō ia i kai e pule ai.

I waena o ko'u pule 'ana, hā'upu ihola au i ka noho 'ana me ko'u kupunahine ma ko'u wā kamali'i. He wahine 'o'ole'a loa 'o ia e kū ana ma kona mana'o pono'ī me ka wiwo 'ole. I kona kuleana ma ka hale pule, 'a'ole 'o ia i pono koho wale aku nō ma mua o ka hoʻoholo ʻana i kāna hana e mālama ai i ia kuleana. Kipa kaʻahele ʻo ia i kona ʻohana a me kona mau hoa hoʻomana. Heluhelu nui ʻo ia i kāna paipala me ka haipule a i ka wā kūpono, puka ka haʻina. Ma ka puka ʻana, kū paʻa maoli ʻo ia ma luna o kāna i hoʻoholo ai ma muli o ke komo pū ʻana o ka ʻike he nui i loko o kāna papahana hoʻoholo piliʻuhane. He mea koʻikoʻi pū ka mālama ʻana i kōā e komo ai ka mana akua i loko o kāna papahana. ʻAʻole wale nō ʻo ia ʻo ka mea hoʻoholo. Hoʻoholo pū ke akua me ia. Pēlā kāna papahana hoʻoholo.

No laila, ma hope o kēia noiʻi nui ʻana a me ka nīnau kaʻahele ʻia o nā hoaloha a me nā kumu nona kēia ʻano ʻike, ua hoʻoholo au i kaʻu hana e hoʻomākaukau ai ia ʻu iho. Ua pono. Ia wā, nūnē ihola au no ke ana e kākau ʻia ana ma koʻu ʻili. I kēlā wā, he mea maʻamau i ka poʻe kākau mīkini haole ke kahakiʻi mua ʻana i ke ana me ka hōʻike pū aku i ke kanaka e kākau ʻia ana. Kainō a e hana ana ʻo Keone pēlā, eia kā ʻaʻole wahi ana i hōʻike ʻia maila. ʻAʻole naʻe au i piʻoloke iki no ka mea ua aʻo au ma koʻu ʻimi ʻana i ka loina kūpono, he ʻikena ʻokoʻa ko ka Hawaiʻi a na koʻu Tūtū kēia ʻikena i hilinaʻi aku. Hoʻoholo ʻia ihola, e hilinaʻi pū au.

I ke kokoke ʻana iho o ka lā kākau, kelepona hou akula au iā Keone (he mea mau ia kelepona ʻana i ia wā haʻalulu o nei keiki ʻo au) e hoʻopaʻa pono ai i nā manaʻo a me nā hana e pono ai iā lā. Wehewehe maila ʻo ia, he ana ke ana i kapa ʻia no ka inoa ʻohana o koʻu Tūtū. No laila hoʻi, inā au manaʻo he kūpono, e kono i nā lālā o ka ʻohana nona kēlā inoa a me koʻu poʻe kākoʻo hou aku. Haʻohaʻo loa koʻu lunaʻikehala i ia mea ʻo ka noʻonoʻo ʻole i ke kono aku i koʻu ʻohana e hele pū mai me aʻu i ka lā kākau. Hōʻeleu hou ʻia maila kēia e koʻu pupuāhulu e kono aku i nā hoahānau a me nā lālā ʻē aʻe o koʻu ʻohana. I loko nō o ka maopopo iaʻu ʻaʻole koʻu ʻohana i hoihoi i kēia ʻaoʻao o ka ʻike Hawaiʻi, ua kono ʻia nō. Ma ka lā kākau, ua kipa mai nō kekahi. Ma muli hoʻi, holo pono akula nā mea a pau. I ka hopena o ka hana o ia lā, ua māʻule.

He kiʻina
I loko o ka palapala a Kawena Pūkuʻi i kapa ʻia ʻo "How Legends Were Taught," kākau maila ʻo ia e pili ana i ke aʻo ʻana i nā moʻolelo. Wehewehe ʻo ia i ka papamanawa aʻo o ka haumāna e aʻo maoli ana i nā moʻolelo a me ke ʻano o ke koho ʻia ʻ ana o ka haumana. ʻŌlelo ʻo ia, ua koho pono ʻia ka haumana, no ka mea he mea nui loa a waiwai loa ka moʻolelo i ka poʻe nona ia moʻolelo. ʻAʻole kēia mau moʻolelo i hōʻike a kūkā wale ʻia aku ma ʻō a ma ʻaneʻi. Ua kiaʻi ʻino ʻia o lilo iā haʻi (1).

I loko o kona ʻohana, ʻo Kawena Pūkuʻi kai aʻo ʻia mai i nā moʻolelo. ʻOiai, he mau inoa kapu no ka ʻohana kai komo i loko o ke aʻo, ʻo ka moʻolelo a me ke aʻo ka mea nui a koʻikoʻi, ʻaʻole ke kanaka. Eia kekahi, ʻaʻole ke ʻano hoʻomīkolohua o ka haʻi moʻolelo ka mea nui (2). Kākoʻo pū ʻo Kaʻaihue ma kāna ʻōlelo penei. Ma ka ʻōlelo wale nō i kaʻa ai ka ʻike mai kekahi hānauna a i kekahi a he nui loa nā ʻoihana kapu kiʻekiʻe i pili i ka ʻōlelo ʻana. ʻIke ʻia ka loea loa o ka poʻe hoʻopaʻa mo'olelo i ka ho'opa'ana'au 'ana, no ka mea ei 'ole lākou, e ola ai ka hapanui o ka 'ike kupuna o kēia wā (10–11).

Wahi a Pūku'i, ma kahi o ka hiki mai o ka wā e piha ai nā makahiki he 'ehiku i ke keikikāne, ua mālama 'ia kekahi 'aha i kapa 'ia 'o ke "Kā I Mua." 'O ka wā kēia i holo ai nā keikikāne i Mua i ka Hale Mua e a'o ai i ke 'ano o nā kāne. 'O ka Hale Mua kahi a nā kāne i 'ai like ai i ka wā i kapu ai ka 'ai pū o ke kāne a me ka wahine (Nānā 2:39; Tengan 129). Ma loko o ia hale i kū ai nā Akua o ia kauhale. Ua a'o mua nā keikikāne i nā pule e mālama ai i nā Akua. Ma kēia wā i ho'omaka maoli ai ka ho'opa'ana'au i mea e kūpono ai ka pule 'ana a me ke kahu 'ana i nā Akua. Wehewehe 'ia i ke keikikāne, inā 'a'ole e mālama pono 'ia ka 'Aumakua a me ke Akua, e ili ana kekahi ho'opa'i 'aumakua ma luna o ka mea hewa. Pēia i pa'a ai ka nohona ho'omana a me ka pilina a ia keikikāne i kona Akua (Pickens 10).

No nei keikikāne, 'o ia ho'i, no nei mea kākau, 'a'ole nō au i kā 'ia i mua e like me ka 'ōlelo a Pūku'i. No laila, ua lilo kēia kākau 'ia 'ana o'u i 'ano 'aha e kā ai ia'u nei i mua. I 'aha pū ia e 'ike ai nō ho'i kēia pūnua manu i ka pa'a o ka 'eheu e lawa ai ka ho'ā'o 'ana e lele. No nei lele 'ana, he lelena e ho'omaka ai i kekahi mau papahana i pili i ka hō'ola 'ōlelo Hawai'i, ka ho'omana kupuna a me ka nohona Hawai'i ma ko'u 'ohana. Ma ka pa'a ho'i o ka uhi i ke kākau 'ia, ua lilo ka mā'ule 'ana i hō'ailona e hō'oia 'ia ai ke ahuwale 'ana a'e o ua mau papahana ala i mau kuleana maoli nō no'u no ia wā aku. Ma kekahi wā koke iho nō, noi 'ia mai nei au e Keone e a'o i ka 'oihana kākau uhi ma lalo ona.

Ka Paia Kū a Kāne

No ke koho 'ia 'ana

E ka mea heluhelu, e hāpai 'ia ana kēia koho 'ia 'ana i mea hanohano ia i ke au ma mua. Hō'ike 'ia ihola e Pūku'i, 'a'ole nō i pono koho wale 'ia aku ke keiki nāna e a'o i ka ho'opa'a mo'olelo. Pēia pū nō ma ka mo'olelo no Kekūhaupi'o i kona wā i 'ike 'ia ai no kona loea lua a me kona 'ano wiwo'ole ho'i. I ke kaua kio 'ana ona me nā keiki 'ē a'e o laila i kai o Nāpo'opo'o, na ke kahuna o ka heiau o Hikiau i hāpai mua i ka mana'o iā Kohāpi'olani, ko Kekūhaupi'o makuakāne, e a'o iā ia i ke koa. 'A'ole nō na Kekūhaupi'o i hāpai mua no kona makemake e a'o i ke koa me ka mākilo pū 'ana i mua o kona makua e like me ko ke au nei po'e kamali'i. Ua koho 'ia 'o ia no kona mau hi'ohi'ona e kū mākaukau ana i kēlā 'oihana (Desha 2).

Kāko'o pū 'ia maila e Pūku'i. Wehewehe maila 'o ia, na nā kūpuna o ka 'ohana i koho i nā keiki lehia i ka ho'opa'ana'au a me ka no'ono'o hohonu ("How" 1). 'Oiai ho'i ua 'ike 'ia kekahi mau hi'ohi'ona ko'iko'i e a'o ai i kēia mau 'oihana 'ike ku'una 'o ke koa a me ka ho'opa'a mo'olelo, kaupaona pū 'ia ihola nā hi'ohi'ona a Keone i 'ike ai i loko o'u e koho 'ia ai au a me koa'u mau hoa papa kākau he 'ehā. Ma ko'u kālailaina, helu akula au 'o ka 'ōlelo a me ka 'ike Hawai'i mua 'ana kekahi mea nui. Eia na'e, 'a'ole wale nō kēlā 'o ke koina e komo ai i loko o kēia papa a'o kākau.

Ua hoʻoholo nā ʻōhua, nā haumāna hoʻi, ʻo ka hoʻomana Hawaiʻi ko mākou hoʻomana i hilinaʻi piha ʻia.

No ke kahua aʻo

I ke au ma mua, he mea nui ke aʻo ikaika ʻia o ka hoʻomana Akua i nā kauhale a me ke kaiāulu no ka mea pēlā i loaʻa mai ai ko ka ʻohana pōmaikaʻi. Ma o kēia ʻano aʻo ʻana i ka hoʻomana, kūkulu ʻia no ke keiki, ka haumana hoʻi, nā palena o kona noʻonoʻo a me kona ʻaoʻao o ka ʻike, ʻo kona kūanaʻike hoʻi (Pūkuʻi, "How"). Na ia ʻano pilina hoʻomana Akua i kūkulu i kona ʻano a ua lilo kēia wā aʻo i mea nui o ke kaumaha a ʻooleʻa nō hoʻi no ke kūʻiʻo o ke kumuhana aʻo. ʻAʻole wale nō kēia wā he wā ʻooleʻa no ka haumana e aʻo ana. He wā pū nō hoʻi kēia e ʻooleʻa ai ka makua, ke kumu hoʻi, e aʻo ana i ke keiki. Ua ʻike ʻia nō ma ko Keone aʻo ʻana, ua noʻonoʻo nui ʻo ia i ka pilina o nā Akua i ke kākau. Ma ko mākou hoʻomaka ʻana i ke aʻo, ua noho mākou i ke alo o ke kumu e hoʻomālō ai i ka ʻili i kona kākau ʻana. Wehewehe maila ʻo Keone e pili ana i ka leleʻoi o kēia kuleana ma mua o ka noho wale ʻana nō ma kekahi papa maʻamau o ke au nei. Ma ia wā, moʻolelo pinepine ʻia akula no ka noho pū ʻana o nā kūpuna a me nā Akua me mākou i ka wā kākau. No laila, ua hoʻonohonoho ʻia mākou me lākou.

I ia wā e noho ai me ia, a me nā Akua, nūnē nui ihola au e pili ana i ke ʻano kapu o ke kākau. Nīnau ihola au iaʻu iho no koʻu pilina i nā Akua kākau a me ka lawena hoʻomana e pono ai. ʻO koʻu kānalua akula nō ia no ka mea ʻaʻole nō au i ʻike leʻa i koʻu pilina i nā mea e noho pū ana me aʻu ma ka moena lauhala like. I loko nō naʻe o koʻu kānalua iho, kaʻu hana maʻamau i ia wā, hoʻomaopopo maila au i koʻu hilinaʻi paulele ʻana i nā haʻawina a Tūtū mā ma mua o ke kākau ʻia ʻana. Ma muli o ia hāʻupu ʻana, koho akula au i ka noho wiwoʻole ʻana ma laila me lākou.

Eia aʻe nā manaʻo i hoʻonā mai i koʻu kānalua. ʻO ka helu ʻekahi, ʻo lākou Akua nō koʻu mau kūpuna. Ua mālama mai ʻo Tūtū ma kona wā ola, e mālama mai ana nō i kēia manawa kekahi. Pēlā nā kūpuna Akua kekahi. ʻO ka helu ʻelua, ola lākou Akua i ka hāhau ʻia o kaʻu pule. I manaʻo maʻamau iā kākou ka makaʻu i ka hoʻomana kupuna ʻoiai ʻaʻohe o kākou ʻike leʻa i ia hana ma hope o kona wāwahi ʻia e Mua mā. He ahuwale naʻe ke kūlana kūpilikiʻi o ka nohona kanaka Hawaiʻi o ke au nei, no laila e huikala ʻia mai ai koʻu hemahema i ke aʻo pono ʻole ʻia. E ʻauamo pū ʻia ka hemahema e ke kanaka a me ke Akua i hoʻoholomua i ke ʻano o ka nohona nei. He koho ke kāhea inoa Akua, a no koʻu koho ʻana e kāhea iā lākou, e mahalo pū ʻia mai koʻu maliu ʻana aku iā lākou me ke aloha. ʻO ke kolu hoʻi, "Aia kinaina i Kahiki" (Pūkuʻi, ʻŌlelo, no. 61). Ola pū au iā lākou. I pau koʻu ola, pau pū ka hiki iaʻu ke hea aku i ko lākou mau inoa. Aia nō ko lākou pono iaʻu i kā lākou pulapula. He kahua aʻo paʻa kēia ʻano o ka hoʻomana no ka mea, e ʻole ke kahua ʻuhane o kā haʻi hana noʻeau Hawaiʻi ola ai ia ʻoihana.

No ke aʻo ʻana

Ma ke aʻo ʻana i nā keiki o ke ao ma mua, ʻo ka nānā ʻana o ka maka o ke keiki kekahi hana mua e aʻo ai (Pūkui, ʻŌlelo, no. 2268). I ka ʻōlelo kaulana, "Nānā ka maka, hoʻolohe ka pepeiao, paʻa ka waha," hōʻike ʻia ke kuleana nui o ka mea e nānā a hoʻolohe ʻia ana. He ʻōlelo noʻeau kēia e hōʻike ai i ke keiki i kona kuleana ma ke aʻo ʻana. E nānā a hoʻolohe i ka mea e aʻo ana iā ia me ka ʻōlelo ʻole aku ma mua o ka hana ʻana i ia mau hana mua a ʻelua. ʻAʻole kēia ʻōlelo he hōʻailona no ka ʻole o ka ʻōlelo ma ka wā aʻo, he kaʻina kēia e hōʻike ai i ke keiki, ka haumana, i ke kaʻina aʻo. ʻO ka mea hoʻohilu ʻia ma nei hana ʻana ka hoʻomākaukau ʻana i kou kahua ʻike ma mua o ka hoʻopuka nīnau wale aku.

Ma loko o kēia kaʻina, e kau nui pū ana ka hana nui ma luna o ka makua e aʻo ana i ke keiki, ʻo ia hoʻi ke kumu. No ka mea, e like ana ka hopena ʻaumākua e kau ana ma luna o nā kumu e aʻo ana i ke keikikāne ma hope o kona kā ʻana i mua ʻoiai ʻo lākou nā kumu ʻike a ia keiki. Ua ʻōlelo ʻia kēia me ke ʻano noʻeau loa, "I maikaʻi ke kalo i ka ʻōhā" (Pūkuʻi, ʻŌlelo, no. 1232), i mea e hōʻoia ai i ke kūlana koʻikoʻi loa o ke aʻo ʻana. ʻAʻole nō i ʻike ʻia ka maikaʻi o kekahi kumu ma loko wale nō o kāna mau hana ponoʻī iho. Ua lilo ka haumana i ana e ʻike ʻia ai ka pono o ke aʻo ʻana o ia kumu a me ka walea o ke kumu ma ia ʻike. Pēlā nō hoʻi nā kūpuna i aʻo ai iā Pūkuʻi i ka hoʻopaʻanaʻau ʻana i kā lākou mau moʻolelo (Pūkuʻi, "How"). Pili ka mākaukau o ka haumāna i ka mākaukau o ke kumu a me ko ke kumu mākaukau i ke aʻo ʻana.

ʻAʻole kēia ʻano aʻo ʻana he mea e pono hana wale ai nō. He mea i kālai ʻia a hoʻomōhala piha ʻia no nā hanauna he nui hewahewa ma mua mai o kākou. I loko o nā moʻolelo Hawaiʻi ka ʻike e pono ai nā Hawaiʻi mai ka wā mai o nā kūpuna a i kēia wā ʻānō. ʻO ka hoʻopaʻanaʻau ʻana a me ka hoʻokikina ʻana aku i ka haumana e hoʻopaʻa pono i ka ʻike i loko ona kekahi mea nui e ʻike ai kākou i ke ʻano aʻo i manaʻo ʻia he aʻo pololei. Ma ka moʻolelo ʻana mai i ka haumana a me ka paipai ʻana iā ia e aʻo aku i kekahi hanauna e like me kona aʻo ʻia ʻana i ka hōʻailona aʻo. He hōʻailona no nā mea a nā kūpuna o ia wā i manaʻo ai he mea nui a kūpono.

I ka noho ʻana i ke alo o kā mākou kumu, ua ʻike mākou i nā mea nui iā ia. Ua hoʻomaka mākou i ke kūkā ʻana a me ka hoʻopaʻanaʻau ʻana i nā pule, nā huaʻōlelo a me nā inoa a pau i pili i ke kākau. ʻO ka mea nui naʻe i ʻike ʻia e mākou ko Keone lawena kākau. Ua hāhai mākou iā ia i loko o nā wahi hana a pau a i mua hoʻi o nā kānaka a pau āna i kākau ai. Ua lohe maila mākou i kāna mau ʻōlelo iā lākou a me kona ʻano i mua o lākou. Ua like nō ia me ke ʻano o ko Kekūhaupiʻo aʻo ʻana i ka lua maiā Koaiʻa mai. Ma ko lāua hoʻokūkū ʻana, ua hiki iā Kekūhaupiʻo ke wānana i nā ʻai lua a Koaiʻa, no ka mea ua ʻapo ʻo ia i ke ʻano o ko Koaiʻa lawena lua (Desha 30–33). I ka hopena o kona aʻo ʻana, ua hele a ʻālike loa ko Kekūhaupiʻo neʻe ʻana me ko Koaiʻa.

He Hale Kanaka

Ka huliau

Ua ulu nō kēia pūnua nei, kēia mea kākau, i loko o ia aʻo ʻana. I ia wā hoʻokahi nō, ua ulu ka ʻohana. Ua hoʻopōmaikaʻi hou ʻia maila mākou e ka hānau ʻia ʻana o kā mākou keikikāne, ʻo Kaʻula. No ka poʻe kākau kekahi, he mea nui ia i ke ola o ka ʻoihana kākau ʻoiai hoʻi he ʻoihana na ke kāne e hana. I loko nō naʻe o ia pōmaikaʻi ʻana, ua ili pū kekahi kuleana nui ma luna o ka mea kākau, no ka mea ua hoʻomaka ko Kaʻula aʻo ʻana i ke kākau mai ka wā mai o kona hanu mua ʻana.

Mai ko Kaʻula wā kamaliʻi, ua hoʻomaka ʻo ia ma ka hoʻopaʻanaʻau ʻana i ka ʻike a pau e pono ai. Hoʻohele pū ʻia akula ʻo ia i mua o Keone a loko pū o ke kākau ʻana. No kēia keiki, ua lilo ke kōʻele a ka hāhau mōlī i kani e nanea ai kona pepeiao. I ka noho ʻana ka hana a kupa i ke alo o ka mōlī, ʻike ʻia akula kona hoihoi a me ke akamai ma ia hana. Ua ʻike pū ʻia kona ʻano mālama kūʻē ʻana i ka ʻike kākau. He mea maoli nō iā ia ke kiaʻi ʻana i kona ʻike a ma ka ʻōlelo hoʻokahi wale aku nō o kona makuakāne, ua lawa nō. Kohu mea ala, ua mākaukau ʻo ia no ke koho ʻia ʻana e aʻo, e like nō hoʻi me koʻu koho ʻia ʻana.

E ka mea heluhelu, ma ko ka mea kākau komo ʻana i kēia au hou ʻo ka makua ʻana, ua lilo naʻe ia i wā e lauwili hou ai ka noʻonoʻo. Ua loli loa ihola ka ʻikena o kēia makuakāne i ka ua mea ʻo ka nohona haumana, no ka mea ua kā hou ʻia nō kēia i ke kūlana kumu. He nani ia, ʻaʻole i noʻonoʻo mua ʻia ke kākau i hana ia e aʻo koke aku ai i kekahi ʻōhua, ua paulele akula ka mea kākau nei i loko o ka ʻimi ʻana i ke kākau "maoli" a "ʻoiaʻiʻo" o ke au nei. Ma ia ala nō naʻe kahi i kuʻia ai koʻu nohona haumana i ka lilo koke ʻana oʻu i kumu na kaʻu kama mai kona wā ʻōkole heleleʻi mai a ʻānō iho nō. I mea ia aʻo ʻana e lilo ai ka ʻikena kākau i nohona maoli nona a paʻa loa.

Ka hoʻoilina

Na ka makuakāne ʻana i hoʻoulu i ke koikoina kālailai o ka mea kakau nei ʻo au. Lilo loa akula nō kā mākou poʻe kākau mau hana a pau i mau kumuhana e kaupaona ai, no ka mea ʻaʻole nō au i manaʻo e lawe ʻia kaʻu keikikāne i ke alo o ka pōʻino. Ma ia ʻano kaupaona ʻana naʻe i ulu ai koʻu hoʻohuoi i nā hiʻohiʻona a pau o ka ʻoihana kākau. Ua ʻōʻili maila kekahi ʻano o ke kālailai ʻana, ʻo ia hoʻi, ua ʻike au i ka mua a me ka hope o nā hana pākahi a pau. Ua ʻono loa koʻu lunaʻikehala i nā haʻina a pau o kāna mau nīnau, eia kā ua makapehu. ʻŌʻili pū maila kekahi nīnau koʻikoʻi. No koʻu kālailai nui ʻana i nā koina e koho ʻia ai ka haumana kākau, ʻaʻole au i noʻonoʻo e pili ana i nā koina e puka aku ai mai ka malu aʻo aku.

ʻAʻole nō i mōakāka ke ākea a me nā palena o ka ʻike a ke kumu e koi mai ana iā mākou e aʻo. I ʻike ia na kā mākou kumu ʻo Keone. Aia hoʻi, hoʻomanawanui ʻia ihola nō kēia mōakāka ʻole, no ka mea e hōʻano hou ana ʻo ia i ka papahana aʻo kākau uhi Hawaiʻi. Ma ka holomua ʻana naʻe o koʻu makuakāne ʻana, me ka ulu pū o ke koikoina kālailai o koʻu lunaʻikehala, ʻaʻole nō i nā koʻu hoʻohuoi no nā lawena e aʻo ʻia ana a me nā haʻawina e aʻo ʻole ʻia ana. Ma waena o māua ʻo kaʻu kumu, ua lilo kēia kālailai ʻana i kumuhana koʻikoʻi e walaʻau nui ai.

I ka lōʻihi ʻana aʻe o ko māua kūkā ʻana no kēia kumuhana, he ʻikea nō, ua ulu ka huoi o koʻu lunaʻikehala i ka paʻa ʻole o ke ala e kaʻi ai ma kēia papahana aʻo. ʻAʻole nō naʻe ia huoi i hopena o ke aʻo hemahema ʻia oʻu. I huoi nō ia i ulu i ka hopena kolonaio, ʻo ia hoʻi, e hoʻohuoi ʻia ana ka maluhia o nā ʻōhua i ke ala waele mua ʻole ʻia, i ka wā hoʻokahi hoʻi o ke ala e ʻimi hou ʻia ana. Ma ke kālailai pū ʻana i ke ala i kaʻi aku nei kaʻu kumu e loaʻa mai ai ʻo kona ʻike kākau, ʻaʻole nō i ʻike ʻia kekahi ala Hawaiʻi piha, ʻoiai hoʻi, ʻaʻole ʻo ia i aʻo wale ʻia nō ma lalo o kekahi malu Hawaiʻi. Ua "ʻuniki" ʻia ʻo ia ma lalo o kāna kumu Kāmoa, ʻo Suʻa Suluʻape Paulo, me ka ʻānoni ʻana i kona ʻike noiʻi kākau Hawaiʻi e like me ko nā kūpuna i moʻolelo aku nei iā ia. ʻAuhea ʻoukou, he mau kūpuna i ʻike lihi wale nō i kēia ʻoihana ʻo ke kākau Hawaiʻi, ua kaʻa ke kuleana hōʻano hou ma luna o ko Keone mau poʻohiwi, ʻo ia hoʻokahi.

Nānā i ke Kumu

Kā Hou i Mua

No laila e ka mea heluhelu, ua hōʻea mai nō ke kuʻina koʻikoʻi loa o kēia palapala. He hulina mākoeā ka ʻimi ʻana i ka mea poʻohala inā ua moku ke kuamoʻo welo. ʻAʻohe ana kahu nānā e ʻailolo i nā ʻōlohe a me nā kāhuna o kēia hope aku. Aia hoʻi, he nui wale nā ʻāpana ʻike i heleleʻi i ke au o ka manawa. Ma ke kālailai ʻana i kēia heleleʻi ʻana o ua ʻike e ʻike ai kākou ē, he hopena kēia i ili wale maila nō ma luna o ka poʻe o ia manawa. He hopena kolonaio i laulaha ma nā ʻāina a pau i hoʻokolonaio ʻia. No laila i lilo ai kēia heleleʻi ʻana i hoapaio na nā lāhui ʻōiwi a pau i pā i kēia hopena kolonaio.

No nā mea Hawaiʻi i kokoke i ka pau loa, e like me ke kākau uhi, he ʻelua wale nō koho. E hiʻi ma ke alo a i ʻole ma ke kua. E waiho hoʻi a pau ia ʻike me nā kūpuna o ka wā ma mua a i ʻole e noiʻi nōwelo i kona hiʻohiʻona kuʻuna a e kūkulu hou i ia ʻoihana no nā hanauna hou aʻe. I loko nō naʻe o ka paʻakikī o kēia ʻano koho ʻana, ua puka maila he kumu hoʻohālikelike kūpono e hoʻohālikelike ai me kaʻu i hoʻomaka ihola i loko o koʻu ʻohana. Ua kokoke loa ka nalo pau o ka ʻōlelo Hawaiʻi. A laila, ua kū maila kekahi hanauna ma mua mai oʻu e hoʻōla i ua ʻōlelo lā me ka ʻike ʻole i ke ala pono e hoʻōla ai a me ka heleleʻi nui pū o ka ʻike ʻōlelo. Eia kekahi, ua hana pū ʻia me ka hānai ʻole ʻia o lākou ma ka ʻōlelo i pūʻā ʻia mai ka wā pēpē mai, e like me nā kumu ʻōlelo o nā hanauna o mua. Ua koho lākou e hoʻōla a ua ola nō.

Me nei ʻano kumu hoʻohālikelike i ʻike ai kēia mea kākau, ʻaʻole ka lāhui e hoʻōla ana i nā ʻoihana pākahi e kuakahi ai. E hoʻōla ana kākou i ke kuanaʻike kupuna holoʻokoʻa ma kona kino piha pono, no ka mea ua pili nā ʻoihana a pau i ia kuana'ike. 'O ka 'ike hula, he mahele. 'O ka 'ike 'ōlelo, he mahele. 'O ka 'ike kilo-lani a me ka ho'okele wa'a, he mau mahele. 'O ka 'ike kākau, ka'u mahele, ko'u ala, e holo pono ai ke ka'i 'ana o ka 'ike piha o ko'u mau kūpuna aloha. 'A'ole ke kākau uhi i ala e ola wale ai nō ke kākau uhi. 'A'ole ka hula i ala e ola wale ai nō ka hula a pēlā aku nō. Aia ho'i, ma ka nānā 'ana i kekahi 'ao'ao o kēia koho 'ana e 'ike 'ia ai ka hakahaka 'ana o ko ka lāhui 'ikena Hawai'i i ka nele. E nele ana ko kākou kahua 'ike i ka piha 'ole o ke kuana'ike Hawai'i, ka 'ike nohona kupuna Hawai'i ho'i. E hihia ana kākou i ka 'ānoni 'ana i ka 'ikena o nā lāhui 'ē a'e i loko o ko kākou no ka loa'a 'ole o ko kākou 'ike pono'ī. Ua lilo akula nō paha ka 'ikena Hawai'i i kama na ka pueo.

No laila, 'oiai na nā kūpuna i koho i ke 'ano o ko lākou nohona, e noi'i a nānā nui i nā po'opo'o a pau o ia 'ikena e holo mua ai 'o ia 'ikena Hawai'i ma kona 'ano piha. 'A'ole e hulikua 'ia lākou kūpuna a me ko lākou 'ano 'i'o nō. 'A'ole nō ho'i e 'ai pākiko wale aku i nā pūpū papa'aina kupuna, 'o ia ho'i, 'a'ole e koho kikokiko 'ia nā 'ano wale nō o nā kūpuna a kākou e 'aelike ai a e makemake ai ho'i i kēia mau lā. I hana ia e paio ai i ka ili piha 'ana o ka 'ikena o ka po'e malihini o nā 'āina 'ē ma luna o nā hanauna hou o kākou. 'O ka nohona ia o ko kākou mua iho. 'O ka nohona nō ho'i ia o ko kēia hope aku. I mea ia e 'ike ai kā kākou mau haunauna hou aku i ko lākou 'ano 'ōiwi iho. I mea nō ho'i ia e kūkulu pono 'ia ai nā 'oihana Hawai'i me nā pono a me nā lako no 'ane'i.

Ho'okumuhonua: Ke kūkulu hou 'ana i nā 'oihana i nalo

I kēia au e nui nei ka 'iha'iha o ka no'ono'o o kānaka no ka hala 'oko'a 'ana o nā 'ōhi'a lehua he nui, ho'omana'o 'ia mai kākou no ka hopena hele loa o nā mea Hawai'i he kini a lehu. Ua hele a nui hewahewa nā mea kanu a me nā mea ola i kokoke loa i ka hala pau. Pākela ho'i ko kākou po'e Hawai'i minamina 'ana i kēia hala loa 'ana o nā lālā 'ōiwi o Hawai'i holo'oko'a. I ka makahiki 1871, kākau mai nei 'o T.N. Penukahi i kekahi palapala i ka nūpepa e pili ana i ka nalowale 'ana o nā manu kama'āina o Mānoa. Hō'ike 'ia mai nei na'e 'o ia ma kāna palapala no kona mana'o e pili ana i ke emi 'ana o ka lāhui 'ōiwi Hawai'i.

> A ke olelo nei au me ka hookamani ole, no ka emi ana o ka lahui, no ka hiki ana mai o na hale ino ma Hawaii nei, na lakou i hoolaha mai i na mai ino…e like me…na manu kamaaina o kakou nei, a me na mea kanu, pela no ka emi ana o ko kakou lahui, ma ka hiki ana mai o na haole ino.

Ma ka wā like o kēia ho'ohalahala 'ana, hāpai pū mai nei 'o ia no ka like o ke kumu i emi ai ka lāhui me ke emi 'ana o nā manu ma Mānoa. Inā 'a'ole i hiki mai ka haole 'ino, inā nō ke emi 'ana o ka lāhui. Ho'omau akula 'o Penukahi me ka minamina, nolaila, ke aloha ae nei au i na wahi manu kamaaina o kuu aina hanau, no ka pau loa i ka nalowale, ke hoohuoi mai nei na wahi kama o keia wa me ka ninau mai, pehea ka ano oia mau manu?

Ho'āla 'ia maila ka mana'o ma ka hopena o kāna palapala no ka ho'oponopono 'ia 'ana o nā kānāwai e ka 'Aha 'Ōlelo i mea e kūpale 'ia ai nā manu kama'āaina mai nā manu haole 'ino. I ke au nei, ke mau nei nō ka ho'ā'o 'ana e mālama 'ia nā manu, e la'a me ka 'Alalā, i 'ole ia e nalowale aku. A'oa'o maila kā Penukahi palapala iā kākou i kēia wā nei e kūpale pono i nā mea kama'āina a me nā mea 'ōiwi, 'o ia ho'i, i nā mea o ko kākou kulāiwi 'o Hawai'i.

No laila ho'i, 'o kā kēia mea kākau nei manu e aloha minamina nei ma nei palapala, 'o ia ka 'oihana kākau uhi Hawai'i i kokoke i ka nalowale. E aha ana lā auane'i ka mea e pono ai kēia 'oihana i kēia hope aku i mea e lohe mau 'ia ai ke ko'ele hiwahiwa? Aia lā ho'i, e ho'omohala hou 'ia ke ala hāiki o kahuna mai kīnohi a pau. E 'imi 'ia nā kānaka nona ka mākaukau e pono ai kēia 'oihana. E ho'opihapiha 'ia nā hakahaka i loa'a ma muli o ka helele'i i ke au kūnewa akula me ko kākou 'ike na'auao o ke au nei. 'A'ole e 'ānoni ho'okalekale i ko kākou 'ike lāhui iho me ko waho 'ike. A 'o ka mea nui loa nō ma luna a'e o nā mea 'ē a'e a pau, e māliu kākou lāhui i ia manu makamae a me nā manu 'ē a'e e nalowale nei.

Hawai'i Pono'ī

Ua 'ōlelo 'ia, "he ali'i ka 'āina; he kauwā ke kanaka" (Pūku'i, 'Ōlelo, no. 531). E nānā kākou i ko kākou mō'ī 'o Hawai'i Pae'āina. Ua kūkala 'ia i ka makahiki 1907, mai ha'alele i ka 'ōlelo makuahine ("Mai"). Eia ke kūkala pū nei, mai ha'alele i kekahi 'ikena o ka Hawai'i. 'O kekahi mana'o ho'olauwili o kēia mau lā ka mana'o no ka hiki i ka Hawai'i ke māliu i kekahi 'oihana me ka hulikua i kekahi. Kohu mea lā, 'eā, 'a'ohe pilina ma waena o nā 'oihana a pau. He pilina ko nā mea a pau i ulu ma Hawai'i mai uka a kai. Pēia pū ka nohona Hawai'i. 'A'ole loa nō nā kūpuna i pono hana wale aku i kekahi mea ma ko lākou nohona. He mau 'āpana nā 'oihana a pau o ke kuana'ike Hawai'i maoli piha. 'A'ole e hiki ana ke kū'oko'a kekahi ma kona 'ano piha kūpono ke 'ole nā 'oihana 'ē a'e.

No laila, e o'u mau makamaka ihu pani o nā mea no'eau kupuna e 'ihi'ihi mau nei, i ko kākou pālama 'ana i nā hakina 'ike kupuna e koe nei, e 'ike kākou ē, ua pili nā 'oihana a pau kekahi i kekahi. 'A'ohe ola o kekahi ke 'ole kekahi no ka mea he mau 'āpana kēia mau 'oihana no'eau o ke kino piha ho'okahi o ke Kuana'ike Hawai'i. Eia kekahi. 'A'ole e wailana 'ia nā hana no'eau me ka mana'o ua 'oi aku ka pono o kekahi ma mua o kekahi. 'O ka 'a'ai 'ia 'ana aku nō ia o ua kino ne-punepu ho'okahi. Na ka 'ike o nā 'oihana a pau e ho'olakolako aku kekahi i kekahi. Na ia mau 'oihana kekahi i kekahi e ho'oikaika. Na ia mau 'oihana waiwai e ho'opa'a i ke kahua Hawai'i 'oia'i'o i 'ole e nāueue a kāpekepeke. Ola nui ka 'ōlelo Hawai'i a me ka 'ike Hawai'i. E ola iā kākou.

Desha, Stephen. *Kamehameha and His Warrior Kekūhaupi'o*. Translated by Frances N. Frazier. Kamehameha Schools P, 2000.

Ka'aihue, Maliakamo'opunawahineopanila DeSoto. *I ka 'ōlelo no ke ola, i ka 'ōlelo no ka make: Deconstructing Hawaiian Children's Literature*. 2010. University of Hawai'i at Mānoa, PhD dissertation.

Krug, [Kalehua] Gary Sherwood, Jr. *He Ha'awina ka Mo'olelo: No ka Ho'okahua 'ana i nā Ha'awina Kaiapuni ma luna o ka 'Ike Kū'auhau o nā Mo'olelo Kūpuna*. 2014. University of Hawai'i at Mānoa, PhD dissertation.

"Mai Haalele i ka Olelo Makuahine." *Kuokoa Home Rula*, vol. 5, no. 12, 22 March 1907, p. 1.

Penukahi, T. N. "He mau wahi kamaaina no ka ua Tuahine, ua nalowale." *Ke Au Okoa*, vol. 7, no. 11, 29 June 1871, p. 3.

Pickens, Alexander L., and David Kemble. *To Teach the Children: Historical Aspects of Education in Hawai'i*. Bishop Museum P. and University of Hawai'i at Mānoa College of Education, 1982.

Poepoe, J[oseph] M[oku'ōhai]. "Ka Moolelo Hawaii Kahiko." *Ka Na'i Aupuni*, Buke 1, Helu 57, 1 February 1906, p. 1.

Pūku'i, Mary Kawena. "How Legends Were Taught." *Hawaiian Ethnographic Notes*, vol. 1, 1602–1606. Bishop Museum Archives, pp. 1–5. http://kumukahi-online.net/haku -olelo-331/na-kumu-ike/mokuna-iv---moolelo-kaao/pukui---how-legends-were .pdf.

———. *'Ōlelo No'eau: Hawaiian Proverbs & Poetical Sayings*. Bishop Museum P, 1983.

Pūku'i, Mary Kawena, E. W. Haertig, and Catherine A. Lee. *Nana I Ke Kumu (Look to the Source)*. 2 vols. Hui Hanai, 1972.

Tengan, Ty P. Kāwika. *Native Men Remade: Gender and Nation in Contemporary Hawai'i*. Duke UP, 2008.

He kupa kēia **Kalehua Krug** nei no ka 'āina 'o Lualualei, Wai'anae ma O'ahu a he kama no Hawai'i pae'āina. No Moloka'i nā kūpuna a he hānai ho'okama na Nānākuli. Nona nō ke aloha nui i ia mau 'āina a pau a me ko laila mau kānaka. 'O ka na'auao 'ōiwi nō kāna e 'imi nei i 'ike e pono ai ka lāhui Hawai'i holo'oko'a. He makuakāne 'o ia i hānai a ho'ohiki i kāna mau keiki 'ekolu ma ka 'ōlelo a me ke 'ano o nā kupuna, 'o ke 'ano ho'i i maopopo iā ia. Mele 'o ia i nā mele Hawai'i. Kūlia 'o ia ma ka 'ōlelo a me ka 'ike o nā kūpuna. Kālele nui 'o ia ma luna o nā 'aumākua a me ona mau akua. Ma kāna mau hana, he alaka'i Papahana Kaiapuni ma mua i kōkua i ke kūkulu 'ia o kekahi hō'ike 'ōlelo Hawai'i no nā kula Kaiapuni a he po'okumu 'o ia i kēia manawa ma ke kula ho'āmana 'o Ka Waihona o ka Na'auao i ke awāwa āiwa 'o Nānākuli nei. 'O ke kākau uhi kāna māhele 'ike Hawai'i e pa'u mau nei ma ka nōelo 'ana, ka ho'opālama 'ana, a me ka ho'opili 'ana i ia hana kupuna.

Hawaiʻinuiākea Series

Editorial Board

Jonathan K. Osorio, Kahikina de Silva, Craig Howes, C. Manu Kaʻiama,
Lia OʻNeill M. A. Keawe, M. Puakea Nogelmeier

The Hawaiʻinuiākea Series provides a multidisciplinary venue for the work of
scholars and practitioners from the Hawaiian community, a platform for thinkers and doers who grapple with real-world queries, challenges, and strategies. Each volume features articles on a thematic topic from diverse fields
such as economics, education, family resources, government, health, history,
land and natural resources, psychology, religion, and sociology. Each volume
includes kupuna reflections, current viewpoints, and original creative expression.

https://uhpress.hawaii.edu/bookseries/hawaiinuiakea/

All volumes in the series are available on Project Muse

Proposals for volume themes may be submitted to:

Dean of Hawaiʻinuiākea School of Hawaiian Knowledge
Hawaiʻinuiākea Series
2450 Maile Way
Spalding 454
Honolulu, Hawaii 96822
hshk@hawaii.edu

Printed in the United States
by Baker & Taylor Publisher Services